SUPERSEX

WORLD COMICS AND GRAPHIC NONFICTION SERIES
Frederick Luis Aldama and Christopher González, editors

The World Comics and Graphic Nonfiction series includes monographs and edited volumes that focus on the analysis and interpretation of comic books and graphic nonfiction from around the world. The books published in the series use analytical approaches from literature, art history, cultural studies, communication studies, media studies, and film studies, among other fields, to help define the comic book studies field at a time of great vitality and growth.

OTHER BOOKS IN THE SERIES

ALLAN W. AUSTIN AND PATRICK L. HAMILTON
All New, All Different? A History of Race and the American Superhero

MATT YOCKEY, ED.
Make Ours Marvel: Media Convergence and a Comics Universe

JORGE SANTOS
Graphic Memories of the Civil Rights Movement: Reframing History in Comics

MARK HEIMERMANN AND BRITTANY TULLIS, EDS.,
Picturing Childhood: Youth in Transnational Comics

BENJAMIN FRASER
The Art of Pere Joan: Space, Landscape, and Comics Form

DAVID WILLIAM FOSTER
El Eternauta, Daytripper, and Beyond: Graphic Narrative in Argentina and Brazil

JAN BAETENS
The Film Photonovel: A Cultural History of Forgotten Adaptations

CHRISTOPHER PIZZINO
Arresting Development: Comics at the Boundaries of Literature

MARC SINGER
Breaking the Frames: Populism and Prestige in Comics Studies

FREDERICK LUIS ALDAMA
Graphic Borders: Latino Comic Books Past, Present, and Future

SUPERSEX
Sexuality, Fantasy, and the Superhero

EDITED BY

Anna F. Peppard

University of Texas Press ⬥ Austin

Copyright © 2020 by the University of Texas Press
All rights reserved
First edition, 2020
First paperback edition, 2023

Requests for permission to reproduce material from this work should be sent to:
Permissions
University of Texas Press
P.O. Box 7819
Austin, TX 78713–7819
utpress.utexas.edu/rp-form

♾ The paper used in this book meets the minimum requirements of ANSI/NISO Z39.48–1992 (R1997) (Permanence of Paper).

Library of Congress Cataloging-in-Publication Data

Names: Peppard, Anna F., editor.
Title: Supersex : sexuality, fantasy, and the superhero / edited by Anna F. Peppard.
Description: First edition. | Austin : University of Texas Press, 2020. | Series: World comics and graphic nonfiction series | Includes bibliographical references and index.
Identifiers: LCCN 2020008797
  ISBN 978-1-4773-2161-4 (paperback)
  ISBN 978-1-4773-2162-1 (PDF)
  ISBN 978-1-4773-2163-8 (ePub)
Subjects: LCSH: Comic books, strips, etc.—United States—History and criticism. | Superheroes. | Superhero films—History and criticism. | Superhero television programs—History and criticism. | Sex in literature. | Sex in motion pictures. | Sex on television.
Classification: LCC PN6714 .S88 2020 | DDC 809/.9352—dc23
LC record available at https://lccn.loc.gov/2020008797

doi:10.7560/321607

To all the space aliens, mutants, sorcerers, inhumans, androids, and cosmic demigods I've loved before. Thank you for your tights, electric skin, supersenses, fur, metallic lips, and occasional thigh-high boots. I couldn't have made it through adolescence or my PhD without you.

To my family: my mother, who took me into my first comic book store; my father, who took me into my first university classroom; and my sister, who has always taken me seriously, even when I'm being ridiculous.

And to this book's wonderful contributors, without whose passion and brilliance this project could not exist.

CONTENTS

INTRODUCTION. Presence and Absence in
Theory and Practice: Locating *Supersex*   1
ANNA F. PEPPARD

PART I. COMICS

1. Tarpé Mills's *Miss Fury*: Costume, Sexuality, and Power   31
   RICHARD REYNOLDS

2. Superman Family Values: Supersex in the Silver Age   57
   MATT YOCKEY

3. A Storm of Passion: Sexual Agency and Symbolic
   Capital in the X-Men's Storm   79
   J. ANDREW DEMAN

4. Dazzler, Melodrama, and Shame:
   Mutant Allegory, Closeted Readers   103
   BRIAN JOHNSON

5. "Super-Gay" *Gay Comix*: Tracing the Underground
   Origins and Cultural Resonances of LGBTQ Superheroes   129
   SARAH M. PANUSKA

6. Parents, Counterpublics, and Sexual Identity
   in *Young Avengers*   151
   KEITH FRIEDLANDER

PART II. FILM, TELEVISION, AND FAN CULTURE

7. X-Men Films and the Domestication of Dissent:
   Sexuality, Race, and Respectability — 175
   CHRISTOPHER B. ZEICHMANN

8. Over the Rainbow Bridge:
   Female/Queer Sexuality in Marvel's Thor Film Trilogy — 199
   SAMANTHA LANGSDALE

9. "No One's Going to Be Looking at Your Face":
   The Female Gaze and the New (Super)Man in
   Lois & Clark: The New Adventures of Superman — 221
   ANNA F. PEPPARD

10. The Visible and the Invisible:
    Superheroes, Pornography, and Phallic Masculinity — 245
    JEFFREY A. BROWN

11. "I Think That's My Favorite Weapon in
    the Whole Batcave": Interrogating the Subversions of
    Men.com's Gay Superhero Porn Parodies — 265
    JOSEPH BRENNAN

12. "That's Pussy Babe!": Queering Supergirl's
    Confessions of Power — 291
    OLIVIA HICKS

13. Meet Stephanie Rogers, Captain America:
    Genderbending the Body Politic in Fan Art,
    Fiction, and Cosplay — 317
    ANNE KUSTRITZ

    EPILOGUE: The Matter with Size — 341
    RICHARD HARRISON

    CONTRIBUTORS — 363

    INDEX — 367

SUPERSEX

INTRODUCTION

PRESENCE AND ABSENCE IN THEORY AND PRACTICE
Locating *Supersex*

ANNA F. PEPPARD

In a now-famous quote from his 1954 bestseller *Seduction of the Innocent*, psychiatrist Fredric Wertham described Batman and Robin as "a wish dream of two homosexuals living together" that "helps to fixate homoerotic tendencies."[1] According to Wertham, "Only someone ignorant of the fundamentals of psychiatry and of the psychopathology of sex can fail to realize a subtle atmosphere of homoeroticism which pervades the adventures of the mature 'Batman' and his young friend 'Robin.'"[2] Wertham interpreted female superheroes such as Wonder Woman and the original Black Cat as similarly, if oppositely, deviant. "Where Batman is anti-feminine," Wertham wrote, "the attractive Wonder Woman and her counterparts are definitely anti-masculine."[3] As with Batman, Wertham linked this gender deviance to homosexuality, writing, "[Wonder Woman's] followers are the 'Holliday girls,' i.e., the holiday girls, the gay party girls, the gay girls."[4] Despite the problematic essentialism of equating gender with sex and sexuality, Wertham's readings of these texts are not, on their own, outrageous. As Darieck Scott and Ramzi Fawaz argue, comics possess an almost unique ability to indulge in "hyperbolic camp visuality or the metamorphosing of human bodies into forms that call into question traditional gender norms."[5] But where Scott and Fawaz celebrate this ability, Wertham condemns it by sensationalistically and speciously linking it to violence and death. Wertham moves quickly from a description of Robin as "a handsome ephebic boy, usually shown in his uniform with bare legs" who often poses with "his legs spread, the genital region discreetly evident,"[6] to describing a thirteen-year-old Batman fan on three years' probation for an incident in which "he and a companion had forced a boy of eight, threatening him with a knife, to undress and carry out sexual practices with them."[7] Wertham states the consequences of reading Wonder Woman comics even more baldly. "For boys," writes Wertham, "Wonder Woman is a frightening image. For girls, she is a morbid ideal."[8]

The moral panic surrounding comic books did not originate with Wertham,[9] nor were superheroes or their sexuality the only target of his ire. Yet given the subject of this volume, it is notable that the sexual possibilities of superhero texts are central to Wertham's condemnation of them. Wertham's critiques also remain notable because *Seduction of the Innocent* is almost certainly the most influential book ever published about either superheroes or American comic books. This will be a familiar story to comics scholars, but it bears repeating: two months after the release of *Seduction of the Innocent,* Wertham was a star witness in a televised and much publicized United States Senate Subcommittee investigation that explored the supposed links between comic books and juvenile delinquency. A few months after that, the American comic book industry saved itself from the threat of government regulation by creating an industry-run censorship program called the Comics Code Authority. Though Amy Kiste Nyberg, among others, has challenged the "persistent belief among fan-historians that the comic book industry was nearly destroyed" by the Code,[10] there can be no contesting the fact that it did profoundly influence the industry's development. From 1954 until a major revision in 1989, the Code prohibited American comic book publishers from depicting "nudity in any form," "illicit sex relations," and a loosely defined and potentially vast array of "sexual abnormalities and perversions";[11] for most of the Code's history, same-sex desire was one such perversion.

The Code was not a law, but rather functioned as a guarantee to concerned parents as well as stores and magazine stands that any comics they were buying or selling were appropriate for children. All comic books bearing the Code's "Seal of Approval" were reviewed by a censorship board that ensured they were not too sexual or violent, and that they upheld positive moral values, such as respect for racial equality, as well as conservative ones, such as respect for authority figures and traditional gender roles. Not all of these strictures were uncalled-for; pre-Code comics were undeniably rife with harmful racial stereotypes and excessive violence, including a great deal of sexualized violence targeting women. Yet it is also undeniable that the Code's emphasis on child appropriateness hampered the creative possibilities of decades' worth of American comic books and helped solidify in the American cultural consciousness the idea that comic books are "kids' stuff," without appeal or value for adult or "sophisticated" readers. Because superhero comics were one of the most popular genres in American comic books and only became more so in the wake of the Code—whose restrictions more severely impacted the competing crime, romance, and horror genres—the American public has long similarly considered them kids' stuff, with all the limitations that assumption implies. Where sexuality is concerned, inasmuch as we assume children do not have sexual identities or imaginations, neither do superheroes.

But of course, assumptions are only that. In reality, even as superheroes' ability to simultaneously show and hide potentially deviant sexualities was a significant factor in the moral panic surrounding comic books and the subsequent development of the Code, it also helped superhero comic books survive and thrive when other genres fell by the wayside. Whereas crime and romance comic books drew a considerable measure of their appeal from the promise of stories based in "real life," and horror depended on overt subversions of morality (however fantastic or tongue-in-cheek), the superhero genre enables rebellions that are at once obvious and elusive, subversive and conservative. By wearing their underwear on the outside and proudly displaying their exaggeratedly hard and sensuous curves inside revealing, skin-tight costumes, virtually all the most famous superheroes openly invite erotic possibilities. Most of the time, these possibilities are sublimated into violence and fantastic metaphors; while superhero bodies routinely swell and shrivel, shoot gooey projectiles and become dramatically entwined with other flamboyantly or scantily-clad bodies, when these bodies get banged up and laid out, it tends to be in a fight rather than the bedroom, and the underwear tends to stay on. Yet to the extent that superhero stories always center around fantastic bodies whose incarnated exaggerations and embellishments are explicitly designed to excite and inspire, their erotic potential is inherent and inescapable. Superhero sexuality is flagrantly present even when it is officially absent. Tellingly, the Code attempted to regulate both sexuality and fantasy. Until 1989, the Code targeted sexual abnormalities alongside "lurid," "unsavory," and "suggestive and salacious" illustration of all kinds.[12] The 1989 revision eliminated this language and finally included "homosexuals" alongside the CIA and FBI on a list of "recognizable national, social, political, cultural, ethnic and racial groups" that must be "portrayed in a positive light."[13] Yet even this comparably liberal revision continued to indicate specific—if flexibly enforced—limits on sexual representations and fantasies. In addition to maintaining total bans on the depiction of "primary human sexual characteristics" and "graphic sexual activity," the 1989 Code reveals a continued wariness regarding comic book superheroes' potential for sexual deviance. Under the 1989 Code, "costumes . . . will be considered to be acceptable if they fall within the scope of contemporary styles and fashions."[14] In other words, costumes must maintain a degree of realism and avoid undue indulgence in fantasy. The 1989 Code also stipulates, "Heroes should be role models and should reflect the prevailing social attitudes."[15] In other words, superheroes may have gay acquaintances but should not be gay themselves.

Yet in any era, and under every version of the Code, the deviant potential of superhero sexuality has proved resistant to erasure. As a case in point: the post-Code Batman comic books tried to address the charge that they promoted a gay atmosphere by incorporating female love interests for Batman and Robin.[16] But rather than quelling the homoerotic atmosphere identified by Wertham, these additions can be seen as multiplying the opportunities for gender and sexual deviance. Before the Code, Batman and Robin had slept in matching twin beds in between clandestine outings in which they donned tights and capes to knock boots with the Joker, a man with the physique of an androgyne, the style of a Victorian dandy, and a literally killer brand of ruby red lipstick. After the Code, they were joined in both their crime-fighting activities and, on occasion, their mansion, by Batwoman and various Batgirls, whose curves and costumes would not have been out of place in contemporary fetish art, yet whose affections Batman and Robin routinely spurn in their superhero identities and court in their civilian ones. Or vice versa; in any case, duality gets in the way. If these characters formed a family, it is a decidedly queer one, wherein everyone has a cave (or closet) for an alternate identity that justifies his or her resistance to the yoke of heteronormativity. Though it took fifty years, Batwoman, at least, did eventually come out.[17]

In addition, the Code did not stop the underground proliferation of sexually explicit comics featuring superheroes. The Tijuana Bibles are the earliest known example of this underground fare.[18] Produced from the 1930s to the 1960s, the Bibles were, in the words of Art Spiegelman, "clandestinely produced and distributed small booklets that chronicled the explicit sexual adventures of America's beloved comic-strip characters, celebrities, and folk-heroes,"[19] including popular superheroes such as Superman, Supergirl, Batman, and the original Captain Marvel (now known as Shazam). Also known as "Eight-Pagers, Two-by-Fours, Gray-Backs, Bluesies, Jo-Jo Books," or simply "Fuck Books,"[20] The Tijuana Bibles were both earnest (i.e., meant to be masturbated to) and parodic (i.e., meant to be laughed at), and generated erotic thrills through their combination of the familiar (i.e., popular characters) and the strange (i.e., seeing those characters engage in graphic sex). Many comic book creators and historians, including Spiegelman, see a connection between the Bibles and the countercultural underground comix movement of the 1960s and 1970s, led by Robert Crumb, Gilbert Shelton, S. Clay Wilson, and others. Like the Bibles, underground comix sometimes featured sexually explicit superhero parodies, but usually with a stronger satirical edge. Perhaps the most famous of these is Sheldon's series of comics starring Wonder Wart-Hog. This porcine parody of Superman first appeared in college humor magazines in 1962, and in various outlets sporadically thereafter, including the famed anthology *Zap Comix* (1968–2005). In a typical Wonder Wart-Hog story from *Zap Comix* #4 (1969), Lois Lane analogue Lois Lamebrain mocks the diminutive size of Wonder's penis. This drives the humanoid warthog from space into a rage, climaxing (literally) in his violent and seemingly nonconsensual deployment of his phallic snout as a substitute; the story concludes with an ejaculative sneeze that sends Lois rocketing out the window, presumably to her death.

Few—if any—underground comix of the 1960s and '70s can be described as depicting superhero sexuality in a positive light. Some stories in feminist underground comix anthologies, such as the groundbreaking one-shot *It Ain't Me Babe* (1970) (the first comic book produced entirely by women) and the long-running *Wimmen's Comix* (1972–1992) embraced, up to a point, female superheroes as symbols of sexualized liberation.[21] Tellingly, though, the version of Supergirl that shows up in *It Ain't Me Babe* requires significant consciousness-raising in order to function as a viable symbol of female empowerment. Generally, underground comix produced by women saw superheroes as representative of the empty promises of the sexual revolution, while underground comix produced by men used superheroes to satirize the conservative morality and hypocrisy of the mainstream culture they were thought to epitomize. Many of these male-produced satires are debatably successful; the Wonder Wart-Hog episode discussed above pillories the superhero genre as hysterically overinvested in the specter of phallic masculinity while simultaneously replicating the misogynistic violence that flows from that investment. Similarly, as Erin Barry documents, even as they implicitly mocked the conservatism of their source texts, the Tijuana Bibles generally embraced patriarchal and misogynistic perspectives that "encouraged the normalisation and glorification of sexual violence as a measure of sexual performance and as an accepted part of a sexual encounter."[22]

Many things have, of course, changed over time. Marvel Comics officially abandoned the Comics Code in 2001, replacing it with their own rating system that includes a category for comics aimed at adult readers; DC Comics followed Marvel's example in 2010. And while much of the sexual content appearing in mainstream superhero texts since the waning of the Code's power in the 1980s has had a decidedly misogynistic[23] or homophobic flair,[24] twenty-first-century superhero comics and the superhero films and television shows they have inspired have slowly begun to feature more optimistic and diverse sexual content. In Marvel and DC's twenty-first-century comic books, She-Hulk has aggressively pursued her own sexual pleasure, Batman analogue Midnighter has openly flirted with Nightwing (a.k.a. original Robin Dick Grayson), the actual Batman has had sex with Catwoman on a rooftop and placed a wedding ring on her finger, and several decades-old superheroes, including the aforementioned Batwoman as well as the X-Men character Iceman and the original Green Lantern, have come out as gay or lesbian. In film, *Superman Returns* (2006) heavily implies the Man of Steel fathered a child with Lois Lane, *Deadpool* (2016) features the title character bending over to celebrate International Women's Day, *Wonder Woman* (2017) features the Mighty Amazon having guilt-free sex with Steve Trevor, and *Thor: Ragnarok* (2017) features a female Asgardian warrior, Valkyrie, who is at least tacitly bisexual.[25] On streaming services and on television, Jessica Jones and Luke Cage's superpowered passion has cracked walls; former Silk Spectre Laurie Blake of HBO's *Watchmen* has been shown worshipping a Dr. Manhattan–inspired dildo; White Canary of the television shows *Arrow* (2012–present) and *DC's Legends of Tomorrow* (2016–present) has had sexual encounters with men and women, including a one-night stand with Supergirl's sister; the *Supergirl* television show (2015–present) features a transgender superhero portrayed by a transgender actor;[26] and a *Batwoman* series starring lesbian and gender-fluid-identifying actor Ruby Rose debuted in October 2019,[27] becoming the first live-action property to star an LGBTQ superhero.[28] Some of these texts, such as the R-rated *Deadpool*, have been marketed to adults; others, such as *Legends of Tomorrow*, are aimed at adults, teenagers, and children alike, acknowledging that sexual identity can be important to persons of all ages.[29] Alongside these official stories and licensed adaptations, the internet has facilitated the ever-widening circulation of superhero porn parodies and fan works featuring myriad forms of eroticism and explicit sex.

Despite these significant changes, the mainstream embrace of sexuality as a meaningful aspect of superheroic identity remains decidedly tentative. Two recent controversies demonstrate the degree to which both producers and consumers continue to perceive superhero sexuality as at once taboo and an open secret, requiring—but also consistently

FIGURE 0.1. Original television Wonder Woman Lynda Carter gives a speech in front of the poster advertising Wonder Woman's honorary UN ambassadorship.

resisting—strong-handed management. The first controversy involves Wonder Woman. On October 21, 2016, the world's most famous female superhero was appointed an honorary UN Ambassador for women and girls. This announcement was accompanied by splashy advertising depicting the Amazon princess clothed in her usual gold and red bustier and accessorized with a shield, a demure cape, and the slogan: "Think of all the wonders we can do. Stand up for the empowerment of women and girls everywhere" (figure 0.1). There was also a well-publicized induction ceremony attended by Lynda Carter, star of the 1970s *Wonder Woman* television series, and current big-screen Wonder Woman, Gal Gadot. The objective of the campaign, according to UN spokesperson Jeffrey Brez, was to use Wonder Woman to draw attention to "UN Sustainable Development Goal No. 5," which "seeks to achieve gender equality and empower all women and girls by 2030."[30] Within days of the announcement, a petition from "concerned United Nations staff members" was formed to have Wonder Woman stripped of her honorary title. According to the petition:

> Although the original creators may have intended Wonder Woman to represent a strong and independent warrior woman with a feminist message, the reality is that the character's current iteration is that of a large breasted, white woman of impossible proportions, scantily clad in a shimmery, thigh-baring body suit with an American flag motif and knee high boots—the epitome of a pin-up girl.[31]

Bolstered by this petition and the considerable publicity it generated, Wonder Woman's induction ceremony was met with physical protests. Two months later, she lost her ambassadorship.

Brez denied that the petition and protests impacted the decision to end the Wonder Woman campaign.[32] One can assume, however, that his office was at the very least unhappy the petition attracted more than forty-four thousand supporters[33] and generated as much media attention as the campaign itself. Certainly, many of the petition's complaints are valid. Wonder Woman is quite obviously a nationalist symbol, as well as a potentially colonialist and white supremacist one. She has also been, throughout her history, a thoroughly problematic feminist. Yet rejecting Wonder Woman as a symbol of empowerment on the basis of her being "scantily-clad" and possessing "large breasts" remains problematic; these criticisms can be seen as defining certain types of female bodies and forms of sexual expression as incompatible with heroism. Significantly, opposing views of Wonder Woman's appropriateness as an ambassador for gender equality specifically highlighted both the fraught history and liberating potential of her sexuality. Fourteen-year-old Tara Peterson's competing petition to reinstate Wonder Woman's honorary title functions as a case in point.[34] In her petition, Peterson writes:

> No matter how she is dressed or how she looks, Wonder Woman's message of peace, justice and gender equality has ALWAYS remained. She is a queer woman and Super Hero who should not be judged (nor should anyone) based on what she chooses to wear or how she looks. She's sexy and confident and by no means does that mean she isn't a FANTASTIC role model for girls AND boys everywhere.[35]

This petition attracted 3,604 supporters before it was closed, something of a drop in the ocean compared to the anti–Wonder Woman petition, but still a strong indicator that the meaning of Wonder Woman's sexuality remains very much up for debate. Where a group of multinational adult UN employees can see a misogynistic pin-up, a fourteen-year-old American girl can see a queer icon.

The second controversy concerns Batman—specifically, a certain part of his anatomy. On September 19, 2018, *Batman: Damned* #1, by Brian Azzarello with art by Lee Bermejo, went on sale, the first of several scheduled releases within DC's newly minted Black Label imprint. According to the company's website, Black Label "will be DC's home for classy, collectible superhero stories aimed at mature readers looking to be challenged and surprised as they're entertained, with an eye for the unique and remarkable."[36] In words less infected with marketing spin: Black Label is a "mature readers" imprint that publishes limited series set outside the main DC continuity, wherein especially popular or critically acclaimed writers and artists are encouraged to put their individual stamp on the company's iconic characters. Part of Azzarello and Bermejo's stamp involved the first on-panel appearance of the Dark Knight's penis (figure 0.2). The context of the scene is not sexual; Batman's penis is clearly but incidentally visible in one panel of a page when Bruce Wayne strips naked so that his computer may scan him for knife wounds. Moreover, the comic's violence (the issue concludes with a splash page presenting the Joker's mutilated and crucified corpse) did not attract any significant criticism. Yet shortly after the release of *Batman: Damned* #1, every major pop and geek culture outlet ran something about the revelation of Batman's penis. Mainstream outlets such as *Vice* and *The Guardian*, as well as talk shows such as *Late Night with Seth Myers*, also picked up the story. The Know Your Meme web page for "Batman's penis controversy" covers several additional flashpoints, including a much-quoted tweet dubbing Batman's penis "L'il Wayne."[37] Given that we exist in what many scholars have described as a "pornified" culture[38] in which pictures and video of virtually any sex act imaginable are only a click away and, as Linda Williams puts it, the formerly "off (*ob*) scene" has become "on/scene,"[39] the uproar over a single, not-overtly-sexual image of Batman's penis does an especially good job of demonstrating the power and danger bound up in superhero sexuality.

Although some reactions to the penis revelation were condemnatory,[40] and most were decidedly juvenile (Myers quipped, "I'm glad his mother's not around to see this"[41]), other fans celebrated it for its subversion of gender and sexual norms. Writing for popular feminist geek website The Mary Sue, Chelsea Steiner pronounced it "refreshing to see a focus on male nudity" in a genre wherein "female bodies are so often exploited."[42] In a related vein, some gay male fans, such as comics writer and cultural critic Anthony Oliveira, saw in *Batman: Damned* #1 a way to rebel against

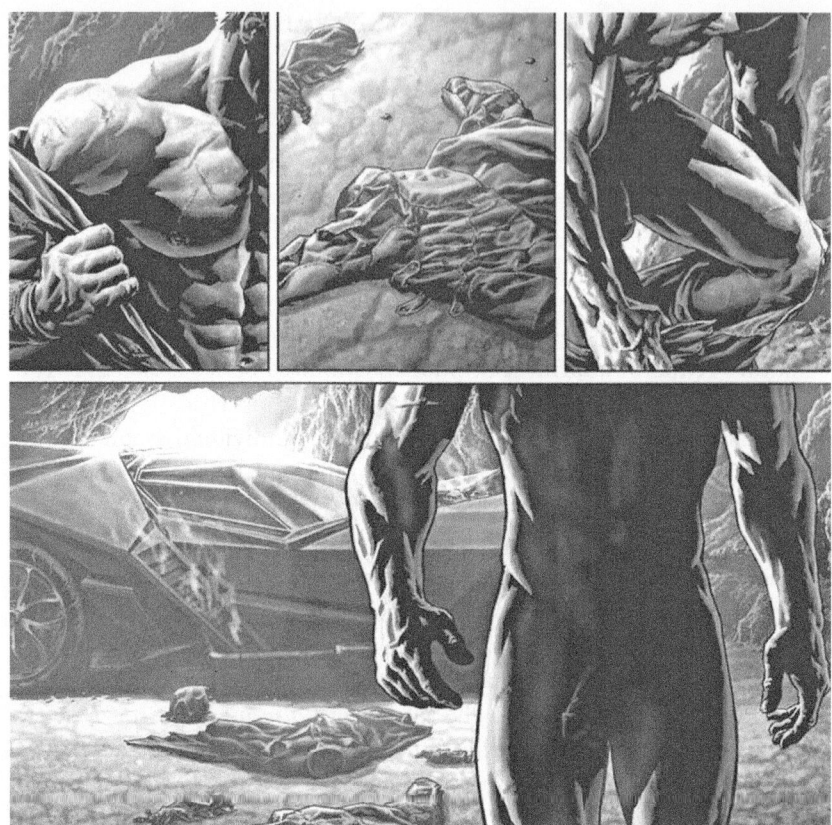

FIGURE 0.2. Wordless preview page featuring Batman's penis. *Batman: Damned* #1 (2018).

superhero fan culture's long-standing homophobia. In a tweet that garnered almost four thousand "likes," Oliveira wrote: "just called my local comic shop to reserve a copy of the book with BATMAN'S PENIS and he muttered under his breath 'this is ridiculous' and i am so glad I get to annoy a straight person AND see Bruce Wayne's peener in the same day."[43] DC's response to the controversy, however, suggests their closer affiliation with the comic book store owner. In an interview with Polygon that appeared on October 8, DC copresident Jim Lee, who provided cover art for *Batman: Damned* #1, blamed the penis scene on "production errors" and said, "It's made us, certainly, look at what Black Label is and think about whether these elements are additive to the story. . . . And that's something that we'll be mindful of going forward, because I don't think we want necessarily a repeat of what happened with the first issue." DC's other copresident, Dan DiDio, was blunter, saying, "It's something we wished never happened."[44] Digital editions and subsequent reprintings of *Batman: Damned* #1 have censored Batman's penis by clouding it in shadow. In some ways, however, this absence has enhanced the presence of "L'il Wayne." The decision to censor the original comic immediately made it a collector's item. At the time of this writing, there are ten eBay users "watching" a mint copy of *Batman: Damned* #1 signed by Lee, Azzarello, and Berjemo, which is listed at $1,749.99 USD. Ironically, the same CGC-certified plastic case that guarantees this comic's mint-ness ensures it can never be read; thus, the visible penis that makes this comic collectible will remain invisible.

From even this brief discussion, it should be clear that the meaning of superhero sexuality is anything *but* clear. Since 1938, when Clark Kent first responded to Lois Lane's rejection by transforming into a gaudily clad Superman who proceeds to reject her, superhero sexuality has been a complicated affair, full of prejudices and possibilities that feed off and reinforce each other. Sexuality cuts to the heart of unresolved questions related to the appropriateness of superheroes as role models and cultural ideals, shining a spotlight on how we define heroism; the fact and nature of superheroes' present yet absent sexuality shows how thoroughly conflicted our society has been and remains about whether heroes should be sexual, and whether sexuality can be heroic. Moreover, that Batman's penis was mostly greeted with laughter while an attempt to use Wonder Woman to spotlight global gender inequality was met with genuine outrage raises questions about which kinds of sexuality might be heroic on which bodies, and in which contexts.

I will leave additional dissecting of these questions to the chapters that follow. The remainder of this introduction will make a case for the value of studying superhero sexuality and how the book you are reading substantiates this value. Because superheroes originated in comic books, and because, as numerous scholars have argued,[45] comic book aesthetics and storytelling strategies continue to influence the depiction of superheroes in other mediums, I will start with what comics can offer the larger study of sexuality.

As Deborah Shamoon observes, to date, porn studies has focused nearly exclusively on "real bodies producing real sex acts" and has "concentrated on the technological capabilities of film as the most appropriate medium for the pornographic imagination."[46] This focus has been limiting, particularly as the multimodal and fragmented nature of comics,[47] which communicate through "sequential patterns, and suggestive, elliptical narration,"[48] has tremendous potential to complicate our understanding of the perceived and possible links—and ruptures—between sex, gender, sexuality, and desire. The unique nature of the comic book form can shed new light on questions that have long troubled porn studies, sexuality studies, and gender studies, such as: Does identification always follow gender? Does desire always align with sexual orientation? In addition, analyzing the depiction of sexual fantasies in comic books compels us to reexamine definitions of pornography and erotica. If erotica "plays to the aesthetic imagination"[49] while a majority of mainstream pornography envisions a "world without empathy"[50] that is fundamentally hostile to self-reflection, comics might never be porn. Yet the special controversy of comic book sexuality nevertheless situates comics as somehow *more* objectionable than other pornographic materials. The depiction and censorship of sexual fantasies in American comics suggests that society creates and consumes such fantasies not only or primarily because of their frequently violent manifestation of what Judith Butler calls the "impossible norms by which [gender] is compelled,"[51] but also because of their potential to rewrite (or redraw) gender norms—a possibility with implications for many fields of study.

The centrality and particular nature of the body in all types of superhero texts contributes to this value. Wendy Haslem, Elizabeth MacFarlane, and Sarah Richardson offer a particularly colorful description of the superhero genre's profoundly visible bodies. The superhero body, they write:

> may defiantly perform impossible acts, may take bullets, may soar into the sky, may stretch itself like elastic, may burst into flames, become as tough as granite, grow into a hulking giant, or shrink to the size of an ant. The body is struck by lightning, submerged in nuclear waste, pierced by the fangs of a radioactive spider, submitted to laboratory procedures, cut apart and engineered, hybridised, and emerges stronger than ever, but forever after not quite human. This is the gift and burden the superhero's body must bear—to be remarkable and remarked upon: capable of amazing feats, incapable of belonging, finding community, or the comfort of anonymity.[52]

These routine (literally generic) interactions, metamorphoses, and hybridities generate a sea of sexual possibilities that lend further credence to Wertham's approach to textual analysis, if not his dire view of its consequences. Scott Bukatman, for instance, argues that superhero bodies are at once "asexual and homosexual, heterosexual, and hermaphroditic";[53] Scott and Fawaz as well as Daniel Stein describe them as inherently queer;[54] and Aaron Taylor characterizes them as nurturing a "bisexual reader subjectivity" and a "polymorphous sexuality."[55] In a more general sense, the superhero genre's mobilization of the body as a cultural text can expose, challenge, and even deconstruct the prevailing logic of mind/body dualism. This logic continues to be exploited in the social, cultural, and political disfranchisement of women, people of color, disabled persons, sexual minorities, and other "others," who are often perceived as "too visible," "too physical," "too bodily," "too present . . . or simply 'too much,'"[56] and even "having *bodies but not minds*."[57] As Butler puts it, within Western patriarchy, "women and slaves, children and animals must be the body, perform the bodily functions, that [the connotatively male body of reason] will not perform."[58] Because the Western world's sexual prejudices are deeply intertwined with these rejections of the body as a meaningful location of culture or identity, unpacking the sexual possibilities of the superhero body can only enhance the value of that body as an object of study.

It is important, however, to keep in mind that the multiplicity of the superhero body allows it to be *both* inherently queer *and* defiantly literal; to repurpose a famous Freudianism, sometimes a flaming teenager is just a flaming teenager. Moreover, while the superhero genre's spectacular violence often expresses its own multiplicity,[59] this violence routinely suggests that some bodies are more redeemably deviant than others. Though both comics and superhero stories "are adept at taking what is real and turning it topsy-turvy to demonstrate the idiosyncrasies or wrongheadedness of our thinking,"[60] because they "rely upon visually coded representations in which characters are continually reduced to their appearances,"[61] comics and superhero stories also "traffic in stereotype and fixity."[62] This fixity is evident in the superhero genre's exaggerated representations of gender norms, and in the related fact that when sexuality is explicitly present in mainstream superhero texts, it is often at the expense of female characters. The hypersexualization of female characters in superhero texts is so pervasive that publicly critiquing it has been known to provoke rape and death threats,[63] and sexually assaulting female characters to motivate male love interests or teammates is so conventional that it has a name—"fridging," coined by writer Gail Simone in honor of a 1994 Green Lantern comic book in which the hero arrives home to find his murdered girlfriend's corpse stuffed in his refrigerator.[64] Fixity is also evident in the superhero genre's representations of supervillains, whose bodies are often strongly associated with prejudices related to disability, racial otherness, or sexual deviance; on the most basic level, countless superhero stories conclude with more acceptable bodies beating, imprisoning, humiliating, or even killing less acceptable ones. In the words of Sheena C. Howard and Ronald L. Jackson II, superhero comics often "tell a story about White heroes and minority villains, White victors and minority losers, White protagonists and perhaps a minority sidekick."[65]

But even if superhero bodies are not automatically progressive, their special visibility is still important to what the superhero genre can offer as a window on the human condition. While most popular texts are polysemic[66] and every long-lived genre will evince the push and pull of changing social and cultural mores, the superhero genre's especially visual bodies means it showcases and negotiates cultural conflicts in ways that are similarly especially visible, and thus especially assessible, for fans and scholars alike. As Deborah Elizabeth Whaley observes, comic books and superhero stories offer "an embellishment of real and imaginary worlds as well as their attendant problems."[67] Anna Beatrice Scott concurs that superhero bodies "function as a fascinating interpolation of fantastical imaginaries and studied anatomical renderings of the unseen, mainly, power."[68] This accessibility is further aided by the fact that the superhero genre generally stars characters who are meant to represent ideal selves and citizens. It is for this reason that Howard and Jackson argue the superhero genre has "the powerful potential to weave imaginary narratives that offer possibilities for seeing Black heroism."[69] Fredrick Luis Aldama has made a similar argument regarding Latinx superheroes,[70] as have several books about female superheroes, most of which agree, in some capacity, with Dawn Heinecken's assertion that "the female hero is a great place to investigate the meanings of female power circulating in society."[71] Wertham's critiques and the dramatic reaction to them show that sexuality has long been one of the most fraught battlegrounds for the superhero genre's negotiation of cultural conflicts; the recent controversies surrounding Wonder Woman's ambassadorship and Batman's penis show that it remains so.

Despite the myriad potential benefits of studying superhero sexuality, the existing academic discourse around comics and superheroes has addressed it only sporadically. Certainly, many individual essays, including Andy Medhurst's much-cited and repeatedly anthologized "Batman, Deviance, and Camp" as well as several contributions to *American Literature*'s recent "Queer about Comics" special issue, have tackled superhero sexuality directly and usefully asserted its relevance to other fields of study.⁷² Superhero sexuality is also discussed in some capacity within many recent academic studies of comics and superheroes, including José Alaniz's *Death, Disability, and the Superhero: The Silver Age and Beyond*; Deborah Elizabeth Whaley's *Black Women in Sequence: Re-inking Comics, Graphic Novels, and Anime*; Ramzi Fawaz's *The New Mutants: Superheroes and the Radical Imagination of American Comics*; Carolyn Cocca's *Superwomen: Gender, Power, and Representation*; and Mel Gibson, David Huxley, and Joan Ormrod's anthology *Superheroes and Identities*. Particular superheroes have also been subject to more sexuality-oriented scholarship than others. As the case studies in this introduction reflect, Batman and Wonder Woman are the most prominent in this regard; Will Brooker's book *Batman Unmasked* features considerable discussion of queer interpretations of the Dark Knight's relationship with Robin, while Noah Berlatsky's *Wonder Woman: Bondage and Feminism in the Marston/Peter Comics*, Jill Lepore's *The Secret History of Wonder Woman*, and Tim Hanley's *Wonder Woman Unbound: The Secret History of the World's Most Famous Heroine* address sexual themes within Wonder Woman stories from various eras. To date, however, only one book, Gareth Schott's *From "Ambiguously Gay Duos" to Homosexual Superheroes: The Role of Sexuality in Comic Book Fandom*, has been published that features superhero sexuality as its central focus, and explores it in conversation with fan culture and a wide sampling of texts. It seems that in academia, superhero sexuality is once again simultaneously present and absent; while sexuality lingers in the background of many explorations of gender, race, and the superhero body, it rarely becomes explicit.

Supersex: Sexuality, Fantasy, and the Superhero makes visible the modes and meanings of the simultaneous presence and absence of superhero sexuality by examining it in as many ways and places as possible. This book includes thirteen chapters, divided into two parts: Part I, "Comics"; and Part II, "Film, Television, and Fan Culture." The collection concludes with an epilogue from poet and scholar Richard Harrison. These multidisciplinary chapters focus on historical and contemporary superhero texts, including mainstream productions as well as those underground, independent, and fan-produced works that have commented on, critiqued, or revised the mainstream. This multidisciplinarity extends to the backgrounds of the contributors, who approach their individual chapters from a variety of fields, including comics studies, film studies, philosophy, ethnography, cultural studies, queer studies, porn studies, and literature. *Supersex* furthermore prioritizes intersectional approaches to the topic; chapters discuss sexuality in conversation with gender, race, disability, and class, among other dynamics. In each section, some chapters consider works that are aimed at adults and/or those which feature explicit or pornographic content. Other chapters consider the sexual themes or implications of "all-ages" works wherein the actual business of sex is only implicitly or metaphorically present. In concert with the collection's multidisciplinarity and intersectionality, comparing explicit and implicit sexual themes and imagery helps highlight the diversity of superhero sexuality and, in so doing, the diversity of the fantasies this genre can and has inspired.

This emphasis on diversity does not ignore the superhero genre's historical and present heterosexism, patriarchy, misogyny, ableism, and white supremacy; many chapters directly address and interrogate these prejudices. *Supersex* does, however, want to challenge prevailing assumptions that the superhero genre has only ever appealed to a narrow demographic of young, straight, white males.[73] Showing the ways in which the superhero genre can appeal to more diverse audiences and experiences is less about celebrating the genre's historical inclusiveness than about spotlighting the aforementioned prejudices and discussing how they might be redressed. In further service of this goal, *Supersex* prioritizes understudied texts and contexts alongside new approaches to familiar topics. Though Superman, Batman, the X-Men, and other iconic characters and franchises are amply discussed in this collection, *Supersex* encourages us to look at individual texts and the superhero genre as a whole with different—and perhaps more lascivious—eyes. For those of us who were already looking lasciviously, *Supersex* acknowledges our gazes, though it does not always sanction them; all of the collection's chapters address the politics of desire.

As this emphasis on seeing differently would suggest, *Supersex* does not limit itself to conventional texts; many of the independent comics and most of the examples of pornography, fan art, fan fiction, and cosplay discussed in this collection do not fit comfortably into conventional understandings of the superhero genre. Yet within its diversity of viewpoints and approaches, *Supersex* defines the superhero in conventional terms: superheroes must have fantastic abilities, have a code name, and wear a costume that reflects what Peter Coogan calls the superhero's "MPI," that is, mission, powers, and identity.[74] "Supersex," then, is the combination of some aspect of those characteristics with some aspect of sexuality, broadly understood as referring to sexual desire, activity, or orientation. Analyzing conventional superheroes within a range of conventional and unconventional contexts is necessary not only to challenge the prevailing neglect of the genre's actual and possible diversity, but also to properly account for the ever-more plentiful ways superheroes are mobilized in this age of convergence culture, wherein popular stories exist within transmedia networks and fan communities have never been more influential. Because superheroes manifest in both mainstream outlets and independent contexts as well as a multitude of formats—including the aforementioned comics, films, television shows, pornography, fan fiction, fan art, and cosplay—they can be used to compare strategies of representation across mediums and styles with different artistic goals, properties, and modes of production and reception; the content and format of *Supersex* encourages such comparisons. This collection does not presume to address every possible permutation of superhero sexuality. It does, however, seek to offer a broad survey and build a strong foundation for future work on the topic; I would like nothing more than for this collection to inspire a flood of books and essays addressing the dynamics it inevitably neglects.

While the contributors to *Supersex* are international, the collection foregrounds the superhero as a quintessentially American (i.e., United States) phenomenon. This focus is not meant to suggest that superheroes do not exist elsewhere or that superhero texts must always reflect American cultural concerns. Yet America invented the superhero and continues to be the most vigorous creator and exporter of superhero texts; as such, aspects of the superhero genre are deeply imbued with American cultural values, including but not limited to America's highly contradictory sexual prudishness. At least since the sexual revolution of the 1960s, American popular culture has tended to allow and even encourage the display and commodification of sexuality even as American society and political institutions attempt to police, regulate, and even criminalize the real diversity of sexual expression; the latter is reflected in ongoing legislative battles over contraception, abortion, and LGBTQ rights. Moreover, because the Comics Code has had a lasting influence on the substance and perception of all types of superhero texts, if superheroes produced within non-American cultural contexts are influenced by the American model, they are influenced by American culture.

The chapters that follow present superhero sexuality as both dangerously exciting and excitingly dangerous, encapsulating the superhero genre's worst impulses as well as its most productively rebellious ones. Taken as a whole, this collection's chapters argue that, for better or worse, superheroes' special ability to negotiate competing demands for sexual liberation and containment—which is reflected in the always-evolving but ever-present play of sexual presence and absence—is vital to their appeal, both historically and in the present moment.

SUMMARY OF CHAPTERS

Part I follows a loosely chronological trajectory, beginning with Richard Reynolds's chapter, "Tarpé Mills's *Miss Fury*: Costume, Sexuality, and Power." Miss Fury is arguably the world's first female superhero and inarguably the first such character created, written, and drawn by a woman. This comic, which ran from 1941 to 1952 as a full-color Sunday newspaper strip, stars the titular Miss Fury, a.k.a. heiress and socialite Marla Drake, who dons a black leopard-skin costume for globe-trotting adventures. Reynolds argues that the real star of the strip, however, is Drake—and her always-glamorous wardrobe, which is informed by Mills's previous work as a fashion illustrator. Reynolds reads Drake's wardrobe as a protest against wartime austerity and an instrument of gender and sexual fluidity within a world where all identities are masquerades. This identity play resonates with many of the most critically lauded contemporary superhero stories, some of which are discussed elsewhere in this collection.

Next, Matt Yockey's chapter, "Superman Family Values: Supersex in the Silver Age," moves the collection into the post-Code era, unpacking the sexual implications of the many wild transformations and fantastic multiplications of Superman and his "family" in comic books from the "Silver Age" of the 1950s and '60s. Yockey argues that the advent and promotion of this decidedly nonnormative family—which includes numerous "Bizarro" doubles and superpowered animals—allows for multiple and diverse forms of identification, what Yockey calls "cognitive reproduction." Rather than lament the conservatism of the era that directly followed the Comics Code, Yockey asserts that it is precisely this era's restrictions that create the need for symbolic alternatives that become, through the absences they both disguise and illuminate, multilayered and highly charged, for children and adults alike.

The next two chapters transition from the Silver Age into the social issues–conscious "Bronze Age" of the 1970s and '80s. J. Andrew Deman's chapter, "A Storm of Passion: Sexual Agency and Symbolic Capital in the X-Men's Storm," argues that the cultural capital of the X-Men franchise is bound up in the transition of longtime team member and sometime team leader Storm—arguably the most prominent Black female superhero in American comics[75]—from a sexual object into a sexually empowered subject. Focusing on comics from Chris Claremont's lengthy and influential run as the lead writer of *Uncanny X-Men*, Deman tracks this transition through Storm's depiction within key relationships—including a potential lesbian relationship with a Japanese ronin—as well as changes in character styling that reflect Storm's (and Claremont's) embrace of queer and alternative culture and the importance of sexual agency as a component of self-making, particularly for female and Black subjects who have historically been denied such agency. Brian Johnson's chapter, "Dazzler, Melodrama, and Shame: Mutant Allegory, Closeted Readers," offers a different perspective on the X-Men's mutant metaphor. Through the example of the X-Men franchise character Dazzler—a mutant disco queen turned rock star with the ability to convert sound into light and energy beams—Johnson discusses the political and personal damage that can result from referencing queer contexts while denying explicit manifestations of queer behavior. Through a historically situated reading of the *Dazzler* solo series published from 1981 to 1985, Johnson details the titular character's emergence as a gay icon and discusses how the positive potential of this identification is undercut by the slipperiness of the mutant metaphor, which enables—and even encourages—hiding as much as showing.

The final two chapters in this section focus on depictions of overtly LGBTQ superheroes in independent and mainstream comics from the 1980s to the twenty-first century. Sarah M. Panuska's chapter, "'Super-Gay' *Gay Comix*: Tracing the Underground Origins and Cultural Resonances of LGBTQ Superheroes," argues that although recent mainstream superhero comic book series should be praised for their inclusions of sexual diversity, this inclusiveness is limited by a paucity of direct references to LGBTQ history and culture. Panuska illuminates these shortcomings through an analysis of the underground anthology comic *Gay Comix* #8, a.k.a. the "Super Gay" issue, originally published in 1986. Produced entirely by LGBTQ-identified creators, the "Super Gay" issue features sexually explicit superhero parodies starring the likes of "Leatherthing," a onetime leather king turned retributive zombie, and "Captain Condom," whose eagerly pursued mission involves demonstrating safe sex techniques amid the AIDS crisis. Panuska's chapter asserts the value and relevance of superhero stories to LGBTQ lives and experiences, and suggests ways contemporary mainstream comics might better leverage that value. Keith Friedlander's chapter, "Parents, Counterpublics, and Sexual Identity in *Young Avengers*," argues that despite their conservative impulses, contemporary mainstream superhero comics can powerfully mobilize superheroic metaphors in ways that are relevant to LGBTQ experiences. Focusing on three *Young Avengers* series—Alan Heinberg and Jim Cheung's original *Young Avengers* (2005–2006), their later crossover event *The Children's Crusade* (2010–2012), and Kieron Gillen and Jamie McKelvie's *Young Avengers* relaunch (2013–2014)—Friedlander argues that in their continuous rebellion against the authority of older heroes who wish them to maintain discrete private lives, the queer teenagers who make up the Young Avengers can be read as forming what Michael Warner terms a counterpublic: a group that defines itself against the dominant (that is, patriarchal and heteronormative) public sphere.

Part II begins with two essays focusing on intersections of gender, race, and sexuality within distinct eras of superhero film production. First, Christopher B. Zeichmann's chapter, "X-Men Films and the Domestication of Dissent: Sexuality, Race, and Respectability," interrogates the problematic intersectionality of director Bryan Singer's critically lauded blockbusters *X-Men* (2000) and *X2: X-Men United* (2003). Situating his analysis within early-2000s identity politics discourse, Zeichmann argues that these films mobilize the elasticity of the mutant metaphor to associate the heroic X-Men with white- and middle-class-dominated struggles for queer rights while associating the villainous "Brotherhood" with the rhetoric of Black liberation movements. Zeichmann's analysis highlights the superhero genre's ability to both disguise political contexts and magnify them, and speculates on how the accusations of sexual assault connected to Singer might affect the legacy of these films. Samantha Langsdale's chapter, "Over the Rainbow Bridge: Female/Queer Sexuality in Marvel's Thor Film Trilogy," explores evolving representations of female strength and sexuality within the Marvel Cinematic Universe using the example of the Thor trilogy, consisting of *Thor* (2011), *Thor: The Dark World* (2013), and *Thor: Ragnarok* (2017). Langsdale argues that the Thor trilogy's unusually complicated and diverse cast of female characters is united by their possession of sexual agency. She also, however, highlights the limits of this agency, which is variously curtailed by romantic frameworks, rendered monstrous, or resigned to the cutting room floor. Ultimately, Langsdale asserts that the Thor films use sexuality to mobilize exciting but incomplete challenges to the superhero genre's historical prejudices and exclusions.

My chapter, "'No One's Going to Be Looking at Your Face': The Female Gaze and the New (Super)Man in *Lois & Clark: The New Adventures of Superman*," shares Zeichmann's and Langsdale's investment in locating superhero comic book adaptations within their specific cultural context. To that end, I revisit the ABC television show *Lois & Clark: The New Adventures of Superman* (1993–1997), a romantic comedy developed by Deborah Joy LeVine, as a rare and historically significant instance of an iconic male superhero being reshaped by women, for women. While I concur with existing scholarship that reads this show's depiction of Lois Lane as emblematic of the political shortcomings of 1990s postfeminism, I argue there is additional progressive potential within *Lois & Clark*'s "new man"–inspired depiction of Superman as the central subject—or object—of its female-driven fantasy. My analysis particularly highlights *Lois & Clark*'s eroticization of masculine transformations; these transformations, I argue, reframe popular understandings of the Man of Steel by complicating the gendered subject/object binaries that traditionally dictate who is permitted to gaze at whom.

From *Lois & Clark*'s family-friendly, officially sanctioned depiction of superhero sexuality, the collection pivots toward two chapters focusing on decidedly unsanctioned pornographic depictions. Jeffrey A. Brown's chapter, "The Visible and the Invisible: Superheroes, Pornography, and Phallic Masculinity," surveys representations of men and masculinity within the increasingly popular subgenre of superhero porn parody films aimed at heterosexual men. Brown argues that while porn parodies might seem to challenge the superhero genre's conventional reification of phallic masculinity by exposing it as attached to a specific body part (i.e., the penis), in fact, the opposite is true; in Brown's reading, pornographic conventions that confer super-ness on the porn star penis serve to reaffirm the superhero genre's phallocentrism. Joseph Brennan's chapter, "'I Think That's My Favorite Weapon in the Whole Batcave': Interrogating the Subversions of Men.com's Gay Superhero Porn Parodies," both complicates and builds upon Brown's conclusions. In his analysis of gender and sex roles within gay superhero porn parodies hosted by the Men.com sub-site Super Gay Hero, Brennan addresses the subversive potential of making the superhero genre's frequently coded gayness explicit. Brennan also, however, considers how these texts replicate the superhero genre's less-than-progressive gender politics by attaching power and victory to sexual "topping" while "bottoming" is almost invariably associated with villainy and vulnerability. Both Brown and Brennan argue that by rendering the power dynamics of the superhero genre (sexually) explicit, superhero porn parodies illuminate key aspects of the genre's continued popularity.

The collection's final two chapters focus on fan works, that is, texts produced by fans for the enjoyment of other fans, without the immediate expectation of financial gain. First, Olivia Hicks's chapter, "'That's Pussy Babe!': Queering Supergirl's Confessions of Power," compares the gender and sexual politics of heterosexual, male-gaze-oriented texts starring Supergirl to those produced within queer and female-dominated communities. Hicks argues that whereas both a majority of mainstream comics and the Tijuana Bibles of the 1950s and '60s present Supergirl's power as a problem that must be contained through sexual conquest (usually at the hands of her older and more powerful cousin, Superman), fan fiction and fan art within the "Supercorp" fandom—which pairs Supergirl with Lena Luthor, the sister of supervillain Lex Luthor, from the *Supergirl* television series (2015–present)—embraces Supergirl's power as a conduit of queer eroticism. Hicks's analysis foregrounds the superhero genre's pervasive misogyny and asserts that listening to the desires of marginalized voices is one of the best ways to combat it. Anne Kustritz's chapter, "Meet Stephanie Rogers, Captain America: Genderbending the Body Politic in Fan Art, Fiction, and Cosplay," shares Hicks's focus on the importance and power of marginalized voices. Kustritz examines how fan works featuring various biological and erotic alterations of the canonically white, straight, and male Captain America comment upon and remake notions of what Lauren Berlant calls the "national imaginary," reconfiguring the intertwined categories of sexuality, gender, race, and the citizen. Kustritz argues that these rewritings/redrawings/reembodiments serve as a form of public pedagogy that makes gender norms strange through reversal, then opens a creative space for imagining women, men, citizens, and strength in new and unexpected ways.

Richard Harrison's epilogue, "The Matter with Size," offers a deeply personal reflection on the inspiration and denigration he has found in male superheroes' beautiful yet sexless (or beautifully sexless) bodies. For Harrison, these bodies reflect both stereotypical masculine power fantasies and a dream of a better masculinity freed from the ugliness of the sexual abuse men continue to be disproportionately responsible for. Harrison's reflections speak directly to a question that animates a great deal of popular culture scholarship, and this collection's scholarship especially: Can we continue to responsibly love stories that we know to be eminently capable of nurturing deeply problematic fantasies? Harrison does not definitively answer this question; nor do the other chapters in *Supersex*. But I am confident that I speak for all contributors when I say that we very much hope we have made a convincing case for it being a question worth asking—of ourselves, our loves, our lusts, and our heroes, "super" or otherwise.

NOTES

1. Fredric Wertham, *Seduction of the Innocent* (New York: Rinehart, 1954), 190.
2. Wertham, *Seduction of the Innocent*, 190–191.
3. Wertham, *Seduction of the Innocent*, 193.
4. Wertham, *Seduction of the Innocent*, 191.

5. Darieck Scott and Ramzi Fawaz, "Introduction: Queer about Comics," *American Literature* 90, no. 2 (June 2018): 201.

6. Wertham, *Seduction of the Innocent*, 191.

7. Wertham, *Seduction of the Innocent*, 192.

8. Wertham, *Seduction of the Innocent*, 193.

9. For detailed histories of the moral panic around comics and juvenile delinquency, see Bart Beaty, *Fredric Wertham and the Critic of Mass Culture* (Jackson: University Press of Mississippi, 2005); David Hajdu, *The Ten-Cent Plague: The Great Comic-Book Scare and How It Changed America* (New York: Picador, 2008); and Amy Kiste Nyberg, *Seal of Approval: The History of the Comics Code* (Jackson: University Press of Mississippi, 1998).

10. Nyberg, *Seal of Approval*, x.

11. Nyberg, *Seal of Approval*, 167–168.

12. Nyberg, *Seal of Approval*, 167.

13. Comic Book Legal Defense Fund, "Comics Code Revision of 1989," http://cbldf.org/comics-code-revision-of-1989/.

14. Comic Book Legal Defense Fund, "Comics Code Revision."

15. Comic Book Legal Defense Fund, "Comics Code Revision."

16. Andréa Gilroy, "The Epistemology of the Phone Booth: The Superheroic Identity and Queer Theory in *Batwoman: Elegy*," *ImageText* 8, no. 3 (2015), http://imagetext.english.ufl.edu/archives/v8_1/gilroy/.

17. The modern Batwoman, introduced in 2006, is officially a different character from the version that appears in the 1950s and 1960s. But a lineage is suggested by the fact that these characters bear the same name in both their civilian and superhero guises (the modern Batwoman is Katherine "Kate" Kane; the original is Kathrine "Kathy" Kane).

18. The name Tijuana Bibles does not reflect these comics' place of origin. Art Spiegelman speculates that they "might have been called Tijuana Bibles as gleefully sacrilegious pre-NAFTA slurs against Mexicans, to throw G-men off the trail, or because the West Coast border towns were an important supplier of all sorts of sin." See Art Spiegelman, "Introduction," in *Tijuana Bibles: Art and Wit in America's Forbidden Funnies, 1930s–1950s*, ed. Bob Adelman (New York: Simon & Schuster, 1997), 6.

19. Spiegelman, "Introduction," 6.

20. Spiegelman, "Introduction," 6.

21. The title is written without the apostrophe (*It Aint Me Babe*) on the cover of the original comic. It is, however, common to include the apostrophe in bibliographic records.

22. Erin Barry, "Eight-Page Eroticism: Sexual Violence and the Construction of Normative Masculinity in Tijuana Bibles," *Journal of Graphic Novels & Comics* 8, no. 3 (May 2017): 227.

23. Despite the Code's seeming disallowance of sexualized exaggeration, female characters are conventionally hypersexualized within the superhero genre. They are also subject to sexualized violence and/or "'killed, maimed, or depowered' at

much higher rates than their more numerous male counterparts, generally as a plot point to further a male character's development." See Carolyn Cocca, *Superwomen: Gender, Power, and Representation* (New York: Bloomsbury, 2016), 12.

24. As a case in point: in the story "A Very Personal Hell" from *Rampaging Hulk* #23 (1980), written by then-Marvel-editor-in-chief Jim Shooter, the Hulk's alter ego, Bruce Banner, is assaulted in a YMCA shower by a pair of men who are strongly signaled to be gay. Many fans read this scene as homophobic. See R. S. Benedict, "That Time the Incredible Hulk Was Almost Raped by Gay Men at the YMCA," Hornet, February 12, 2017, https://hornet.com/stories/time-incredible-hulk-almost-raped-gay-men-ymca/.

25. As Samantha Langsdale discusses elsewhere in this volume, though a scene was filmed that would have made this character's bisexuality manifest, it was ultimately cut, reportedly because producers considered it a "distraction."

26. The character Nia Nal/Dream Girl is portrayed by activist-turned-actor Nicole Maines.

27. Laurie Sandell, "What Ruby Rose Really Thinks about Speaking Out on Social Media," *Cosmopolitan*, February 1, 2017, https://www.cosmopolitan.com/entertainment/a8659262/ruby-rose-march-2017/.

28. The authors of this collection are aware that the acronym LGBTQ does not include every identity along the sexuality spectrum. Yet within the mainstream political and cultural discourses that are the main focus of this book, the nonnormative and/or marginalized sexual identities that comprise the LGBTQ acronym are the most commonly recognized; as such, this collection generally employs *LGBTQ* as a common point of reference. However, individual chapters discuss additional sexual identities and mobilize different interpretations of the terms that compose the LGBTQ acronym. This collection encourages these differences. Where appropriate, authors explain their divergences from common usage or demonstrate their interpretation of terms through their approach to analysis.

29. The website Common Sense Media, which advertises itself as "the leading independent nonprofit organization dedicated to helping kids thrive in a world of media and technology," indicates that "parents say" *Legends of Tomorrow* is appropriate for ages 13+, while "kids say" the show is appropriate for ages 11+. Parent commentators on the site express concern for the show's violence and sexuality. About the latter, opinion is, unsurprisingly, divided; some parents praise the show's depiction of same-sex relationships, while others cite it as central to their disapproval. "Parent Reviews for DC's Legends of Tomorrow," Common Sense Media, accessed March 15, 2019, https://www.commonsensemedia.org/tv-reviews/dcs-legends-of-tomorrow/user-reviews/adult.

30. Elizabeth Roberts, "UN Drops Wonder Woman as Honorary Ambassador," CNN, December 13, 2016, https://www.cnn.com/2016/12/13/health/wonder-woman-un-ambassador-trnd/index.html.

31. "Reconsider the Choice of Wonder Woman as the UN's Honorary Ambassador for the Empowerment of Women and Girls," Care2 Petitions, accessed March 15, 2019, https://www.thepetitionsite.com/en-gb/741/288/432/reconsider-the-choice-of-honorary-ambassador-for-the-empowerment-of-women-and-girls/.

32. Erin McCann, "U.N. Drops Wonder Woman as an Ambassador," *New York Times* online, December 13, 2016, https://www.nytimes.com/2016/12/13/world/un-wonder-woman-campaign.html.

33. Roberts, "UN Drops Wonder Woman."

34. Roberts, "UN Drops Wonder Woman."

35. Tara Peterson, "Make Wonder Woman a UN Ambassador Again," Change.org, accessed March 15, 2019, https://www.change.org/p/united-nations-make-wonder-woman-a-un-ambassador-again.

36. Tim Beedle, "Shedding New Light on DC Black Label," DC Comics online, June 15, 2018, https://www.dccomics.com/blog/2018/06/15/shedding-new-light-on-dc-black-label.

37. "Batman's Penis Controversy," Know Your Meme, accessed March 15, 2019, https://knowyourmeme.com/memes/events/batmans-penis-censorship-controversy.

38. See Pamela Paul, *Pornified: How Pornography Is Transforming Our Lives, Our Relationships, and Our Families* (New York: St. Martin's Griffin, 2006).

39. Linda Williams, "Proliferating Pornographies On/Scene: An Introduction," in *Porn Studies*, ed. Linda Williams (Durham, NC: Duke University Press, 2004), 3.

40. One of the most condemnatory statements came from the Genital Rights Association, which decried the fact that Batman's penis was circumcised. Nicole Drum, "Genital Rights Organization Upset over New Batman Comic," Comicbook.com, September 28, 2018, https://comicbook.com/dc/2018/09/23/batman-penis-controversy-genital-rights-group/.

41. "Trump Visits North Carolina, Batman's Penis—Monologue," *Late Night with Seth Myers*, YouTube video, September 20, 2018, https://www.youtube.com/watch?v=ZPjBsw1RVX4.

42. Quoted in Alison Flood, "Holy Backtrack, Batman! DC Withdraws Caped Crusader's Nude Scene," *Guardian*, September 21, 2018, https://www.theguardian.com/books/2018/sep/21/batmans-genitals-dc-withdraws-nude-scene-damned.

43. Flood, "Holy Backtrack, Batman!"

44. Susan Polo, "Batman's Nudity Controversy Made DC Comics Publishers Reassess Other Black Label Books," Polygon, October 8, 2018, https://www.polygon.com/comics/2018/10/8/17952834/dc-comics-batman-nudity-black-label-jim-lee-dan-didio. Rich Johnson, founder and lead writer of Bleeding Cool, speculated that the controversy was likely to generate creative crackdowns across the board in the interests of deflecting further negative attention. Rich Johnson, "NYCC Bar Talk: How Batman's Penis Is Damaging DC Comics from Within," Bleeding Cool, October 5, 2018, https://www.bleedingcool.com/2018/10/05/nycc-batman-penis-destroying-dc-comics-within/.

45. For example, see Dru Jeffries, *Comic Book Film Style: Cinema at 24 Panels per Second* (Austin: University of Texas Press, 2017); and Blair Davis, *Comic Book Movies* (New Brunswick, NJ: Rutgers University Press, 2018).

46. Deborah Shamoon, "Office Sluts and Rebel Flowers: The Pleasures of Japanese Pornographic Comics for Women," in *Porn Studies*, ed. Linda Williams (Durham, NC: Duke University Press, 2004), 77.

47. For its multimodal nature, see Dale Jacobs, *Graphic Encounters: Comics and the Sponsorship of Multimodal Literacy* (New York: Bloomsbury, 2013). For its fragmented nature, see Barbara Postema, *Narrative Structure in Comics: Making Sense of Fragments* (Rochester, NY: RIT Press, 2013).

48. Jared Gardner, *Projections: Comics and the History of Twenty-First-Century Storytelling* (Stanford, CA: Stanford University Press, 2012), 86.

49. Alyce Mahon, *Eroticism and Art* (Oxford: Oxford University Press, 2005), 15.

50. Robert Jensen, "Pornography Is What the End of the World Looks Like," in *Everyday Pornography*, ed. Karen Boyle (New York: Routledge, 2010), 112.

51. Judith Butler, *Excitable Speech: A Politics of the Performative* (New York: Routledge, 1997), 68.

52. Wendy Haslem, Elizabeth MacFarlane, and Sarah Richardson, "Introducing the Superhero Body," in *Superhero Bodies: Identity, Materiality, Transformation*, ed. Wendy Haslem, Elizabeth MacFarlane, and Sarah Richardson (New York: Routledge, 2018), 2.

53. Scott Bukatman, "X-Bodies: The Torment of the Mutant Superhero," in *Matters of Gravity: Special Effects and Supermen in the 20th Century* (Durham, NC: Duke UP, 2003), 49.

54. Scott and Fawaz, "Introduction"; Daniel Stein, "Bodies in Transition: Queering the Comic Book Superhero," in "Queer(ing) Popular Culture," ed. Sebastian Zilles, special issue, *Navigationen* 18, no. 1 (2018): 15–38.

55. Aaron Taylor, "'He's Gotta Be Strong, and He's Gotta Be Fast, and He's Gotta Be Larger Than Life': Investigating the Engendered Superhero Body," *Journal of Popular Culture* 40, no. 2 (April 2007): 346, https://doi.org/10.1111/j.1540-5931.2007.00382.x.

56. Sander L. Gilman, *Making the Body Beautiful: A Cultural History of Aesthetic Surgery* (Princeton: Princeton University Press, 1999), 111; Jeffrey A. Brown, *Black Superheroes, Milestone Comics, and Their Fans* (Jackson: University Press of Mississippi, 2001), 170; Susan Bordo, *Twilight Zones: The Hidden Life of Cultural Images from Plato to O.J.* (Berkeley: University of California Press, 1999), 130.

57. Kobena Mercer, quoted in Brown, *Black Superheroes*, 173.

58. Judith Butler, *Bodies that Matter: On the Discursive Limits of Sex* (New York: Routledge, 2011), 22.

59. As Carolyn Cocca observes, violence within the superhero genre routinely causes female characters, in particular, to "[exaggerate] traits associated with masculinity and femininity simultaneously." Cocca, *Superwomen*, 12.

60. Sheena C. Howard and Ronald L. Jackson II, "Introduction," in *Black Comics: Politics of Race and Representation*, ed. Sheena C. Howard and Ronald L. Jackson II (New York: Bloomsbury, 2013), 2.

61. Marc Singer, "'Black Skins' and White Masks: Comic Books and the Secret of Race," in *African American Review* 36, no. 1 (2002), 107.

62. Frances Gateward and John Jennings, "Introduction: The Sweeter the Christmas," in *The Blacker the Ink: Constructions of Black Identity in Comics and*

Sequential Art, ed. Frances Gateward and John Jennings (New Brunswick, NJ: Rutgers University Press, 2015), 2.

63. A notable example is the reaction to Janelle Asselin's critique of the cover of *Teen Titans* #1, which appeared on the popular website Comic Book Resources in 2014. The level of vitriol leveled at the article, and at Asselin specially, contributed to the website shutting down all of its forum pages and relaunching them with a new anti-harassment policy. See David Mann, "An Almost Unnoticed Side-Effect: Thoughts on the Janelle Asselin/Teen Titans Cover Controversy," Sequart, May 25, 2014, http://sequart.org/magazine/43814/thoughts-on-the-janelle-asselin-teen-titans-cover-controversy/.

64. Gail Simone, Women in Refrigerators, blog, https://www.lby3.com/wir/.

65. Howard and Jackson II, "Introduction," 2.

66. John Fiske, *Television Culture* (New York: Routledge, 1989), 16.

67. Deborah Elizabeth Whaley, *Black Women in Sequence: Re-inking Comics, Graphic Novels, and Anime* (Seattle: University of Washington Press, 2016), ix.

68. Anna Beatrice Scott, "Superpower vs. Supernatural: Black Superheroes and the Quest for a Mutant Reality," *Journal of Visual Culture* 5, no. 3 (2006): 296.

69. Howard and Jackson II, "Introduction," 1.

70. See Frederick Luis Aldama, *Latinx Superheroes in Mainstream Comics* (Tucson: University of Arizona Press, 2017).

71. Dawn Heinecken, *The Warrior Women of Television: A Feminist Cultural Analysis of the New Female Body in Popular Media* (New York: Peter Lang, 2003), 21.

72. Medhurst's essay appears in *The Many Lives of the Batman: Critical Approaches to a Superhero and His Media*, ed. Roberta E. Pearson and William Uricchio (New York: Routledge, 1991), 149–163; and *The Superhero Reader*, ed. Charles Hatfield, Jeet Heer, and Kent Worcester (Jackson: University Press of Mississippi, 2013), 237–251.

73. For documentation and analysis of the neglect of female superhero comics readership by both the comics industry and academia, see the following: Karen Healey, "When Fangirls Perform: The Gendered Fan Identity in Superhero Comics Fandom," in *The Contemporary Comic Book Superhero*, ed. Angela Ndalianis (New York: Routledge, 2009), 144–163; Anna F. Peppard, "'This Female Fights Back!': A Feminist History of Marvel Comics," in *Make Ours Marvel: Media Convergence and a Comics Universe*, ed. Matt Yockey (Austin: University of Texas Press, 2017), 105–137; and Suzanne Scott, "Fangirls in Refrigerators: The Politics of (In)visibility in Comic Book Culture," *Transformative Works and Cultures*, no. 13 (2013), http://journal.transformativeworks.org/index.php/twc/article/view/460/384.

74. Peter Coogan, *Superhero: The Secret Origin of a Genre* (Austin, TX: MonkeyBrain, 2006), 33.

75. In this collection, the authors capitalize *Black* as an identity category but do not capitalize *white* in the same context. Decisions about which identities to capitalize are inevitably political and always imperfect. The authors view capitalizing *Black* as a gesture of respect that acknowledges this term's affirmative reclamation and the deep importance of that reclamation within the context of the centuries-long

efforts of Western societies and cultures to suppress positive affirmations of Black identity. Not capitalizing *white* risks shielding whiteness from interrogation, which in turn risks upholding problematic assumptions about its universality. Yet we view capitalizing white as a more dangerous proposition. At the time of this writing, the most common voluntary use of *white* as an affirmative identity is within white supremacist groups. We do not wish to lend any legitimacy to these ideologies by sharing their method of capitalization. For a concise summary of contemporary debates surrounding the capitalization of *Black* and *white*, see Merrill Perlman, "Black and White: Why Capitalization Matters," *Columbia Journalism Review*, June 23, 2015, https://www.cjr.org/analysis/language_corner_1.php.

PART I

COMICS

1

TARPÉ MILLS'S *MISS FURY*
Costume, Sexuality, and Power

RICHARD REYNOLDS

Superheroes don't put on costumes to fight villains—superheroes fight villains so that they can put on costumes!

> Scott Bukatman, speaking at New York's
> Metropolitan Museum of Art, 2008

Miss Fury was a syndicated weekly newspaper comic strip that ran from 1941 to 1952. At its peak, the strip was featured in over one hundred American Sunday papers; material was also repackaged to make up eight issues of a Timely comic book, also called *Miss Fury*, which appeared between 1942 and 1946.[1] Miss Fury has a claim to being the first significant female superhero. She was unquestionably the first female superhero to be written and drawn by a woman.[2]

Tarpé Mills (1918–1988), the series' writer-artist and auteur, was a graduate of Pratt Institute and had worked in the fashion industry as a model and illustrator before becoming involved in the mushrooming comics business. Mills's first comics characters—starring in strips such as *The Purple Zombie* and *Daredevil Barry Finn*—were unremarkable genre productions.[3] But in 1941, Mills hit the big time by selling her *Black Fury* concept (as the strip was initially known)[4] as a syndicated newspaper strip.

Launched in April 1941 by the Bell syndicate, *Miss Fury* predates Wonder Woman by more than six months. The widely syndicated strip ran for eleven years and some 480 weekly episodes (with a hiatus from October 1947 to January 1949).[5] *Miss Fury* is a high-adventure, glamorously staged espionage thriller set in international locales. In many ways, it has more in common with Milton Caniff's action-adventure strip *Terry and the Pirates* or even Dale Messick's "working girl"/action strip *Brenda Starr* than with the superhero genre, which was being developed and elaborated contemporaneously within the comic book market. Using examples from throughout the entire 1941–1952 run of *Miss Fury*, this chapter will examine these comics' presentation of relationships between identity, fashion, performance, and sexuality. This examination will argue that *Miss Fury* was ahead of its time, but not in the way one might, at a first glance, assume. Unlike its superhero comics contemporaries, *Miss Fury* is less interested in singular transformations denoting binary differences than in exploring fluid identities denoting the possibility of infinite change. *Miss Fury*'s title character may be a proto-feminist, but she is also a woman luxuriating in her spectacular femininity, finding power in glamor and resistance in denying the allure of the black leopard-skin costume that on discrete occasions affords her a more connotatively masculine form of physical power. *Miss Fury* is thus an atypical costumed adventurer. Her alter ego, rich heiress Marla Drake, normally prefers to avoid donning her costume and becoming Miss Fury. For Drake, switching to the persona of the masked vigilante is a strategy of last resort, only adopted when all other approaches to a problem have been thwarted. Her costume is also said to bring bad luck, and this injunction against overuse of her secret identity is something that Marla Drake takes seriously. Drake's reluctance to get into costume also highlights the strip's wider fixation with identity and the processes through which costume and fashion are used as markers of selfhood.

"WHAT SHALL I WEAR TO THE MASQUERADE?"

Mills's focus on fluid personal identity begins with an exploration of tropes already made familiar by the emergent superhero genre. The strip's original setup resembles the original setup of Batman's comic book adventures, which preceded *Miss Fury* by two years. Strip 1 introduces the reader to Marla Drake, bored heiress and socialite, in the moment of discovering that she has chosen the same dress as another guest for a masquerade party (figure 1.1). Appalled, she accepts the suggestion of her maid and confidant, Francine, and switches clothes, donning an African heirloom from her uncle: a pitch-black, skin-tight leopard-skin costume that incorporates a mask, ears, and a whip-like tail. The panther suit turns out to have mysterious superpowers, and Drake is immediately drawn into

FIGURE 1.1. Marla Drake rejects her eighteenth-century ball gown in favor of the black catsuit sourced by her maid, Francine. *Black Fury* (a.k.a. *Miss Fury*) #1 (1941).

crime fighting, spending the evening beating and capturing a criminal instead of attending the fancy-dress party. The reader infers that Ms. Drake has discovered a much more exciting kind of masquerade. Absent from this story is any awareness of the implied appropriation in this plot device. Like most popular creators from the period, Mills does not interrogate contemporary assumptions about race or ethnicity; Drake's access to the power of masquerade flows, unquestioned, from both her wealth and her whiteness. Also absent from this origin story is any explicit "motivation" for the protagonist to become a costumed vigilante or crime fighter. Drake simply puts on the costume, and everything flows from this choice. The imperative to perform when in costume is more fundamental to the story than any ethical, social, or political agenda. Life for Marla Drake is a nonstop masquerade—a performance in which personal loyalties and feelings determine moral choices.

Despite its grounding in class and racial privilege, this transition from street garb to superhero costume can be interpreted as a metaphor for the (supposedly) universal fluidity and malleability of metropolitan identity.[6] The urban superhero, in such a reading, is a kind of modern flaneur: the hidden face in the crowd, the masked avenger who makes manifest the will of the anonymous urban landscape. Numerous Batman, Daredevil, and similar "street level" superhero stories explore this theme. Miss Fury's mask and catsuit also evoke the persona of the femme fatale, whose "seductive power," as Mary Ann Doane notes, ". . . confounds the relation between the visible and the knowable."[7] Miss Fury's battles repeatedly involve the uncovering of truth and the removal of deception. She fights silently, and the panels depicting her fighting sequences involve repeated mirroring of her opponents' movements, who also regularly duplicate or imitate Miss Fury's own appearance.[8] For Marla Drake, Miss Fury affords a brief passage into a looking-glass world. The boudoir vanity mirror and its reflections are also used as a repeated trope to signal the identity transformations of both Drake and her supporting characters.[9] *Miss Fury* evokes this notion of urban masquerade even while its protagonist is "out of costume." One might say that Tarpé Mills's characters are *always* "in costume": their identities are constructed from the costumes they wear to perform their roles in the complex, gendered melodramas of their lives. In this regard, *Miss Fury* is far ahead of its time, exploring themes of identity and sexualization through a fetishization of costume and dress that would not become central to the superhero genre until decades later, in texts such as *Watchmen* and *The Sensational She-Hulk*, and in movies such as *Batman Returns*.[10]

Mills represents dress as a tool her characters use in the performance of their identities. As Mills is more concerned with character development and suspense than with action, the tangled relationships of her characters generate the rich variety of psychological (and occasionally physical) confrontations and dramatic reversals. These webs of entanglement frequently involve overlapping or double relationships, in which characters serve multiple generic roles simultaneously (i.e., cop/lover, friend/enemy, prisoner/lover, maid/companion), colliding with each other in unpredictable ways. Power relationships between characters—and the eroticization (and fetishization) of power and the body through dress, fashion, and uniform—remain key throughout the series.

As a former professional fashion illustrator, Mills was exceptionally well placed to use costume to explore relationships between appearance and identity. For Marla Drake, the performance of identity does not begin with putting on her black catsuit: it is enacted every day when she prepares fastidiously to confront the world as a perfectly groomed and fashionably attired young society heiress. Drake could be said to embody Simone De Beauvoir's famous dictum, "One is not born, but rather becomes, a woman."[11]

For example, during the strip's first story arc (encompassing strips 1 to 54, when the action is mainly set in New York), Mills depicts Drake in day dresses and evening gowns that are absolutely on trend with the spring and fall 1941 fashions. Spring 1941 was the first spring season after the fall of Paris to the invading German army, and fashion journalists unabashedly invited the American woman to assume the mantle of global fashion leadership. A *Vogue* editorial published in March 1941 asserts,

> This is a spring different from all the springs that have gone before: different from any spring that may come after. . . . The way you think and feel, this spring, is important. . . . Your clothes have their part. You won't let them be an obsession with you, but because three-quarters of the world is askew, you will try to make your own part of it inviting, engaging, as nearly normal as possible.[12]

Bright color and bold contrasts were crucial to achieving this look, according to *Vogue*'s April 1941 editorial: "Perhaps a violet suit or coat. Grey with honey-yellow. Black and pink. . . . Clear, sharp prints on light or white backgrounds."[13] This could be a description of Marla Drake's wardrobe in the early months of the strip. Such bold colors and contrasts work well on the printed page.[14] In strip 5, Mills depicts Drake in an asymmetrical yellow suit with a yellow and black cloche hat and black fur stole. Strip 13 sees her in a (borrowed) red suit with black trim and a matching red and black leopard-skin beret. Strip 25 sees Marla in a crimson shirtwaist dress, a style *Vogue* declared to be the "dress that all America loves."[15] Strip 39 has Drake dressed in a flowing, full-skirted evening gown in dark blue with diagonal black stripes—a silhouette and pattern that was all over the fashion magazines for autumn 1941. Fashion for Marla Drake is a form of theater, a public performance of identity. Her clothes are meaningless without an accompanying narrative, as contemporary fashion writers were also at pains to emphasize. This is how a *Harper's Bazaar* editorial characterized the "Spring afternoon": "When the city glows with a luminous blue light, you'll break out of uniform. You'll emerge a pretty, feminine, leisurely creature. . . . This is the hour that can lengthen into restaurant and theatre evenings."[16] Spring evenings are also characterized as an occasion for performance: "A spring night creeps in, stoled figures waft out of apartment houses and into taxis, slim black columns drift into theatres, big splashy prints move to new rhythms over the dance floors."[17] The warm and glowing background tones of Mills's strips echo the words of the fashion writers, capturing the twilight moments that are so often the stage for both Marla Drake's and Miss Fury's performances. Without explaining why, *Harper's Bazaar* asserts, "Wartime has given this twilight-to-midnight dressing great importance"[18]—possibly because this time of day brings the male and female, or the uniformed soldier and civilian, into social contact. In her "Lines to a Woman" from the same issue of *Harper's Bazaar*, fashion guru Pauline Potter asserts that a woman's fashion choices are an index of her inner character: "To intimates and outsiders her clothes will sum up her moods, her most private tastes, her character. . . . If she lets these clothes create a misunderstanding between herself and the world she is guilty . . ."[19]

A statement such as this invites a reading inflected by Judith Butler's distinction between performance and performativity, Butler's thesis being that gender (and the associated discourses of fashion) are performative in the sense that there is no performer who "precedes the performance."[20] Mills makes such performance a key element in the diegetic spectacle of her narrative. The very first panels of the series depict Marla Drake in her boudoir, rejecting one fancy-dress costume (a baroque-style dress, complete with an enormous cage crinoline) in favor of the catsuit that will become her fighting costume. The decision itself is arbitrary, and it is only through wearing the catsuit (complete with its menacingly phallic tail) that Drake comes to perform the role of the superhero. The "wardrobe" metaphor that Sarah Salih uses to interpret Butler's notion of performativity seems especially pertinent to Drake's transformation:

> If we compare gender to choosing an outfit from a limited wardrobe, then once again we must ask who or what is doing the choosing? My example of a person who stands in front of a wardrobe of clothes and chooses what to wear that day, implies the existence of a subject or an agent that is *prior* to gender . . .[21]

Drake's catsuit was a supposedly random choice, just another performance of fashion in the theater of metropolitan life. Yet it is a transformative decision that unlocks a hitherto unexplored identity and is thus purely performative in Butler's terms. There was no Miss Fury until Marla Drake chose to put on the costume.

THE PERFORMANCE OF IDENTITY

Mills is fascinated by identity—and by identity exchange. Identity exchange is a factor in Mills's choice of professional name. Tarpé was June Tarpé Mills's middle name, which she used for professional purposes.[22] Unlike June, Tarpé is not gender specific, being so unusual that it does not automatically conjure up a male or female persona. Mills believed that the reception of her work might be affected negatively by her identity as a woman. But it is intriguing that, while disguising her gender, Mills did not choose an unequivocally masculine pen name. She chose a name that was elusive, ambiguous.

From its opening pages, *Miss Fury* is packed with examples of individuals with multiple, mirroring, or ambiguous identities. Drake has barely settled down from her initial adventure when a second Black Fury appears, usurping Drake's costume and committing crimes that place Drake in danger of arrest. Grace, wife of soon-to-be-appointed Special Prosecutor James Dana, is being blackmailed by a gangster known as Miguel Rico. Rico turns out to be connected to Baroness Erica Von Kampf, Drake's archnemesis. Like Marla Drake, Baroness Erica lives the life of a wealthy New York socialite, but under her veneer of respectability she is a spy, passing on information to the Nazis.

Drake instructs her maid, Francine, to run up a second Black Fury costume so she can track down the imposter and clear her name, thus reconfirming her original decision to wear the costume. In socialite mode, she pretends to be attracted to Rico, luring him away from his home so that, in her Black Fury persona, she can recover the blackmail letters that Rico holds over Grace. But Drake's battle to regain the sole right to the Black Fury identity uncovers another identity swap (figure 1.2). While Marla Drake suspects that the bogus Miss Fury is the duplicitous Baroness Erica, it is, instead, the blackmailer and gangster, Rico: a male villain masquerading as a female vigilante.

Meanwhile, after a botched assassination plot involving her employer, General Bruno Beitz (strip 20), Baroness Erica flees New York for Rio De Janeiro. There, she effects another identity swap, transforming herself

FIGURE 1.2. Francine is on the lookout while Miss Fury battles with her own mirror image: a male villain who has appropriated her fighting costume. *Black Fury* (a.k.a. *Miss Fury*) #32 (1941).

into the wife of Gary Hale, Marla Drake's former admirer. The baroness marries Hale to expedite her return to the United States. Baroness Erica is cornered by her disappointed Nazi paymasters, and they brand her forehead with a swastika symbol in revenge. She is initially dismayed. But a strategy for dealing with the situation is quickly devised:

FIGURE 1.3. Promotional paper-doll fashion cutouts of Marla Drake and Baroness Erica, 1942–1946. The symmetrical layout emphasizes how the two characters mirror each other's chic styles. Reprinted in Tarpé Mills, vol. 1, 11.

> BARONESS ERICA
> This won't be difficult to hide . . . at least until I get to the United States . . . a good plastic surgeon will do the rest![23]

Three panels later we see the baroness dressed and ready to make her getaway. A chic cloche hat, a black demi-veil, and the curls of her ash-blonde hair conveniently hide her telltale swastika. The baroness is ready to re-enter the drama of the city—any city—and play a new role. Mills situates in the modern metropolis the power to reinvent one's identity almost without constraint.[24]

Later, in the extended Brazilian interlude (strips 54 to 214, published between early 1942 and the spring of 1945), Drake is held captive by General Bruno. Separated from her luggage, Drake keeps up appearances by wearing a series of glamorous outfits borrowed from Baroness Erica's wardrobe (the two women must be the same size—suggesting yet another multiplication of identity). This fashion show only enhances Drake's allure in the eyes of the general (figure 1.3).

Mills plays with other variations on the theme of multiple identities.

Tarpé Mills's *Miss Fury*   39

On her eventual return to New York in 1945, Marla encounters Charlie (or "Sharlie"), the portly, perfumed, dog- and child-hating proprietor of a high-class fashion salon in New York. Sharlie is fencing artworks looted by the Nazis and reselling them to well-heeled collectors. Sharlie is overdetermined as a gay character through a host of negative stereotypes. He is also double-crossing his own accomplices as well as his clients. When things become too hot for him in New York, Sharlie attempts to escape south to Miami. During this escape, Sharlie transforms into a well-padded *grande dame*, with a practiced ease that suggests cross-dressing is familiar to him.[25] Although Sharlie's genderbending escapade is informed by predictable stereotypes, the naturalness of gender is subverted by his ability to "pass" as female with flying colors. Nobody reads him as male or cross-dressing on the journey to Florida.

The Sharlie plotline and performance is followed immediately by another identity swap, which involves a gang of villains incarcerating Marla Drake so that an exact double can impersonate her (and not, on this occasion, the costumed Miss Fury).[26] The plan is for the gang to collect the fortune that Drake is due to inherit on her twenty-third birthday. As in the Sharlie plotline, this story presents identity exchange and identity theft as disturbingly easy to pull off. Even Drake's faithful maid, Francine, fails to realize that the woman who arrives at her apartment in strip 279 is not the real Marla Drake.

Three other men who are not what they seem appear in the subsequent *Miss Fury* story arc, which ran from strips 291 to 323. One of these is a German war criminal, hiding in the New York area. He seeks the assistance of two wealthy young men, one of whom, Thebold, is in the process of courting Era,[27] Marla Drake's Brazilian rival and antagonist from her South American interlude. Thebold and his friend Karvun are scientists who, at some point in the early nineteenth century, discovered an elixir of life; in the timeline of the strip, they are two hundred years old. This plotline is representative of the science fiction and gothic fantasy elements that periodically intrude into the glamorous film noir atmosphere of Mills's work. But even in this story arc, Mills is less interested in the scientific or ontological implications of immortality than in the opportunities it affords for mistaken identity; for Mills, immortality is yet another way of presenting a fluid character who is two or more persons in one. The drawbacks of immortality have been presented in many different guises in fiction,[28] but Mills portrays eternal life as a loss of identity. Mills's immortals spend their whole existence pretending to be someone else, unable to reveal their true selves or their true ages. This is an immortality kept firmly in the closet, and at the conclusion of the story line, the characters in question decide that an immortal life is not worth living and allow themselves to die of old age. Besides a potential commentary on the psychological harm that can come from hiding one's true self, this story line could be read as Mills commenting ironically on the seemingly eternal youth enjoyed by Marla Drake; in *Miss Fury*, history marches on (World War II comes to an end), but the characters remain frozen at a certain age.

Strips 378 to 415 deal with another kind of identity swap, in this case involving a down-on-his-luck ventriloquist, Red Devlin, who is befriended by Marla Drake, Francine, and Marla's adopted child, Darron. Red is falsely accused of murder and is blackmailed by a relative of the real killer. Even though the identity swap theme does not actually revolve around the ventriloquist's profession, it is characteristic of Mills that she should choose a ventriloquist as the protagonist for one of her plots. Red's ventriloquism becomes yet another way to explore the theme of one character speaking through another, or becoming someone else. A ventriloquist "wears" a separate identity as easily as a change of clothing.

Of course, the key double identity in these strips is that of Miss Fury/Marla Drake. Mills elegantly reproduces the Batman/Bruce Wayne trope of the bored socialite as alibi for a secret identity. But whereas Golden Age comics starring Batman, Superman, and Wonder Woman play up a warrior/wimp dualism that uses the wimp half of the equation primarily as a means to dramatize and emphasize the greater (literally superheroic) agency of the warrior half, Miss Fury's secret identity is just one element in a web of relationships that impact each other in unexpected ways. For Miss Fury's rarely seen but highly balletic fighting sequences, Mills mutes her color pallet, emphasizing the contrast between the performances of fashion and the darker performance of physical combat. Marla Drake is diminished by her transformations into Miss Fury. She becomes more interesting (and has more agency) as Marla, the heiress and adventuress for whom clothes and makeup effect a transformation even more empowering than physical combat.

MALE IDENTITY IN *MISS FURY*

In *Miss Fury*, everyone is performing gender, for every viewer's gaze. As a Bell Syndicate advertising blurb for the series proclaims: "MISS FURY brings to any colored comic section a sparkling beauty and a story of spies, scoundrels, and plenty of admirers. MISS FURY is always up to her beautiful neck in a fast-moving, suspense-packed drama[,] . . . always surrounded by an aura of mystery that keeps readers coming back for more."[29]

One of the strip's chief scoundrels—who becomes yet another of Drake's admirers—is the aforementioned General Bruno Beitz, the German officer leading a covert operation to invade Brazil on behalf of the Axis Powers. Over time, Bruno becomes leader and spokesman for patriotic Germans who are opposed to Hitler and the Nazis. By the latter part of 1943, Bruno has in captivity not only Miss Fury but also her friend and admirer, Dan Carey, now of the US Marines. Bruno—who is missing an arm from the failed assassination plot in strip 20—threatens to have Carey's arm surgically removed and attached to himself. This improbable idea is a ruse to bully Drake into revealing everything she knows about a chemical agent that devours all metals—including armor for tanks.

Carey agrees to fight Bruno for possession of his arm. Both men will fight one-handed, with Carey's left arm restrained by a straitjacket. The fight becomes a symbolic struggle for Drake's affections, with both men required to perform their masculinity while symbolically emasculated by their real or temporary loss of a limb. The immaculately uniformed Bruno—his bullet-shaped head closely shaved, his sleeve neatly tied and tucked where his missing arm should be—refuses to allow Drake to witness the fight, declaring that "a battle between two men is no spectacle for a woman to watch!"[30] But he gives Drake his word "as an officer and a gentleman" that Carey will receive "fair play."

Bruno's fluid characterization is transformed into something more elemental than mere villainy. To maintain command of his secret army, Bruno must become the superlative of hypermasculinity. His masquerade of military power is an assemblage of signs: physical appearance, uniform, and habits of speech. Bruno is encoded as a villain but becomes far more alive in his hypermasculine sexuality than the various "good guys" that Mills puts up against him—in other words, he is the classic "Byronic" male villain.

The men in Tarpé Mills's series share a masculinity that is similarly overdetermined. The key American male characters—Carey, Hale, and Fingers Martin—carry their suits in angular, rigid shapes, posing their bodies and articulating their gestures and body language in ways that emphasize their broad shoulders and solid thighs. These men present the counterpoint to Marla Drake's fluid shapes. When Carey changes into evening dress in strip 52,[31] his heavily defined shoulders project far beyond his hips, while the arms of his black dinner jacket are so solidly defined they could be molded from concrete. In the same episode, in a lower tier of panels, we can see the relatively emasculated Gary Hale dancing with the trickster and villainess Baroness Erica Von Kampf. Hale wears a white tuxedo, and the cut and positioning of his arms in each panel echo

FIGURE 1.4. The mirroring of Marla Drake and Baroness Erica encompasses both their wardrobes and their love lives. *Miss Fury* #52 (1942).

the poses of Carey, but with less rigidity and masculine definition. Hale's performance of sexuality on the dance floor is visibly inferior to Carey's. Consequently, we read him as the gullible dupe of the scheming baroness.

As Hale and the baroness are leaving the nightclub, Erica pretends to stumble on her high heel and falls elegantly into Hale's waiting arms. They kiss. He has become trapped in her web, as suggested by the sheer gossamer-lace sleeves and bodice of the baroness's floor-length evening gown.[32] In another example of mirroring, the similarly cut gown that Marla Drake wears on the same page features a pattern of curling black lines on a white background in which the black and white elements remain clearly demarcated (figure 1.4). The sheer lace of Baroness Erica's bodice and sleeves tangles everything together. Erica complicates and confuses identities and situations, while Marla reinforces and polices the requisite boundaries.

DRESSING FOR PLEASURE?

The stylized qualities of Mills's characters—including what the contemporary eye might see as their excesses and overdetermined constructions of gender—reflect the characteristic fashions of their era. As fashion historian Valerie Steele has argued, there is no way for male or female bodies to be perceived or even exist outside the formal preoccupations of their period: "It is apparently a difficult concept for most people to accept that there is no 'natural' way for men and women to look. . . . The 'natural' human body does not exist; but most people accept as natural the clothed figures that they are accustomed to seeing, or, to some extent, they would like to see."[33] The performance of gender and sexuality is, in other words, always determined by the historic and social conditions in which that performance takes place,[34] which in turn shapes the prevailing styles and fashions of the age. Steele draws attention to the historical mechanisms that make the fashions of previous eras appear artificial. It is easier to perceive the element of gender performance in the dress of a historical era, as we do not automatically contextualize such fashion choices within our own everyday experience. Nevertheless, a debate about what is acceptable or proper in the performance of one's gender and sexuality is articulated as a discourse between the characters in Mills's text. Other characters comment on—and criticize—Marla Drake's fixation with her own appearance.

This debate emerges between Marla Drake and Era, one of the leaders of the opposition to the German Fifth Column in Brazil who holds Miss Fury captive during the Brazilian plotline (strips 62 to 96). An amusing panel, published in strip 68 (July 1942), shows Marla holding up two chic dresses—on hangers—from her traveling wardrobe (echoing the choice she made at the very beginning of the saga). Choosing which to wear is a tough decision, even though Marla—whose captors wrongly believe her to be a Nazi spy—would seem to have bigger problems on her hands. Era is not amused by her prisoner's vanity:

ERA
My! My! You Yankee women must find it quite costly to keep up your glamour! Hmph![35]

And later, as Drake puts on her makeup in front of a vanity mirror:

ERA
Just exactly who is all this primping for?

MARLA
Why I . . . I always put on a bit of powder![36]

In a different kind of story, and if Drake truly was a Nazi spy, her obsession with appearances might be a sign of a narcissistic or corrupt inner character. Mills, however, is defending a woman's right to take pride in her appearance, even during wartime (figure 1.5). Marla primps herself and performs her sexuality for her own gratification: her performance is not for the male gaze alone. In scenes such as these, Marla Drake embodies an empowering—although also problematic—fantasy of independent female glamor and wealth, as offered for the reader's gaze. This affluent heroine never needs to resort to a line of gravy-browning painted down the back of her leg to simulate the seams of her silk stockings. Drake's unabashed enjoyment of her traveling wardrobe, even while spy-hunting in Brazil, celebrates her irrepressible taste for extravagance. Ironically, Era later makes her own performance—in a full-blown Carmen Miranda–style "Brazilian" costume.[37]

We should take note here of the conflicted, ideologically contested nature of the fashion and beauty industries in the 1940s, both in America and elsewhere. The world was enduring the horrific reality and the impoverished aftermath of a savage and destructive global war. Rationing of food and clothes had affected even the affluent United States. The fashion industry is a luxury industry, and as such it was seen by many as both fundamentally reactionary and standing in opposition to the progress (or even the rebuilding) of civilization and the improvement of the lot of the common man and woman. George Orwell captures this mood in a 1946 tirade against American fashion magazines in his *Tribune* column "As I Please":

FIGURE 1.5. Lauren Bacall in smart but practical fashion that perfectly mirrors the editorial promotion of the American Red Cross. Front cover of *Bazaar*, March 1943.

> Someone has just sent me a copy of an American fashion magazine which shall be nameless. . . . One striking thing when one looks at these pictures is the overbred, exhausted, even decadent style of beauty that now seems to be striven after. Nearly all of these women are immensely elongated. . . . Evidently it is a real physical type, for it occurs as much in the photographs as in the drawings.[38]

Sadly, I have not been able to locate the precise magazine that Orwell was describing. But in his description of this image, Orwell lifts the lid on another, noneconomic aspect of haute couture that might be regarded as subverting the patriarchal order:

> On the front cover there is a coloured photograph of the usual elegant female standing on a chair while a grey-haired, spectacled, crushed-looking man in shirt-sleeves kneels at her feet, doing something to the edge of her skirt. If one looks closely one finds that actually he is about to take a measurement with a yard measure. But to a casual glance he looks as though he were kissing the hem of the woman's garment—not a bad symbolical picture of American civilization, or at least one important side of it.[39]

The style of fashion photography to which Orwell is responding began to emerge in the 1940s almost in step with the realization that the Allies would win the war. By the 1950s, it had developed into the "dirt beneath my feet" school of fashion modeling: the implicitly fetishized presentation of "models in their mid-thirties . . . cinched into a tight 'Merry Widow' girdle and stiffened satin,"[40] whose inaccessible beauty epitomized the luxury and glamor of the couture garments they displayed.

The origins of this postwar style of photography lie in the collision between fashion, portraiture, and surrealism in the 1930s, as evidenced in the work of Man Ray, Lee Miller, Horst P. Horst, Edward Steichen, and others. The utility fashions of the war years and the "active" style of modeling that went with them can be seen with hindsight as a digression from the development of the sensuous cutting and draping of 1930s couture into the ultrafeminine and languid fashions of the postwar period.

The surrealists and those they influenced decontextualized the body and its clothed contours, presenting it as a ductile and malleable shape. Such shaping was accentuated by the draping and sculptural qualities of silks and satins cut on the bias. This sculptural draping was the signature style of Madeleine Vionnet,[41] and—in a different way—of Elsa Schiaparelli, as well as those they influenced in Hollywood and elsewhere, such as Adrian, Alix, and Charles James. The visual "double take" of an accessory such as Schiaparelli's famous shoe-hat introduces a ludic sense and a delight in transformation and double meanings, which Caroline Evans and Minna Thornton describe as "choreographed deception [that is] . . . self-conscious, constructive and critical."[42] Such work positions the couturier (and by extension the photographer and the model) as exponents of high culture. In the photographic worlds created by Miller, Horst, and others, haute couture becomes a means of projecting an image and an identity that stands on an equal basis with other art forms.

An alternative school of fashion photography in the war years located the model within public action and economic activity.[43] Civilian dress for women echoed the cut of military uniforms. Imagery involving locomotives, jeeps, aircraft, and other forms of machinery was much used, hinting at a mobility and utility supportive of the war effort.[44] Rosie the Riveter in her dungarees and headscarf is an iconic image of this era, but much fashion photography of the war years was intended to suggest that women (and men) could be glamorous and desirable without wasting resources and derailing the war effort.

The prospect of peace saw the reappropriation of imagery that had been abandoned in the war years and the eventual emergence of a new generation of supermodels: Lisa Fonssagrives, Suzy Parker, Jean Patchett, Mary Jane Russell, and many others. These "haughty, high-cheekboned, neurasthenic models" captured the spirit of Dior's "New Look" and other extravagant postwar fashions as photographed by Clifford Coffin, Irving Penn, and others.[45] There was a partial return to the heavy chiaroscuro and other dramatic lighting and contrast effects of the 1930s to capture the exaggerated qualities of cut and shape embodied in these new fashions. The collaboration of Fonssagrives with her photographer-husband, Irving Penn, resulted in a new language of high-contrast black-and-white fashion imagery, epitomizing the look that Orwell found so vexatious (figure 1.6). The sexualized power that resides in this type of subliminally fetishized imagery is something that Orwell clearly apprehends—as did Tarpé Mills. The power of such a clearly articulated and performative sexuality can also be traced in Hollywood's film noir cycle, and in the iconic and immaculately groomed women portrayed by Rita Hayworth, Lizabeth Scott, Barbara Stanwyck, Lana Turner, and other movie stars of that era, whose performances evoke the "deception, instability and unpredictability" that Doane identifies as characteristic of the femme fatale.[46] Mills's heroine combines the identity of the visibly active woman with the unknowable femme fatale in a discourse that spans three separate phases of fashion history. Just like Vionnet, Schiaparelli, Man Ray,

FIGURE 1.6. Lisa Fonssagrives, epitomizing the mood of postwar fashion photography that was regarded as both decadent and vexatious. Photographed by her husband Irving Penn, *Vogue*, 1950.

and Lee Miller, Mills takes a ludic delight in transformations and double meanings.

Sexualized haute couture—as envisioned by Mills—can be read as a double-pronged attack on the forces of patriarchy. It disavows the goals of the war machine and the nation-state.[47] It undermines the power of the patriarch himself by making him appear submissive, enslaved by his male gaze. General Bruno, Mills's most hypermasculine and patriarchal creation, is regularly tamed and controlled by his own gaze as it falls on Marla Drake's performance of her sexuality. By giving a glamorous woman agency and the protagonist's role in her adventure series, Tarpé

FIGURE 1.7. Marla Drake embraces the influence of Dior's "New Look"—and the romantic and ultrafeminine styles of the postwar period. *Miss Fury* #318 (1947).

Mills subverts the usual relationship between the subject, the object, and the reader's gaze. Presented as a perfectly styled exemplar of female fashion and beauty, Drake is a focus for the gazes of characters throughout the saga as well as for readers. Yet this object of attraction is also the subject of its own discourse, capable of taking heroic action (figure 1.7).

Despite—or, in fact, because of—the strip's consistent privileging of Marla Drake, there is no split (as with some portrayals of Wonder Woman) between the glamorous superwoman and a mousy alter ego. Miss Fury has agency and glamor as a costumed heroine. Marla Drake has agency and glamor as a rich socialite.

CONCLUSION

The twenty-first-century reader who comes to *Miss Fury* with the expectation of encountering a prototype of a kick-ass female superhero is setting themselves up for possible disappointment. Miss Fury and her alter ego, Marla Drake (the true protagonist of the series), have a much more complex and ambivalent relationship with the social forces of the 1940s that—driven by the demands of a war economy—were advancing the social and professional prospects of women in the United States. Most of the time, Marla Drake is not the late twentieth or early twenty-first century's ideal of a liberated woman, fighting crime in her black catsuit. She spends more of her time attending to her appearance and thinking about her relationships with men. Drake also spends a great deal of time as a captive. And her conversations with other women regularly fail the Bechdel test, as their most frequent topic is men.[48]

So is *Miss Fury* simply a relic of a bygone era? If so, it is a misunderstood relic that lends itself to contemporary misrepresentation because of the protagonist's (rarely seen) cool costume and the assumptions that can be made about the series because its creator was a woman. Happily, there is a lot more to *Miss Fury* than this. Beneath its glossy surface, the series unpicks the interlinked issues of (white) gender, identity, and power, and does so through the lens of Tarpé Mills's knowledge of haute couture and other forms of dress. *Miss Fury* is the first superhero narrative to explicitly concern itself with issues of personal identity from a female perspective, and to explore the mechanisms through which power and gender are performed in the theater (or masquerade) of daily life.

The most mysterious and ambiguous character in the *Miss Fury* saga is Marla Drake's French maid, Francine. As the narrative develops, their relationship becomes that of close friends, or perhaps that of a wealthy lady and her paid companion. Francine waits faithfully in New York for three years for Drake to return from Brazil.[49] She does not seek another employer, and she happily accepts the responsibility of looking after Marla's adopted child when her employer finally reappears. Throughout the rest of the saga, the two women look out for each other, regularly coming to each other's rescue. By the time of the *Miss Fury* adventures published in the early 1950s (the Red Devlin plot and the subsequent trip to Europe), Francine has effectively become Drake's partner—a handy combination of Alfred and Robin to Marla Drake's Batman. A farewell scene at the airport as Francine departs for France prompts Drake to reflect on their relationship:

DRAKE
Whenever I needed anything, Francine was always there—yet now when *she* needs someone, I've let her go off alone![50]

In an unobtrusive way, Mills's narrative slowly works toward the depiction of a stable same-sex relationship between Marla Drake and Francine, and the construction of a nuclear family—Marla, Francine, and adopted son Darron—that can happily exist without the need for an adult male presence. There are no explicitly amorous scenes between Marla and Francine,[51] although we do on occasions share Francine's admiring gaze toward her employer at her toilette, attired in her signature satin and lace lingerie.[52] Besieged by suitors in the early years of her strip (Hale, Carey, Bruno, and others), Marla succeeds in preserving herself forever as a young heiress, always on the cusp of womanhood. As time passes, the male admirers are ever more successfully kept at arm's length. The life she constructs for herself with Francine and her adopted child appears to be completely satisfying to Marla. This may be Marla Drake's ultimate masquerade: to be a deeply encoded queer character who negotiates her transgressive identity within the rules of genre fiction and the performance of gender and sexuality that prevailed in her time.

NOTES

1. The covers of the Timely *Miss Fury* comics, believed to be the work of Alex Schomburg, portray a violent, belligerent, costumed Miss Fury, and their regular reproduction has been responsible for some of the widespread misunderstanding of the actual content of the *Miss Fury* newspaper strips, such as Denis Gifford's erroneous description of the series in *The International Book of Comics* (London: Hamlyn, 1984), 124.

2. Mills's creation has been overlooked by many of the key academic critics of the female superhero. See Jeffrey A. Brown, *Dangerous Curves: Action Heroines, Gender, Fetishism, and Popular Culture* (Jackson: Mississippi University Press, 2011); Cocca, *Superwomen*; Jennifer Stuller, *Ink-Stained Amazons* (London: IB

Tauris, 2010). Mike Madrid, *The Supergirls: Fashion Feminism and the History of Comic Book Superheroines* (Exterminating Angel, 2016), and Valerie Frankel, *Superheroines and the Epic Journey* (Jefferson, NC: McFarland, 2017), pay more attention to Miss Fury but fail to give the character the primacy she merits as the first significant female superhero and the first written and drawn by a woman.

3. For a good sampling of these early works by Mills, see Tarpé Mills, *Miss Fury: Sensational Sundays 1944–1949*, ed. Trina Robbins (San Diego, CA: IDW, 2011), 8–9; and Tarpé Mills, *Miss Fury: Sensational Sundays 1941–1944*, ed. Trina Robbins (San Diego, CA: IDW, 2013), 12–21. For the purposes of referencing the *Miss Fury* strips in chronological order, I refer here to the Robbins volume covering the years 1941 to 1944 as volume 1 and the volume covering 1944 to 1949 as volume 2.

4. The series title changes from *Black Fury* to *Miss Fury* in strip 37, published December 1941. It is unwise to try to date the *Miss Fury* strips precisely, as exact publication dates varied from one newspaper to another. This article uses the numbering system introduced by Robbins for the strips that she reproduces in her 2011 and 2013 edited volumes. With the indispensable help of comics scholar Guy Lawley—and generous access to Guy's *Miss Fury* archive—I have continued this numbering system into the material not included in the Robbins volumes.

5. The hiatus occurs between strips 326 and 327.

6. See, for example, Scott Bukatman, *Matters of Gravity* (Durham, NC: Duke University Press, 2003), 184–223.

7. Mary Ann Doane, *Femme Fatales* (New York: Routledge, 1991), 46.

8. See, for example, Mills, *Miss Fury*, vol. 1, 55–56.

9. See Mills, *Miss Fury*, vol. 1, 37, 44, 70, 71, 91, passim.

10. In Alan Moore's *Watchmen* (London: Titan, 1987), Moore and artist Dave Gibbons focus on the relationship between Nite Owl (Dan Driberg) and Laurie Juspeczyk—and the effect on Dan's libido when both characters are in costume. "Did the costumes make it good?" Laurie memorably inquires after their first successful sexual encounter. John Byrne's *Sensational She-Hulk* (Marvel, 1989–1994) explores its protagonist's sexualization in both body and costume: for an interesting discussion of this series, see Madrid, *The Supergirls*, 259–266. In *Batman Returns* (Warner Bros, 1992) the agency acquired by Selina Kyle through her transformation into Catwoman is linked explicitly to her creation of a fetishized costume. As Kyle says to her cat, Miss Kitty, on first wearing the costume: "I don't know about you Miss Kitty but I'm feeling . . . so much yummier." These instances are just a tiny sampling: see Andrew Bolton, *Superheroes: Fashion and Fantasy* (New York: Metropolitan Museum of Art, 2008) for an in-depth discussion of the fetishization of female superhero costumes.

11. Simone de Beauvoir, *The Second Sex* (London: Vintage Classics, 1997 [1949]), 295.

12. *Vogue*, March 1941, 45.

13. *Vogue*, April 1941, 51.

14. For a color strip such as *Miss Fury*, the writer/artist would have supplied

a color guide to the engraver, who would then complete the color-separations for the printer.

15. *Vogue*, April 1941, 82.
16. *Harper's Bazaar*, March 1941, 57.
17. *Harper's Bazaar*, March 1941, 69.
18. *Harper's Bazaar*, March 1941. 57.
19. *Harper's Bazaar*, March 1941, 55.
20. Judith Butler, *Gender Trouble* (New York: Routledge, 1990), 25.
21. Sara Salih, *Judith Butler* (New York: Routledge, 2002), 51.
22. See Mills, *Miss Fury*, vol. 2, 7–8.
23. Mills, *Miss Fury*, vol. 1, 71.
24. See, for example, Jonathan Raban, *Soft City* (London: Harper-Collins, 1974), 64–67.
25. The "Sharlie" plotline thus anticipates Billy Wilder's *Some Like It Hot* (United Artists, 1959).
26. Strips 278 and 279 show Drake chained by her foot in a basement, in a rare appearance of the bondage theme in *Miss Fury*.
27. A quite separate character from Baroness Erica.
28. The first to do so may have been Jonathan Swift in *Gulliver's Travels* (London, 1726).
29. Mills, *Miss Fury*, vol. 2, 10.
30. Mills, *Miss Fury*, vol. 1, 158.
31. Mills, *Miss Fury*, vol. 1, 75.
32. Mills, *Miss Fury*, vol. 1, 75.
33. Valerie Steele, *Fashion and Eroticism* (New York: Oxford University Press, 1985), 244.
34. Judith Butler takes up an equivalent position in *Gender Trouble*, 163–180.
35. Mills, *Miss Fury*, vol. 1, 90.
36. Mills, *Miss Fury*, vol. 1, 91.
37. Mills, *Miss Fury*, vol. 1, 114–115.
38. George Orwell, *Collected Essays, Journalism and Letters* (London: Penguin, 1968), 4:273.
39. Orwell, *Collected Essays*, 274.
40. Alison Lurie, *The Language of Clothes* (London: Bloomsbury, 1981), 78–79.
41. Vionnet's famous twisted and knotted evening gown epitomizes this style. For a description and critical reading of this garment, see Caroline Evans and Minna Thornton, *Women and Fashion: A New Look* (London: Quartet, 1989), 120–121. The villainous Baroness Von Kampf has several analogues of this dress in her wardrobe, such as the ball gown she wears in strip 21 (Mills, *Miss Fury*, vol. 1, 44).
42. Evans and Thornton, *Women and Fashion*, 139.
43. The work of the (female) fashion photographer Toni Frissell epitomizes this approach.
44. This trend was arguably an acceleration of a tendency that had begun in the 1930s, alongside the surrealist-inflected fashion image. Polly Devlin, for

example, characterizes the late 1930s as an era when "models stood in actual railway stations, about to board the trains; they no longer stood poised and exquisite by the side of swimming pools, but plunged in." Polly Devlin, *Vogue Book of Fashion Photography* (London: Condé Nast, 1979), 119.

45. Lurie, *Language of Clothes*, 78.

46. Doane, *Femme Fatales*, 46.

47. The War Machine's relationship to the nation-state is explored in Gilles Deleuze and Félix Guattari, *A Thousand Plateaus*, translated by Brian Massumi (London: Athlone Press, 1988), 351–423.

48. Also known as the Bechdel-Wallace test, this process—named after the American cartoonist Alison Bechdel—establishes whether any specific fictional narrative includes a scene in which two or more women hold a conversation with each other about something other than a man.

49. Three years in terms of elapsed publishing time.

50. Strip 415, October 22, 1950. The numerical reference here is to Guy Lawley's numbering of the latter years of the *Miss Fury* strip.

51. It would be easy to construct a sexualized/fetishized reading of the dominant Marla, the mistress attired in her black catsuit, and the submissive Francine, dressed in her maid's costume. Perhaps another scholar or critic will feel moved to explore further this aspect of the narrative.

52. See, for example, Mills, *Miss Fury*, vol. 2, 86, 159, 180.

2

SUPERMAN FAMILY VALUES
Supersex in the Silver Age

MATT YOCKEY

The back cover of *Superman Annual* #6 (1962–1963) features an image by artist Curt Swan titled "The Superman Family" (figure 2.1). In the illustration, Superman holds hands with his Kryptonian cousin Supergirl while Mister Mxyzptlk, an imp from the Fifth Dimension, reclines on a cloud above them. To Superman's right stand Beppo, the super-monkey from Krypton; Superman's adoptive Earth parents, Martha and Jonathan Kent; his "pal" Jimmy Olsen; Olsen's occasional love interest Lucy Lane; *Daily Planet* Editor-in-Chief Perry White; Superman's "girlfriend," Lois Lane; and Lois's primary rival for Superman's affection, Lana Lang. Above this group are Krypto the Superdog, Streaky the Super-Cat, and Comet the Super-Horse. To Supergirl's left stand Professor Potter, Bizarro Superman, and Superman's Kryptonian birth parents, Lara and Jor-El, while Lori Lemaris, a mermaid whom Superman once romanced, relaxes in a pool of water. Meanwhile, five members of the Legion of Super-Heroes (a super-team of teenagers from the thirty-first century) hover in a bubble above the group.

This image, which was reprinted multiple times in Superman comic books of the 1960s, is striking for its representation of the dialectic of the familiar and the strange. This dialectic defines Superman titles of the Silver Age, a period that most comics scholars describe as running from 1956 to the early 1970s. Everything marked as heteronormative in this image is inflected with a strong sense of the uncanny, and that

57

FIGURE 2.1. "The Superman family." *Superman Annual* #6 (1962–1963).

which is unfamiliar is coded as part of the heteronormative. Figurative and literal reproduction is essential to an understanding of the dialectical relationship between the familiar and the unfamiliar in Silver Age Superman comic books. The "family" here is quite literal in many respects; in addition to Superman's two sets of parents and his cousin, Lucy and Lois are sisters and Potter is Lana's uncle. At the same time, the family figuratively extends to members who clearly exist outside the boundaries of the heteronormative, such as Mxyzptlk and Lori Lemaris. Meanwhile, the bestiary of super-pets exists as a hyperbolic affirmation—or absurdist parody—of suburban American ideals of the period.

Superman himself asserts the hegemonic power of white masculinity prevalent in Silver Age superhero comic books. The majority of the characters in this tableau, including the alien Kryptonians, are depicted as white. Moreover, the only nonwhite-skinned character, the Legionnaire Chameleon Boy, confirms Marc Singer's observation that such ostensible racial diversity is negated by its clear and obvious fantasy juxtaposed with the equally clear and obvious reality of whiteness, which is the only racial category that overlaps with this image and the real world. This intense privileging and normalizing of whiteness means that figures such as Chameleon Boy differ "from the normative white characters only in the exotic pastel colors of their skin."[1] Disability is rendered in similar terms; a mentally challenged version of Superman, Bizarro Superman, stands in for and erases an actual disabled community. In a similar vein, when Superman first meets Lori Lemaris, she hides her mermaid identity by using a wheelchair and covering the lower half of her body in a blanket.

These ideologically fraught erasures speak to what Richard Reynolds recognizes as the essential contradictory nature of the superhero as "both the exotic and the agent of order."[2] If Superman represents "truth, justice, and the American way," as the radio series *The Adventures of Superman* first asserted in 1942, then Silver Age Superman comic books strongly suggest that the "American way" is decidedly strange. Within the liminal space of the self/other binary produced by Superman's family resides the reader, who is positioned as both part of the heteronormative and outside of it by virtue of their consumption of these Superman texts. This chapter will argue that the symbolic reproductive capacity of these comic books is a primary aspect of their appeal for the young readers they directly solicit by suggesting these readers' ability to be incorporated into the Superman family. In their figurative, nonnormative representation of reproduction, Silver Age Superman comic books routinely allow young readers to symbolically affirm their own powers of cognitive reproduction—that is, their desire and ability to imagine multiple and nonnormative subjectivities. Through a survey of typical imagery and themes from Silver Age Superman comic books, I argue that this space for cognitive reproduction is produced (and reproduced) not despite, but rather *because of* the medium and genre's overarching conservatism, as highlighted by its restrictions on overt representations of sex. It is precisely these restrictions that create the need for symbolic alternatives that become, through the absences they both disguise and illuminate, multilayered and highly charged.

FIFTY SHADES OF KRYPTONITE

Swan's illustration is emblematic of the transformation of Superman comic books under the stewardship of editor Mort Weisinger. Starting in 1945, Weisinger served as coeditor of all Batman and Superman titles; in 1958, he assumed full editorial control of all Superman comic books. Weisinger's tenure saw the expansion of Superman-related titles with the introduction of *Superman's Pal Jimmy Olsen* in 1954 and *Superman's Girl-Friend Lois Lane* in 1958. Superman comic books were so popular during this period that by 1961 both *Jimmy Olsen* and *Lois Lane* regularly outsold *Batman*.[3] Weisinger and his staff of writers—including Otto Binder, former writer of the original Captain Marvel; space opera novelist Edmond Hamilton; and Superman cocreator Jerry Siegel—were responsible for important changes to the Superman mythos, including the introduction of Supergirl as Superman's cousin, the miniaturized bottled Kryptonian city of Kandor, the Phantom Zone, and various colors of kryptonite and their often unpredictable effects on Superman. Yet perhaps the most significant addition to the Superman metatext was a conceit that allowed for changes outside of his mythos: non-canon "Imaginary Stories" that offered radical deviations from Superman continuity. Many of these tales are explicit reversals of Superman continuity, and some of the most notable ones concern Superman and Lois Lane marrying and, often, having children. A Superman/Lois wedding was the subject of the very first Imaginary Story, "Mr. and Mrs. Clark (Superman) Kent!" from *Superman's Girl-Friend Lois Lane* #19 (1960). Superman's love life entered more emotionally complex terrain in other stories, such as "The Three Wives of Superman!" from *Superman's Girl-Friend Lois Lane* #51 (1964), in which the Man of Steel weds Lois Lane, who subsequently dies. He then turns his romantic attentions to Lana Lang, who also dies shortly after they are married. Finally, Superman weds Lori Lemaris, with the same tragic result.

In "The Three Wives of Superman!" Superman's profound grief over the deaths of his brides extends what had, by the 1950s, become a central aspect of Superman's mythos—namely, the loss of his home planet and his ongoing melancholic desire to restore it in some way—into the realm of the human and the sexual. During this era, Superman's reproductive desires are intimately linked to his irrecoverable Kryptonian past, a past that was given ever more narrative prominence under Weisinger's watch. The bottled city of Kandor alone reifies the perpetual influence of Krypton as an emotional force in Superman's life that can never be fully integrated in his psyche, just as the city itself can never be restored to its normal state. Conversely, the desire on the part of human characters such as Lois to marry Superman indicates their attraction to Superman's innate superiority as a Kryptonian. Superman is rendered as an ideal object of romantic desire by virtue of his Kryptonian heritage, and it is this heritage that also makes him unobtainable as such. Unsurprisingly then, the desire to marry Superman is deferred within the Superman canon by Superman's insistence that he can never wed, as it would endanger his bride's life. The only way by which such a desire can be realized is by Lois becoming superpowered herself, a transformation only permanently allowable in the fantasy space of Imaginary Stories. Thus, Superman weds Lois in "The Three Wives of Superman!" after he concocts a super-serum that gives her powers similar to his own. However, after a medical examination by a Kryptonian doctor in Kandor, Lois learns that "one of the elements in the serum your husband gave you has a deadly side effect he did not anticipate! You will die in eight days!" Thus, the story reinforces the barrier between the super (i.e., the Kryptonian) and the normal that defines Superman's relationships with Earthlings in the Superman canon. In this story, Krypton is the motivating device for reproduction inasmuch as Superman's desire to create his own super-family can be read as connected to his need to recover from the psychic trauma of its loss; it is also the barrier to that reproduction.

Other Imaginary Stories more fully realize their potential to reverse the rules of Superman continuity, particularly in respect to the relationship between reproduction and Krypton. Consider "The Amazing Story of Superman-Red and Superman-Blue!" from *Superman* #162 (1963), in which Superman is challenged by the citizens of Kandor to fulfill his long-standing promise to restore their city to its original size. In order to acquire the necessary intellect to devise a reversal of Kandor's plight, Superman submits himself to the rays of his brain-evolution machine, which Supergirl warns "is powered by the rays of all varieties of kryptonite! It's dangerous!" Upon being doused by the machine's rays, Superman splits into two beings—the aforementioned Superman-Red and Blue—who are different only in the primary color of their costumes. Working together, the "twin Supermen" fulfill key goals of Superman: they restore Kandor to normal, they find a cure for green kryptonite (exposure to which is fatal to Superman), and they eradicate evil. With these tasks accomplished, Superman-Blue advises Superman-Red, "We can fulfill another ambition! We can get married!" Superman-Red decides to ask Lois Lane to marry him, while Superman-Blue elects to propose to Lana Lang. In this way, Superman's twin romantic desires, as well as those of the women who routinely compete for his affections, are fulfilled. Significantly, the planned double wedding becomes a triple wedding after Lucy Lane agrees to marry Jimmy Olsen. Lucy tells Jimmy, "For years you've been asking me to marry you, but I've always turned you down because I wanted to wait until my sister Lois was married! Well now, it's happened at last! So if you still want me!" Thus, the satisfaction of non-superpowered Jimmy Olsen's romantic desires can only be fulfilled by the satisfaction of Superman's utopian desires. The story concludes with Superman-Red and Lois moving to the planet New Krypton (created by

FIGURE 2.2. The theme of doubling is compounded in "The Amazing Story of Superman-Red and Superman-Blue!," *Superman* #162 (1963).

both Supermen after the restoration of Kandor) and raising their twins, while Superman-Blue and Lana remain on Earth to raise their own twins. Compounding the theme of doubling, both couples have a boy and a girl who are visually rendered as child-versions of each parent (figure 2.2).

The significance of this story's imagining of two Superman families is elucidated, in part, by the fact that Weisinger predicated much of his editorial approach on what he concluded children wanted to read based on personal interviews with them as well as consultations with his young son. Weisinger also created the first letter page in a Superman comic book, dubbed the "Metropolis Mailbag," in 1958, affording him another opportunity to receive feedback from readers. In a 1962 interview with the *New York Times*, Weisinger observed, "The kids still love this sort of stuff. But in putting together the book we have to bear in mind that the kids are much more sophisticated than they were 20 years ago."[4] He also noted that his comic books were likely being read by adults as well as children:

"The old folks now and then peek over the shoulder of their kids and get a nostalgic twinge. I think the parents help us sell the magazine."[5] Silver Age Superman stories have been dismissed by many as childish dross of a less sophisticated period in the comic book industry. Comic book historian Bradford W. Wright, for example, contrasts Weisinger's Superman with the original social crusader of the 1930s: "As the series veered ever further into flights of unreality, so too did its ability to work within a social context. Whereas the original series created by Siegel and Shuster had been a modern social fantasy, the Weisinger series amounted to a modern fairy tale."[6] In a more nostalgic mode, comic book author Mark Waid opines that "under Weisinger's watchful eye, the Superman universe was one of awe and wonder, a fairy-tale existence . . . giving youngsters a safe and simple retreat from an outside world growing darker and more confusing."[7] Both Wright and Waid equate the Weisinger-era stories to fairy tales in ways that suggest such stories are "safe" or simplistic fantasies. But these observations fail to account for the fact that fairy tales are often Freudian fever dreams that reveal the messy processes of the human psyche. As Bruno Bettelheim observes, the symbolic language of fairy tales allows a child "to gain a preconscious comprehension of matters which would greatly perturb him if they were forced into his conscious attention. . . . In such a manner, fairy tales are an ideal way for the child to learn about sex in a fashion appropriate to his age and developmental understanding."[8] From this perspective, the "fairy tale" qualities of Silver Age Superman comic books amplify and deepen the potential value of their preoccupation with reproduction.

Certainly, Weisinger's observations about adult readers, and his interest in learning what younger readers wanted, suggests that the appeal of Silver Age Superman stories may be broader, and their content more complex, than critics have typically allowed for. To be clear, my contention that these stories are complex should not be confused with an assertion of critical deconstruction or political subversiveness. Weisinger's Imaginary Story conceit is predicated on radically subverting Superman continuity while not necessarily destabilizing Superman mythology. The very notion of Superman marrying Lois Lane and raising children on New Krypton is, moreover, completely consistent with the logic of the prevailing Superman metatext; this story line actualizes Superman's ongoing defense of heteronormative values (i.e., "the American way") and affirms his superior Kryptonian pedigree as a utopian ideal. Consequently, tales such as "The Amazing Story of Superman-Red and Superman-Blue!" can be regarded as an actualization of the inherent promise of Superman comic books, a promise that is forestalled by the dictates of comic book industry moral standards rather than the Superman mythology itself.

As discussed in the introduction to this collection, the Comics Code Authority that was established in 1954 provided a self-regulating set of industry rules that forbade "suggestive and salacious illustration" and the portrayal of "illicit sex relations," "sexual abnormalities," and "sex perversion." But no Superman comic books were depicting any such content at any point before the creation of the CCA. In fact, DC's longstanding editorial standards became part of the testimony during the 1954 Congressional Hearing on Juvenile Delinquency that led to the creation of the CCA. The twin concerns of sex and violence are articulated in the document's summary statement: "In general, the policy of Superman D-C Publications is to provide interesting, dramatic, and reasonably exciting entertainment without having recourse to such artificial devices as the use of exaggerated physical manifestations of sex, sexual situations, or situations in which violence is emphasized sadistically."[9] Silver Age Superman comic books always operated within their own system of repression, and the Weisinger-era proliferation of increasingly strange concepts speaks to Weisinger's desire to rejuvenate Superman titles in order to maintain the interest of young readers within that system. Recalled Weisinger: "I would bring out a new element every six months to keep the enraptured kids who were our audience involved."[10] Thus, market demands for constant revision work in symbiotic alignment with the thematic concerns of reproduction in Silver Age Superman comic books as determined and disciplined by heteronormative hegemonic standards.

In this way, these stories confirm Umberto Eco's assertion that Superman comic books are both novelistic and mythic;[11] it is not incidental that when these stories took up the entire content of an issue, they were called "Imaginary Novels." At the same time, Imaginary Stories such as "The Amazing Story of Superman-Red and Superman-Blue!" not only embrace the novelistic change that Eco contends would be fatal to Superman (e.g., marrying Lois Lane), but also imbricate those alterations with the Superman myth. At the end of the story, two divergent Superman fantasies are realized: he gets to live a normal-yet-extraordinary life on New Krypton, wherein he is non-superpowered but culturally pure Kryptonian, as well as an extraordinary-yet-normal life on Earth, wherein he is a retired superhero with superpowered children. In both cases, Superman retains a link to the mythic—symbolized by Krypton and his superhero identity—and has a doppelgänger son to serve as a marker of mythic and novelistic continuity into the future. Further, Superman-Red's decision to live on New Krypton speaks to the nostalgic value of new Superman stories, while Superman-Blue's decision to raise superpowered children on Earth appeals to young readers who can identify with those children in terms of fantasies of the self in the present while also identifying with Superman-Blue as a model for future adulthood. Both possible futures encourage cognitive reproduction: the adult imagines a child-self, the child an adult-self.

As "The Amazing Story of Superman-Red and Superman-Blue!" suggests, the "naturalness" of heterosexuality (and the institution of marriage itself) is constantly questioned in canonical Superman comic books of the period because of the constant deferral of its consummation and its perpetual displacement into the realm of fantasy (e.g., Imaginary Stories). But these Imaginary Stories, which exist as fantasies embedded within fantasies, are perhaps most revealing of a deeply rooted desire within both Superman himself and the young readers of his comics to actualize reproductive agency. Non-sexual reproductive acts in Silver Age Superman comic books frequently serve as substitutes for sexual reproduction. Scott Bukatman rightly points out that superheroes embody "the displacement of sexual energy into aggression."[12] Given that Silver Age Superman stories rarely feature the kind or degree of physical violence that is a primary characteristic of superhero comics, the displaced sexual energy in these stories is rendered in different psychic terms: the violent destruction of a planet is bound up with sexual reproduction. Indeed, symbolic reproduction is readily apparent in many canonical (i.e., non-"Imaginary") Superman stories of the period. For example, Superman builds a number of robotic versions of himself and is sometimes assisted by the Superman Emergency Squad, a group of miniature Kandorians in Superman costumes. Moreover, while it is the Imaginary Story conceit that allows for the actualization of sexual reproduction, it is the symbolic reproduction of Superman into Blue and Red iterations that leads to sexual reproduction. It is additionally significant that in "The Amazing Story of Superman-Red and Superman-Blue!" Superman must literally *and* figuratively split from himself in order to consciously recognize and pursue his desire for sexual reproduction. Essential to the splitting of Superman into two equal selves is the act of self-recognition produced by self-alienation. It is important that these two Supermen are virtually identical but also bear a single characteristic that defamiliarizes each one to the other and to readers. Thus, physical reproduction leads to cognitive reproduction; new ways of being offer new ways of seeing, and vice versa. In this way, the conceit of Imaginary Stories compels readers to recognize different cognitive and symbolic spaces that Superman can occupy, and in their identification with Superman, readers are encouraged to recognize the inherent fluidity of their own subjectivities.

BIZARRO LOVE TRIANGLE

Crucial to these new ways of being and of seeing is these comics' representation of Superman as a contradictory signifier of the heteronormative and the nonnormative. In either case, Superman is a figure of excess; he is a template for idealized difference who is simultaneously inside and outside of the heteronormative. Consequently, his "family" embodies an especially complex relationship with the social and with Superman as an emblem of social law. According to Michel Foucault, the laws of a land are confirmed and legitimated through the bodies of its most transparently subjectivized citizens, yet the discipline asserted thusly must also be resisted symbolically as a necessary component of its continuation[13]—hence the value of culture to circulate representations of such bodies, marking them in equal parts as abject and desirable. Superman's body signifies both disciplining law and an American ethos of liberty; the bifurcation of Superman and Clark Kent indicates the open secret of the presence of the law as inscribed on the bodies of all its citizens. According to Gilles Deleuze, law is "an empty form of difference" that "compels its subjects to illustrate it only at the cost of their own change."[14] The law compels its various subjects to both adapt to it and to violate it in order to constitute its boundaries. Thus, the law can only exist by being followed *and* broken. It also demands general conformity *and* requires individual repetition. Consequently, the nation as a discursive expression of the law becomes a trap; the concepts of individualism and liberty (the repetitions of each citizen that are the same and also different) are central to confirming the power of the law. In form and content, the comic book superhero offers a symbolic escape from this trap through excessive repetition. This symbolic value represented visually and narratively within Silver Age Superman comic books substantiates a comparable effect of consumption and production. Repetition in consumption both asserts individual subjectivity and confirms the integrity of a collective.

As Deleuze argues, "the simulacrum is not just a copy, but that which overturns all copies by *also* overturning the models: every thought becomes an aggression."[15] Thus, each reproduction of Superman is simultaneously a repetition (stable) and a challenge (unstable) to the law; repetition becomes the aggressive act that satisfies Bukatman's displacement of sexual energy. According to Deleuze, repetition challenges the law through the inevitable production of difference, but this can also confirm that repetition itself can be the law, and/or that the law *requires* repetition. Such a requirement is apparent in the demands (or the laws) of mass culture and serial comic book production, and in the necessary acts of symbolic reproduction performed by Superman as a means of contending with his traumatic past. In this sense, the law as a discursive property of the social and of a genre produces its own difference. This understanding of the law is of particular value in examining the majority of Silver Age Superman comic books that are not Imaginary Stories but instead conform to Superman continuity and its laws.

In Silver Age comic books, Superman's relationship to the law is bound up in his Kryptonian heritage, which marks him as both physically and ideologically superior to Earthlings. Moreover, his Kryptonian past is an idealized heteronormativity centered around his parents, Jor-El and Lara, and Superman's desire to realize the utopian ideal of his birth planet is defined by the impossibility, per the laws of utopia, of recovering the past through biological reproduction. Given Superman's value as a physical and moral utopian ideal, it is worth noting Fredric Jameson's observation that representations of utopia are not "the exhibit of an achieved Utopian construct, but rather the story of its production and of the very process of construction as such."[16] The value of utopia resides in our imagining it and our desire for it, not its impossible realization. All representations of utopia are critiques of the moment of their expression. As Jameson argues, utopian politics is about "the dialectic of Identity and Difference, to the degree to which such a politics aims at imagining, and sometimes even at realizing, a system radically different from this one."[17] Consequently, when characters in Silver Age Superman comic books attempt to realize their utopian imaginings as represented by Superman, the result is a radical reproduction of that utopian ideal. Bizarro Superman, or simply Bizarro, who made frequent appearances in Silver Age Superman comic books, is one of the most prominent expressions of this utopian desire that manifests as an ostensibly dystopian iteration of Superman's Kryptonian past. Bizarro shares Superman's innate goodness but is an explicit inversion of the aesthetic and intellectual ideals embodied by the Man of Steel. As such, Bizarro is a subversive Silver Age comic book reduction and complication of the self/other dialectic. The character was created in 1958 for the Superman newspaper strip by author Alvin Schwartz, who saw Bizarro in expressly psychological terms. For Schwartz, the character was a "deconstruction of Superman, that is, a breaking up of the meaning embodied in the whole idea of the character. . . . I was striving, you might say, for that mirror-image, that opposite. . . . I was certainly inspired to some degree by C. G. Jung's archetype of 'the shadow'—and Bizarro certainly reflected that, as well."[18]

The character was introduced to comic book readers in "The Boy of Steel vs. the Thing of Steel" from *Superboy* #68 (1958), in which a scientist accidentally uses "an imperfect duplicator ray" on Superboy, "creating an unloving bizarre imitation" of him composed of "non-living matter." Borrowing heavily from the Universal Studios Frankenstein films of the 1930s that starred Boris Karloff as the monster, the well-meaning Bizarro roams Smallville in search of friendship but is met with fear because of his grotesque appearance; his only friend is a blind girl who recognizes his benign nature and need for love, seeing in him what the scientist who created him cannot. In this latter aspect, Bizarro is most subversively an inversion of Superman, who, in his interactions with Lois Lane, constantly asserts that he does not need love at all. Bizarro's attempts to win the favor of others result in various catastrophes, and Superboy determines that he must destroy this distorted version of himself. After discovering that Bizarro is immune to the adverse effects of kryptonite, Superboy finally realizes that he can be destroyed by fragments of the exploded duplicator ray that created him. Just as pieces of kryptonite are deadly to Superboy, pieces of the exploded duplicator ray can fatally weaken Bizarro; in both cases, power is tied to a reproductive symbol that is subsequently transformed into a threat with the potential to cancel its own reproductive outcomes. However, before Superboy can use the deadly fragments, Bizarro, described as a "perilous, yet pathetic, creature," chooses to destroy himself by deliberately flying into the large piece of duplicator ray held by Superboy. This "super-collision" creates a "shock wave" that "stimulate[s]" the blind girl's optic nerve "back to life," restoring her vision, confirming that, at least in this first story, one of Bizarro's values is to figuratively and literally erase actual disability. Superboy even conjectures that Bizarro intuitively understood that his death in this manner would produce such an outcome.

The corollary of Krypton and the duplicator ray as both the source of life and a potentially deadly threat for Superboy and Bizarro, respectively, indicates that reproductive power has the potential to negate itself, a point reinforced by the fact that Superboy—Bizarro's "father"—spends much of this story devising ways to destroy Bizarro. As a physically grotesque version of Superboy derived *from* Superboy, Bizarro can be regarded as a reification of Superboy's melancholic longing for Krypton. Bizarro becomes another iteration of a yearning for utopia that is necessarily a monstrous reversal of that ideal. While Bizarro is identified as monstrous, his essential association with Superboy—specifically, Superboy's reproductive ability—confirms the latent monstrous potential of Superboy, whose body is always outside the boundaries of the social. In this respect, Silver Age Superman comic books can be regarded in terms of Mikhail Bakhtin's grotesque body of carnival. Bakhtin asserts that "the grotesque body . . . is a body in the act of becoming. It is never finished, never completed; it is continually built, created, and builds and creates another body. Moreover, the body swallows the world and is itself swallowed by the world."[19] Bizarro as a reversal illustrates the degree to which Superman's body is grotesque, as well as the integral relationship of that body to readers, who are Bakhtin's swallowed and swallowing body. In his inability to sexually reproduce per the law of utopia, Superman is perpetually located in an affective space defined by a reproductive desire forestalled by melancholia.

In "The Boy of Steel vs. the Thing of Steel," Bizarro only exists because Superboy does, and, according to narrative logic, only Superboy has the ability to understand how this grotesque version of himself can be destroyed. The Superboy/Bizarro relationship confirms Bukatman's observation regarding displacement and condensation, but at the same time, the creation of Bizarro demonstrates that these are reproductive mechanisms that can function symbolically for comic book readers as much as for superheroes. Deleuze notes that "repetition is the thought of the future."[20] Despite his original untimely death and Superboy's certainty of the necessity of that demise, Bizarro, like the various iterations of Superman in Imaginary Stories, represents the possibility of difference positively for young readers. The reproductions of Superman in the comic books of this period confirm Deleuze's argument that "real opposition is not a maximum of difference but a minimum of repetition—a repetition reduced to two, echoing and returning on itself; a repetition which has found the means to *define* itself."[21] Readers can identify with Bizarro in his desire and inability to be like Superman; Bizarro is also a reductive reification of Superman's own desire to reproduce. The repetition is reduced to two in the act of reading this story and identifying with Superman and his reproduction. Readers occupy a dialectical point of identification in reading acts of interiorization that mirror Superman's own interiorization, as represented by Imaginary Stories—which can be regarded as the expression of both Superman's and readers' desires—and reified by figures such as Bizarro.

This point is made all the more evident by the return of Bizarro and a pivotal change made to the character: the capacity for sexual reproduction. An adult version of Bizarro debuted in "The Battle With Bizarro!"

from *Action Comics* #254 (1959). As in the character's first appearance, Bizarro is centrally characterized by a strong desire for love. In this story, Lex Luthor makes a copy of the duplicator ray used to create the Bizarro Superboy to make a Bizarro Superman. Described again as a "thing of steel," Bizarro mistakenly believes that Lois Lane loves him and proceeds to court her and ask for her hand in marriage. Rebuffed, Bizarro then uses the duplicator ray on himself to make a physically perfect version of himself, an iteration that looks like Superman but has Bizarro's diminished mental capacity. In the conclusion to the story, "The Bride of Bizarro!" from *Action Comics* #255 (1959), Bizarro and his "perfect" duplicate of Superman fight it out after Lois spurns the latter. The imperfect "perfect" Superman duplicate is destroyed and Bizarro then battles Superman to a stalemate. To resolve this dilemma, Lois uses the duplicator ray to create a Bizarro version of herself. Bizarro Superman and Bizarro Lois immediately fall in love and fly into space to find a planet where they can live by themselves.

Less than a year later, in *Action Comics* #263 and #264 (1960), readers learn that Bizarro Superman (now referred to as Bizarro #1) and Bizarro Lois (similarly renamed Bizarro Lois #1) have used a duplicator ray to populate an entire planet called Htrae ("Earth" spelled backward) with duplicates of themselves. This concept is extended and deepened in "The Son of Bizarro" from *Superman* #140 (1960), in which the Bizarros are apparently no longer creatures of "non-living matter." In this story, Bizarro Lois #1 gives birth to a son who, much to the distress of the rest of the Bizarro population, looks like a normal human being but has Superman's powers. Because the other Bizarros want to use a ray to change this boy into Bizarro form, his father places him on a satellite that takes him to Earth. The story then reiterates Superman's origin story, as a caption informs us: "Strangely, it is almost like when the Krypton rocket of Jor-El landed his infant son on Earth." Just as the Kents found the infant Kal-El, a middle-aged couple discovers Superbaby and takes him to Midvale Orphanage, where he wreaks havoc. He then flies to Metropolis, where he encounters Superman, who exclaims, "Great Scott! Am I . . . I seeing things? That flying child almost looks like me when I was Superbaby in Smallville!" Supergirl takes the infant to the Fortress of Solitude, and Superman stammers, "We'll be the . . . er . . . foster parents of that super-child!" The remainder of the plot is given over to a series of reproductive acts: Supergirl seemingly turns Superbaby into a Bizarro baby, who then creates a Bizarro Supergirl, using the original duplicator ray kept in the Fortress of Solitude. Eventually, it is discovered that Bizarro babies change over time from human to Bizarro in appearance. Superman notes,

FIGURE 2.3. The Bizarros are bound by the laws of natural reproduction. "The Son of Bizarro," *Superman* #140 (1960).

"It's not magic, but just a law of nature with certain species of life!" This confirms that Bizarros are now understood to be wholly living and bound to natural laws, including those of sexual reproduction (figure 2.3).

In this story, Superman's repressed powers of sexual reproduction are displaced onto the Bizarros, making them superior to Superman inasmuch as they actualize the utopian ideal he cannot achieve (the best he can do is suggest adopting Superbaby with his cousin). Significantly, Htrae is a distorted version of Earth (specifically, the middle-class, white American ideal that defines Smallville and Metropolis equally), not Krypton. As described in "The Shame of the Bizarro Family" from *Adventure Comics* #285 (1961), "astonishingly, everything on this cube-shaped world is a whacky version of Earthly civilization! City skyscrapers lean crookedly at all angles! For the pathetic Bizarro people hate perfection!" As flawed reproductions of Superman, the Bizarros confirm the impossibility of readers to become Superman and are, as such, potentially more identifiable—or at the very least, differently attractive—than Superman. This is an act of cognitive repetition as reproduction; a renewed sense of self is achieved by the reader in the acts of self-alienation and self-recognition ("I am not Bizarro; I am Bizarro" and "I am not Superman; I am Superman"). As Deleuze observes, "self-consciousness in recognition appears as the faculty of the future or the function of the future, the function of the new."[22] Just as with Imaginary Stories, the Bizarro tales provide a space for imagining a possible future self and tie cognitive reproduction directly to expressions of sexual reproduction.

WEIRD LOVES AND STRANGE ROMANCES

This function of the carnivalesque bodies of the Bizarros is carried over into another trope of Silver Age Superman comic books: the radical transformation of Lois Lane's body. In Weisinger-era stories, Lois temporarily becomes a "Madame Jekyll," a centaur, an infant, a mermaid, and a hyper-evolved "super-brain" being, to name only a few of her many transformations. Her radically changing body is particularly useful for understanding how the process of self-alienation/self-recognition is carried out in Silver Age Superman comic books. Superman's desire to avoid the reiteration of trauma bound up in the loss of family is most potently realized through the figure of Lois, who, in her desire to marry Superman, represents the most direct possibility of such a recurrence; if Superman does not marry Lois and have children, he will not risk the possibility of again losing his family. Her body equally contains the possibility of utopia (sexual reproduction) and dystopia (death of the family). Consequently, her body bears the burden of reproduction in its constant transformations that work to circumvent the possibility of sexual reproduction with Superman; at the same time, these transformations mark her as cognitively fertile. Importantly, per the dictates of genre conventions and iterative narration, Lois cannot marry and reproduce with Superman; it is only her desire that can be reproduced. The knowledge of this (both on the diegetic and extra-diegetic registers) marks both Lois and readers (who are compelled to identify with Lois via her comparative humanity and love of Superman) as inherently subversive subjects who push back against the heteronormativity represented by Superman's utopian body and subjectivity.

Through Lois, it becomes especially clear that what is being repressed in these comic books is sexual reproduction within the confines of heteronormativity. As noted in Superman's mythos, reproduction is grounded in trauma, and the reproduction of self is inherently traumatic inasmuch as it compels cognitive transformation. Such cognitive transformation is made manifest in the radical body transformations of Lois, which in fact represent Superman's trauma. In myriad ways, Lois becomes the subject of Superman's displacement and condensation. His traumatic past, which is papered over by his resolutely integral, superior body, reemerges in the traumatic forms taken on by Lois. It is important that this trauma is manifested by the character most strongly defined by an attachment to Superman, for her own desire to be closer to Superman compels this bodily transaction. Sex and trauma are explicitly conflated in the relationship between Superman and Lois because her desire must necessarily be marked as impossible, and because Superman's reproductive potential would at least partially ameliorate the trauma of the destruction of Krypton but is similarly impossible. In a sense, Superman is defined as "super" as much by this trauma as by his extraordinary powers; in order to remain Superman, he must remain fixed as the perpetually traumatized subject. Unsurprisingly, this fundamental but essentially unresolved trauma is often worked out on his body. For example, red kryptonite routinely alters his body, such as when he acquires the physical characteristics of an ant in *Action Comics* #296 (1963) as a result of his exposure to it (figure 2.4). Yet Lois's comparable transformations confirm that all social subjects are traumatized by their submission to the law. The regulation of cognitive difference—represented by Superman's Kryptonian past—links Lois to Superman and is affirmed by their perpetually deferred and mutual sexual attraction to one another.

Lois's transformations destabilize socially constructed gender differences that mark the female body as expressly different from the male

FIGURE 2.4. Superman under the influence of red kryptonite. *Action Comics* #296 (1963).

body. Judith Butler contends, "The heterosexualization of desire requires and institutes the production of discrete and asymmetrical oppositions between 'feminine' and 'masculine.' . . . The cultural matrix through which gender identity has become intelligible requires that certain kinds of 'identities' cannot 'exist.'"[23] Lois routinely assumes such impossible identities, whether as a superwoman à la Superman or in other nonhuman forms, frequently as an expression of her desire to be romantically closer to Superman. Such changes can be represented as directly beneficial to Superman, as in the story "Beware of the Bug-Belle!" from *Superman's Girl-Friend Lois Lane* #69 (1966), in which Lois decides to assume Superman's heroic duties while he is away on a mission in outer space. In other words, she chooses to reproduce her own subjectivity, a repetition of both herself and Superman marked by radical difference. She borrows Lana Lang's Insect Queen costume and her "bio-genetic ring" given to Lana by "an insect man from another world," which allows the wearer to "temporarily change into any arthropod form." Lois's decision is marked by a vexed matrix of feelings: she wishes to help others in a manner similar to Superman (and Lana), and she must also overcome her

FIGURE 2.5. Lois Lane and Lana Lang as heroic bug women. "Beware of the Bug-Belle!," *Superman's Girl-Friend Lois Lane* #69 (1966).

personal disgust for insects ("They give me the creeps," she shudders). With the ring, Lois changes herself into a variety of different kinds of insects, retaining the upper half of her human form while being a "dragonfly girl," a "hawk moth maid," and a "mosquito maid." She retains only her head when she changes into a "scorpion girl" and a "water beetle woman" to stop a gang of armed thieves. However, a woman intent on collecting the Anti-Superman Gang's million-dollar bounty on Superman steals the ring and, using information on Krypton found in the book *All About Krypton* written by Superman, assumes the form of a "scarlet spinner of Krypton" and ensnares Superman in an indestructible web. In response, Lois and Lana transform themselves into Kryptonian insects and rescue Superman, an act that realizes not only their shared love of Superman but also their desire to be superheroes themselves (figure 2.5).

CONCLUSION

Lois's and Lana's transformed bodies are the realization of a reproductive agency that resists the laws of utopia. In remediating sexual desire as the production of the grotesque body linked to but also removed from Krypton, "Beware of the Bug-Belle!" actualizes the inherent utopian appeal of Silver Age Superman comic books also evident in Imaginary Stories and figures such as Bizarro. This appeal is predicated on the notion that radical bodies as reifications of new subjectivities allow readers the ability to imagine new social possibilities for themselves.

Indeed, the Superman stories of this era retain this symbolic potency in their affirmation of the liberating possibilities attached to the reimagined body to this day. Compare, for example, the tales examined here to a contemporary story, "The Thousand Deaths of Lois Lane" from *Superman Giant* #7 (2019), in which Superman repeatedly imagines Lois's torture and brutal murder at the hands of Lex Luthor. This story explicitly and brutally asserts the long-standing law that Superman and Lois can never fulfill their romantic and sexual desires for one another. Modern Superman comic books such as this one strive to achieve an "adult" sense of realism, but their representation of "mature" content results in the suppression of the fertile reimaginings of self that define Weisinger-era Superman comic books. Rather than a recursive recapitulation of trauma, these Silver Age stories offer a means by which trauma can work in service of renewal and regeneration, of life rather than death. If readers in the 1950s and '60s were encouraged to consider themselves part of a

Superman family, the invitation remains perpetually open to any readers willing to imagine themselves and the very meaning of being super in different ways.

NOTES

I am indebted to Michael Dibble for his invaluable research assistance and to Joyce Kaffel, who generously shared memories of her father, Mort Weisinger, and his working methods during Superman's Silver Age.

1. Singer, "'Black Skins,'" 110.
2. Richard Reynolds, *Super Heroes: A Modern Mythology* (Jackson: University Press of Mississippi, 1992), 83.
3. "Comic Book Sales Figures for 1961," Comichron, accessed January 23, 2020, https://www.comichron.com/yearlycomicssales/postaldata/1961.html.
4. Quoted in Will Murray, "Superman's Editor Mort Weisinger," in *The Krypton Companion*, ed. Michael Eury (Raleigh, NC: TwoMorrows Publishing, 2006), 12.
5. Murray, "Superman's Editor," 13.
6. Bradford W. Wright, *Comic Book Nation: The Transformation of Youth Culture in America* (Baltimore, MD: The Johns Hopkins University Press, 2001), 60–61.
7. Mark Waid, "Introduction," in *Superman in the Sixties* (New York: DC Comics, 1999), 9.
8. Bruno Bettelheim, *The Uses of Enchantment: The Meaning and Importance of Fairy Tales* (New York: Vintage Books, 1977), 279.
9. Quoted in Joe Sergi, "The Amazing Adventure of the Man of Steel and the Psychiatric Censor—Superman vs. Doctor Wertham," Comic Book Legal Defense Fund, September 19, 2012, http://cbldf.org/2012/09/the-amazing-adventure-of-the-man-of-steel-and-the-psychiatric-censor-superman-vs-doctor-wertham/.
10. Quoted in Les Daniels, *Superman: The Complete History* (San Francisco: Chronicle Books, 1998), 103.
11. See Umberto Eco, "The Myth of Superman," *Diacritics* 2, no. 1 (1972): 14–22.
12. Bukatman, *Matters of Gravity*, 185.
13. Michel Foucault, *Discipline and Punish: The Birth of the Prison* (New York: Vintage Books, 1995).
14. Gilles Deleuze, *Difference and Repetition*, trans. Paul Patton (New York: Columbia University Press, 1994), 2.
15. Deleuze, *Difference and Repetition*, xx.
16. Fredric Jameson, *Archaeologies of the Future: The Desire Called Utopia and Other Science Fictions* (New York: Verso, 2007), 217.
17. Jameson, *Archaeologies of the Future*, xii.
18. Quoted in Mike Conroy, *500 Comic Book Villains* (Hauppauge, NY: Barron's Educational Series, 2004), 244.

19. Mikhail Bakhtin, *Rabelais and His World*, trans. Hélène Iswolsky (Bloomington: Indiana University Press, 1984), 317.
20. Deleuze, *Difference and Repetition*, 7.
21. Deleuze, *Difference and Repetition*, 13.
22. Deleuze, *Difference and Repetition*, 15.
23. Butler, *Gender Trouble*, 17.

3

A STORM OF PASSION
Sexual Agency and Symbolic Capital in the X-Men's Storm

J. ANDREW DEMAN

In recognizing our sexual appetites as normal, we might lose a sense of ourselves as the victims of sex.

Paula Webster, quoted in Hillary L. Chute,
Graphic Women: Life Narrative and Contemporary Comics

Recent studies of Chris Claremont's writing for *Uncanny X-Men* have revealed a complex array of subversive messages about female sexuality within a patriarchal culture.[1] While most of these studies have focused on Jean Grey/Phoenix, the character Ororo Munroe/Storm is far more prominently featured throughout Claremont's sixteen-year run as the lead writer of the X-Men comic book franchise. Storm also represents multiple important cultural milestones. Storm is one of the first female superhero team leaders in American comics and the first Black superhero team leader. She is also, in the words of Carolyn Cocca, the "first major black superheroine."[2] Despite this position of prominence, Storm has not always lived up to expectations for progressive representation. Her potential has been particularly restricted by how often she has been written to reflect the sexual fantasies of a straight white male comics readership. In this chapter, I argue that the key to Storm's symbolic capital is her transition from a passive sexual fantasy object to a dynamic character with sexual agency. I additionally argue that this transition has cascading, far-reaching effects and implications for the symbolic capital of the larger X-Men comics universe and, quite possibly, superhero comics in general. I will perform this analysis using examples taken from Chris Claremont's run on *Uncanny X-Men* from 1983 to 1984. During this time, the character of Storm comes to the forefront of the series and challenges entrenched perceptions within the comics form, thus creating an enduring legacy that continues to influence contemporary portrayals.

SYMBOLIC CAPITAL

In *The Greatest Comic Book of All Time*, Bart Beaty and Benjamin Woo build on the work of Pierre Bourdieu to develop a series of questions about the manner in which various institutions attribute value to particular comics over others. If we measure value by sales alone (a cynical proposition, but one allowed by Beaty and Woo's method), then the X-Men franchise is automatically a juggernaut. The flagship *Uncanny X-Men* dominated comics sales charts for the majority of Claremont's tenure as its writer, and the title's 1991 relaunch as *X-Men* #1 holds the Guinness World Record as the top-selling single-issue comic book of all time, with an estimated 8.1 million copies sold. Using Bourdieu's work as a template, Beaty and Woo ultimately suggest that symbolic capital is a product of some combination of "economic capital (sales)" and "cultural capital (prestige)."[3] The evidence is clear that Claremont's *X-Men* has accrued unparalleled economic capital, but what of its cultural capital?

Cultural capital is, as Beaty and Woo note, more abstract than economic capital. But the case for Claremont's cultural capital is easily made through the emergent field of "Claremont studies," a broad term for scholars who have been tracing the unique contribution of Claremont to popular culture; this scholarship has been partly enabled by the acquisition of Claremont's papers by Columbia University. The enduring legacy of Claremont's stories is further evinced by the fact that they continue to be retold in film and television adaptations. Moreover, as Paul Levitz, former president and publisher of DC Comics, notes, Claremont's work "played a pivotal role in assembling the audience that enabled American comics to move to more mature and sophisticated storytelling, and the graphic novel."[4] If this is true, then how did Claremont create a more mature and sophisticated X-Men? I am putting forward Storm's sexual awakening as one potential answer to this question.

The cultivation of Storm's sexual desire allowed her character to become the iconic superhero she is today, while also allowing X-Men comics to reflect a greater complexity of character and character relationships. In his description of the enduring influence of X-Men comics, Roger Sabin identifies "the fact that they fell in love, fell out, got married, gave birth, died and, above all, experienced discrimination from prejudiced humans" as major contributing factors.[5] Jason Powell, Sean Howe, and Joseph Darowski similarly identify the increasing complexity, depth of character, and thematic darkness of Claremont's run as significant factors in the franchise's combination of record-breaking sales and critical adulation.[6] Carol Cooper sees sexual politics as another major factor, noting, "Shifting attitudes toward sex and women became a big part of the book's increasing appeal once Claremont began scripting the X-Men."[7] These critical summaries suggest there is a confluence of factors pushing X-Men from a poor-selling single title on the verge of cancellation to arguably the most important superhero comics franchise of the Bronze Age.[8] Storm is located at the very center of this confluence.

IN THE BEGINNING

As noted by Lillian Robinson, beginning in the 1960s and extending well into the 1970s, Marvel Comics tend to place female superheroes in subservient roles, often of a domestic nature.[9] We can see this in examples of other Marvel superhero teams throughout the 1960s and 1970s. The Wasp, for example, plays a highly maternal role within the Avengers, as does Sue Storm/the Invisible Girl (later the Invisible Woman) within the Fantastic Four. These trends did not, however, begin with Marvel. Instead, they belong within a broader tradition that can be traced back at least as far as *All Star Comics* #13 from 1942, wherein Wonder Woman is invited to join the Justice Society of America as the otherwise all-male team's secretary.[10]

This same tradition of placing female team members into subservient roles can be seen in Storm's early appearances. Though scholars such as David Lambkin, Blair Davis, and Anita McDaniel have celebrated Storm's significant cultural achievements, it is important to keep in mind that those achievements took a long time to develop. Certainly, she is a touchstone character for Claremont's initial run on *Uncanny X-Men*; along with Wolverine, she is the only character to remain in Claremont's X-Men for the entirety of his sixteen-year run (minus two issues during which she is believed to be dead), and she is the leader of the team for the majority of that time. Yet as Cocca notes, Storm's "introduction is highly stereotyped."[11] The racial stereotypes informing Storm's early appearances in

X-Men stories are articulated by Davis in his article "Bare Chests, Silver Tiaras, and Removable Afros: The Visual Design of Black Comic Book Superheroes," as well as in my own earlier work on the subject in *The Margins of Comics*. Cooper provides a succinct perspective on the subject in saying that Storm "somehow got cast as the mythic earth-mother/matriarch figure critiqued by many black feminists as both unrealistic and racist in its glib projection of inhuman perfection."[12]

From the perspective of gender, Storm's early appearances are equally unrealistic and problematic. This is something that Richard Reynolds speaks to directly in *Super Heroes: A Modern Mythology*:

> Storm is . . . a focus for the opposing themes and mythologies which the X-Men embody; her character reconciles a whole gamut of conflicting myths and ideologies. An elemental force of nature, she is the least spontaneous and most withdrawn of the X-Men. Asexual (even for a superheroine); she sports perhaps the most revealing and fetishistic black costume of any 1970s Marvel or DC character. As with the Scarlet Witch, Storm's exotic sexuality is offered in the context of family and domestic life: the family being in this case the X-Men themselves. She occupies a quasi-maternal role in the dynamics of the group, distantly tolerant of the flirtatious sexuality of Nightcrawler or Wolverine.[13]

Darowski supports Reynold's conclusion, noting that Storm "codes" her relationship to the other X-Men as asexual by referring to the male members of the team as "brother."[14] Visually, Storm's depiction falls into Richard Lupoff's definition of "good girl art."[15] Storm's original costume, with thigh-high black leather heeled boots, cut-outs, and plenty of skin, presents Storm as an object of male gaze–directed sexual fantasy, even as her behavior remains steadfastly asexual. Reynolds argues that this combination of visual sexual objectification and narrative asexuality is typical of good girl art. According to Reynolds, good girl art "takes the signs of pornographic discourse (whips, chains, spiked heels, beautiful but blank faces) and integrates them into the context of non-pornographic stories. "In this way," continues Reynolds, "the sign of pornography (never explicitly delivered) comes to stand in for an entire pornographic subtext, a series of blanks which readers remain free to fill in for themselves."[16] Reynolds further suggests that good girl art is commonly used to resolve "the amalgam of sexual fear and desire" held by the presumed majority comics readership in the late 1970s/early 1980s.[17] Like other contemporary female superheroes, the original version of Storm is designed to appeal to the fantasies of an adolescent male readership and written as aggressively asexual in order to alleviate the fear of sexuality inherent in that same presumed audience. She is, in other words, drawn to be sexy for the sake of the readers but is not represented as having any sexual desires of her own. This approach to sexuality typifies the first eight years of Storm's existence.

TURNING POINT

As mentioned, Storm's turn away from this passive sexuality is enabled, in part, by the sheer scope of the Claremont run.[18] As detailed in Howe's *Marvel Comics: The Untold Story*, Claremont was not interested in retelling the same X-Men stories over and over; instead, he was motivated by a desire to shake up the characters,[19] even when his illustrators and editors did not support such rejections of the status quo. In the early 1980s, Storm was the primary focus of Claremont's experimentation. Because Storm is the leader of the X-Men during this time and is a central character within the overarching story that comprises the Claremont run, the reconfiguration of her character reflects—and directs—the reconfiguration of X-Men comics as a whole. Powell singles out the transformation of Storm from "a naïve virgin/goddess figure into a mohawk-wearing, weapon-wielding 'punk'" as evidence of Claremont's commitment to changing up the X-Men stories.[20] Powell further suggests that the redevelopment of Storm's sexuality is central to her transformation. This redevelopment occurs through two key relationships, one subtextual and one textual.

YUKIO

In *Uncanny X-Men* #172–173 (1983), Storm is separated from the rest of the X-Men and has an adventure with an androgynous young woman named Yukio, a character who had only recently been cocreated by Claremont and Frank Miller for the first *Wolverine* mini-series. Canonically, this is not a romance. Yet the story is frequently discussed in terms of queer coding in comics. Writes Cocca: "Storm's romantic life is multifaceted and complicated in the comics. The first time she really seems to be taken with someone is with female Japanese ronin Yukio. Fans have certainly read into the relationship between Storm and Yukio since the 1980s."[21]

FIGURE 3.1. Storm meets Yukio. *Uncanny X-Men* #172 (1983).

Writing for the Eisner Award–winning website Comics Alliance, Andrew Wheeler asserts that "Storm's transformation from elemental goddess to mohawk leather punk is one of the queerest stories ever told in comics."[22] Jay Edidin of the popular podcast *Jay and Miles Xplain the X-Men* states the issue even more directly: "[Storm and Yukio] are 100 percent totally doing it." In support of this reading, Edidin notes, "The first time they meet, Storm rescues Yukio from falling off a building, and seriously could this be any more like the classic romantic arc?"[23]

A close reading of the scene in question bears out Edidin's argument. In the story, Yukio is acrobatically leaping among the rooftops of Tokyo after spying on the X-Men and their adversary. As she loses her footing, she falls from a skyscraper only to be rescued at the last moment by Storm swooping in to catch her. Yukio is delighted by the experience, remarking, "What a ride—one in a million—I loved it!" As Storm protests that Yukio almost died, the ronin proclaims, "Life is the ultimate adventure, wind-rider, and death the prize that awaits us all," before cartwheeling away while laughing. Storm, in astonishment, reflects, "The woman is mad . . . and yet, I wish I could laugh so" (figure 3.1).[24]

In Yukio and Storm's next encounter within the same issue, Storm again intervenes to help Yukio but is electrocuted to the point that her clothes burn off. It is significant to note that Storm is electrocuted by her own power, which is manipulated through the intervention of a villain. Storm's costume has important symbolic implications. As Reynolds notes, it is innately "fetishistic,"[25] speaking to sexual fantasy at the expense of character relatability. Thus, the fact that Storm, to some degree, destroys her own costume is similarly symbolic; in essence, Storm is destroying her old self. This time, Yukio is the savior, leaping to rescue the now-naked and vulnerable Storm. In a gesture with echoes of masculine chivalry, Yukio wraps Storm in a kimono to preserve her modesty and ushers her to safety. In the following issue of the story, Storm begins to exhibit characteristics and behaviors learned from Yukio. When the pair are confronted in an alley by a gang of knife-wielding men, Storm thinks, "Oh, well—you only die once."[26] After the men are defeated, Storm confides to Yukio, "I have never used my powers to deliberately inflict pain." Yukio explains that the men deserved it, to which Storm replies, "You know . . . I think you're right! Whatever it means—this madness of yours that has infected me—I welcome it!" The next time we see Storm, she has adopted a punk-inflected costume very different from her original one (I will discuss the significance of this costume in more detail below). Following this, Yukio and Storm do not appear together again in X-Men comics for many years. However, in *Uncanny X-Men Annual* #11 (1987), each X-Man is shown his or her deepest longing, and Storm's is Yukio. Within a dream, she remarks, "I never knew truly how to laugh before I met Yukio. In many ways I have never been as happy since. I want to join her" (figure 3.2).[27]

Storm's character continues to change upon her return from Japan. In *Uncanny X-Men* #174 (1983), it is revealed that she has cleaned out her attic garden. She explains to her teammate, Kitty Pryde, "As I have changed little one . . . I have changed my home to match."[28] As identified by Ramzi Fawaz, Storm's garden is an important symbol of her previous

FIGURE 3.2. Storm's greatest desire. *Uncanny X-Men Annual* #11 (1987).

character. Fawaz describes the garden as a place of autonomy and "a space of contemplation and connection to nature."[29] In earlier issues, the garden features prominently in scenes devoted to Storm's characterization, establishing and reestablishing her primordial connection to nature and her command over the elements, both of which align Storm with cultural stereotypes about Africanness. In addition, Storm frequently refers to her plants as her children and talks to them as such. Thus, in abandoning her garden, Storm can be seen as rejecting both her connection to primordial nature (a connection steeped in gender, racial, and ethnic stereotypes) and her connection to the traditionally feminine nurturer role. With each rejection and subsequent reinvention, Storm becomes a more complex and sophisticated character. All of these changes, and all of this growth, are initiated by her subtextual sexual awakening.

COSTUME CHANGE

In the wake of her subtextual sexual encounter with Yukio, Storm adopts both the philosophy and androgynous appearance of her symbolic lover, and she creates a new costume for herself (figure 3.3). As mentioned earlier, Storm's original costume aligned her with the concept of good girl art, which shows "superheroines [who are] as exciting for their looks as for their villain-bashing exploits."[30] Superheroes' costumes are, arguably, the most iconic aspect of their characterization. McDaniel notes in her discussion of Storm, "The costume is designed to define the character's purpose and affiliation. . . . The costumes are important because they highlight the superhero identity elements that are valued by the reader."[31] With regard to Storm, though, McDaniel argues that the character's sexualized display undermines her value as a person. McDaniel notes that "a costume that exposes a lot of skin draws the reader's attention toward less-valued, human elements such as race, gender, and physical attractiveness, whereas a costume that covers the body and hides the identity draws the reader's attention toward the more valued, superhero elements such as strength and the ability to perform heroic acts."[32] The math here is simplistic but holds up pretty well: as Storm transitions from "goddess-garb to punk rock duds,"[33] the reader comes to identify with Storm rather than just eroticize (or exoticize) her.[34]

In addition to Storm's punk costume revealing less skin and more character, the sexual politics of the punk movement and its active resistance to gender binaries and sexual repression function as a potent symbol of opposition to the gendered stereotypes that had previously defined Storm. The punk aesthetic for women is traditionally used to "destabilize static sociogendered identities."[35] We can see this reflected in the androgyny of Storm's punk haircut and boxy leather vest as well as her general embrace of a type of biker aesthetic that was also embraced by both gay "clone culture" and "butch" lesbians; these queer associations either/both magnify or are magnified by the sexual subtext of the relationship with the ronin punk Yukio. Given the new and different connotations it evokes, it is not surprising that Storm's sudden costume transition was jarring to many X-Men readers in the early 1980s. This reaction is perhaps best illustrated through the audience stand-in character of Kitty Pryde, who in issue #173

FIGURE 3.3. Storm's original costume versus her punk costume. *Uncanny X-Men* #173 (1983).

confronts Storm's new look and runs off screaming, "Your clothes! Your . . . hair! What have you done?!! How—could you!?!"[36] Storm's costume change is rendered additionally jarring and significant by established patterns of symbolic meaning in X-Men costuming. Barbara Brownie and Danny Graydon suggest that costumes in the X-Men universe symbolize the competing forces of social otherness and team unity, arguing that "the wearing of the uniform expressed identification with a shared set of values, and a willingness to actively participate in the role assigned to them by the rest of the team."[37] Consequently, when X-Men change their costumes to something more unique or perhaps even deviant, it reflects a desire to "proclaim individuality."[38] This is certainly true of Storm, who, in the *Uncanny X-Men* #172–173 story line, rejects the costume she had worn throughout her previous tenure as an X-Man, which was designed for her by Professor Xavier, in favor of a costume she designs herself.

The radicalness of Storm's costume change is historically significant.

In describing the depiction of women in comics memoir from the 1970s and 1980s, Hilary Chute notes that "today's readers of graphic narrative may not know how hard-won the opportunity was to visualize non-normative lives of women in an aesthetically engaged format during the significant period when comics shifted from the strictly commercial to the politically and artistically revolutionary."[39] While Chute is speaking to the specific context of graphic memoirs by female artists, the same logic could apply to the new Storm, as could the same identification of a culturally significant depiction in comics history. As Fawaz notes, "Storm's feminist sensibility, then, did not emerge as a wholesale abandonment of all gendered relations but from her demand to be a free agent who chooses her own affiliations rather than allowing them to be dictated by social expectations."[40] Storm embodies the punk mentality by choosing to define herself. McDaniel sees this development as directly connected to Storm's costume change, arguing that her 1980s outfit "may be most salient rhetorically when discussing her ascendency in superhero status. Storm adopted this look to symbolize her need to reclaim her spiritual self as a woman—to reconnect with her emotions and how they influence her ability to control her powers."[41] In addition, the choice to articulate these changes through punk style speaks to an ambition to expand ideas about what superhero comics could be. Chute notes, "Punk profoundly influenced comics, and comics profoundly influenced punk. Today, punk rock's historical era is over, but comics is an art in which we can recognize its values—the weirdness and alterity along with the accessibility—while comics also extends its reach into the mainstream, abandoning none of punk's energy while also creating new models for art."[42] Each of the punk values that Chute identifies are key to the significance of Storm's transition. The weirdness and alterity that she projects (again evidenced by Kitty Pryde's reaction) allow her to step down from the idealized goddess stereotype and declare her unwillingness to conform to the social expectations that Fawaz describes above.

In *The Margin of Comics*, I compare the intersections of Storm's sexuality and ethnicity to Jan Pieterse's reading of Josephine Baker's *La Revue Negre*, a burlesque show performed in Paris in which Baker appeared topless with a skirt made of bananas and the occasional jungle cat. Pieterse notes that "this ambivalent sexual exoticism that was racist and at the same time biologized by what was, allegedly, 'primitive' and 'savage,' was characteristic of the epoch."[43] As I conclude in that text, "Storm in 1970s America channels her savage, primitive and exotic character elements toward a complex eroticism that is rooted in the audience's fascination with her Otherness."[44] Storm's adoption of the punk aesthetic for the 1980s subverts this previous performance of exotic sexuality, replacing it with an aesthetic known for declaring a resistance to conformity and consumerism. Consequently, Storm's costume change can be read as the character declaring noncompliance to the sexual-fantasy role she had previously occupied. Although her new costume carries with it signifiers of another sexual fantasy (with possible BDSM signifiers), the signifiers of power and resistance associated with the punk imagery give Storm a new sense of sexual deviance and agency. When she dons the punk costume, she is no longer a passive or traditional sexual fantasy.

What Chute calls punk's "accessibility" is equally important to Storm's development. Storm was, prior to her transformation, dehumanized by her inaccessibility, as demonstrated by her conformity to the good girl aesthetic. By donning the signifiers of a punk mentality, Storm declares her desire to be less distant and detached from the world, to interact with the world in the same human ways that her male teammates have been allowed to interact with the world. Far from conforming to cultural stereotypes, Storm moves from being behind the curve to ahead of it. As Michael Campochiaro notes, "she is an early signifier of third-wave feminism, a black woman in America of African heritage and upbringing whose sexuality cannot be easily categorized (I think she's straight but has had a great and enduring love for several women), and who represents a challenge to previously accepted notions of what a feminist is and is not."[45] In this sense, Storm's costume change signals a radical recontextualization of the way her character interacts with the discourse of women in comics.

Beyond her costume change, Storm's identity is likewise refined by Claremont at the narrative level in the wake of the encounter with Yukio. During this period, Storm transitions from goddess to human in a way that makes her more identifiable, relatable, and flawed. Humanizing Storm helps cement both the economic and cultural capital of X-Men comics. Campochiaro describes the effect as such:

> And in Storm, the X-Men finally had a character who makes explicit all of the mutants-as-minority themes that the book had been pursuing since its inception in the 1960s. With Storm, we have a character who isn't nominally Other while still white, but instead one who *is* Other, a nonconformist minority character who doesn't abide by the stated political and social power structures but instead acts as a role model for how the disenfranchised can push back against these oppressive norms. And when Storm sports the Mohawk and leather jacket, she creates an iconic representation for readers on the margins, both female and male.[46]

In this sense, then, the quality of Storm's characterization has a direct effect upon the quality and resonance of X-Men comics' central metaphor, thus opening important new venues for the creators to explore by connecting the series more directly to a nonconformist (we might also say "queer") audience.

FORGE AND "LIFEDEATH"

As much as Storm developed and changed in the wake of her encounter with Yukio, her first canonical romantic pairing would not occur until two years later, with the publication of the now-famous story titled "Lifedeath" in *Uncanny X-Men* #186 (1984). Powell describes "Lifedeath" as "among Claremont's most prized of his own X-Men work" and "one of Claremont's most deeply felt and personal stories" (figure 3.4).[47]

The significance of this story is evident in the fact that it appears in a special double-size issue illustrated by Barry Windsor-Smith, whose visual sensibility immediately sets the tone for the treatment of Storm within the narrative itself. As Osvaldo Oyola describes:

> [Windsor-Smith] draws Storm in a way that makes her more real. She is less a voluptuous superheroine in bathing suit and cape, and a more sinewy, lean, strong-looking one. She is still attractive, but the depictions of her, even in the nude, while beautiful, are never overtly sexualized. She is not infantilized either, despite her vulnerable state. Instead, she contains an impressive maturity and authority, even when she is unsure of how to go on.[48]

This strategy of visual representation is particularly important to note in the context of Black female sexuality in comics. Deborah Elizabeth Whaley notes that "calls for positive or desexualized vestiges of blackness, though well-intentioned, risk foreclosing the artistic possibilities of visual culture. Offering the idea of Black women as sequential subjects interrogates problematic characterizations of difference while insisting upon the way those same characterizations are pregnant with possibilities."[49] By portraying Storm's sexual awakening in comics without subjecting her to the tropes and clichés of the masculine gaze, Windsor-Smith's art can very much be read in this light.

Windsor-Smith's art style goes a long way to making this story possible, as some of the plot elements of the narrative are, from the perspective of gender, problematic at best. Forge is a Cheyenne mutant

FIGURE 3.4. "Lifedeath" cover art. *Uncanny X-Men* #186 (1984).

with the vaguely defined power of "technomancy," which enables him to create whatever technological device he requires. In the issue prior to "Lifedeath," a device that Forge has created is used, much to Forge's dismay, in an attack on Storm's teammate Rogue. While Forge attempts to stop the attack, Storm attempts to save Rogue, which results in Storm being struck by the weapon and stripped of her superpowers. Convoluted mitigating circumstances aside, the basic fact remains that before Storm falls in love with Forge, Forge is quite literally responsible for taking her power away from her. At best, this is problematic; at worst, it can be read as "fridging," a narrative trope in which a female character is depowered or subjected to violence in order to advance the story of a male character.[50] In addition, "Lifedeath" frequently features Forge explaining Storm's innermost feelings to her in a manner that sounds a lot like mansplaining. Edidin goes so far as to describe Forge's behavior as "gaslighting."[51] Conversely, Cooper suggests that losing her superpowers actually empowers Storm as a human being: "Deprived of her elemental powers as both reason and tool for sexual sublimation, Storm spent the next few issues of a story arc initially entitled 'LifeDeath' as neither goddess nor X-Man, and began therefore to discover the power of the kind of romantic love she'd been hitherto denied."[52] Thus, even though the gender politics of "Lifedeath" are problematic, they do not negate the further development of Storm's character through her awakening sexuality. Additionally, it is important to note that the controlling behaviors exhibited by Forge are the exact reasons that Storm leaves him at the end of the story, asserting her power within the relationship and her unwillingness to settle for a man with Forge's condescending, patriarchal tendencies. The opening splash page of the issue shows Storm waking up in bed in Forge's apartment, in a visual depiction that is highly reminiscent of Lord Leighton's painting "Flaming June" (figure 3.5). The opening narrative caption sets the tone of emotional gravity that will dominate the issue: "Once upon a time, there was a woman who could fly." The image features potential erotic signifiers, with Storm curled up among silk sheets, naked. While the caption helps orient the image in a different direction, its sexual undercurrents are thematically important; the complex interaction between sexuality and the gravity of human emotion is central to "Lifedeath."

The semantics of the opening caption are also important in terms of the fairy tale tradition that Claremont is drawing on. This is true in two ways:

1. The use of "once upon a time" (referring to previous issues when Storm could fly) characterizes Storm's previous existence as a

FIGURE 3.5. Windsor-Smith's art juxtaposed with Lord Leighton's. *Uncanny X-Men* #186 (1984).

    fairy tale. This conforms with my argument that earlier incarnations of Storm were distant and dehumanized by way of being unrealistic.
2. The fairy tale tradition normally begins with "Once upon a time, there was a girl . . ." By identifying Storm as a "woman" instead of a girl, Claremont subverts this tradition and further humanizes Storm, signaling to the reader that she is not to be infantilized.

Similarly, though Windsor-Smith's opening splash page references Leighton's painting, it also significantly revises it. While Leighton's painting is frequently interpreted as depicting a mythological nymph, Milene Fernandez suggests it is possible that the painting "indicates the dangers of a man's doomed infatuation with an unavailable woman or a femme fatale." Either way, the visual intertextuality is apt for the story ahead. On the comics page and in contrast to the female character in Leighton's painting, Storm is upside-down; this is an important signifier of her mental state and another effective way to signify that she is not the idealized feminine mythological object or femme fatale we might be tempted to read her as. In this position, Storm is unable to perform Flaming June.

The story that unfolds from that opening splash page is complicated. Forge conceals from Storm that he was the one who invented the weapon that depowered her, and he seeks to rehabilitate her from both her physical injuries and the suicidal depression she experiences as a result of losing her powers. Forge is motivated in this issue by both his own sense of guilt for his role in depowering Storm and his infatuation with her. Thinks Forge: "Lord, she's beautiful, with a soul as lovely as her body. The personification of life itself. She changed last year. Her goddess-like serenity gave way to an all too human passion. It made her lovelier than ever."[53] As much as Forge's motivations are suspect here, it is important to note that he views Storm's character development (he is referring to the post-Yukio transformation) as making Storm more attractive, not less. Thus, he is tacitly supporting the metatextual development of Storm's character from simple object of desire to complex female character.

Claremont loads the story with traditional romantic trappings. Storm and Forge share a swim in the pool that leads to them discussing and bonding over their respective traumas, which in Forge's case includes the amputation of his leg and hand due to injuries suffered in the Vietnam war; this is followed by a dinner date in which Storm dons a pink dress, sent to her by Forge. The costume change from her punk attire signifies her desire to inhabit (if temporarily) a different role—that of the traditional female romantic lead. When she looks at herself in the mirror, Storm's reciprocal affection toward Forge comes out: "I wonder what he will think?" When she next descends the staircase toward the apartment's living quarters, Forge is startled to the point of cutting his finger with a kitchen knife. When she notices Forge staring at her, Storm suddenly becomes self-conscious, a characteristic antithetical to a character who, in her previous incarnation, would routinely swim naked in front of the other X-Men. She excuses herself to change, thinking, "Stupid, stupid woman! No, not a 'woman' at all, but a foolish child trying desperately to impress. Why do I so crave his approval? It is not like me."[54] Storm's insecurity, combined with her hyperawareness of said insecurity, showcases how unaccustomed she is to the romantic feelings that she experiences with Forge. This action is also in keeping with what Anna Peppard sees as a major theme of the "Lifedeath" story: a sense of corporeal existence that is uncommon within superhero comics. She writes, "In 'Lifedeath,' although neither Storm nor Forge want to be limited by the perceived or actual capabilities of their respectively powerful but unstable and/or incomplete bodies, their emotional healing cannot be separated from their corporeal experiences."[55] Where the pre-Yukio Storm could wear her highly sexualized costume unabashedly, the Storm we see in "Lifedeath" has become hyperaware of both her body and her attire.

After removing the highly feminine dress and replacing it with a pair of overalls—an outfit that is much more in keeping with her adopted punk aesthetic—Storm tells Forge, "This . . . is more comfortable." In rejecting traditional femininity in favor of something more androgynous, Storm is expressing her resistance to the traditional heteronormative romance story that seems to be unfolding around her. She is also, however, keeping Forge at a distance due to her own sense of insecurity. Nonetheless, by exploring her feminine identity by wearing the dress in the first place, Storm shows her desire to explore different aspects of herself. Appropriately, the dress does not suit her, but with a new outfit (or, a new costume) in place, she is able to continue the exploration of her romantic/sexual desires on her own terms, arguably better off for having experimented in the first place.

As the renewed date continues, Storm has another bodily experience through her first alcoholic drink and again acts out of character. She thinks, "My heart is pounding—I feel flushed and giddy—It must be the wine."[56] Over drinks, the characters confide in each other, Forge opening up about his Cheyenne heritage and Storm about her childhood trauma. Then, Storm explains to Forge the transformation that she experienced after her encounter with Yukio, while conveniently neglecting to mention Yukio:

> I have been living on the raw edge of my emotions . . . feeling . . . reacting . . . to everything as intensely as can be. The first lesson I learned—and a very harsh one it was too—was that my elemental abilities were bound up with my emotions. The greater my feelings the more extreme the atmospheric response. To protect myself and those around me, I cultivated an absolute serenity of mind and body so much that I lost virtually all awareness of myself as a woman. A few months ago, I cast away those restraints. I could no longer endure my self-enforced spiritual celibacy . . . so I rebelled. I cut my hair, changed my clothes—like you, I denied as completely as I could my old world and self and beliefs.[57]

This dialogue can be seen as either Claremont retconning Storm's earlier lack of humanity and committing to a new direction for the character, or a sincere explanation for how he perceived his creation. Either way, the characterization of Storm's previous state as "spiritual celibacy" is telling of the significance of the literal celibacy that also defined her earlier incarnation. Appropriately, it is at this moment that Forge leans in and kisses her.

In keeping with X-Men comics' commitment to melodrama, things very quickly fall apart. Forge gets a phone call, and Storm accidentally overhears that Forge was the one who made the gun that depowered her. She laments opening her heart to him and walks away from him, declaring:

> To be loyal, you must believe in something. Anything! You are hollow form without substance. You cannot believe, because there is no "you" . . . We are much alike, Forge. I see in you a "me" that might have been. I choose to walk another road. My feet may never leave the ground . . . but someday, I shall fly again.[58]

Thus ends "Lifedeath."

In spite of ending before Forge and Storm's physical intimacy can progress beyond a rather chaste kiss, the second sexual awakening of Storm depicted in "Lifedeath" plays a notable role in the further development of her character. Following her romance with Forge, Storm decides not to return to the X-Men and instead embarks on a yearlong pilgrimage to discover herself. She notes in *Uncanny X-Men* #189 (1985), "I must rebuild my life. And the best place for that is Africa, my mother's home, where I grew to womanhood."[59] Storm's journey becomes a b-story throughout X-Men comics over the next year (a sort of solo series within a series) that culminates in "Lifedeath II" in *Uncanny X-Men* #198 (1985), a Storm solo story that takes place in Kenya and solidifies her repatriation with her African heritage. As Oyola notes, "'Lifedeath II' is a narrative departure from the rigmarole of X-Men continuity—taking a breath to try to examine the disjuncture between Ororo's African origins and her superhero identity." In "Lifedeath II," Storm's African-ness is recontextualized in order to detach her from the tropes of the indigene that had defined her earliest incarnation. Oyola observes that the effort does not produce perfect results because "it still reinforces a narrative of Africa as impoverished and superstitious."[60] Despite this, the story does complicate the relationship between culture and identity, further distancing Storm from racial and ethnic stereotypes. Describes Oyola: "Ororo goes on this journey to find herself after her loss of powers, but discovers that the hybrid-self made of different cultural influences cannot be tied to any one place." In this way, Storm and the reader discover simultaneously that her character can no longer be defined exclusively by her African-ness. As a result of "Lifedeath II," Storm is no longer confined to the African stereotypes that limited her previous characterization. This is an important development for a character that Whaley sees as a tool of American nationalism and colonialism in her earliest incarnation, conforming to stereotypes of the "magical negress."[61]

CONCLUSION

Ultimately, it is through her pilgrimage to Africa that Storm 2.0 returns to the X-Men ready to lead them again: "She winds up finding a rebirth of sorts, one that leads to an inner calm and a greater self-awareness."[62] Upon her return, Storm challenges Cyclops for leadership of the X-Men and wins, despite the fact that she does not have any powers.[63] For several years afterward, Storm becomes the centerpiece of X-Men comics. Importantly, Storm's transformation is total. According to Peter Coogan's well-accepted definition of the superhero, there are three things that define what a superhero is: mission, powers, and identity.[64] Claremont breaks down each of these three things and builds them anew in order to create the enduring and iconic character that Storm has become. As I have demonstrated, this process of reconstitution is driven by Storm's sexual self-discovery.

Within both of Storm's sexual encounters, we see the kind of complex intersectionality that Christopher D. Zeichmann, writing elsewhere in this volume, finds lacking in the early filmic adaptations of X-Men stories. Storm is a highly gendered, highly sexualized character who holds a position of rare prominence in superhero comics as a woman of color whose initial (implied and actual) sexual attractions are both with people of color, one of whom is coded as bisexual, the other disabled. Storm's aesthetic transition from African Princess to Punk Warrior adds further complexity to the configuration of discourses through which this character (and her love life) passes. In the end, the relationships that Storm forms do not easily cohere to any existing stereotypes, archetypes, or tropes, and in that, the character becomes truly compelling and individualized, further extending her agency.

As McDaniel notes, "Storm is an important black female character in the Marvel Universe because she has been drawn and written to be important. Few black or female characters (not to mention black *and* female characters) have achieved her status as a superhero."[65] In this chapter, I have argued that Storm was not written to be important in her initial incarnation. Instead, she was written to conform to stereotypes of exoticism and feminine domesticity in accordance with the perceived fantasies (and insecurities) of the majority comics readership of the time. By giving Storm passion, Claremont gave her purpose, resonance, and humanity, which, in turn, gave X-Men comics as a whole a similar purpose, resonance, and humanity. As Whaley notes, "Storm's metamorphosis over the years represents a visionary social subject that propels social change."[66]

This metamorphosis was and remains essential to the enduring symbolic capital of the X-Men comic book franchise and its many offshoots, within both comics and other media. In the end, Storm's sexual awakening can be seen as a potent symbol of how popular media can reinvent itself in order to achieve a greater sense of both resonance and relevance. The passion of Storm forever changed comics—and superheroes—in ways that are still being felt today.

NOTES

1. Ramzi Fawaz, *The New Mutants: Superheroes and the Radical Imagination of American Comics* (New York: NYU Press, 2016); Miles Booy, *Marvel's Mutants: The X-Men Comics of Chris Claremont* (London: Toris, 2018); Cocca, *Superwomen*; Jason Powell, *The Best There Is at What He Does: Examining Chris Claremont's X-Men* (Edwardsville, IL: Sequart Organization, 2016); and Joseph Darowski, *X-Men and the Mutant Metaphor: Race and Gender in the Comic Books* (Lanham, MD: Rowman & Littlefield, 2014).

2. Cocca, *Superwomen*, 125.

3. Bart Beaty and Benjamin Woo, *The Greatest Comic Book of All Time: Symbolic Capital and the Field of American Comic Books* (New York: Palgrave Pivot, 2016), 11.

4. Calvin Reid, "X-Men Writer Chris Claremont Donates Archive to Columbia University," *Publisher's Weekly*, November 14, 2011, http://www.publishersweekly.com/pw/by-topic/industry-news/comics/article/49499-x-men-writer-chris-claremont-donates-archive-to-columbia-university.html.

5. Roger Sabin, *Comics, Comix and Graphic Novels: A History of Graphic Novels* (London: Phaidon Press, 1996), 159.

6. Jason Powell, *The Best There Is at What He Does: Examining Chris Claremont's X-Men* (Edwardsville, IL: Sequart Organization, 2016), 157; Sean Howe, *Marvel Comics: The Untold Story* (New York: HarperCollins, 2013), 286; Joseph Darowski, *X-Men and the Mutant Metaphor: Race and Gender in the Comic Books* (Lanham, MD: Rowman & Littlefield, 2014), 85.

7. Carol Cooper, "Leading by Example: The Tao of Women in the X-Men World," in *The Unauthorized X-Men*, ed. Len Wein (New York: Smart Pop, 2005), 195.

8. The Bronze Age of comics is generally thought to begin in 1970 and continue until approximately 1984. "Bronze Age of Comic Books," Wikipedia, accessed January 23, 2020, https://en.wikipedia.org/wiki/Bronze_Age_of_Comic_Books.

9. Lillian S. Robinson, *Wonder Women: Feminisms and Superheroes* (London: Routledge, 2006), 88–94.

10. Gardner Fox, *All-Star Comics*, no. 13 (New York: DC Comics, 1942).

11. Cocca, *Superwomen*, 125.

12. Cooper, "Leading by Example," 189.

13. Reynolds, *Super Heroes*, 94.

14. Darowski, *X-Men and the Mutant Metaphor*, 168.

15. Richard A. Lupoff, *The Great American Paperback, Art, Collectibles, Pop Culture* (Portland, OR: Collectors Press, 2001).

16. Reynolds, *Super Heroes*, 34.

17. Reynolds, *Super Heroes*, 84.

18. Cocca, *Superwomen*, 125.

19. Howe, *Marvel Comics*, 286.

20. Powell, "Best There Is," 157.

21. Cocca, *Superwomen*, 132.

22. Andrew Wheeler, "Mutant & Proud: Understanding the Queerness Of The X-Men," Comics Alliance, June 30, 2014, http://comicsalliance.com/mutant-proud-xmen-lgbt-rights-identity-queerness-transformation/.

23. Jay Edidin and Miles Stokes, "25: The Best at What He Does," *Jay & Miles Xplain the X-Men*, podcast, MP3 audio, 47:49, accessed October 12, 2018, https://www.xplainthexmen.com/2014/10/25-the-best-at-what-he-does/.

24. Chris Claremont, *The Uncanny X-Men Omnibus: Volume 3* (New York: Marvel Comics, 2015), 686.

25. Reynolds, *Super Heroes*, 94.

26. Claremont, *Uncanny X-Men Omnibus*, 706.

27. Chris Claremont, *Uncanny X-Men Annual*, no. 11 (New York: Marvel Comics, 1987), 34.

28. Claremont, *Uncanny X-Men Omnibus*, 740.

29. Ramzi Fawaz, *The New Mutants: Superheroes and the Radical Imagination of American Comics* (New York: New York University Press, 2016), 151.

30. Reynolds, *Super Heroes*, 34.

31. Anita McDaniel, "Negotiating Life Spaces: How Marriage Marginalized Storm," in *Heroines of Comic Books and Literature, Portrayals in Popular Culture*, ed. Maja Bajac-Carter, Norma Jones, and Bob Batchelor (Lanham: Rowman & Littlefield, 2014), 121.

32. McDaniel, "Negotiating Life Spaces," 121.

33. Osvaldo Oyola, "Imperfect Storm (Part One): Exploring 'Lifedeath,'" The Middle Spaces, June 30, 2018, https://themiddlespaces.com/2015/06/30/imperfect-storm-part-one/.

34. It is worth noting here that Ramzi Fawaz has a different interpretation, seeing Storm's original costume as empowering: "Storm's embodiment of the black female 'disco diva' that dominated gay and African American visual culture . . . positions her as a figure capable of taking pleasure in the performance of a variety of racial and gender identities." While I acknowledge this symbolic potential, I

would argue, in keeping with Reynolds, that this costume did far more to situate Storm as the object of a gaze, if only through the manner in which Storm was posed within it.

35. Shehnaz Suterwalla, "Cut, Layer, Break, Fold: Fashioning Gendered Difference, 1970s to the Present," *WSQ: Womens Studies Quarterly* 41, no. 1–2 (2013): 267–284. doi:10.1353/wsq.2013.0047, 271.

36. Claremont, *Uncanny X-Men Omnibus*, 721.

37. Barbara Brownie and Danny Graydon, *The Superhero Costume: Identity and Disguise in Fact and Fiction* (London: Bloomsbury, 2016), 151.

38. Reynolds, *Super Heroes*, 26.

39. Hillary L. Chute, *Graphic Women: Life Narrative and Contemporary Comics* (New York: Columbia University Press, 2010), 26.

40. Fawaz, *New Mutants*, 150.

41. McDaniel, "Negotiating Life Spaces," 124.

42. Hilary L. Chute, *Why Comics? From Underground to Everywhere* (New York: Columbia University Press, 2018), 236.

43. Nederveen Pieterse, *White on Black: Images of Africa and Blacks in Western Popular Culture* (New Haven, CT: Yale University Press, 2006), 143.

44. J. Andrew Deman, *The Margins of Comics: The Construction of Women, Minorities, and the Geek in Graphic Narrative* (Toronto: Nuada Press, 2015), 106.

45. Michael Campochiaro, "On X-(Wo)Men and Third-Wave Feminism," Sequart Organization, February 6, 2016, http://sequart.org/magazine/62699/on-x-women-and-third-wave-feminism/.

46. It is important to note that otherness in X-Men comics can be inherently fictive, with characters being persecuted for being blue or furry, or having blasts shoot out of their eyes. Storm's minority status is different from these purely metaphorical depictions in the sense that she is a Black woman in America, a literal embodiment of a prominent real-world minority group. Campochiaro, "On X-(Wo)Men."

47. Powell, *Best There Is*, 121.

48. Oyola, "Imperfect Storm (Part One)."

49. Whaley, *Black Women in Sequence*, 182.

50. Gail Simone, Women in Refrigerators, accessed October 12, 2018.

51. Jay Edidin and Miles Stokes, "180: Lawful Badass," *Jay & Miles Xplain the X-Men*, podcast, MP3 audio, 105:39, accessed October 12, 2018, https://www.xplainthexmen.com/2018/01/180-lawful-badass/.

52. Cooper, "Leading by Example," 194.

53. Chris Claremont, Arnold Drake, and Barry Windsor-Smith, *X-Men: Lifedeath* (New York: Marvel Worldwide, 2011), 7–8.

54. Claremont, Drake, and Windsor-Smith, *X-Men: Lifedeath*, 29.

55. Anna F. Peppard, "Reading the Superhuman: Embodiments of Multiplicity in Marvel Comics," PhD diss., York University, 2017, 220.

56. Claremont, Drake, and Windsor-Smith, *X-Men: Lifedeath*, 30.

57. Claremont, Drake, and Windsor-Smith, *X-Men: Lifedeath*, 32.

58. Claremont, Drake, and Windsor-Smith, *X-Men: Lifedeath*, 42.
59. Chris Claremont, *Uncanny X-Men*, no. 189 (New York: Marvel Comics, 1985), 6.
60. Osvaldo Oyola, "Imperfect Storm (Part Two): Exploring 'Lifedeath II,'" The Middle Spaces, July 17, 2018, https://themiddlespaces.com/2015/07/14/imperfect-storm-part-two/.
61. Whaley, *Black Women in Sequence*, 107.
62. Campochiaro, "On X-(Wo)Men."
63. Chris Claremont, *Uncanny X-Men*, no. 201 (New York: Marvel Comics, 1986).
64. Peter Coogan, "The Definition of the Superhero," in *A Comics Studies Reader*, ed. Jeet Heer and Kent Worcester (Lexington: University of Mississippi Press, 2009), 77.
65. McDaniel, "Negotiating Life Spaces," 121–122.
66. Whaley, *Black Women in Sequence*, 107.

4

DAZZLER, MELODRAMA, AND SHAME
Mutant Allegory, Closeted Readers

BRIAN JOHNSON

[Dazzler's] journey of struggling for acceptance from a dismissive father and longing for the love of her missing mother was something that queer readers, who only years earlier could have been arrested for showing signs of affection toward a member of the same sex in public, connected with. Embracing your sexuality had to happen in dark, sweaty nightclubs with disco music blaring, or, for younger gay men far from the metropolises of New York and San Francisco, it could occur in their childhood bedrooms, reading Dazzler's exploits in between more butch fare like X-Men and Spider-Man that wouldn't get them bullied.

Ira Madison III, "The Queer Importance of Dazzler, Marvel's Disco-Inspired, Roller-Skating Superheroine," MTV.com

Queer, I'd suggest, might usefully be thought of as referring in the first place to . . . [a] group of infants and children . . . whose sense of identity is for some reason tuned most durably to the note of shame.

Eve Kosofsky Sedgwick, *Touching Feeling: Affect, Pedagogy, Performativity*

Ira Madison III's recent appreciation of "the queer importance of Dazzler, Marvel's disco-inspired rollerskating superheroine" captures in passing something vital but largely neglected in discussions of how queer fans have historically read superhero comics, namely the disconcerting proximity between "embracing your sexuality" via the transformational protocols of queer reading and a more fundamental—at once necessarily prior and troublingly persistent—experience of gay shame. Back in the early 1980s, when Dazzler debuted, the "younger gay men far from the metropolises of New York and San Francisco"—too isolated and too young to find love in "dark, sweaty nightclubs with disco music blaring" that Madison's article conjures—may well have thrilled to a kind of queer demotic pedagogy and the reparative pleasures of self-recognition afforded by the comic book adventures of Dazzler, a.k.a. Alison Blaire. I certainly did—at least, to an extent. White, male, lower middle class, eldest son in a four-person nuclear family, resident of a WASP-y neighborhood in a large Canadian prairie city, anxious about a gender role to which I could not adequately conform and uncertain of my sexuality, I was eight when Dazzler first appeared in the pages of *Uncanny X-Men* #130 in 1980 and fourteen when her forty-two-issue solo series concluded in 1986. To me, Madison's sketch of the furtive young *Dazzler* fan with no illusions about schoolyard bullies or the stigmatizing power of object choice strikes a chord. As I was to learn, however, the closets of nightclub and childhood bedroom have less in common than Madison's remarks suggest and imply very different moments in the dialectic of concealment and revelation that is so determining of the specific shape, history, and texture of a queer life. Of the two, only the shielded collective space of the disco affords the possibility of a social experience of liberating recognition; the childhood bedroom cum secret library indexes a prior and more ambiguous moment of queer self-apprehension often still tethered to homophobic disavowal, a moment in which the act of reading can, at best, offer only obscure intimations of a community that might—or might not ever (have to?)—arrive to help deliver the nascent queer subject from a difficult present where anxiety, loneliness, and shame are regular companions.

    The project of this chapter is to explore the formal and diegetic conditions of superhero comics that structure negative affects like these insofar as such affects emerge within and come to organize the reading practices of queer youth, especially those children, like myself, for whom adolescence did not mark the beginning of self-understanding or self-acceptance, but rather a period of intense sexual confusion, shame-consciousness, and normalizing self-discipline. Broadly speaking, it proceeds from my own attempt to remember what it was like to read *Dazzler* as a queer/questioning child in the early 1980s in order to reflect upon how the ad hoc technique of queer reading so widely celebrated within comics studies (and within queer geek subcultures and queer theory more broadly) breaks down, devolving from a reading practice that opens the queer subject onto more secure positions of self-recognition and self-validation into one that points the way to greater self-betrayal. Although what follows is informed by my own necessarily partial memory of being a young reader and fan of superhero comics during that period of stifled self-becoming/negation and is inevitably colored by a thirty-year struggle to even acknowledge, much less fling wide, the closet door, it is not predominately a work of autoethnography. Rather, its focus is on the ways the ongoing series *Dazzler* (1981–1986) and Marvel Graphic Novel #12, *Dazzler: The Movie* (1984), exemplify the contradictions that young queer readers encountered in the mutant superhero allegory's unstable structuring of queer desire, recognition, and shame in the early 1980s, offering such readers potentially enabling but necessarily treacherous ground upon which to cultivate their "queer world-making projects."[1]

It may sound like I am intending to challenge the experiences of queer comics readers who find in superhero and mutant metaphors a panacea of queer belonging. I am not. Nicholas E. Miller's brilliant cultural history of Dazzler's still-evolving queer reception, to which I refer below, leaves no room to doubt the extraordinary role Dazzler has played (and continues to play) as an imaginative resource for a wide range of queer fans.[2] Nor am I claiming, perversely, and contra articles like Madison's or Miller's, that *Dazzler* "made me" a closet case, or that reading her adventures as a gay child amounted to a kind of workaday conversion therapy. But just as Dr. Fredric Wertham's once-scandalous imputation that Batman and Robin's domestic relationship was "like a wish dream of two homosexuals living together" has found itself ironically affirmed by queer comics creators' and scholars' celebration of the liberating charge produced when readerly desire meets the homosocial imaginary of superhero comics,[3] so too, I argue, must we take seriously the lingering and contradictory effects of the often-homophobic representations upon which queer worlding performs its secular identitarian magic. The specific challenge that such semantically and ideologically contradictory texts pose for young queer readers becomes acutely visible, I suggest, in the socially progressive mutant allegories of the 1980s, and perhaps nowhere more symptomatically than in comics starring Dazzler. In what follows, I concur with Madison and Miller that early-1980s Dazzler was an exemplary, and even liberating, site of self-recognition for gay male fans. Ultimately, however, my goal is to read against the grain of reparative queerings of Dazzler in order to focus more deliberately on the ways in which the character's corporate origins, narrative history, editorial management, and allegorical structuration complicate her function as a gay icon.

COMICS READERS, SUPERHEROES, AND THE RHETORIC OF SHAME

Shame has been on the agenda of queer studies for some time now, at least since 1993, when Eve Kosofsky Sedgwick argued, "If queer is a politically potent term, which it is, that's because, far from being detached from the childhood scene of shame, it cleaves to that scene as a near-inexhaustible source of transformational energy." Shame and its transformational energies have been important points of reference within geek culture and comic book fan studies as well, where the long history of anti-comics stigma and the pathologization of fans have generated a plethora of "performative identity vernaculars" and rhetorical countermoves to redeem the medium and, in Paul Lopes's memorable formulation, "demand respect."[4] The convergent ways in which queer performative identity vernaculars and superhero comic fandom (and geek culture more generally) demonstrate the psychic necessity of working through stigmatizing social scripts rather than simply discarding them affirms Chad Bennett's suggestion that "there is something queer about fandom in general," especially insofar as fans "structure their fandom in relation to shame and shame-related affects that hover around their erotically charged, overlapping fan activities—including viewing, reading, listening, writing, fantasizing, role playing, and archiving."[5] Similarly, the overlapping implication of queer men and male geeks in heteronormative cultural scripts about "subordinate masculinity" or gender failure points to shared sources of shame-consciousness informing the performative identities of heterosexual geeks, queers, and queer fans.[6] As Anthony Lioi puts it, "relative to normative American masculinity, nerd affect is queer because it involves the expression of love for cultural artifacts and practices associated with childhood, and not with the adult masculine role of producer and reproducer."[7]

Despite such suggestive convergences between queerness, fandom, and shame, however, queer scholarship on superhero comics has bifurcated in a way that discourages engagement with the persistence and implications of shame-based rhetorics in some of the comics most privileged and celebrated by queer readers. On the one hand, queer comics scholarship engages implicitly with the shaming effects of superhero comics when it pursues the historicist path laid out by Marxist, feminist, and anti-racist cultural studies that focuses heavily on the politics of representation. Kara Kvaran's "SuperGay: Depictions of Homosexuality in Mainstream Superhero Comics" epitomizes this disciplinary habitus, which characteristically submits the history of its subject to a survey of absences, a critique of stereotypes, and a cautious assessment of recent progress in the realm of representational inclusivity and nuance. Within such accounts, an awareness of the relation between superheroes and shame inheres in the identification of homophobia at the level of figural representation and characterization and the roles played by creators, social commentators, and institutional practices in abetting or ameliorating the representational field of sexualities. Dr. Wertham's fearmongering about the homosexual subtexts of popular fantasy, the Comic Magazine Association of America's self-censoring proscription against "sex perversion" from 1954 to 1989 (homophobic stereotypes excepted), and the gradual appearance of out and (mostly) proud LGBTQ superheroes following Northstar's historic voicing of what was already an open secret in a 1992 issue of *Alpha Flight* all feature prominently in this archive. Within its melioristic metanarrative of gradual, albeit uneven, progress, buttressed by the critic's own "paranoid" position of wise suspicion, such criticism tacitly relegates queer shame either to a past that has been largely overcome or to the position of bad object that can be confidently rejected.[8]

Meanwhile, complementing the study of representations of queer figures (or their absence), a second queer approach to superhero comics takes its cue from the disciplinary consolidation of fan studies (with its interest in what readers do with texts, rather than in what texts do to readers) and a more general multidisciplinary shift away from ideology critique and its "paranoid" textual-critical agon in favor of what Sedgwick, following the pioneering psychoanalytic work of Melanie Klein and Sylvan Tomkins, calls "reparative" reading. To read reparatively, in Sedgwick's influential formulation, is "to unpack the local, contingent relations between any given piece of knowledge and its narrative/epistemological entailments for the seeker, knower, or teller," provisionally deemphasizing the critical will to master a text's ideological horizon in favor of understanding how such "narrative/epistemological entailments" participate in "what Foucault calls 'care of the self,' the often very fragile concern to provide the self with pleasure and nourishment in an environment that is perceived as not particularly offering them."[9] Unlike studies of "representations of homosexuality" in superhero comics, this approach focuses precisely on figures that the diegesis identifies (or presents in an unmarked way) as heterosexual and on periods in which homosexuality is officially disavowed by publishers and creators as a feature of the textual world, locating in this unlikely soil nourishment for queer appetites and privileged sites of self-recognition among hermeneutically industrious queer readers. Lee Easton's affecting account of queering the homosocial bonding of Captain America and the Falcon as a boy in "Sharing a Quick Look: A Gay Man Reads His Comics" exemplifies this style of autoethnographic reading that thrives on what, in a different context, David Halperin has described as the "queer world-making" process whereby "gay men appropriate non-gay cultural forms and bring out the queerness they find in them" to "escape from their personal queerness into a larger, universal, non-stigmatizing queerness."[10] Within this nostalgic tradition of queer superhero comic studies, which joins with the more general tradition of comic book fan memoir and fan-scholar autoethnography exemplified by Scott Bukatman, Henry Jenkins, and the authors of Sean Howe's *Give Our Regards to the Atomsmashers!*, a return to the scene of childhood reading redeems the illegitimacy of the medium, bypasses the issue of homophobic representation, and relegates queer shame to a world beyond the panels in a fell swoop.[11]

Ramzi Fawaz's recent study of postwar superheroes "and the radical imagination of American comics" bridges the gap between these two approaches to queer shame, but in a way that at times elides their methodological distinctions between historicist suspicion (what texts say) and reparative sociology (what readers do).[12] Fawaz argues that World War II–era comics' jingoistic, racist, heteronormative celebration of the superhero as a "triumphant embodiment of American ideals" gave way in the postwar decades to a new breed of superheroes "framed as cultural outsiders and biological freaks capable of upsetting the social order in much the same way that racial, gendered, and sexual minorities were seen to destabilize the image of the ideal U.S. citizen." In Fawaz's reading, comics like *Fantastic Four*, *Justice League of America*, and *Uncanny X-Men*, among others, "articulated the tropes of literary and cultural fantasy to a variety of left-wing projects for political freedom."[13] These celebrations of "implicitly queer and nonnormative affiliations that exceeded the bounds of traditional social arrangements such as the nuclear family and the national community," Fawaz suggests, "facilitate[d] the reinvention of the superhero as a distinctly 'queer' figure."[14] Even as "readers came to 'relish, learn from, or identify with' this expansive collection of queer beings," however, the celebration of Johnny Storm, Ben Grimm, and the X-Men as queer figures, which extends the X-Men's "radicalized" mutant allegory to an entire "mutant generation" of postwar superheroes, risks overestimating the socially progressive ambience of the Marvel revolution and its aftershocks at DC Comics.[15] As accounts like Kvaran's remind us, the representational status of "homosexuality" in mainstream superhero comics during this period differed significantly from that of "racial minorities and women"; indeed, it was virtually invisible and, until 1989, when revisions to the Comics Code Authority rescinded the ban on "sexual abnormalities," literally unspeakable.[16] Moreover, when homosexuality did appear as an implied object of representation in rare moments of envelope-pushing in the early '80s, it did so either as a narratively unmarked open secret or as unapologetic homophobia. Marvel editor in chief Jim Shooter's infamous Hulk story of 1980, ". . . A Very Personal Hell," in which Bruce Banner is nearly raped by two men who cruise the YMCA showers (a setting evidently calculated to evoke the Village People's gay disco anthem of 1978) suggests that the editorial environment at Marvel Comics remained hostile toward "abnormal" or "perverse" sexualities during what might otherwise have been one of its most "radical" periods.[17] At the same time that racial minorities and women were becoming more visible and being presented more self-consciously within a liberal imaginary that emphasized tolerance and respect, Marvel's editor in chief could reportedly still decree, turning a blind eye to one of his own scripts, "There are no gays in Marvel Comics."[18]

In other words, it is easy to agree with Fawaz that postwar superheroes complicated and even—if only through the alchemy of readerly desire—"radicalized" the race and gender politics of an earlier era of normative superhero figures. But the industry's self-censoring ban on sympathetic (or even direct) representations of homosexuality makes it difficult to see the so-called "queerness" of superheroes during the same period as radical in quite the same way. That is because, in addition to adopting the more capacious definition of queerness, which now becomes synonymous with the performance of "disorienting" nonconformity,[19] "the reinvention of the superhero as a distinctly 'queer' figure" must now more heavily privilege reader consumption over industry production, even as the legibility of queerness within the pages of superhero comics requires that readers vibrate between the melodramatic lingua franca of postwar superhero comics and a new, more indirect register: allegory.

Fawaz's interventions are clearly essential to explaining why superheroes have for so long occupied a place of profound and intimate meaning in the lifeworlds of gay geeks and queer fans. Yet the semantic ambiguity of allegory means that the legibility of queerness within superhero comics whose creators are editorially constrained to tell stories as if they have never heard of nonnormative sexualities will vary dramatically in relation to the sagacity and receptivity of those comics' readers. Simply put: the "queerness" of heroic monsters like the Human Torch or the Thing may only be visible from the position of a subject already attuned to oblique intimations of same-sex love and open to the reparative hermeneutic these can nourish. As interpretive operations go, queering even as suggestive a text as *Uncanny X-Men* is quite different from apprehending the blackness of the Black Panther or the femininity of the Invisible Woman. Visually overdetermined representations of "racial minorities and women" and semantically underdetermined allusions to gays and lesbians whose existence can only (and at best!) be signaled indirectly through the allegory of "mutant" activism require different interpretive protocols. Readers who were less competent or more resistant presumably passed over these potential sites of queer world-building without pause—or, if they did pause, as I did, it was not to build worlds, but to register a furtive vibration, intuit the danger of such an enterprise, retreat from the recognitions upon which it rested, and grasp at convoluted justifications for a suspect readerly pleasure. Such self-evasions did not unfold unattended: the gloriously hysterical "mutant" superbodies capable of magnetizing the creative labor of queer allegorizing in the early 1980s were ideologically contradictory things: polymorphous and strange, certainly, but at the same time always already entangled in an aesthetics of disavowal. Their normative silence on the figure of "the homosexual," like the tacitly homophobic presentations, narratives, and paratexts that framed their adventuring, ensured that even the emancipatory strangeness of these mutant superbodies competed, semantically, with the whole familiar apparatus of homosexual panic, queer shame, and normative interpellation.

Whereas Fawaz's defiantly utopian account of postwar superhero comics tacitly enlists queer readers who have already "come out of shame,"[20] my concern in what follows is to strike a less utopian, less nostalgic note by asking how such obliquely "queer" figures looked to younger and/or less self-possessed readers. I am thinking specifically of those "naïve," misfit, acutely shame-conscious readers in whom the intuition of queer identity was still experienced as a hazard that might yet be avoided, and for whom "growing up" evoked a homophobic fantasy of repression and sexual self-discipline that blinded itself to even the limited affective freedoms that a cathexis on the closet as a metaphor of self-positioning might enable. It asks: What was it like to navigate the ideological contradictions of comics starring Dazzler in situ, not as a queer adult reader who has gone a considerable way toward developing a practice if not a politics of queer identity (however provisional this kind of identity work must necessarily be), but as a "queer child," that is, a far less certain subject-in-becoming for whom the "dark, sweaty nightclubs with disco music blaring" were as yet barely imagined.

DAZZLER WITHOUT DISCO: CHEESECAKE FEMINISM AND FANBOY FANTASY

The notion that Dazzler could function as a locus of repressive pedagogy sounds apocryphal at a time when Dazzler's status as a gay icon among queer superhero fans has never been more self-evident. The butterfly eye makeup and mirrorball romper worn by Lady Gaga during her gravity-defying 2017 Superbowl Halftime Show, for instance, prompted immediate social media comparisons between the singer/LGBTQ activist and Marvel Comics' disco-inspired, X-Men–affiliated mutant singer/superhero. Mash-ups of Gaga's performance with classic *Dazzler* covers like the one by pop culture parody Tumblr Entertain Me Weakly (figure 4.1) made the "Disco Stick" pop singer/"Disco Dazzler" superhero analogy explicit.[21] So too did queer writer and cultural commentator Anthony Oliveira's much-shared Twitter meme that captioned side-by-side images of Lady Gaga and Dazzler, "when u gotta do the #Superbowl halftime at 9 but gotta stop the Sentinels from persecuting x-gene carriers at 10" (@meakoopa, February 5, 2017)—itself a riff on a 2013 April Fool's joke by bisexual film director Bryan Singer, who teased that he had cast Lady Gaga as Dazzler ("one of my all-time favorite characters") in his then-upcoming X-Men film *Days of Future Past* (@BryanSinger, April 1, 2013). Moreover, the camp allure that Lady Gaga and Dazzler share as embodiments of disco's queerly inflected stylistic excess accounts for only part of what makes such comparisons seem so apt. As Oliveira's meme suggests, Gaga's performance of her "little monsters" songbook medley, especially her queer anthem "Born This Way," to a global Superbowl audience in the aftermath of the 2016 US presidential election was no less politically symbolic than the X-Men's decades-long struggle against mutant-persecuting "Sentinels" and their allegorical counterparts had ever been.[22]

The product of a later-scuttled intercompany imbroglio in which Marvel was to invent a disco-singer/superhero persona that Casablanca Records would cast and produce, Dazzler was originally to be a condensation of disco's hip, hit-making flashiness and the oddball swagger of late-'70s Marvel try-anything superhero strangeness. Insofar as disco was also a cultural watershed in the "broaden[ing of] the contours of blackness,

FIGURE 4.1. Lady Gaga/Dazzler mashup. Entertain Me Weakly on Tumblr.

femininity, and male homosexuality,"[23] Dazzler's musical gimmick seemed also to predispose the character to the sort of counterhegemonic cultural work now regularly attributed to the X-Men, whose ability to function as a queer allegory is a familiar part of pop mythology.[24] It is therefore hardly surprising that Dazzler ultimately saw print as a mutant, premiering in the pages of *Uncanny X-Men* #130 in 1980, introduced by an afroed announcer in full disco drag (figure 4.2).[25] Where better to premiere a character originally modeled on Jamaican-born disco artist, gender outlaw, and Studio 54 icon Grace Jones,[26] hyped in a gonzo film treatment for a never-to-be-produced Dazzler feature by then-Marvel editor in chief and Dazzler cocreator Jim Shooter (with the roles for Casablanca talent like Cher, Donna Summer, and the Village People!)?[27] Small wonder, either, that contemporary queer appreciations like Madison's or those of Lady Gaga's meme-generating fans find Dazzler as antithetical to Trump's America today as she must have been to the "straight white men who pledged their allegiance to rock music" and symbolically detonated a crate of disco records in Comiskey Park on so-called "Disco Demolition Night," July 12, 1979, to specularize the racist, homophobic recoil of the "Disco Sucks" moment of which they were the vanguard.[28] Dazzler's disco backstory and affiliation with the perpetually persecuted X-Men are mutually reinforcing, leaving little room to doubt that the character's principal function for queer readers is as a site of pleasurable and emancipatory recognition.[29]

By the time Dazzler's solo series debuted, however, disco was all but over and the "mutant songbird's" gimmick had become something of a liability. As original series writer Tom DeFalco recalls, even in 1979, when Shooter first announced at a writer's meeting that Marvel was going to produce a new title called *Disco Queen*,

> nobody wanted to have anything to do with it. . . . I don't think the word "Disco" is really mentioned in the first book. She sings in a Disco, but she is not a "Disco Singer." She is a singer. . . . We decided very early on not to make it a real Disco book because . . . we figured that by the time the book came out Disco would be dead.[30]

In 1981, when the turbulent Dazzler project finally saw print as issues #1 and #2 of Dazzler's own series, Casablanca had withdrawn from the collaboration and a tactical retreat from the original concept is already visible in the tension between the story's completed artwork and final script. Whereas the plot and artwork of those issues root the story in the

FIGURE 4.2. Dazzler as disco queen. *Uncanny X-Men* #130 (1980).

disco setting already established by the character's pre-series appearances when the Marvel-Casablanca collaboration was still salient, the final script indicates a different musical trajectory for the singer. In the first issue alone, *Dazzler* references rock, new wave, and soft rock acts like Pink Floyd, Blondie, and Billy Joel, making no mention of disco as a musical style at all, despite the story's mise en scène.[31] The cover text for the second issue, which concludes the material developed out of the Casablanca misadventure, blares "Last Stand in Discoland!" but also ironically commemorates the last stand *of* discoland for a character who, in subsequent issues, was to be given an all-male backup band and rebranded as a rock act by DeFalco and his successor, Danny Fingeroth.[32] By the third issue, Dazzler's new manager, Harry Osgood, had extricated her altogether from the New York nightclub scene, booking her a gig at the United Nations opening "a UNICEF benefit concert"—a detail likely inspired by the Music for UNICEF concert held at the UN General Assembly Hall or the Paul McCartney UNICEF Concert for Kampuchea (Cambodia), both in 1979.[33] Later issues amplified Dazzler's reimagining as a generic rock act (taking a brief detour through country music in issue #6), with references to "Rock and Roll" almost entirely replacing allusions to "disco" in scripts. Symptomatically, "the height of the disco craze" is explicitly presented as ancient history by Dazzler's manager, who reflects on the unfortunate origin of cybernetic adversary Techmaster, a former disco lightshow technician whose handsome face was disfigured by an accident with indoor "lightening" effects he was recklessly attempting to create for a "Donna Gaynor" disco performance in a period preceding the diegetic time of the series.[34] As Dazzler's own career becomes more closely aligned with Beatles covers and benefit concerts,[35] her increasingly abject disco origin appears only as a sartorial remainder in attire like her (less frequently featured) silver jumpsuit, mirrorball necklace, and roller skates, or in displaced and repudiated form as a monstrous disco-themed villain like the Techmaster, who stages an uncanny return of the repressed.

The swift demonization of disco in favor of a more generic rock aesthetic within the first year of Dazzler's solo series reflects the general cultural ascendancy and homophobic backlash of reactionary Chicago radio DJ Steve Dahl's rock-oriented "Disco Sucks" movement. The sexual politics of the national shift in musical tastes from the racially diverse and sexually liberated beats of disco to the mainstream semiotic of '80s "rock" were fortuitous for an editorial will keen on creating an ongoing serial whose protagonist would be generic enough to attract a wide mainstream audience. In DeFalco's words, which expand on initial series editor Louise Jones's observation that "music styles come and go," "[Dazzler] will always represent someone who is struggling for a dream. In her case her dream is music."[36] Implicit in the watering down of Dazzler's musical aesthetic to make her into a generic "singer" is the subtle heteronormative management of potentially radical images and scenarios associated with the disco scene. The "Grace Jones" Dazzler was never to be; in the end, Marvel modeled its singer/superhero on the mainstream appeal of blonde American actor and sex symbol Bo Derek. Thus, within the solo series, Dazzler's queer associations received no explicit diegetic or editorial sanction. With the notable exception of Ann Nocenti, who wrote a queer-coded Dazzler-Beast romance in the eccentric *Beauty and the Beast* limited series of 1984–1985 at the height of the AIDS epidemic,[37] Dazzler's creators generally disavowed her ties to queer histories and identities, reframing her as, paradoxically, a liberal feminist subject and an object of heterosexual fantasy.

The editorial will to reorient Dazzler from queer subject to normative object was especially evident in the series' reactionary deployment of a mode of "cheesecake" feminism that objectified Dazzler even as it promised to liberate her. On the one hand, Alison Blaire's struggle to pursue her singing career in defiance of patriarchal edict while navigating gender inequality and sexual harassment in the music industry is immediately graspable within the framework of second-wave white liberal feminism. Dazzler's periodic rescuing of hapless bohunk and road manager Lance Steele epitomizes these comics' pop feminist gender role reversals, as does the frequent evocation of a PG variation on American cinema's rape-and-revenge motif in depictions of Dazzler being cornered in dark alleys and empty buildings by threatening gangs of men on whom she ultimately turns the tables. One the other hand, like Marvel's other female-helmed superhero series of the late '70s and early '80s—*Ms. Marvel* (1977–1979), *Spider-Woman* (1978–1983), and *The Savage She-Hulk* (1980–1982)—*Dazzler* occupied a contradictory position with regard to gender ideology, torn as it was between Marvel's corporate commitment to liberal tolerance and the market reality of producing mass fantasies for an audience presumed to be composed primarily of young heterosexual men.[38] As Miller's rereading of Marvel Graphic Novel #12, *Dazzler: The Movie* (1984), in terms of the more recent #MeToo movement's focus on gender-based violence and toxic (especially workplace) masculinity correctly suggests, *Dazzler*'s feminism is ambivalent.[39] Such ambivalence is most infamously evident in the tension between the liberal feminist inflections of the scripts and

FIGURE 4.3. Cheesecake art. *Dazzler: The Movie* (1984).

artist Frank Springer's cheesecake illustrations of Dazzler, which characteristically fetishized Alison as a sexual object in scenes of gratuitous seminudity and autoerotic self-regard (figure 4.3).[40] Similarly, Dazzler's sleuthing adventure team-ups with fellow leading ladies Spider-Woman (a private detective) and She-Hulk (a lawyer) during the second year of the series appropriated the "jiggle TV" idiom of *Charlie's Angels* (1976–1981), though not without exposing subtle differences in objectifying strategy between Marvel's assorted female superheroes. *Savage She-Hulk*, *Ms. Marvel*, and *Spider-Woman* all solicited a "red-blooded" fanboy gaze, too, but the softcore sexualization of *Dazzler* as a Bo Derek–style pinup in Springer's "good girl" art emphasized Dazzler's embodiment of feminine clichés of softness and vulnerability in ways that the more overtly sadomasochistic visual themes of *Spider-Woman* did not.[41] In the context of Dazzler's potential association with disco's queer signification, Alison's visual identification with the "girl-next-door" pinup conventions of heteronormative femininity played a dual role, at once advertising her sexual availability to a randy fanboy gaze and disavowing her potential connection to deviant (and thus "queer") sexualities like those suggested by the fetishistic bondage motifs of *Spider-Woman*—a brand of kink permissible in that comic only because Spider-Woman was already so firmly anchored in the heterosexual imaginary that for Dazzler was more uncertain.

Given the striking ambivalence characterizing even Dazzler's liberal feminism, it is not surprising that the series tends to demonize feminist collectivity by refracting it in a parade of female villain collectives like "the Grapplers," "the Sisterhood," and "the Racine Ramjets." Shouldering the symbolic burden of Dazzler's own potentially threatening association with more radical forms of feminist politics, these lesbian-coded cabals helped make Dazzler more palatable to fanboy readers. In "Brawl!," for instance, Dazzler (out of costume as Alison Blaire) rescues a fellow waitress from abusive roller derby champions "The Racine Ramjets" while serving tables at Femmes, which its vampy, caped proprietor coyly describes as "a women-only club," adding, "There are hundreds of men-only establishments! Why not a place exclusively for women?"[42] The implicit vilification of lesbianism in this story, which relies on stereotypes of lesbians as slinky vampires or masculine women to signify danger, is supplemented by the disavowal of homosexuality that is enacted by the Femme proprietor's disingenuous recoding of gay bars as homosocial gentleman's clubs to mask the queer implications of her own "women-only" space under a pretense of sexually innocent "exclusivity." Such discursive contortionism makes the editorial constraints on queer representation in Dazzler abundantly clear. At once depraved and unspeakable, lesbianism is, at one level, coyly evoked as a come-on to heterosexual fantasy before it is paraded as a monstrous spectacle of gender confusion. Meanwhile, the potentially queer/radical implications of second-wave feminism that were already emergent in the early '80s, coincident with Dazzler's heyday, are safely embodied in "loud, obnoxious women" who are no match for the more conventionally beautiful, liberal, feminine, heterosexual heroine (figure 4.4).[43] As Miller argues in his reading of this episode, the climactic fight scene at Femmes is at once phantasmatic, allegorical, and managerial: "We might imagine this confrontation as one in which Shooter makes Dazzler battle her own queerness."[44] How fitting, then, that the intolerable roller derby team should also evoke the repudiated world of the roller disco, particularly in Bill Sienkiewicz's subversive cover painting for that issue (figure 4.5), which depicts a dreamlike and counterhegemonic condensation: a non-diegetic scene in which an out-of-continuity long-haired Alison Blaire (looking as she did at the beginning of her series, prior to her hair's restyling in the *Dazzler* graphic novel) skates *with*, rather than clashing *against*, the roller derby team—pursued by them yet also ambiguously incorporated into their queer-signifying context.[45] It is only a dream, unfortunately; this cover, like all of Sienkiewicz's painted *Dazzler* covers, evokes an aesthetically exceptional paraspace adjacent to official narrative continuity and thus operates in tension with the issue's more conservative ideological presentation.

As the tension between the homophobic script of "Brawl!" and the queer utopianism of Sienkiewicz's cover for that issue suggests, *Dazzler*'s queer resonance was at best a partial and contradictory affair. Such is particularly the case within *Dazzler*'s ongoing domestic melodrama, where the thematic constellation of shame, disappointment, and yearning for reconciliation with the estranged nuclear family made a queer reading persistently but obliquely available over the first two years of the series. In these issues, Alison is presented as a melancholy subject, tormented by the wound of paternal disapproval inflicted by her father, Judge Carter Blaire, who forbids her from pursuing her dream of a music career and disowns her when she refuses to study law. This archetypal conflict, familiar in its emotional torsions to both female and queer children of conservative families, is repeatedly specularized in Dazzler's reluctant grappling with a sequence of villainous father substitutes, most notably Doctor Doom and Galactus, each of whom belittles her as "insignificant" or "inconsequential," monstrously exaggerating her father's wish to override her will and compel her obedience. Doctor Doom's haughty commands as he sends

FIGURE 4.4. The Racine Ramjets. *Dazzler* #35 (1985).

FIGURE 4.5. Cover art by Bill Sienkiewicz. *Dazzler* #35 (1985).

Dazzler to Nightmare's "Dream Dimension" to locate a McGuffin called "the Merlin Stone," for instance, are simply more potent versions of her father's edicts. In the pop-unconscious of Nightmare's extra-dimensional realm, Dazzler is immediately confronted with her own psychodrama: accusing images of her father that flood paraspace and heckle her, "You'll never amount to anything!" "You've always been a disappointment!"[46] In a later adventure, the aloof cosmic entity and world-devourer Galactus is so indifferent to Dazzler's personhood and desires than he does not even acknowledge or address her directly, and he makes her feel like "a can-opener." This "godly" habitus, like Doctor Doom's, is rhymed with scenes of Alison's aloof, sulking father who confirms the family referent of these phantasmatic conflicts, sullenly declaring: "I have no daughter."[47] Queer shame is so archetypally bound up in such scenes of parental disappointment that *Dazzler*'s thematic orientation around this devastating scenario in the symptomatic register of soap opera made the series irresistible to me as a queer/questioning boy. That my queerness already expressed itself in a preference for female friendships—a preference whose social corollary was being known as "just one of the girls" or, more simply, "faggot"—made my cross-gender identification with Alison Blaire all the more spontaneous and inevitable. Yet Dazzler's capacity to function as a reparative mirror within my as yet half-cognized/half-resisted queer allegorizing was precarious—and not only because my naïve readerly erotics were obviously still so nebulous and conflicted. As we have seen, Dazzler herself was hardly unambiguous as a signifier of queer self-acceptance, and the narrative resolution of *Dazzler*'s queer-resonant domestic melodrama was similarly equivocal. The "SHAMEFUL SECRET OF DAZZLER'S PAST!" that incites the father to decree that Alison renounce her desire and cleave to the law turns out to have been the betrayal by her delinquent mother, who abandoned the family to pursue her own catastrophic singing career years earlier.[48] Culminating in a special double-size issue with an unusual photo cover to signal its "special event" status, this revelation of the "selfish" (read: queer) mother at the origin of the broken family permits a reconciliation between father and daughter. The wayward mother, too, is recuperated, but conditionally: first, she must express contrition, capitulate to patriarchal norms, dress like a church-matron, and do penance as a spectator to Alison's own swan song as a musical performer. As unexpected as this latter development might seem, the script has Dazzler decide independently of her father, in a characteristic moment of ideological closure, that she has doubts about her musical dream and about an industry that she increasingly sees as sexist and abusive. Patriarchy, it seems, is not so bad or even so misguided in its paternalism, so long as its violence is (eventually) justified by good intentions and a tearful apology. Just as pertinently for my younger queer self, another equally dubious moral flickered on the horizon: the queer shame of family breakdown can be avoided, so long as desire can be foreclosed.

"THE WISDOM OF CAUTION": ALLEGORY, SILENCE, AND THE PEDAGOGY OF THE CLOSET

In the end, Dazzler's structural fragility as a site of queer identification in the 1980s does not so much negate as complicate her status as a queer icon. Clearly, queer comic fans and fan scholars have no difficulty making Dazzler legible as a site of recognition. Yet as I have argued, the indirect, allegorical framework in which such recognition occurred in the early '80s made Dazzler's inconsistent and often contradictory queering of the X-Men's mutant allegory an unstable proposition, especially for those readers whose relation to their own desire was already fraught. The ground for a confused cluster of ambivalent self-recognitions and evasions, *Dazzler* was, in my own archive of feeling, slippery affective terrain, the emotional coloration of which today calls to mind the governess's description of her notoriously ambiguous ghost story in Henry James's *The Turn of the Screw*: "a succession of flights and drops, a little seesaw of the right throbs and the wrong."[49] Among the flights were those moments of naïve and dimly cognized "queering" in which I made the first tentative steps toward appropriating both the limited liberationist promise of Dazzler's white liberal feminism and the objectifying eroticism of Springer's art as imaginative building blocks for a future self I could not yet name "homosexual." At its most daringly transgressive (for so it seemed), this allegorizing transformation of Dazzler's person, desires, woes, and adventures reveled in the series' extravagant celebration of romance comics and soap opera, effectively placing me alongside Alison in Warren Worthington's strong arms as we soared on his "Angel" wings over Manhattan on a dinner date fit for mutant superheroes (figure 4.6). Such forbidden flights inevitably seesawed into drops, however, as I was dragged down to earth by the cartoon anvils of self-shaming scripts that relentlessly posed the Jamesian question: Which were the right throbs, and which the wrong? Thus did queer longing rush to extinguish itself, temporarily, in the safety of more normative generic pleasures: the age-old contest of good and evil, the hypnotic spectacle of a superpowered laser show.

While the homophobic disavowal and even punishment of queerness

FIGURE 4.6. Dazzler and Angel. *Dazzler* #17 (1982).

over the course of Dazzler's solo series was instrumental to the reversal whereby imaginative flight might suddenly give way to the terror of free-fall, the fact that an incipient queer identification with Dazzler remained vulnerable to the counterforces of denial inheres in the transformative nature of queer allegorizing itself. Occasioned by an unspoken absence that communicates only through the ambiguous implication of symbolism and referential underdetermination, the allegorical meaning-making native to queer reading is only as certain as the conviction of its readerly coconspirator. Indeed, even for the most determined reader, queer allegorizing remains structurally haunted by the very textual silence for which interpretive transformation compensates, and this haunting is not necessarily benign or empowering. "Silence," as Gershen Kaufman and Lev Raphael underscore in their psychoanalytic account of queer negativity, "breeds shame every bit as much as shame breeds further silence";[50] and so, the unspoken opens ambiguously onto the unspeakable. In other words, the mutant allegory's silence—its constitutive deniability with respect to queer reference—cuts both ways, thereby structuring an ambivalent pedagogy: on the one hand creating a site of potential self-recognition for queer fans by circumventing the corporate prescription on representing homosexuality, and on the other, through its very performance, suggesting that queerness (narratively, diegetically) is officially not to be spoken, by implication validating the shaming scripts of the homophobic culture in which it stages its paradoxical nonappearance.

CONCLUSION

The tacit attachment of Dazzler's "mutant secret" to the trope of the gay closet in Shooter and Springer's Marvel Graphic Novel *Dazzler: The Movie* epitomizes the treacherous deniability of allegory's bait and switch. Although flagrantly implied by Dazzler's "outing" as a mutant, the queer referent in Shooter and Springer's seductive but reactionary graphic novel remains an unspoken final taboo—very different from the overt thematics of post-Holocaust Jewish identity that defines *X-Men*'s Kitty Pryde or the transparently feminist subversions of Phoenix and Storm. Another scene from the *Dazzler* graphic novel summarizes the dilemmas of an emancipatory allegorical structure that can so easily collapse into a pedagogy of the closet: flopped on the couch at the X-Mansion, Storm phones up Alison and frets that the current "wave of anti-mutant sentiment sweeping the country" puts Alison at risk because, she says, "You flaunt your mutant ability in public." Alison replies that "there's nothing to worry about! When I do my light tricks on stage, people in the audience presume it's just a stage gimmick!" But Storm remains worried: "Nonetheless, be careful Alison! Times are not good for our kind! You would be safer here in Westchester with us in our secret stronghold! Consider it . . . please! I wish you well . . . good-bye." After hanging up, Storm concludes that Alison will probably not take her advice because she is "a willful young woman, driven hard by her dreams." "Such people," says Storm, "can seldom be convinced of the wisdom of caution!" Reading this exchange as an eleven-year-old, the implication of Storm's "wisdom" was not entirely lost on me. It seemed odd, even at the time, that Storm should advocate the "wisdom of caution" to a fellow mutant who dared to reveal her powers in public. Even her characterization of Xavier's School for Gifted Youngsters as a "secret stronghold" for mutants evokes something closer to the pedagogy of the closet than the liberating space of subcultural safety. "Look at it this way," the blue furry elf-like mutant Nightcrawler consoles her, "at least a mutant like her isn't quite as obvious as I am!" "True," Storm concedes, "but if she continues publicly displaying her power long enough, sooner or later *someone* will suspect."

This was wisdom I immediately understood. "YOU read *Dazzler*??" a schoolmate once shrieked at me in disbelief when, in an unguarded moment, I let her look through a pile of comics I had secreted in my knapsack. She had clocked me, and we both knew it. But I rallied, playing butch: "Sure. She's a mutant, like Wolverine." She let it go. But it was a long time before I flaunted my powers publicly again.

NOTES

1. David Halperin, *How to Be Gay* (Cambridge, MA: Belknap Press of Harvard University Press, 2012), 114.

2. Nicholas E. Miller, "Disco, Derby, and Drag: The Queer Politics of Marvel's Dazzler," in *The Oxford Handbook of Comic Book Studies*, ed. Frederick Luis Aldama (Oxford, UK: Oxford University Press, forthcoming). I am grateful to the author for sharing an advance draft of this article.

3. Wertham, *Seduction of the Innocent*, 190.

4. Eve Kosofsky Sedgwick, *Touching Feeling: Affect, Pedagogy, Performativity* (Durham, NC: Duke University Press, 2003), 60; Paul Lopes, *Demanding Respect: The Evolution of the American Comic Book* (Philadelphia, PA: Temple University Press, 2009), xxi–xxii.

5. Chad Bennett, "Flaming the Fans: Shame and the Aesthetics of Queer Fandom in Todd Haynes's *Velvet Goldmine*," *Cinema Journal* 49 (Winter 2010): 18–19.

6. Benjamin Woo, "Nerds, Geeks, Gamers, and Fans: Doing Subculture on the Edge of the Mainstream," in *The Borders of Subculture: Resistance to the Mainstream*, ed. Alexander Dhoest, Steven Malliet, Barbara Segaert, and Jacques Haers (New York: Routledge, 2015), 17.

7. Anthony Lioi, *Nerd Ecology: Defending the Earth With Unpopular Culture* (New York: Bloomsbury, 2016), 62.

8. Kara Kvaran, "SuperGay: Depictions of Homosexuality in Mainstream Superhero Comics," in *Comics as History, Comics as Literature: Roles of the Comic Book in Scholarship, Society, and Entertainment*, ed. Annessa Ann Babic (Madison, NJ: Fairleigh Dickinson University Press, 2013), 143–145, 149; on the "paranoid" position of "the hermeneutics of suspicion" as a critical stance, see Sedgwick, *Touching Feeling*, 124–128.

9. Sedgwick, *Touching Feeling*, 124, 137.

10. Lee Easton, "Sharing a Quick Look: A Gay Man Reads His Comics," in *Secret Identity Reader: Essays on Sex, Death, and the Superhero*, Lee Easton and Richard Harrison (Hamilton, Ontario: Wolsak and Wynn, 2010), 135–153; Halperin, *How to Be Gay*, 113, 114.

11. Scott Bukatman, "Secret Identity Politics," in *The Contemporary Comic Book Superhero*, ed. Angela Ndalianis (New York: Routledge, 2009), 109–125; Henry Jenkins, "Death-Defying Heroes," in *The Wow Climax: Tracing the Emotional Impact of Popular Culture* (New York: New York University Press, 2007), 65–74; Sean Howe, ed., *Give Our Regards to the Atomsmashers! Writers on Comics* (New York: Pantheon, 2004).

12. Fawaz, *New Mutants*.

13. Fawaz, *New Mutants*, 8, 11.

14. Fawaz, *New Mutants*, 4, 22.

15. Fawaz, *New Mutants*, 33, 15.

16. Revisions to the 1989 version of the Comics Code specified that "character portrayals will be carefully crafted and show sensitivity to national, ethnic, religious,

sexual, political and socioeconomic orientations." "Comics Code Revision of 1989," Comic Book Legal Defense Fund, http://cbldf.org/comics-code-revision-of-1989/.

17. Jim Shooter (w), John Buscema (p), Alfredo Alcala (i), "... A Very Personal Hell," in *The Hulk Magazine* #23 (October 1980); See Kvaran, "SuperGay," 145–146.

18. Kvaran, "SuperGay," 146.

19. Fawaz, *New Mutants*, 14–15, 32–34, 83–84.

20. Gershen Kaufman and Lev Raphael, *Coming Out of Shame: Transforming Gay and Lesbian Lives* (New York: Doubleday, 1996), 11.

21. "Flame On!," Entertain Me Weakly (blog), Tumblr, February 8, 2017, https://entertainmeweakly.tumblr.com/post/156974908275/flame-on-johnny-storm.

22. See also Madison's celebration of the character as a queer emblem of inclusive politics desperately needed in an America faced with Donald Trump's "courtship of white supremacists" and rampant "fearmongering about the progression of civil rights that benefit blacks, Latinos, Muslims, women, and LGBT individuals." Ira Madison III, "The Queer Importance of Dazzler, Marvel's Disco-Inspired, Roller-Skating Superheroine," MTV, July 28, 2016, http://www.mtv.com/news/2911767/the-queer-importance-of-dazzler-marvels-disco-inspired-rollerskating-superheroine/.

23. Alice Echols, *Hot Stuff: Disco and the Remaking of American Culture* (New York: Norton, 2011), xxv.

24. See essays by J. Andrew Deman and Christopher B. Zeichmann in this volume. See also Michael J. Lecker, "'Why Can't I Be Just Like Everyone Else?': A Queer Reading of the X-Men," *International Journal of Comic Art* 9, no. 1 (2007): 679–687; and Anthony Michael D'Agostino, "'Flesh-to-Flesh Contact': Marvel Comics' Rogue and the Queer Feminist Imagination," *American Literature* 90, no. 2 (2018): 251–281. I concur with Miller's observation that Dazzler's extraordinary capacity to telegraph queerness to gay fans owes not just to her similarity to the X-Men (as a mutant), but to her difference from them (as a performer rather than a superhero) (see Miller, "Disco, Derby, and Drag"). Dazzler's foundational association with disco and her solo series' generic intensification of romance and melodrama unwittingly and unavoidably queered the mutant allegory that *Uncanny X-Men* had established most explicitly in the domains of race, gender, and class—those identities most conducive to direct visual and narrative representation and not subject to the same degree of editorial censorship.

25. Chris Claremont (w), John Byrne (e), Terry Austin (i), "Dazzler," *The Uncanny X-Men*, no. 130 (New York: Marvel Comics, February 1980), 11.

26. *Modern Masters Volume 18: John Romita Jr.*, ed. George Khoury and Eric Nolen-Weathington (Raleigh, NC: TwoMorrows, 2008), 18.

27. Jim Shooter, "The Debut of Dazzler," JimShooter.com, July 4, 2011, http://jimshooter.com/2011/07/debut-of-dazzler.html/.

28. Madison III, "Queer Importance."

29. For a detailed reading of this history of Dazzler's early and still evolving history as a site of reparative identification for queer readers, see Miller, "Disco, Derby, and Drag."

30. Richard Howell and Carol Kalish, "Dissecting Dazzler: Interview with Tom DeFalco, Louise Jones (Simonson), and Roger Stern," *Comics Feature* 7 (November 1980).

31. Tom DeFalco (w), John Romita Jr. (p), Alfredo Alcala (i), "So Bright This Star," *Dazzler*, no. 1 (New York: Marvel Comics, March 1981), 2, 4, 10.

32. DeFalco wrote *Dazzler* 1–5 and scaled back his contribution to "plotter" for issues 6–11, during which time he was joined by Fingeroth as "scriptor." Fingeroth assumed all writing duties for issues 12–26, succeeded by Frank Springer and Jim Shooter.

33. Blue Chevigny, "Rock and Roll Benefit Concerts: Music to UNICEF's Ears," Unicef, last modified December 7, 2006, https://www.unicef.org/people/index_37418.html.

34. Donna Gaynor is evidently a portmanteau name combining disco luminaries Donna Summer and Gloria Gaynor. Tom DeFalco and Danny Fingeroth (w), Frank Springer (p), Vincent Colletta (i), "Hell . . . Hell Is for Harry!," *Dazzler*, no. 8 (New York: Marvel Comics, October 1981), 9.

35. Tom DeFalco and Danny Fingeroth (w), Frank Springer (p), Vincent Colletta (i), "The Hulk May Be Hazardous to Your Health!," *Dazzler*, no. 6 (New York: Marvel Comics, October 1981), 2.

36. Howell and Kalish, "Dissecting Dazzler."

37. See Miller, "Disco, Derby, and Drag."

38. Fawaz, *New Mutants*, 20.

39. Nicholas E. Miller, "'Is There Anything Left to Be Shattered?': Reading Dazzler in the #MeToo Moment," The Middle Spaces, April 10, 2018, https://themiddlespaces.com/2018/04/10/dazzler-in-the-metoo-moment/.

40. Jim Shooter (w), Frank Springer (p), Vince Colletta (i), *Marvel Graphic Novel 12: Dazzler: The Movie* (New York: Marvel, October 1984).

41. I am grateful to Anna Peppard for pointing out this difference.

42. Jim Shooter (w), Frank Springer (p), Vincent Colletta (i), "Brawl!," *Dazzler*, no. 35 (New York: Marvel, 1985), 13.

43. Shooter, Springer, and Colletta, "Brawl!," 13.

44. Miller, "Disco, Derby, and Drag."

45. For another account of Dazzler's queer relation to disco and roller derby, see Miller, "Disco, Derby, and Drag."

46. Tom DeFalco (w), Frank Springer (p), Danny Bulanadi and Armando Gil (i), "Here Nightmares Abide!," *Dazzler*, no. 4 (New York: Marvel, June 1981), 11.

47. Tom DeFalco and Danny Fingeroth (w), Frank Springer (p), Vince Colletta (i), "In the Darkness . . . A Light!," *Dazzler*, no. 10 (New York: Marvel, December 1981), 12.

48. The cover copy of *Dazzler* #21 reads: "SPECIAL DOUBLE-SIZED ISSUE" and "REVEALED . . . THE SHAMEFUL SECRET OF DAZZLER'S PAST!"

49. Henry James, *The Turn of the Screw* (New York: Dover, 1991), 6.

50. Kaufman and Raphael, *Coming Out of Shame*, 103.

5

"SUPER-GAY" *GAY COMIX*

Tracing the Underground Origins and Cultural Resonances of LGBTQ Superheroes

SARAH M. PANUSKA

The last decade has seen both Marvel and DC Comics jump on the gay superhero bandwagon with their renditions of what an LGBTQ superhero might look like.[1] After many decades of official and tacit exclusion of LGBTQ characters from the comic book universes of the Big Two publishers, readers can finally turn their high-gloss pages to see superheroes in skintight costumes saving the world and coming home to the domestic comfort of a person of their own sex, or even a partner that reflects the ever-wider expansion of gender and sexual identities.[2] And yet there is something about these portrayals that strikes some readers—including this one—as a bit unsatisfying. These characters might be out and proud, but beyond the moment of coming out or some brief moments of intimacy, most contemporary LGBTQ superheroes are LBGTQ in name alone. This is partly due to the unique challenges of representing nonnormative communities within a popular medium and genre with a long and complicated history of controversy and censorship. Creators at the Big Two publishers must portray their LGBTQ superheroes in ways that do not alienate the predominately straight (and male) audience that has long consumed their comics. Yet if they want their LGBTQ superheroes to appeal to LGBTQ readers and/or the increasing number of current and potential readers who sympathize with LGBTQ concerns, they also must also ensure their representations do not stray into the realm of stereotypes. Because of these different and sometimes competing agendas, the LGBTQ characters in mainstream superhero comics can sometimes appear to exist in a vacuum. While many of these characters proudly proclaim their queerness, expressions of intimacy are rare, as are direct references to contemporary or historical LGBTQ culture.

Marvel's 2006 series *The Young Avengers*, created by gay-identifying writer Allen Heinberg and artist Jim Cheung, is emblematic of this bind.[3] This series centers on a group of teens who fight crime while paying homage to the main (older) Avengers team. Two of these teens are Teddy Altman and Billy Kaplan, a.k.a. Hulkling and Wiccan. Teddy and Billy's involvement in a budding romance is alluded to throughout the series. But compared to the heterosexual romances between teammates Nathaniel Richards and Cassandra Lang, a.k.a. Ironlad and Stature, as well as Eli Bradley and Kate Bishop, a.k.a. Patriot and Hawkeye, Hulkling and Wiccan's relationship is relegated to innuendo and implication. While other members might kiss or flirt, Hulkling and Wiccan's relationship is, in general, only discernable through the intensity of each teen's fear for the safety of the other.[4] While Hulkling and Wiccan's lives as teen superheroes provide enough danger to ensure their concern for each other is expressed quite often, the means Hulkling and Wiccan have to show concern or care for each other are bound up in fear of loss and death, as if the threat of death sanctions (or excuses) the teens' recognition of their love. Furthermore, though Hulkling and Wiccan are very often portrayed next to each other in different panels throughout the comics, there is very little in the way of relationship-specific dialogue. In the first twelve issues of Heinberg and Cheung's *Young Avengers* series, Hulkling and Wiccan's relationship is only directly addressed twice. The characters do not share their first on-panel kiss until the final issue of the mini-series *Avengers: The Children's Crusade*, released in 2012[5]—six years after they were first introduced.

In his chapter elsewhere in this volume, Keith Friedlander correctly observes that subsequent *Young Avengers* series—in particular, Kieron Gillen and Jamie McKelvie's 2013 reboot—bring sexuality and sexual diversity more to the forefront. Friedlander also argues that Gillen and McKelvie's series builds on previous series in exploiting conflicts of private and public identity that can resonate strongly with LGBTQ experiences. Yet even Friedlander admits, "While Gillen and McKelvie's series features plenty of images of Hulkling and Wiccan kissing, the characters' romance still takes a backseat to action sequences and humor. If you want outright erotica, or even a simple image of Hulkling and Wiccan casually holding hands, you will only find it in fan art." I do not wish to demean the complexity or importance of Hulkling and Wiccan's relationship,[6] either as outlined by Friedlander or as it exists in the hearts and minds of its fans (of which there are many).[7] Nor do I want to suggest that the quest for better representation could—or should—be fulfilled merely with the addition of more graphic sexual content. I do, however, want to argue for the importance of making LGBTQ sexuality *visible*, and that this visibility depends on something that remains missing from most contemporary depictions of LGBTQ superheroes—namely, a willingness to accurately reference and reflect real-life LGBTQ community and culture.

Mainstream superhero comics have not been totally devoid of such references. For instance, in the Young Avengers mini-series *The Children's Crusade* (2010–2012), there are moments in which Heinberg and Cheung make nods to the ways that Hulkling and Wiccan, as gay teens, are connected to a larger gay male culture that has its own traditions and history outside the pages of Marvel comics. In one instance, Wiccan uses his power to generate a disguise for the Young Avengers as they attempt to keep a low profile. As Wiccan's powers mist and twinkle, the group's new look is revealed, and his friends' reactions are incredulous. Hawkeye looks down at her newfound guitar case and is exasperated, saying, "Really, Billy? *The Sound of Music*?" Hulkling explains in a groan, "It's his favorite movie," to which Wiccan replies, "It is NOT. It's *one* of my favorite movies."[8] Though the Young Avengers traipse through the hills of Transia as Von Trapps for only a few panels, this scene does successfully negotiate a gay cultural tradition[9] while also resisting the full punch of stereotypes (after all, Hulkling's reaction indicates that *The Sound of Music* is probably not one of *his* favorite things). This is an example of how comics creators can sprinkle in elements that link characters to LGBTQ culture, which in turn helps make these heroes *culturally visible*.

But it will take more than a sprinkling of references to meaningfully improve the representation of LGBTQ superheroes within mainstream comics. While the past decade has seen a marked increase in the number and diversity of characters with nonnormative sexual and gender identities,[10] the Big Two publishers have, to date, largely relied upon spotlighting the former (numbers) to demonstrate their attention to the latter (diversity). In this chapter, I contend that the *sheer number* of LGBTQ heroes should no longer be a measure of progress. Rather, it is the *quality* of LGBTQ representations in comics that now needs to be evaluated. This chapter will argue that in addition to increasing the number of LGBTQ characters within mainstream comics, there should be attention paid to representing and contextualizing these superheroes within LGBTQ culture. While LGBTQ culture often goes unrepresented in mainstream comics, underground and independent comics published by LGBTQ creators in the last decades of the twentieth century not only featured overt depictions of nonnormative sexualities and identities, but also contextualized their characters within traditions of gay and lesbian cultures and subcultures.[11] With regard to the specific intersection of LGBTQ culture and superheroes, *Gay Comix* #8, the "Super Gay" issue, can be considered exemplary. This chapter examines the various ways in which *Gay Comix* #8 presents parodies of superheroes that are explicitly, unmistakably, and unapologetically "Super Gay"—not only with regard to the proclivities of the characters but also in terms of the ways these characters reflect and resonate with gay culture. I emphasize the importance of *Gay Comix*'s strategies of representation through a comparison with two recent Marvel series, *Iceman* (2017–2018) and *America* (2017–2018), both of which are penned by LGBTQ-identifying writers yet continue to struggle to find a place and a voice within the contemporary landscape of mainstream American superhero comics.

"SAY, MISTER, DO YOU HAVE SUPER POWERS OR ARE YOU JUST GAY?": *GAY COMIX* #8 AND "SUPER GAY(NESS)"

Superheroes and LGBTQ culture converged in complex ways in the 1980s in the underground anthology aptly named *Gay Comix*. First published by Kitchen Sink Comix and later published by Bob Ross, *Gay Comix* ran from 1980 to 1998 and provided, throughout its tenure, an important outlet for gay and lesbian artists to develop their own stories, characters, and culture.[12] The series was created by gay and lesbian artists, with the first several issues edited by Howard Cruse, who was responsible for the anthology's tongue-in-cheek tagline, "Lesbians and Gay Men Put It on Paper." The "It" in this tagline refers to the entire glorious gamut of gay life. Admittedly, *Gay Comix* does not always live up to this promise; throughout the 1980s, the series prioritizes white gay male desires and experiences. Yet *Gay Comix* does depict a diversity of perspectives within this limited focus; the series' mix of one-off short stories as well as ongoing, serialized narratives depict the highs and lows of dating, the party scene, and the general, day-to-day ups and downs of gay life in ways few other visual mediums or genres were concurrently doing.

Despite the significant historical and thematic interconnections between superhero comics and gay culture, gay superheroes did not find their way into *Gay Comix* until its eighth issue in 1986.[13] Unlike the Big Two's twenty-first-century LGBTQ superheroes, the superheroes that appear in *Gay Comix*'s "Super Gay" issue are deeply imbricated in the gay culture of their day.[14] These superheroes thrive within the practices, values, and institutions that were central to the era's gay culture. It is also important to note that the stories in *Gay Comix* #8 are, almost without exception, superhero parodies.[15] Parody allows the anthology's contributors creative freedom, which is exploited in the following ways: (a) it allows contributors to apply many of the conventions of the superhero genre—which was otherwise almost exclusively straight during this time—to gays and the gay community; (b) it allows contributors to poke fun at the increasing self-seriousness of superhero comics' mythologies; and (c) it allows contributors to use superhero metaphors to talk about issues relevant to LGBTQ culture, mainly the impact of HIV and AIDS on the gay community. Created and designed by Kalynn Campbell and Robert Triptow for the double-size *Gay Comix* #8—whose title is changed, for one issue only, to "Super Gay Comix" (figure 5.1)—the cover art for the issue is typical of the series as a whole in the way it depicts situations common to gay life but exaggerates them with a tinge of dark humor.[16] The cover depicts a man dressed in superhero garb. He wears a yellow suit with pink polka-dot tights and cape. He has two wiry antennas on his head. His goggles are pushed up on his forehead as he enjoys his "Super Muscle" comic, though he is, at the same time, attempting to look inconspicuous, positioning the comic so that it covers most of the lower half of his face. The man's thought bubble, which features a Supermanesque character flexing his bicep in a blue suit and red cape, indicates both how engrossed he is in the comic book and the substance of his interest. To the right of this man is a large rack of "Kids Comics" with "wholesome" titles like "Sick Fantasies," "Grotto Girl," "Career Girl Love," "Tales of Useless Lives," "Wimp," "Everyone Dies," "Getcha Red Hot," and "Biker Gang Shock." To the left of the cape-wearing man reading the "Super Muscle" comic is a small boy wearing a shirt that labels him as part of the "Howdy Doody Fan Club." The small boy looks quizzically up at the man and asks, "Say, Mister, do you have super powers or are you just gay?"[17]

There are several different layers of humor here. First, there is commentary on the "adult" content of comics that are commonly sold to kids. Part of this commentary is a not-so-subtle claim that, despite popular assumptions about superhero comics being written by and for heterosexual males, there is a lot about superhero corporeality, fashion, and

FIGURE 5.1. Cover by Kalynn Campbell and Robert Triptow. *Gay Comix* #8 (1986).

themes that have relevance to gay people and their lives.[18] Additionally, the "Super Muscle" comic book functions as a multivalent disguise for the man reading it; the comic both masks his queer gaze and suggests ways superhero comic book fandom might provide a "beard" for queer desires. A second layer of humor highlights the irony that comics featuring gratuitous violence—often as a central selling point—are routinely marketed as "Kids Comics," while homosexuality is forced to remain underground. The third and primary joke (i.e., the punchline) revolves around the small boy's inability to ascertain whether the grown-up is a superhero or "just gay." The man reading the comic is construed as a superhero due to his costume, his muscles, and his cape, and as gay due to his costume, his muscles and . . . his cape. This insightfully foregrounds the similarity between being spectacularly superheroish and spectacularly gay; implicit in this comparison is the proposition that the superhero, on the basis of aesthetics as well as metaphor, might be somewhat inherently "gay."

The parody in the cover of the "Super Gay" issue is lighthearted; it does not attempt to take on hard-hitting issues. It does, however, include an implicit critique of the gender and sexual politics underpinning the conventions of the superhero genre, knowingly poking fun at which persons and actions might be worthy of the superhero label. In applying superhero conventions to gay lives and communities, this story shows the relevance of those conventions to gay lives and demonstrates their ability to address certain problems specific to gay life.

Between the covers of *Gay Comix*'s "Super Gay" issue, the illuminating parody continues. In stories such as "The Adventures of Captain Condom!," "A Midsummer Night's Super Stud," and "Leatherthing," superhero parody is used to celebrate the major and minor heroics that accompanied gay existence at this particularly volatile time in the community's history. While the bulk of this section will take up the most substantial of these parodies ("Leatherthing"), a brief examination of "The Adventures of Captain Condom!" and "A Midsummer Night's Super Stud" will further demonstrate the common and diverse ways in which *Gay Comix* #8 uses superheroes to reframe the big and small struggles that went hand in hand with gay culture during this era.

Some of the most impactful parodies in *Gay Comix* #8 link the superheroic with the sexual precautions being promoted in light of the emergence and deadly impact of HIV/AIDS. Jeff Jacklin's "The Adventures of Captain Condom!" functions as an example. This story follows Captain Condom on a routine flight through the city. Captain Condom is portrayed by Jacklin as a version of Superman merged with 1980s "clone" stylings, that is, close-cropped hair and the iconic clone mustache. During

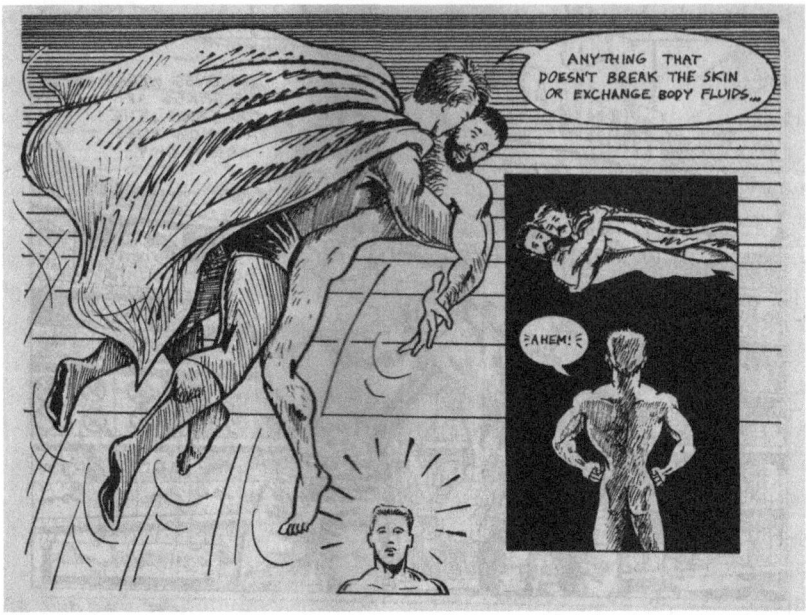

FIGURE 5.2. A scene from Jeff Jacklin's "The Adventures of Captain Condom!" (1986).

his patrol, Captain Condom overhears two men having a discussion about whether or not they should use condoms.[19] Once Captain Condom realizes the two men are not in agreement, he intervenes, taking it upon himself to fly into the (very naked) duo's bedroom and ask, "What's wrong with condoms?" One of the men replies that he would rather forgo condoms because "they just seem so straight" and "they take all the fun out of sex." Captain Condom then describes the various ways the reluctant condom user and his partner can have sex while hindering the exchange of fluids and/or making sure skin does not break. As Captain Condom explains various techniques of "hugging," "caressing," "cuddling," "body rubbing," "wrestling," and "jacking off together," his explanation becomes a demonstration with the reluctant condom user—until his partner interrupts with an annoyed "Ahem!" (figure 5.2). Captain Condom then departs, and the soon-to-be bedfellows go to the pharmacy, where they are presented with another dilemma: what type of condoms to get.

"The Adventures of Captain Condom!" exemplifies *Gay Comix*'s approach to humor. In this story, the serious and poignant are enfolded in the exaggerated, the outrageous, and the bizarre. And yet, as it reframes superhero conventions (in this case, the convention of the single-minded do-gooder) to reflect cultural concerns within the 1980s gay community, the concerns it highlights are far less trivial. The humor in this story is located, in part, in the silliness of Captain Condom—as a visual and as a concept—juxtaposed with the seriousness of the threat he confronts. While conventional superheroes take on supervillains, gangs, and monsters, Captain Condom fights a real-world disease that was taking a tremendous toll on the real-life gay community. Published roughly nine months before the Food and Drug Administration approved AZT as a means to prevent and treat HIV, and when nearly twenty-five thousand people had already died due to HIV and related illness,[20] "The Adventures of Captain Condom" uses the figure of the superhero to promote small but important ways of battling the epidemic. It also suggests that changing the culture around certain sexual practices within LGBTQ communities might be celebrated as an act of everyday heroism.

Kurt Erichsen's "A Midsummer Night's Super Stud" is a lighter story with a deceptively deep meaning. This is the story of one horny gay urbanite's transformation from dud to stud. Jeff, due to his looks and lack of fashion sense, has not been allowed entry into a hip club in his neighborhood, run by a queen named the Duchess.[21] With the help of his clique, made up of his pals Vernon, Lee, Murphy, and Sid, Jeff is transformed into Super Stud, finally taking his game to a level worthy of entry into the Duchess's bar. "Super Stud" does not attempt to take on hard-hitting issues. It does, however, use superhero parody to assert the value of gay cultural practices. In contrast to Peter Coogan's insistence that a superhero's pro-social mission "must not be intended to benefit or further his own agenda,"[22] the gay society represented in "A Midsummer Night's Super Stud" is one in which a certain self-centeredness is allowed and an individual's social status is very important; as such, this story incorporates superhero imagery and conventions while ensuring that the hero's relevance to his community ultimately takes priority. The story's parody has a number of targets. It subverts the stereotype that all gay men have a great sense of aesthetics; it also shows a (relatively) true-to-life example of the way that members of LGBTQ communities frequently rely on their friends and chosen families to get through moments of adversity. Furthermore, while this story uses parody to gesture toward the shallowness of Jeff's problem in comparison with the literally earth-shattering crises that superheroes routinely face, comparing Jeff to a superhero embraces the fact that his problems have genuine social ramifications within gay male culture. At the same time that this story pokes fun at both Jeff and the superhero genre, it uses the superhero genre to suggest Jeff's problems are, within the context of gay culture in the 1980s, genuinely serious; similarly, Jeff's ability, with a little help from his friends, to overcome these problems can be seen as heroic.

Though we all know size is not everything, one of the lengthier superhero parodies in the "Super Gay" issue, "Leatherthing" by Vaughn Frick, is also one of the issue's most narratively meaty stories.[23] Frick's "Leatherthing" differentiates itself from the issue's other stories in its gestures toward cultural diversity and the range of sexual expressions within the LGBTQ community. As all superhero comics readers know, every superhero has an origin story, and Leatherthing is no exception. But Leatherthing's origin story is a bit different (figure 5.3). This titular superhero's parents are not shot dead in front of him, nor does he barely escape his home-planet's destruction or receive a magic word from a wizard in a secret subway tunnel. Instead, Leatherthing's origin is, paradoxically, also his demise.[24] Lenny, a leather-shop proprietor, narrates Leatherthing's story. Lenny tells us that Leatherthing started out in "a sexually liberated place and time" as a "young clone" whose enthusiasm for leather led him to purchase an entire leather body suit. While this reference to a "sexually liberated place and time" can be seen as a general nod to the sexual openness of the 1960s and '70s, it is also, given the content of the story, a direct reference to the heyday of leather culture, which was a thriving, radically sexual subculture during the 1970s.[25] In the changing sexual landscape of the 1980s, Leatherthing's link with the leatherman subculture has particular ramifications. Unfortunately for the soon-to-be Leatherthing, "the sexually liberated place and time" that was vital to his transition from clone to leather daddy vanished because "the dark cloud of AIDS settled over the scene," which leaves "our leather bound lad trapped inside of a tomb of leather, a deflated specter of a time once removed." This tale literalizes, through superhero metaphor, how HIV/AIDS impacted the sexual culture of gay men in the mid-1980s, which resulted in some sexual practices being deemed particularly hazardous and unsafe. Leatherthing represents a darkly humorous vision of the fate that might await those holdovers who cannot, or will not, change their sexual practices in the wake of HIV. In addition, the way in which Leatherthing is entombed, out of place and lost to time, implies something of the nature and scale of the tragic losses the gay community suffered during this time in its history.

"Leatherthing" also parodies the comic book superhero trope that Joseph Campbell calls "the call to adventure."[26] While many superheroes have signals or senses that send them into action against the forces of evil, Leatherthing is awakened from his slumber by some inquisitive "yuppie developers" who find him in the remains of the BlowHole club. After stumbling upon the dormant Leatherthing as they inspect the potential of the

FIGURE 5.3. The origin story of Vaughn Frick's "Leatherthing" (1986).

abandoned sex club for redevelopment, the yuppie developers are quick to label the forgotten BDSM garb "a public embarrassment" that clashes with their "first-rate" vision of "chrome lining, zebra prints, turquois and pink." Though the yuppies are not explicitly labeled as gay, their gayness is heavily telegraphed through their demeanor and styling. Furthermore, Frick uses the yuppies to connote the disconnect between the youthful gays of the mid-1980s and the old relic that Leatherthing has become. This is communicated through the yuppies' interest in aesthetics, which includes their tight jeans and popped collars, as well as their knowledge about what Leatherthing was, what era he represents, and the like. The yuppies also know party drugs when they see them. While stumbling around their new investment property, they try to "revive" Leatherthing by giving him something he might have encountered in his past as a part of the underground sex scene—poppers. The party drug does the trick, and Leatherthing is, indeed, revived; he leaves the interrupted solitude of his tomb-like lair and begins to roam the streets.

Leatherthing eventually runs into an evil hairstylist named Vic Voo, a catty queen who uses his "attitude" to cause unsuspecting gays and lesbians mental anguish. Voo's evil power is the shade he throws at LGBTQ community members he does not like. He is very thin and angular with long limbs and hands that look like they might cut you just like the scissors he uses to cut hair. Wearing loud, patterned, low-buttoned shirts with popped collars and sporting a pompadour that resembles a squirrel's tail on the top of his head, Voo is shown knocking an older gay man and a butch lesbian unconscious with the force of his shade. Similar to how making Leatherthing a leatherman points to the ways that LGBTQ communities in the 1980s were fraught with tensions and their own socially imposed stigmas and prejudices, Leatherthing's adventures underscore how certain sexual communities faced criticism and discrimination at the hands of others within the larger gay community. Within the context of "Leatherthing," our leather-clad hero faces the most adversity from those *within* the gay community—first the yuppie developers who want to ruin his abode in the remains of the BlowHole, then Vic Voo, who wants to end his existence. After seeing Leatherthing for the first time, Voo belittles him, calling him "a dinosaur" and remarking that he thought all the "leather queens died out." He then sets about trying to make this last leather queen "become extinct." Rather than meet Leatherthing with compassion, Voo makes it clear that Leatherthing's outmodedness, his existence beyond use, makes him deserving of death. There is a sense that, for Vic Voo, Leatherthing's affiliation with the leather community makes him more like a piece of folklore, something fabled that is seen as out of fashion in the contemporary moment.

Leatherthing is ultimately exceptional—or "super"—in part because he is able to survive not only Voo's attacks but also the change in sexual trends and the HIV/AIDS epidemic. Leatherthing may be a "dinosaur," but he is still animated—alive, in some sense, when so many others are not. When Voo's attempts to snub Leatherthing are unsuccessful, he removes Leatherthing's mask. The emptiness that Voo finds inside the suit provokes his own undoing. Lenny the leather shop owner's story concludes by informing us of Voo's fate. Readers are told that "Voo aged a lifestyle overnight and spent the rest of his days cruising under-aged chicken in noisy bars." Yet Frick leaves the fate of Leatherthing ambiguous. The only insight Lenny offers is the phrase, "As for Leatherthing well . . ." The final panels of the story show both Leatherthing and Voo—protagonist and antagonist—out of time and out of place in the landscape of a rehabilitated nightspot. While Voo's "aging of a lifestyle" puts him quite literally outside the youth-oriented gay social scene, Leatherthing also remains dislocated from a sexual community that has been altered, reevaluated, and reimagined after the HIV crisis (figure 5.4).

Perhaps more than any other story in *Gay Comix* #8, "Leatherthing" demonstrates that gay superheroes do not have to manifest from the clash between a normative, homophobic society and a presumptively progressive LGBTQ community. The conflict in "Leatherthing" is, instead, between different factions of the LGBTQ community. "Leatherthing" features clashes between old and new forms of being gay and between a culture and its subcultures. This makes for a more authentic story, inasmuch as it lessens the burden of representation and helps ground representation within a specific history, time, and place. While parody functioned within "The Adventures of Captain Condom!" and "A Midsummer Night's Super Stud" to play with conventional definitions of the trivial and the heroic, Frick's "Leatherthing" uses superhero parody to reflect on gay culture's biases as well as what communities and sexual practices were lost due to HIV. The superhero parody helps make this tale accessible, enabling the story's grim critique of the community through a fusion of humor and poignancy. As much as the circumstances of Leatherthing's origins might seem completely outlandish, Frick is able to mobilize this fantastical aura that congeals around the superhero mythos to account for practices, communities, and lives that were decimated by the emergence of HIV and the ways these communities continue to live on in the present despite the tragedies of the past.

FIGURE 5.4. Viv Voo having "aged a lifestyle overnight." Vaughn Frick's "Leatherthing" (1986).

BACK TO THE (QUEER) FUTURE

To this point, this chapter has argued that what is missing in many contemporary mainstream superhero comics is LGBTQ culture—shout-outs, Easter eggs, references, and jokes that tie these characters to LGBTQ history and community. I would like to both bolster and qualify this claim with some examples of contemporary LGBTQ superhero comics envisioned by LGBTQ creators.

Marvel's 2017–2018 *Iceman* series, which follows from a 2015 story outing the titular original member of the X-Men, shows that the company has become less wary of depicting LGBTQ lives and desires. Penned by gay-identifying writer Sina Grace with art by Robert Gill, *Iceman* includes a marked effort to surround the title character with LGBTQ cultural contexts. The through-line of this series is the long-closeted Iceman starting to address his identity as a gay man. And while several of Marvel's standby techniques for representing nonnormative superheroes are present in the majority of Iceman's adventures,[27] there are some promising moments where gay culture is allowed to inflect the series. During a story arc spanning issues #6 and #7 that sends Iceman to Los Angeles, the newly out superhero finally meets his community. This culminates with Iceman chatting up, flirting with, and setting up a date with a hunky gay named Judah.[28] The two guys bring their crews to a West Hollywood gay bar. Even the iconic corner captions are in the spirit of the evening, indicating that Iceman's next social adventure is taking place in "*West Hollywood. Den of Gay Dudes.*"[29] Over the course of the night, Iceman is sweetly incredulous about his date arriving late, he dances the night away with Judah, and—following a brief battle with fake sentinels scavenged by a desperate filmmaker—the two guys tuck into some frozen yogurt before opting to "Netflix and chill."[30]

While the relationship between Iceman and Judah is short lived, the events that take place over these two issues show just how much can be gained by having gay characters engage with their communities. Iceman still has his action-packed showdown with some sentinels, but he also learns about his community and its social patterns (being late, how to date, etc.). Though the issue leaves some ambiguity about what, exactly, Bobby and Judah did together while Netflix-and-chilling, we can *see* Iceman as a gay man, beyond his sexual proclivity. We can recognize him as an LGBTQ superhero in more than name alone.

Another, quite different, example is Marvel's *America* (2017–2018), written by queer-identifying Gabby Rivera and penciled by Joe Quinones.[31] This series chronicles the post–*Young Avengers* adventures of America Chavez, a.k.a. "Miss America," as she heads west, trading in an East Coast metropolitan existence for California's Sotomayor University. Campus life affords Chavez the time and space to evolve her powers, reconnect with old friends, and make new ones,[32] as well as uncover more information about her origins. *America* is laudable in its multifaceted representations of people of color and its embrace of intersectionality, especially compared to the dominance of white gay male concerns in both *Iceman* and *Gay Comix*. Intersectionality is a term developed by Kimberlé Crenshaw in 1989 to account for how most approaches to gender and race fail to account for the ways these factors intersect in the discrimination faced by Black women.[33] Intersectionality has since been taken up in legal, academic, and activist contexts, wherein it refers to the multivalent and interwoven structures of oppression that affect different marginalized communities. Though America Chavez is a fictional character—and an alien to boot— her story offers ways to think through multiple forms of interconnected identities and prejudices.

Born on a world called the Utopian Parallel that is populated solely by women, America Chavez is forced to make her way through the universe on her own after her mothers, Amalia and Elena, seal the Utopian Parallel with their love to protect it from invaders. America eventually arrives in the Bronx. Through a flashback that takes place at the beginning of *America* #3, America explains, "After my moms died, I left the parallel. I found spaces on Earth where little brown girls blend into the scenery and became part of the family. . . . [I] didn't even know what a Puerto Rican was. I just knew these folks look like me and let me in."[34] After punching her way through dimensions and arriving amid the Santana family BBQ, America Chavez meets Abuela Santana and is offered food and a place to stay. Ironically, though, this moment of acceptance also marks America Chavez's entry into a system where she will, as a queer woman of color, experience prejudices she would not have known on her home planet.

Like *Iceman*, *America* makes a significant effort to flesh out a queer context. *America*'s creators fashion an origin story for their queer Latina superhero that is steeped in the Sapphic. As mentioned above, America is born of two mothers in a world where lesbianism is unstigmatized. Over the course of the series, America discovers the full potential of her power and the world where others like her originated. After America meets her punching, stomping, and suplexing grandmother, Madrimar, she accepts the luchadorcoque Fuertona's help to understand her powers. *America* #7 opens with Madrimar and America visiting the Ancestral Plane—"a metaphysical space that holds the history of Madrimar's people."[35] While exploring the plane called Planeta Fuertona, grandmother and granddaughter witness the origin of their people and the planet responsible for their ass-kicking powers (figure 5.5). Madrimar explains that two spirit women, Berraca and Sanar, created Planeta Fuertona through their union. Madrimar tells America:

> Sanar felt Berraca's energy through the portal just as the planet she was creating neared completion. Esa fuerza was what her dreams were made of. And in that moment, Berraca caught a glimpse of the very being who would change the course of her destiny. . . . They didn't even realize they had fallen in love between them until . . . Planeta Fuertona bloomed between them.[36]

As this story makes clear, love between women is responsible for America's life but also the rich culture that she rediscovers through her grandmother. The creators of *America* have not only put a new spin on the trope

FIGURE 5.5. Madrimar and America visiting the Ancestral Plane, "a metaphysical space that holds the history of Madrimar's people." *America* #7 (2018).

of the superhero origin story but created an entire culture initiated by and supportive of emotional and sexual love between women.

It is not the purview of this chapter to see America Chavez's Sapphic cultural origin story as anything other than a step forward for LGBTQ representation in mainstream superhero comics. *America* certainly offers, in the words of Fredrick Luis Aldama, a "rich, compelling, and kinetic Latino superhero comic book [storyworld]."[37] I would, however, note that despite its rich metaphor and healthy abundance of characters who can be read as LGBTQ, *America* makes few references to everyday contemporary LBGTQ life and culture. While *America*, like many of Marvel's other recent series, has embraced social media culture with characters who "beam" each other, communicate through text messages, and have their social media represented for the reader, references to LGBTQ culture remain scarce, despite the fact that this culture has a much longer history than social media.[38] One of *America*'s few nods to LGBTQ culture or community occurs toward the beginning of issue #1. After saving the planet Maltixa with the aid of Spectrum (Monica Rambeau) and Captain

Marvel (Carol Danvers), America Chavez stops over at the apartment of her girlfriend, Lisa, in New York City. As the couple reunite at the entry of Lisa's building, a rainbow flag is seen hanging on the left side of the door. While the symbolism here is obvious—America and Lisa represent the LGBTQ community just as the rainbow flag does—this scene is also an example of *America* relying on fairly generic symbols and fashion references to make LGBTQ culture legible.

What is missing is more specific and grounded cultural resonance. This is where contemporary comics featuring LGBTQ superheroes could take a page from the work of underground gay and lesbian comics. Obviously, underground creators like those featured in *Gay Comix* #8 were working within different creative parameters than contemporary creators of mainstream superhero comics; these creators were not worried about alienating straight audiences, and they could take more liberties in depicting nudity, sex, and so forth.[39] Yet it is not merely the presentation of gay sex but also the references to specific histories, practices, and common associations/jokes of gay culture that make *Gay Comix* #8 an explicitly gay comic. Though comic book series like *Iceman* and *America* have found inventive ways of incorporating nonnormative relationships into superhero mythologies, to take representation out of the realm of diversity and into the realm of true inclusion, this author hopes that future series will be even more overt and enthusiastic about incorporating LGBTQ culture.

I also hope mainstream publishers will demonstrate a stronger commitment to this cause. Despite both *Iceman* and *America* being pitched as ongoing series, neither made it past twelve issues. Yet even these failures reveal the fact and importance of cultural resonance. In 2018, real-life LGBTQ folks and allies mounted a successful campaign to resurrect the *Iceman* series.[40] In effect, a fictional gay superhero inspired the real-life LGBTQ community to come to his rescue. And it worked—at least for now.

CONCLUSION

In their introduction to the special issue of *American Literature* titled "Queer about Comics," Darieck Scott and Ramzi Fawaz stress the radically queer nature of comics as a medium. They do this not only by linking the comics medium to queer theory, but also by theorizing queerness as "a social force, a complex network of erotic and affective ties, or an entire shared culture."[41] Scott and Fawaz argue that comics' fantastical capabilities allow the medium to depict "a vast array of nonnormative expressions of gender and sexuality—from the most metaphoric . . . to the most literal."[42] I do not want to contest or detract from the valuable work that Scott and Fawaz undertake to move comics studies and queer studies forward. I would only insist that we do not forget the culture that I, along with Scott and Fawaz, place at the heart of queerness. Given the expansive possibilities of the comics medium as highlighted by Scott and Fawaz, it seems reasonable to ask the medium, and specific genres within that medium, to represent LGBTQ cultures imaginatively and vibrantly, as well as truthfully. Looking backward to underground comix like *Gay Comix* suggests the usefulness of combining fantasy with reality to create LGBTQ imaginaries that might authentically reflect our histories and multiplicities, and inspire our ever-emerging and evolving futures.

NOTES

1. From *Alpha Flight*'s and *Uncanny X-Men*'s Northstar to the coupledom of Hulkling and Wiccan in Marvel's *The Young Avengers*, Gareth Schott tracks the emergence of industry-created LGBTQ superheroes and the impact these changes have on comic book fandom. For more, see Gareth Schott, "From Fan Appropriation to Industry Re-Appropriation: The Sexual Identities of Comic Superheroes," *Journal of Graphic Novels and Comics* 1, no. 1 (2010): 17–29.

2. As exemplified by the increasingly common expansion of "LGBTQ" into "LGBTQQIP2SAA," standing for "lesbian, gay, bisexual, transgender, queer, questioning, intersex, pansexual, 2-spirited, asexual, and allies." In this chapter, I have opted to use "LGBTQ" in order to show the wealth and breadth of sexualities and identities that our contemporary moment has to offer. Others might have used "queer" to do this, but I feel this too closely aligns with the identity category "queer." I have decided to present the community through the acronym in order to demarcate our different and wondrous variety while still attesting to our shared goals and values.

3. The Young Avengers franchise both includes one of comicdom's most famous gay couples in Wiccan and Hulkling and is representative of a tempered but clear effort to involve more LGBTQ creators in telling LGBTQ stories.

4. A typical example occurs during a scene in which the Young Avengers battle Kang the Conqueror in *The Young Avengers* #5. As Wiccan attempts to use his newly discovered spellcasting abilities to disable Kang's force field, his body violently collides with said force field, accompanied by an off-panel scream from Hulkling. The following panel shows Hulkling and Hawkeye assessing the condition of their battered colleague. Hulkling is the closest character to Wiccan, and he touches the spellcaster's shoulder with a look of concern on his face. The first speech bubble the reader encounters in this panel features Hulkling asking Wiccan, "You okay?" See

Allan Heinberg (w) and Jim Cheung (a), *The Young Avengers* (New York: Marvel Comics, 2006), 12.

5. Allan Heinberg (w) and Jim Cheung (a), *Avengers: The Children's Crusade*, no. 9 (New York: Marvel Comics, 2012).

6. The importance of Hulkling and Wiccan's relationship lies in its boundary-breaking uniqueness and continued controversy. The kiss the characters share in *Children's Crusade* #9 was the first on-panel same-sex kiss in mainstream superhero comics. With regard to controversy: in September 2019, Marcelo Crivella, the mayor of Rio de Janeiro, attempted to have the graphic novel featuring Hulkling and Wiccan's first kiss banned from book fairs; in retaliation, Brazil's largest newspaper, *Folha de S.Paulo*, ran an image of the kiss on the front page. For more discussion of this controversy, see "Brazil Paper Publishes Gay Kiss Illustration in Censorship Row," *Guardian*, September 8, 2019, https://www.theguardian.com/world/2019/sep/08/brazils-biggest-paper-publishes-illustration-gay-kiss-front-page.

7. As Friedlander observes, Heinberg and Cheung's series was awarded the 2006 GLAAD Media Award and the 2006 Harvey Award for Best New Series. Gillen and McKelvie's series also had an intensely passionate fandom, remnants of which are still very visible on Tumblr.

8. Allen Heinberg and Jim Cheung, *Young Avengers: The Children's Crusade*, no. 2 (New York: Marvel Worldwide Inc., 2017).

9. The affinities that gay males have for musicals are taken up throughout David Halperin's work on the complexities of gay male culture. For more, see Halperin, *How to Be Gay*.

10. See Keith Friedlander's and Brian Johnson's contributions to this volume for a more detailed history and analysis of these developments.

11. You might have noticed a shift from *LGBTQ* to *gay and lesbian* here. This is done in reference to two prominent identity categories and sexualities in the last two decades of the twentieth century, and I have used it to mark my turn toward a historical consideration of *Gay Comix*. I certainly do not wish to alienate folks who do not consider themselves gay or lesbian, but this section comprises a historical consideration of a comic that was mostly about gay (and some lesbian) life.

12. Ross more famously cofounded and published the *Bay Area Reporter*.

13. In the 2018 special issue of *American Literature* titled "Queer about Comics," Darieck Scott and Ramzi Fawaz write that despite "the prevailing assumption that mainstream comics (namely the superhero genre) embody nationalistic, sexist, and homophobic ideologies," throughout comic history "comic books have been linked to queerness or broader questions of sexuality and sexual identity in US society" (197–198). For more, see Scott and Fawaz, "Introduction: Queer about Comics."

14. I want to stress that what might seem like a fast-and-loose use of *gay* here—and in the rest of this section—is reflective of *Gay Comix*, primarily its representation of gay (male) creators and comics that reflected gay male life in the last two decades of the twentieth century. There were a few exceptions to this. For example, Alison Bechdel had a comic, "The Crush," published in *Gay Comix* #10.

15. An exception to the outright parody of other comics included in *Gay Comix*

#8 is the PSA created by Jennifer Camper, "Ironwoman's Safety Tips for Gals," which provided information/advice for dealing with a potential rapist.

16. The covers from the early issues of *Gay Comix* were wonderfully dense and spectacularly rendered. Folks so inclined should take a turn through the issues archived in the Comic Art Collection at Michigan State University.

17. Kaylann Campbell and Robert Triptow, cover, *Gay Comix*, no. 8 (Kitchen Sink Comix, 1986).

18. In the chapter "Bodies in Transition: Queering the Comic Book Superhero," Daniel Stein brings queerness and queer theory to bear on comic book superheroes. Stein writes,

> As a biological misfit, the superhero inhabits a body that deviates from real-life bodies and may therefore queer mainstream views of gender and sexuality rooted in references to the physical body. As a social outcast who must hide or sublimate a secret (and occasionally sexual) identity and is burdened by the great responsibilities that come with superhuman powers, the superhero has the potential to queer normative notions of male and female corporeality despite its overt promotion of an idealized and hypersexualized heteronormative body.

See Stein, "Bodies in Transition," 20.

19. Jeff Jacklin, "The Adventures of Captain Condom," *Gay Comix*, no. 8 (Kitchen Sink Comix, 1986), 17–21.

20. "Thirty Years of HIV/AIDS: Snapshots of an Epidemic," amfAR, https://www.amfar.org/content.aspx?id=3598. See also Meecha Corbett, "A Brief History of AZT," *Smithsonian*, September 9, 2010, http://americanhistory.si.edu/blog/2010/09/a-brief-history-of-azt.html. See also "HIV/AIDS Historical Timeline," US Food and Drug Administration, https://www.fda.gov/forpatients/illness/hivaids/history/ucm151074.htm.

21. Kurt Erichsen, "A Midsummer Night's Super Stud," *Gay Comix*, no. 8 (Kitchen Sink Comix, 1986), 8–16.

22. Peter Coogan, "The Definition of a Superhero," in *Superhero: The Origin of a Genre*, 31.

23. Vaughn Frick, "Leatherthing," *Gay Comix*, no. 8 (Kitchen Sink Comix, 1986), 1–5.

24. This refers to the origin stories of Batman, Superman, and Captain Marvel, respectively.

25. Gale Rubin, in her essay "The Catacombs: A Temple of the Butthole," writes that the 1970s were an important time for the development of sexual subcultures. Rubin writes, "In the decade after Stonewall and before AIDS, gay communities generally underwent explosive growth in terms of population, economic power, and political self-confidence. Leather communities were similarly robust. . . . At night, leathermen owned those streets, prowling easily among the bars, sex clubs, bath houses, and back alleys." For more, see Gayle Rubin, "The Catacombs:

The Temple of the Butthole," in *Deviations: A Gayle Rubin Reader* (Durham, NC: Duke University Press, 2011), 224–240.

26. Campbell writes, "The first stage of the mythological journey—what we have designated 'the call to adventure'—signifies that destiny has summoned the hero. . . . The hero can go forth on his own volition to accomplish the adventure . . . or he may be carried and sent abroad by some benign or malignant agent." See Joseph Campbell, "The Call to Adventure," in *Hero of a Thousand Face*s (Novato, CA: New World Library, 2008), 48.

27. By this I mean the focus on Iceman "coming out" to friends and family, the fusion of mutant acceptance within society paralleled to the acceptance of LGBTQ identities and lifestyles within dominant culture, puns and jokes, etc.

28. See Sina Grace (w), Robert Gill (a), and Kevin Wada (c), "Champions Reunited, Part 1," *Iceman*, no. 6 (New York: Marvel Characters Inc., 2017).

29. Grace, Gill, and Wada, "Champions Reunited, Part 1."

30. See Sina Grace (w), Robert Gill (a), and Kevin Wada (c), "Champions Reunited, Part 2," *Iceman*, no. 7 (New York: Marvel Characters Inc., 2017), 11–12.

31. These are the credits for *America* #1–6 as collected in *America: The Life and Times of America Chavez* (Quebec: Solisco Printers, 2018).

32. This includes her old friends from the *Young Avengers* Kate Bishop, a.k.a. Hawkeye, and David Alleyne, a.k.a. Prodigy.

33. Kimberle Crenshaw, "Demarginalizing the Intersection of Race and Sex: A Black Feminist Critique of Antidiscrimination Doctrine, Feminist Theory and Antiracist Politics," in *University of Chicago Legal Forum* 1, no. 8 (1989).

34. Gabby Rivera, Joe Quinones, and Stacy Lee, *America*, no. 3, in *America: The Life and Times of America Chavez*, 3.

35. Gabby Rivera and Jen Bartel, *America*, no. 7, in *America: Fact and Fuertona* (Quebec: Solisco Printers, 2018), 2.

36. Rivera and Bartel, *America*, no. 7, 4.

37. Aldama, *Latinx Superheroes*, 179.

38. Other contemporary issues or trends in popular culture are referenced in *America*. America is seen wearing a "Nasty" hat, punching Nazis, and evoking Beyoncé by referring to a reluctant ally as "Becky." We later learn that Becky's last name is Goodhair.

39. One example of this would be in *Gay Comix*'s first issue, which centered on the worries, fears, and uncertain future generated by the impact of HIV. Another example would be Howard Cruse's "Ready or Not Here It Comes: Safe Sex," which appeared in the fourth issue of *Gay Comix*.

40. For an interview with Grace about the campaign to resurrect *Iceman*, see George Gene Gustines, "Iceman Came Out. Now He's Coming Back in His Own Series," *New York Times*, June 28, 2018, https://www.nytimes.com/2018/06/28/books/iceman-new-comic-book-series.html.

41. Scott and Fawaz, "Introduction: Queer about Comics," 200.

42. Scott and Fawaz, "Introduction: Queer about Comics," 201.

6

PARENTS, COUNTERPUBLICS, AND SEXUAL IDENTITY IN *YOUNG AVENGERS*

KEITH FRIEDLANDER

Although its initial run lasted for only twelve issues, Allan Heinberg and Jim Cheung's 2005 series *Young Avengers* introduced a cast of young superheroes that would go on to feature heavily in Marvel crossover events and mini-series over the following years. One reason for the team's continued popularity was the refreshingly modern depiction of a same-sex romance between Teddy Altman (a.k.a. Hulkling) and Billy Kaplan (a.k.a. Wiccan). This relationship was refreshing, in part, simply because it existed. At the time, Marvel's roster featured few gay superheroes, and none of these were in meaningful relationships with one another. The mere presence of Hulkling and Wiccan's relationship indicated a significant step toward representing more sexual diversity. This was not, however, a simple act of tokenism. Hulkling and Wiccan's popularity can partly be attributed to the understated depiction of their relationship. Rather than sensationalizing this relationship, Heinberg and Cheung depicted it as a healthy, stable constant. In an interview with the *Gay Times*, during which he discusses his own experiences growing up as a closeted gay teen, Heinberg explains, "My approach to Wiccan and Hulkling . . . was to make their sexuality beside the point. While they are open about their sexuality and their relationship, they're by no means defined by it."¹ The characters do not struggle to come to terms with their sexual identity; they are not afraid to come out to their loved ones, and there are no dramatic revelations. They are simply two gay heroes in love. By normalizing the characters' sexuality and romance, Heinberg struck a chord with readers and critics, and *Young Avengers* went on to be awarded the 2006 GLAAD Media Award and the 2006 Harvey Award for Best New Series.

However, this narrative surrounding the characters' appeal is not uncontested. A number of critics have pointed out that Hulkling and Wiccan's romance is represented so subtly that the characters' sexuality is effectively hidden from view. Esther De Dauw argues that Heinberg and Cheung's depiction of Wiccan and Hulkling's relationship reinforces a trend of tailoring gay identity to appease conservative, middle-class sensibilities. According to De Dauw, attempts to create positive depictions of gay characters by downplaying their sexuality "are, perhaps inevitably, reductive and restrictive because they are based on conservative gender roles."² Far from a frank depiction of a homosexual relationship, Wiccan and Hulkling's romance is consistently concealed from the public gaze. In the first volume of *Young Avengers*, their relationship is typically only hinted at in oblique remarks. It is not until the final issue of the *Children's Crusade* mini-series, seven years after the characters' first appearance, that we finally see them share a kiss. For De Dauw, this understated approach demonstrates a neoliberal mind-set that legitimates homosexual relationships only when they are carried out discretely, in private settings. Accordingly, the only scene from the original series that directly addresses Hulkling and Wiccan's sexuality is set in the latter's home. Interrupting a conversation about secret identities and superheroism, Wiccan's parents mistakenly assume the secret being discussed is the teens' relationship. They quickly assure the young men that they know they are gay and completely support their relationship. In this scene, though Hulkling and Wiccan's homosexuality is acknowledged and accepted, the normative aegis of domesticity and parental approval looms large. Thus, De Dauw concludes that *Young Avengers* promotes a particularly normative image of gay identity at the cost of other, bolder representations. "[I]n *Young Avengers*," writes De Dauw, "homosexuality is socially acceptable as long as it cannot be seen."³ Elsewhere in this volume, Sarah Panuska similarly criticizes the depiction of Hulkling and Wiccan's relationship as overly tame, further noting that it includes few—if any—references to historical or contemporary queer culture. Panuska rightly ties this particular failing to a broader trend of popular superhero comics glossing over their LGBTQ characters' sexuality for fear of alienating straight readers.

De Dauw and Panuska's critiques prompt critics to reconsider what qualifies as progressive representations of same-sex relationships in superhero comics. Did Hulkling and Wiccan's popularity simply result from a lack of available alternatives in 2005? Does Heinberg's approach to making "their sexuality beside the point" do a disservice to Marvel fans eager for more diverse—and manifest—depictions of sexuality? While these are legitimate concerns, this line of reasoning overlooks a subtler critique of the superhero genre's heteronormative values that play out across a decade of *Young Avengers* comics. While accepting that Hulkling and Wiccan constitute a homonormative depiction of gay romance, this chapter seeks to complicate De Dauw's assertion that the series "clearly follows the private/public split where sexual/romantic conduct between consenting homosexuals in a relationship is allowed in private but not in public."[4] Rather than reinforcing a clear division between private and public spheres that has traditionally been used to depoliticize and silence LGBTQ voices, comics starring the Young Avengers exploit the trope of the superhero's secret identity to challenge and break down this distinction. Though Wiccan/Billy's parents accept his homosexuality, they are far less accepting of his superheroism. In fact, Billy and the other Young Avengers perpetually struggle against the authority of parental figures that would limit their access to the public sphere; consequently, the Young Avengers repeatedly resist the suppression of nonnormative identities to private spaces. Heinberg and Cheung use the superhero genre to demonstrate that private matters cannot be separated from public identity. In doing so, they manifest Michael Warner's concept of a counterpublic: a subcultural public that defines itself in opposition to a dominant social order. The Young Avengers' defiance of parental authority and public acts of self-representation as a superhero team mirror the historic processes by which LGBTQ communities have organized as counterpublics. While Heinberg and Cheung's series do shy away from explicitly addressing Hulkling and Wiccan's sexuality, from a thematic perspective, these series are very much about the heroism of stepping out, claiming public space, and making private matters of identity political.

In the introduction to their "Queer about Comics" special issue of *American Literature*, Darieck Scott and Ramzi Fawaz observe a synergistic relationship joining queer theory and comics studies. Emphasizing comics' status as a marginal art form, presumably patronized by outcasts and minorities, they ask, "How might the medium's courting of marginal and outsider audiences allow for the formation of queer counterspaces?"[5] The Young Avengers demonstrate that potential by complicating private/public dichotomies to create a superhero narrative directed at young queer audiences. Accordingly, this chapter will examine the interaction of heteronormative superhero traditions and disruptive counterpublics across three Young Avengers series: Heinberg and Cheung's original *Young Avengers* (2005–2006), their later crossover event *The Children's Crusade* (2010–2012), and Kieron Gillen and Jamie McKelvie's *Young Avengers* relaunch (2013–2014).

HEINBERG AND CHEUNG'S *YOUNG AVENGERS*: COMING OUT AS SUPERHEROES

In the original *Young Avengers* series, Heinberg and Cheung use the superhero device of secret identities as a metaphor for sexual identity. This metaphor is most clearly established in the previously mentioned "coming out scene," in which Billy's parents reassure their son that they accept his relationship with Teddy. This scene's humor comes from the fact that Billy and Teddy are actually discussing revealing their secret identities as Wiccan and Hulkling when they are interrupted. The implication is that it is easier for Billy's liberal parents to accept and support a gay son then it would be for them to accept him as a magically powered vigilante. As De Dauw points out, this joke serves to downplay the characters' sexuality, rendering it a nonissue and normalizing Billy and Teddy as socially acceptable models of homosexuality. Yet, even as this scene depoliticizes Billy and Teddy's sexuality, it also establishes a parallel between sexual identity and superhero identity that is central to the series' commentary on sexuality and identity politics. Over the next decade of Young Avengers story lines, the characters' secret identities serve as a device for connecting themes of closeted living, intergenerational conflict, and fights for public representation.

From the outset of their superhero career, the Young Avengers struggle to fully realize and take ownership over their public identities. Throughout each series, they are placed in conflict with parental figures they both admire and resent as normative archetypes. In an effort to gain legitimacy and present themselves as proper superheroes in the public eye, the Young Avengers initially model themselves after the adult Avengers; each team member has a code name, costume, and superpower that references one of the adult heroes. Patriot, for instance, throws star-shaped shuriken and wears an altered version of the costume originally worn by Bucky, Captain America's WWII-era sidekick. Similarly, the Asgardian (who will later change his code name to Wiccan) flies around wearing a winged helmet and shooting bolts of lightning, much like Thor, while Hulkling appears as a spitting image of the Incredible Hulk, but with softer features and a cooler haircut. It is quickly revealed, however, that the Young Avengers have no affiliation with the actual Avengers; they have simply co-opted their gimmicks in order to pass as legitimate superheroes. In reality, the Asgardian is not actually from Asgard, and Hulkling did not gain his superstrength from exposure to gamma radiation. Over the span of the twelve-issue series, all of the Young Avengers reveal their true origins and eventually differentiate themselves from their adult counterparts.

When Captain America confronts Patriot regarding his use of the Bucky costume, Patriot resents the implication that he has any relation to Steve Rogers. Instead, he reveals that he is Eli Bradley, the grandson of the first Captain America, African American Isaiah Bradley.[6] He claims he gained his superpowers after receiving a blood transfusion from his grandfather and wears the Bucky mantle to honor Isaiah. Though it is later revealed that there was no blood transfusion (Eli's agility and strength are the effects of an illegal street drug that he takes in order to be a superhero), this does not change the fact that Eli's efforts to establish his own identity as Patriot are motivated by conflicted feelings of insecurity, reverence, and resentment toward the predecessors that serve as his role models. Similarly, Iron Lad has no relation to Iron Man but simply mimics his armor. In actuality, he is a young version of the time-traveling supervillain Kang the Conqueror. When Iron Lad learns from his adult self that he will grow up to become a tyrant, he travels back in time to form the Young Avengers and change his destiny. Thus, his entire motivation for becoming a superhero is to defy the expectations of a controlling adult authority in the form of his older self, whom he eventually murders in an attempt to gain autonomy. For each of the Young Avengers, the initial, superficial connection to an adult superhero only masks a more complicated and fraught child-parent relationship that must be confronted before each character can establish his or her own autonomy as an individual.

This mimetic drive to both meet and defy the expectations of parental figures escalates when the Young Avengers come up against the authoritative control of the Avengers. According to Captain America and Iron Man, the Young Avengers are too young and inexperienced for the responsibility and danger that come with being superheroes. This delineation between an adult world of costumed heroism and an adolescent world of private citizenship is a recurring theme in superhero comics. In his essay "The Naked Hero and Model Man: Costumed Identity in Comic Book Narratives," David Coughlan argues that the act of donning a costume signifies the superhero's transition from the feminine, domestic scene of the private sphere into the masculine, adult world of the public sphere. Superhero narratives repeatedly reiterate a male fantasy of entering into adult manhood, gaining the public agency associated with masculinity, and regressing back into adolescence when the adventure is over. According to Coughlan, this establishes a gendered binary that devalues the emotional labor and adult responsibilities of the domestic sphere by consistently prioritizing the hero's world-saving adventures. Traditional superhero narratives are often driven by the tension between these two irreconcilable identities. In one classic example, Peter Parker's ability to achieve domestic bliss is constantly being disrupted by the weight of his responsibilities to the public as Spider-Man. The potential threat to Parker's family and friends demands he hide his superhero identity and keep his private life separate from his career as a hero. While these two worlds inevitably clash, the superhero is faced with an imperative to keep them separate: "The comic book hero's costume . . . constructs him as a man exactly because it marks him as a public figure. In this way, comics suggest that strength in the masculine public sphere is the truest sign of manhood."[7] It is worth noting that when Captain America does censure the Young Avengers, he expressly forbids them from donning their costumes: "If you *ever* put those uniforms on again, Iron Man and I will do everything in our power to shut you down for good."[8]

Captain America is determined to check the Young Avengers' heroic pursuits because they defy the traditional private/public binary in two ways. First, the teenage heroes are simply too young. If the superhero costume is meant to signal the individual's status as an adult and agency within the public sphere, then Captain America serves as the model par excellence of a gatekeeper, determining who is worthy of adult status and limiting those who deviate from the norm. Second, the Young Avengers consistently show a disregard for the separation of the public business of superheroism from the private world of familial connection. As Coughlan notes, the traditional private/public binary promotes a regressive standard of maturity, whereby adult masculinity is characterized by a retreat from domestic matters of emotional openness and personal connections.[9] In traditional superhero narratives, especially those starring male heroes coming to terms with their masculinity, the decision to consistently prioritize protecting the world over commitments to loved ones is framed as the mature, responsible decision, implying that social influence is a surer sign of adulthood than healthy personal relationships. *Young Avengers* questions this hierarchy by repeatedly showing how private and public matters overlap.

The Young Avengers' struggles to assert their autonomy repeatedly

FIGURE 6.1. Captain America and Hulkling fighting back to back. Heinberg and Cheung's *Young Avengers* #12 (2006).

demonstrate how private matters of familial connection and personal identity are often inseparable from public matters. For example, in the concluding arc of the original series, Hulkling discovers that his green skin and shape-changing superpowers are a result of his genetic background. He is actually a multiracial extraterrestrial, half Skrull and half Kree. When these two warring alien races both send agents to reclaim Hulkling so that he can take his place in their respective societies, the matter of birthright threatens to reignite an intergalactic war. Once Hulkling's racial and familial status becomes a matter of public debate, the Avengers intervene to act as the presiding authority. In the ensuing battle, Captain America once again commands the Young Avengers to remove themselves, but Hulkling insists that his involvement is necessary because he is at the root of the conflict (figure 6.1). There is a subtle shift in the way these two heroes are juxtaposed here versus the series' first story arc. When Hulkling first encounters Captain America, the latter is typically depicted in a position of dominance, standing in the foreground, imposing his authority over the young heroes. In these first few issues, Hulkling is still sporting dark green hair as part of his act to pass as a younger version of the Hulk. Here, for the first time in the series, a Young Avenger is depicted on equal footing as Captain America, as Hulkling fights alongside him. Posed predominantly in the foreground with his shock of blond hair, Hulkling stands his ground against both his attackers and his idol. In the story's climactic battle, the Avengers are unable to divorce the private controversy surrounding Hulkling's identity from concerns of public safety and interstellar politics; the inescapable intertwining of these matters helps the Young Avengers effectively assert their public agency.

In this way, Heinberg and Cheung's first *Young Avengers* series breaks down the binary between private life and public duty characteristic of traditional superhero narratives. In doing so, the comic presents a critique of the superhero genre's commitment to a normative monoculture. Susan Hekman explains that the concept of a clean division between public and private worlds is grounded in the neoliberal ideology of a neutral, objective standard of justice. In both Heinberg and Cheung's *Young Avengers* and subsequent stories starring its titular characters, Captain America represents a neoliberalism that defines the public world as completely separate from the private sphere, imagining it as a polity grounded in reason and unaffected by matters of personal identity or bias. Within this ideology, the ideal public citizen is expected to remain objective and act from a position of impartiality when addressing political matters. According to Hekman, "central to the justice voice is the reliance on a single, universal standard that applies equally to all. Opening up discourse in the public sphere to the personal and the particular challenges this universal standard."[10] This notion of universal citizenship is rooted in the misconception that the personal need not be political, that citizenship can be based on an all-inclusive model that is not affected by gender, race, or sexuality. In actuality, however, the universal citizen of liberalism is modeled after the experiences of a specific demographic: the normative model of the straight, white male.

The traditional superhero's struggle to maintain a clear separation between a private life as a real person with complex relationships and a public life as an icon of justice is informed by this liberal ideology of universal citizenship. To return to the previous example, Peter Parker hides his superheroism from those closest to him so that Spider-Man can realize his potential as a detached paragon of justice. While Spider-Man comics typically illustrate the unrealistic nature of this goal (supervillains repeatedly disrupt Parker's private life), Captain America is, in general, able to realize this notion of objective public justice. Interpreting

Captain America through the lens of Aristotelian moral virtues, Mark D. White asserts that Cap's most essential characteristic—indeed, his true superpower—is his unfailing moral compass. More than any other hero in the Marvel Universe, Captain America is able to achieve an objective moral outlook. A related key characteristic of Captain America, however, is his lack of a complex private life. As a man out of time, having left his family and friends behind in the 1940s after being frozen in ice for several decades, Captain America is able to fully embody his superhero persona because he has no private life to compromise it. He is the universal citizen made flesh; consequently, he is an impossible model for other heroes to aspire to. In this regard, he acts as a perfect foil for the Young Avengers. Whereas Spider-Man stories often illustrate the difficulty of achieving public agency wholly divorced from one's private identity, the Young Avengers subvert the very ideal of the universal citizen by declining to pursue it. Hulkling's refusal to follow Captain America's example presents an alternative model of superhero identity that embraces the overlapping complications of private identity and public responsibility, confronting both simultaneously.

There is a similar story line regarding Wiccan's family background in the crossover series *Avengers: The Children's Crusade*, in which it is revealed that he is actually the son of the Scarlet Witch. Due to the events of the *House of M* story line, during which the Scarlet Witch reshapes reality and wipes out the world's mutant population, the Avengers decide that both she and Wiccan, who appears to have inherited her powers, are too powerful to be allowed to remain free. In their effort to find and redeem Wiccan's mother, the Young Avengers are once again forced to defy the Avengers and become fugitives. With both the Avengers and the X-Men claiming the authority to determine the Scarlet Witch's fate, private aspects of Wiccan's identity—his parentage, his status as a mutant—become matters of contention for supposedly impartial arbiters of public justice. In this story line, the analogy between superhero identity and sexual politics is very apparent, as the private aspects of Wiccan's life are investigated, policed, and contested by the same authorities that deny him public agency. Discussing multiple high-profile court cases involving gay and bisexual individuals, Eve Kosofsky Sedgwick notes that bodies of authority historically alternate between designating sexuality as a public or private matter based on practicalities of control. In 1985, a guidance counselor who was fired for coming out as bisexual did not fall under the protection of the First Amendment because her admission was not considered a public matter. However, in 1986, Michael Hardwick was found guilty on charges of sodomy when a court decided that his sexual practices were not protected as a private matter.

If homosexuality is not, however densely adjudicated, to be considered a matter of *public* concern, neither in the Supreme Court's binding opinion does it subsist under the mantle of the *private*. The most obvious fact about this history of judicial formulations is that it codifies an excruciating system of double binds, systematically oppressing gay people, identities, and acts by undermining through contradictory constraints of discourse the grounds of their very being.[11]

Heteronormative (read: dominant) culture, operating from a position of public authority, adjudicates on the rights of the LGBTQ community while, at the same time, denying the political nature of sexuality and demanding silence. The Young Avengers repeatedly find themselves navigating a similar double bind. While Wiccan's attempts to save his mother have nothing to do with his sexuality, Heinberg and Cheung draw upon the same contradictory power dynamics described by Kosofsky to complicate his public agency. The Avengers decide that the Scarlet Witch's fate is a matter of public import while barring Wiccan's involvement in making such decisions based on his personal background.

The Young Avengers are repeatedly left with no other recourse than to evade the Avengers' supervision and operate on their own. In doing so, they complicate the model of public agency upheld by the conventional superhero. As Hekman notes, asserting an objective standard of justice requires one to invest in the notion of a single public that applies equally to all people. However, as Warner argues, there is no singular public sphere. Instead, there are multiple publics that organize themselves across different groups: "A public is a space of discourse organized by nothing other than discourse itself. . . . It exists only as the end for which books are published, shows broadcast, Web sites posted."[12] In other words, publics are self-organized by groups, projected into being as audiences for speakers, and defined through differentiation from other publics. Due to their exclusion from the larger public order constituted by the authority of the Avengers, the Young Avengers demonstrate how public organization takes place across multiple spheres of action. In the place of a singular public sphere, they constitute themselves as a counterpublic. According to Warner, a counterpublic is formed by "an awareness of its subordinate status. The cultural horizon against which it marks itself off is not just a general or wider public but a dominant one."[13] Banned from participating in the dominant public sphere by Captain America and the other Avengers, the Young Avengers begin meeting in parks and city streets to organize themselves in secret. It is in these anonymous public spaces, away from the scrutiny of adults, that they formalize their own independent identities, coming up with new code names and donning new costumes distinct from the adult Avengers.

Warner's research traces the importance of counterpublic spaces to the development of queer culture. As one example, he describes how circles of drag queens would gather for photo shoots in the 1960s, forming their own public in the face of a repressive society. In *Young Avengers* #6, as the team puts on their new costumes in the shadows of an abandoned warehouse, Wiccan asks if they will tell their parents that they are superheroes. Reiterating the sexual identity analogy established earlier, Hulkling responds, "We're gonna have to come out to them at some point." More than a humorous metaphor, this scene can be read as an allusion to a history of clandestine self-organization and self-fashioning that made it possible for LGBTQ communities to take root. Moreover, it posits an alternative model of public agency for the modern superhero while highlighting the limitations and potentially draconic implications of the old model.

GILLEN AND MCKELVIE'S *YOUNG AVENGERS*: LIVING OUT LOUD

Kieron Gillen and Jamie McKelvie's 2013 relaunch of *Young Avengers* maintains the thematic focus on youthful resistance to adult authority and the contested status of public spheres. However, in this more recent series, the sexual subtext of the original becomes text. With a revised cast of sexually diverse characters, romantic incidents and sexual histories play a more pivotal role in the plot. Whereas Wiccan and Hulkling were the only LGBTQ characters in the original series, the cast of Gillen and McKelvie's series represents a diverse—and seldom stable—spectrum of sexualities. In addition to Wiccan and Hulkling, the new *Young Avengers* includes America Chavez, a.k.a. Miss America, a dimension-hopping, Latina-presenting superwoman who describes herself as having experimented with men before coming to identify firmly as a lesbian; Noh-Varr, a.k.a. Marvel Boy, an alien who admits to experimenting with other men during his travels through space;[14] and David Alleyne, a.k.a. Prodigy, an African American mutant who once possessed the ability to psychically absorb and mimic the knowledge and talents of others, and who comes out as bisexual following a romantic encounter with Hulkling.[15] The team also includes a young version of Loki, the Norse god of mischief, who has been depicted as gender-fluid in previous Marvel Comics. Loki explains to Prodigy, "My culture doesn't really share your concept of sexual identity. There are sexual acts. That's it."[16] Kate Bishop, a.k.a. Hawkeye, the only white human member of the team, also claims to be its only straight member. Yet in the closing issue of the series, America Chavez observes, "I've seen the way you look at me. You're not that straight."[17] Thus, in addition to representing a broad spectrum of sexual identities, the new Young Avengers demonstrate that such orientations are not fixed. Rather, they fluctuate and develop over time.

Perhaps as a response to the original series' hesitancy to depict sexual content, the opening scene of *Young Avengers* consists of Kate Bishop waking up in Noh-Varr's bed after a night of casual sex. The tone is distinctly sex positive, as Kate quickly dismisses any feelings of shame for having hooked up with a virtual stranger and enjoys her present situation: "I lie in the strange bed and watch this beautiful alien boy dance to the music my parents loved, and think . . . this is everything I always hoped for."[18] This opening scene sets a different tone for the new series in which key moments of character development often revolve around romantic trysts, confrontations with angry ex-lovers, and moments of sexual discovery.[19]

While the tone and content of the new series is more overtly sexual, Gillen and McKelvie continue to address many of the same themes of public citizenry discussed in the previous section. Once again, the central conflict of the story focuses on the Young Avengers' resistance to the authority of parental figures and their subsequent organization as a counterpublic. In keeping with the series' more explicit content, however, these themes become considerably more overt, signaling superheroics as an analogy for passionately embracing an authentic identity and actively resisting heteronormative culture.

Following the events of *The Children's Crusade*, which concluded with a number of Young Avengers losing their lives, Wiccan decides to retire from superheroism and live his life as Billy Kaplan.[20] When Teddy begins to sneak out at night to continue his crime-fighting activities as Hulkling, Billy confronts him. In the ensuing argument, Teddy describes Billy's retreat from superheroism in terms of self-closeting: "You're so scared of yourself it breaks my heart. I'm not going to spend the rest of my life in the phone booth. I'm not living a lie."[21] Billy's decision to live a private life, away from the public world of superheroism and his identity as Wiccan, is, according to Teddy, a regressive attempt to conform to a normative lifestyle.

In this series, just as superhero identity once again signifies entry into public life, the primary threat facing the Young Avengers again serves as a metaphor for a repressive monoculture. Indeed, Gillen and McKelvie create a supervillain that serves as an even balder analogy for normative values than Captain America. Following their argument, Wiccan uses his magical powers to bring Hulkling's adoptive mother back to life by pulling her from another timeline. While the woman Wiccan summons initially appears to be Hulkling's dead mother, it is soon revealed that she is actually an interdimensional parasite named Mother. Chiding the young heroes for staying up late and dating at such a young age, she proceeds to entrap them in her pocket dimension, where she plans to consume their life force. Her mere presence has a brainwashing effect on all adults; this results in Wiccan's parents and even the Avengers becoming Mother's agents and attempting to subdue the Young Avengers on her behalf. When Mother does capture Wiccan, she sends him to his "room"—a featureless box in her dimension.

Mother serves as an embodiment of a dominant conservative public order that seeks to confine and assimilate deviance. Her ability to effortlessly control adults speaks to the ubiquitous influence of normative values, as every figure of parental authority in the Young Avengers' lives automatically bends to her homogenizing will. It seems Mother can control adults because they are old enough to live comfortably within conformity. Even as they forcefully subdue the young heroes, the grown-up Avengers dismiss their complaints with gentle, condescending bromides. As he abandons the Young Avengers to Mother, a brainwashed Captain America tells Wiccan, "Be a grown-up, William" and "We've all been young once [. . .] it's not the end of the world."[22] Cap's tone alludes to the complacency of a privileged class that cannot perceive the hardships of an aberrant individual. At the heart of this conformity is Mother's home dimension, a colorless void of white tendrils and boxes that reflexively seek to enclose the Young Avengers (figure 6.2). It is a bland monotony that feeds on their youth and passion.

When Wiccan attempts to secretly contact the Scarlet Witch for help, he is immediately set upon by Mother and forced to flee; in this series, no adult can be trusted. The pervasiveness of Mother's influence forces the Young Avengers to once again run away from their homes and live off the grid. Yet whereas the original *Young Avengers* series depicted the heroes' flight from authority as a desperate, high-stakes bid to save the world,

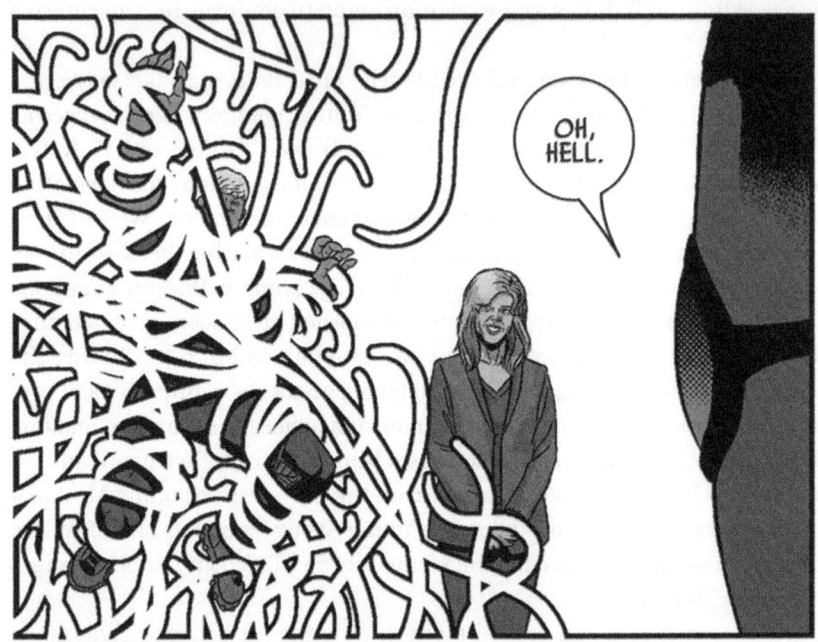

FIGURE 6.2. Hulkling ensnared by Mother's pocket dimension. Gillen and McKelvie's *Young Avengers* #8 (2013).

the new series is decidedly more joyful and upbeat, depicting escape from parental authority as a riotous adventure of friendship and self-discovery. The public spaces occupied by these new Young Avengers are more colorful and varied. Rather than gathering in parks and city streets, they journey through outer space and alternate dimensions. These adventures are also shared online; presented in a series of Instagram-like posts, the Young Avengers' fugitive existence sees them going to concerts, celebrating birthdays, and enjoying their escapades as young superheroes (figure 6.3). Where Heinberg and Cheung have been criticized for hiding Wiccan and Hulkling's romance in private settings, Gillen and McKelvie tellingly have the characters post a picture of themselves kissing online for the world to see. Rather than focusing on the hardships of a life on the run, the new series portrays alternative public spaces as liberating opportunities for personal expression and growth. This notion of defying normative society as a celebratory act reaches its apotheosis in the series' concluding issues when, upon defeating Mother, the Young Avengers throw an outdoor rave for all the teenage heroes of the Marvel universe.

FIGURE 6.3. The Young Avengers post their adventures on faux Instagram. Gillen and McKelvie's *Young Avengers* #7 (2013).

In their essay "Sex in Public," Lauren Berlant and Michael Warner describe how the sanctification of family values in American culture speaks to the desire for a homogenous monoculture. In order to accomplish this, heterosexual culture relegates intimacy and sexuality to the private sphere: "By making sex seem irrelevant or merely personal, heteronormative conventions of intimacy block the building of nonnormative or explicit public sexual cultures."[23] Like the blank white boxes that Mother uses to trap the Young Avengers, mainstream culture erases diversity by hiding sex behind closed doors. Once isolated and denied access to a community, the individual becomes easier to control and exploit. Mother's stated goal of draining the heroes of their life force alludes to mainstream culture's parasitic appropriation of the subaltern. In order to resist this monoculture, LGBTQ culture must undertake world-building projects, constructing alternative spaces and discourses that "allow for the concretization of a queer counterpublic."[24] This work cannot be done in private. The community must have places to gather and organize, to imagine and realize alternative models of intimacy. By necessity, these spaces have historically been mobile and transient: dance halls, drag shows, parades. "If we could not concentrate a publicly accessible culture somewhere," Berlant and Warner write, "we would always be outnumbered and overwhelmed."[25] In a similar vein, the Young Avengers remain mobile, leading lives of public resistance, perpetually at risk of being overwhelmed and absorbed into Mother's hive mind. Using America Chavez's ability to kick open dimensional portals, they embark on a continuous road trip, jumping from alternate reality to alternate reality. By the end of their journey, the Young Avengers have experienced sexual awakenings, personal epiphanies, and relationship crises. Before the ultimate party, their road trip concludes with them returning to rally other young heroes and form a body of resistance that is not dependent upon the approval of the Avengers and other established, adult heroes. Unlike traditional superheroes, Gillen and McKelvie's Young Avengers do not engage with the public sphere in order to maintain a status quo. Instead, their diverse, exuberant public lives provide spaces for self-actualization and mobilization.

Throughout all of their iterations, the Young Avengers reimagine the superhero's relationship with the public. Heinberg and Cheung's series focuses on challenging the old model represented by Captain America by demonstrating its incompatibility with the politicized identities of a younger and more diverse generation. The traditional superhero's ability to divide a public life as an objective icon of justice from a private life is a function of privilege that does not apply to LGBTQ superheroes. In presenting this deconstruction, however, Heinberg and Cheung's *Young Avengers* series ultimately strikes a conservative tone, focusing more on the limitations facing the young heroes than on the potential of what they might become. Gillen and McKelvie pick up where the previous creative team left off by using the superhero genre's capacity for fantastical reinvention to show what an alternative, youthful model of superheroism might actually look like. Explicit, colorful, and irreverent, Gillen and McKelvie's series presents young heroes who live their lives out loud and in public. In this series, maintaining an identity as a superhero is not defined by hiding one's personal drama from sight, but rather involves airing grievances and building relationships. As a result, this series more frankly—and comprehensively—depicts the diverse sexuality represented by its cast.

One final comparison will help emphasize the important difference between these two versions of the Young Avengers. In *The Children's Crusade*, the call to adventure comes from Wiccan's grandfather, Magneto. Intent on finding and redeeming his daughter, Magneto encourages the Young Avengers to run away from their adult counterparts and join him in his quest to find the Scarlet Witch. The invitation is an ominous one; joining forces with an infamous supervillain foregrounds the risk of moral compromise that comes with defying the authority of the Avengers. By contrast, in Gillen and McKelvie's *Young Avengers*, the call to adventure comes from Noh-Varr. After saving Wiccan and Hulkling from Mother's agents in an acrobatic shoot out, he stands astride his spaceship in a sexy action pose that highlights his taught posterior and beckons to the couple, "Come with me if you want to be awesome."[26] Where the former series depicts the formation of a counterpublic as fraught with complications and danger, the latter presents it as an exciting and alluring opportunity to realize one's best life.

CONCLUSION

Commenting on the image of Hulkling and Wiccan sharing their first on-panel kiss in the final issue of *The Children's Crusade*, prominent gay comic critic and creator Andrew Wheeler explains that it is a remarkable moment "because it took seven years to show a kiss between two characters who must kiss each other every day. It's a remarkable kiss because of all the times we haven't seen it."[27] In part, this kiss had impact because fans—especially LGBTQ fans—had waited for this significant moment, which built anticipation. Yet, as Wheeler observes, there are other reasons this kiss was particularly meaningful that are related to the willingness of Marvel editorial to publish such an image. Wheeler points out that when *Young Avengers* was first published, Marvel was in the practice of placing "mature reader" labels on titles featuring gay characters.

In examining how various series starring the Young Avengers represent (or fail to represent) LGBTQ characters, it is important to situate the series between two competing forces: a conservative publisher cautiously testing the waters and a fan base eagerly imagining a more diverse range of representation. Between the introduction of Hulkling and Wiccan in 2005 and the characters' first on-panel kiss in 2012, Marvel had undergone shifts in editorial outlook and reader demographics.[28] Thus, it is possible that Heinberg and Cheung delayed this kiss and offered an overall subtler approach to Hulkling and Wiccan's relationship because they were measuring the receptiveness of their audience and publisher; it is also possible that Gillen and McKelvie would not have been able to create one of the most explicitly queer-positive superhero series in mainstream comics without the prior existence of subtler approaches. I would argue that Heinberg and Cheung were, on a fundamental level, less interested in explicit representation and more interested in creating a story that challenged the heteronormative traditions of the genre. Building upon Heinberg and Cheung's deconstruction of the neat public/private distinction that informs the traditional superhero's depoliticized identity, Gillen and McKelvie's *Young Avengers* imagines new spaces for young, queer heroes to unapologetically express themselves.

None of this is to suggest that Gillen and McKelvie's series represents an unimpeachable peak—that it is the most we can aspire to in terms of representing LGBTQ identities in superhero comics. I concur with Sarah Panuska's assertion in the preceding chapter that fans and critics should not be satisfied with the mere existence of LGBTQ superheroes but must now keenly scrutinize the quality of their depictions. In his survey of the representation of gay superheroes, Gareth Schott notes the mixed reader responses to Heinberg and Cheung's original *Young Avengers* series, with some fans canceling their subscriptions in protest of gay superheroes and others demanding more explicit content. Relating the lack of intimate exchanges in this original series to broader trends in superhero comics, Schott concludes, "Industry penned representation of gay superheroes to-date suggests that fan intervention still remains necessary. Industry acknowledgement of sexuality is simply that, having done little to further challenge the identity of the superhero and its portrayal in the long term."[29]

FIGURE 6.4. "Holding Hands," fan art of Wiccan and Hulkling sharing a quiet moment. Image by Cris-Art from DeviantArt, 2012.

This support for the necessity of fan interventions can apply equally well to Gillen and McKelvie's *Young Avengers*. While Gillen and McKelvie's series features plenty of images of Hulkling and Wiccan kissing, the characters' romance still takes a backseat to action sequences and humor. If you want outright erotica, or even a simple image of Hulkling and Wiccan casually holding hands, you will only find it in fan art (figure 6.4).[30]

Following *Young Avengers*, America Chavez received her own solo comic series. While many fans celebrated Marvel's decision to assign the series to Gabby Rivera, a queer Latinx writer, *America* was canceled less than a year into its run. Marvel cited the title's lagging sales as the reason for the cancellation, but critics pointed out that the series was canceled before the release of its first trade paperback, which would have allowed it to develop a larger audience in the book market.[31] Hopefully, series like

Young Avengers will serve as a foundation for more candid, varied depictions of LGBTQ characters in mainstream superhero comics, but this will depend on the publishers' willingness to support such titles.

NOTES

1. Rich Johnston, "Allan Heinberg—The Gay Times Interview," Bleeding Cool, February 24, 2011, https://www.bleedingcool.com/2011/02/24/allan-heinberg-the-gay-times-interview/.
2. Esther De Dauw, "Homonormativity in Marvel's Young Avengers: Wiccan and Hulkling's Gender Performance," *Journal of Graphic Novels and Comics* 9, no. 1 (2018): 63.
3. De Dauw, "Homonormativity," 66.
4. De Dauw, "Homonormativity," 66.
5. Scott and Fawaz, "Introduction: Queer about Comics," 199.
6. Isaiah Bradley first appears in *Truth: Red, White, and Black* (2003) by Robert Morales and Kyle Baker. In this limited series, it is revealed that the super-soldier serum that was used to create Captain America but subsequently lost was tested on African American soldiers in an attempt to re-create it. The sole survivor of the test program, Isaiah gains superpowers and dons Captain America's uniform, but is later court-martialed and imprisoned by the American government.
7. David Coughlan, "The Naked Hero and Model Man: Costumed Identity in Comic Book Narratives," in *Heroes of Film, Comics and American Culture*, ed. Lisa M. DeTora (Jefferson, NC: McFarland, 2009), 238.
8. Allan Heinberg and Jim Cheung, *Young Avengers*, no. 6, in *Young Avengers: The Complete Collection* (New York: Marvel Comics, 2016).
9. Coughlan, "The Naked Hero," 241.
10. Susan Hekman, *Private Selves, Public Lives* (University Park, PA: Penn State University Press, 2004), 66.
11. Eve Kosofsky Sedgwick, *Epistemology of the Closet* (Berkeley: University of California Press, 1990), 70.
12. Michael Warner, "Publics and Counterpublics," in *Publics and Counterpublics* (Brooklyn, NY: Zone Books, 2002), 67.
13. Warner, "Publics and Counterpublics," 119.
14. However, it is later revealed that all of Noh-Varr's major relationships were with women.
15. Prodigy loses his power as a result of the *House of M* crossover event. However, he does retain the knowledge and skills that he had previously absorbed.
16. Kieron Gillen and Jamie McKelvie, *Young Avengers*, no. 15, in *Young Avengers Omnibus* (New York: Marvel Comics, 2014).
17. Gillen and McKelvie, *Young Avengers*, no. 15.
18. Gillen and McKelvie, *Young Avengers*, no. 1.
19. Andrew Wheeler (2014) describes the depiction of Noh-Varr, and this scene

in particular, as an attempt to create a sex symbol that would appeal to a new audience of female and gay readers.

20. During the final battle of *The Children's Crusade*, Dr. Doom kills Cassie Lang (a.k.a. Stature), the size-shifting Young Avenger and daughter of Scott Lang (a.k.a. Ant-Man). After Dr. Doom is defeated, Iron Lad destroys Vision for preventing him from using his time-traveling powers to save Cassie. Following the deaths of his two teammates, Eli retires his identity as Patriot and leaves the team.

21. Gillen and McKelvie, *Young Avengers*, no. 1.

22. Gillen and McKelvie, *Young Avengers*, nos. 2 and 12.

23. Lauren Berlant and Michael Warner, "Sex in Public," in *Publics and Counterpublics*, auth. Michael Warner (Brooklyn, NY: Zone Books, 2002), 193.

24. Berlant and Warner, "Sex in Public," 199.

25. Berlant and Warner, "Sex in Public," 204.

26. Gillen and McKelvie, *Young Avengers*, no. 4.

27. Andrew Wheeler, "At Last: Hulkling and Wiccan Share First Kiss in 'Young Avengers: The Children's Crusade' #9," Comics Alliance, March 8, 2012, http://comicsalliance.com/hulkling-wiccan-first-kiss-young-avengers/.

28. For a full account of the rise of female readership over the past decade, see Tim Hanley, "The Evolution of Female Readership," in *Gender and the Superhero Narrative*, ed. Michael Goodrum, Tara Prescott, and Philip Smith (Jackson: University of Mississippi Press, 2018), or Stephanie Orme, "Femininity and Fandom: The Dual-Stigmatisation of Female Comic Book Fans," *Journal of Graphic Novels and Comics* 7, no. 4 (2016): 403–416. According to these sources, women now constitute 40 percent of comic shop customers and roughly half of comic convention attendees. While there is less available statistical evidence of increases across other demographics, the creation of expressly inclusive fan spaces (e.g., Flame Con), retailers (e.g., Books with Pictures in Portland, Oregon, and Amalgam Comics and Coffeehouse in Philadelphia, Pennsylvania), and publishers (e.g., Beyond Press and Lion Forge Comics) over the past decade indicate similar trends.

29. Schott, "From Fan Appropriation," 25.

30. In their online galleries and self-published sketchbooks, DeviantArt user Cris-Art depicts Teddy and Billy in a full range of intimate moments, from casual embraces during holidays to various sex acts. The range of Cris-Art's works underscores the relative lack of romantic depictions in the actual comics, as well as fans' desire for more. Cris-Art, "Holding Hands," DeviantArt, 2012, https://cris-art.deviantart.com/art/Holding-Hands-330121836. See cris_art on Instagram for more examples of the artist's work.

31. Susana Polo, "Marvel Exec Insists Wave of Cancellations Not Motivated by Book Diversity," Polygon, December 22, 2017, https://www.polygon.com/comics/2017/12/22/16810138/marvel-exec-insists-wave-of-cancellations-not-motivated-by-books-diversity.

PART II

FILM, TELEVISION AND FAN CULTURE

7

X-MEN FILMS AND THE DOMESTICATION OF DISSENT
Sexuality, Race, and Respectability

CHRISTOPHER B. ZEICHMANN

Bryan [Singer] embraces this Martin Luther King versus Malcolm X approach to the values that are being presented.

> Ralph Winter, producer of *X-Men* (2000) and *X2* (2003)

"Mutant" was a stand-in for "gay."

> Bryan Singer, director of *X-Men* (2000) and *X2* (2003)

One of the most iconic properties in the world of Marvel Comics is the X-Men, a superheroic team composed of mutants born with the capacity for superpowers. Created in 1963 by Stan Lee and Jack Kirby, hot on the heels of their cocreation of the Hulk, the Fantastic Four, Thor, Iron Man, and many others, the X-Men have long engaged in social justice rhetoric built around identity politics, with the franchise's main characters marginalized due to their status as mutants. This marginalization frequently manifests in stories where the X-Men and other mutants must navigate state violence or its threat, such as anti-mutant legislation, anti-mutant policing (e.g., the robot Sentinels programmed to find and kill mutants), hate crimes tacitly accepted by the state (e.g., Friends of Humanity, an anti-mutant hate group), and the prospect of state-sponsored suppression or genocide (e.g., the "Mutant Control Act"). Because otherness and persecution have long been central to the characterization of mutants in Marvel Comics, the X-Men franchise has taken to analogizing mutants with various real-world emancipatory projects. Stories of the X-Men and other mutants commonly evoke discourses of racial liberation, post-Holocaust Jewish politics, disability, and queerness.[1] A Jim Crow metaphor, for instance, can be read in stories where humans attempt to segregate mutants from humanity. Similarly, Black separatist or Zionist discourse can be read into X-Men archnemesis Magneto's founding of a mutant-only nation of Genosha; disability themes are present in stories centered on Professor Xavier's paraplegia; and queer themes are available in numerous stories involving the necessity of mutants hiding their powers from their friends, family, or government, and/or "coming out" to those same people and institutions. These stories vary in their message, ranging from narratives of hope and resilience to those of loss and fear.

The X-Men, however, are hardly the only mutants affected by persecution. The primary opponents of the X-Men are Magneto and his variously named Brotherhood of (Evil) Mutants. X-Men stories featuring Magneto often explore differing approaches to the threat of state violence. Whereas Professor Xavier and his X-Men generally advance peaceful approaches to mutant political liberation, Magneto and the Brotherhood commonly exhibit a greater willingness to enact violence against their oppressors. Critics and fans have often viewed Professor Xavier and his X-Men as an analogue for Martin Luther King Jr. and Magneto as an analogue for Malcolm X, inasmuch as Xavier advocates reconciliation with mutants' human oppressors (e.g., making peace whenever possible), whereas Magneto advances a more separatist and nationalist approach to mutant identity (e.g., exhibiting hostility toward humans and founding the mutant-only country of Genosha).[2] Like Martin and Malcolm, Xavier and Magneto have a friendly and respectful rivalry within and despite their distinct approaches to state violence. The remarks of John Trushell represent a common interpretation of this dynamic:

> Professor Xavier and his X-Men, who sought accommodation with homo sapiens, recalled moderate elements of the civil rights movement of the 1960s as exemplified by Martin Luther King, Jr. King, head of the Southern Christian Leadership Conference,

maintained during the March on Washington for Jobs and Freedom in August 1963 that "the Negro dream is rooted in the American dream." Militant mutants such as Magneto and his Brotherhood of Evil Mutants, who "disdained to cooperate with homo sapiens", resembled increasingly radical elements. These included the Nation of Islam whose best-known spokesperson, Malcolm X, advocated black nationalism, and the Student Non-violent Coordinating Committee, latterly headed by Stokely Carmichael who, in Canton, Mississippi, publicly proclaimed "Black Power" in 1966.[3]

X-Men cocreator Stan Lee expressed sympathy for Magneto in similar terms:

> I did not think of Magneto as a bad guy. He, according to his philosophy and [how he] saw the world, was a good guy. He was just trying to strike back at the bad people who were so bigoted and so racist . . . against the mutants. . . . He was a menace, but I never thought of him as a villain, as "bad."[4]

Granting Lee the benefit of considerable hindsight—Lee was the one who decided that Magneto's team was named the Brotherhood of *Evil* Mutants, after all—it is clear that the X-Men and the Brotherhood were meant to represent differing approaches to the experience of prejudice and persecution.

But how does this Martin-Malcolm distinction fit within the broader political analogies of the X-Men franchise, which now includes dozens of long-running, serialized comic books as well as multiple cartoons, video games, television shows, and films? As mentioned, X-Men stories evoke a number of real-world social concerns, including issues related to gender and sexual identity, racism, post-Holocaust Jewish identity, and disability. Should the reader infer that the franchise prioritizes one of these over the others, or are we to interpret X-Men stories as a commentary on generalized notions of oppression? Erik Dussere, for instance, claims that across the history of X-Men stories, "the most forceful metaphor represented by mutanthood is homosexuality. Homosexuality, like mutancy, is a hidden difference—gays walk among us, and we never know who might be one. It is a condition that manifests itself in adolescence, and when it does, it frequently causes the confused and scared young person to be ostracized from both community and family."[5]

Martin Lund responds to claims that X-Men stories are built around a single, dominant experience of oppression by highlighting the danger of conflating distinct depictions of the X-Men across time. As Lund observes, the X-Men's comic book stories have been written and drawn by many different people across what is now a nearly sixty-year history; to suppose that these comics all address the same real-world sociopolitical context is untenable. Racial, queer, Jewish, and other issues were not equally important to all creative teams, so one should expect differing emphases and analogies in different stories. Lund argues that scholars should attend to the distinctive social-historical contexts in which X-Men stories are produced to avoid grand generalizations based on cherry-picking texts across a substantial period of time. As a case in point, it is telling that X-Men stories came to depict their human opponents in the vein of Christian "hate groups" during the time of the Moral Majority, and that mutant heroes became celebrities during the early years of reality television. Lund argues that both fan-based and scholarly analyses tend to link the X-Men with whatever political project the commentators in question are most sympathetic to. As such, producing a more accurate sociopolitical history of the X-Men franchise must include a more self-conscious method of analysis, one that is capable of guarding against commentators projecting their own preferences onto the stories.

 This chapter embraces Lund's methodological challenge by examining a distinct corpus of texts within the X-Men franchise, ascertaining the sociopolitical context within which they were produced, and theorizing the social interests that propel their politics. Specifically, this chapter will examine discourse on state violence in the first two X-Men films, *X-Men* (2000) and *X2: X-Men United* (2003), in conversation with the sexual and racial politics of the context in which these films were produced. These films have much in common, including the bulk of their cast as well as director Bryan Singer, screenwriter David Hayter, and producers Lauren Shuler Donner and Ralph Winter. The films feature discrete stories but operate with a shared continuity, with character arcs and stories initiated in the first film continued and developed in the second. Consequently, it may be helpful to understand the movies as a single and coherent corpus. Singer and Hayter had little involvement in the third film in the series (*X-Men: The Last Stand* [2006]), by which point the original films' story lines were retconned to serve the storytelling needs of the series' new filmmakers; as such, it is reasonable to limit present analysis to the first two films.

 This chapter argues that although they also develop other themes, these two films have a particular interest in conflating varied emancipatory projects into the purportedly universal category of "mutant," and in doing so, conceal how they moralize and prioritize real-world interests differently. Specifically, the films draw valorized parallels between contemporary struggles for queer rights and the X-Men's tensions with state and society, but associate the series' mutant antagonists with the "bad" rhetoric and politics of Black liberation movements. This bifurcated analogy associates queerness with whiteness and moralizes white queerness as "good" in contrast to the analogically "Black" Brotherhood of Mutants. In their ultimate aim to reconcile the white queer X-Men with the US state, the films tacitly condone the state's violence against the Brotherhood and reject its calls for racial liberation and self-determination. These political choices reflect a constellation of discourses specific to the early twenty-first century discourse. This chapter will interrogate the mechanics of those discourses, including methods of justifying old power hierarchies by disguising them as something new.

QUEER LIBERATION IN X-MEN FILMS

From the beginning of the first *X-Men* film, self-identification as a mutant is linked with sexuality: Dr. Jean Grey asserts that "mutations manifest at puberty," and early in the movie, the teenage mutant Rogue's first kiss reveals previously unknown powers. The association of the mutant condition with sexuality becomes more overt and more clearly linked with queerness throughout the films. For instance, the discourse on "passing" as a regular human/nonmutant often serves to associate mutants with same-sex desire, with Professor X asserting that "anonymity is a mutant's first defense against the world's hostility." But while humans are generally oblivious to the true nature of mutants successfully passing, mutants recognize each other as such. For instance, Rogue and Wolverine have an unspoken recognition of their shared nature before they even speak, wherein one is reminded of "gaydar." The queer subtext becomes more explicit in *X2*, where there is a significant subplot concerning Iceman "coming out" as a mutant to his family, culminating in some on-the-nose dialogue with his mother that evokes early twenty-first-century discourse on sexual determinism. In this scene, Iceman's mother speaks the following lines: "When did you first know you were [a mutant]? We still love you. . . . [But] have you tried *not* being a mutant?" Following this uncomfortable exchange and a betrayal by his brother (who alerts police to the presence of Iceman and other mutants), Iceman leaves his childhood home to be with those more understanding. It is implied that the household of Iceman's friend Pyro was even less accepting, as Pyro examines with resentment a smiling family portrait of Iceman's family. Locating one's "birth family" as the site of misunderstanding and potential hostility speaks to a widespread queer experience. This may be further implied with gestures toward "conversion therapy." Case in point: in the same film, the mutant-phobic villain William Stryker is revealed to have overseen the lobotomization of his mutant son, Jason.

The queer subtext of the X-Men films has consequently been a popular topic of discussion. *X-Men: First Class* screenwriter Zach Stenz, who identifies as gay, claims that "Bryan Singer wove his own feelings of outsiderdom as a gay man into the movie series."[6] In an interview contemporaneous with the release of the first film, Singer himself states that "'mutant' was a stand-in for 'gay.'" Film critics across the political spectrum have also noted the propensity of the X-Men films to use such metaphors. Chad Thompson, who self-identifies as "ex-gay"—a social project whereby people experiencing same-sex attraction convert to evangelical Christianity and renounce their previous desires—says that he "saw the movie and discovered that almost every scene in it somehow parallels the struggle to integrate gay and lesbian people into society."[7] A great many think-pieces about the links between the first two X-Men films and queer politics of liberation have also appeared on various websites, message boards, and blogs, as will be seen below. Many film reviews similarly mentioned these connections. A queer subtext seems entirely predictable given the people responsible for the films' production. The director of *X-Men* and *X2*, Bryan Singer, is an openly bisexual man—frequently (mis)identified as gay—and several prominent members of the cast are also positioned along the LGBTQ spectrum. Magneto is played by the openly gay actor Ian McKellen, Rogue is played by the openly bisexual actress Anna Paquin, and Nightcrawler is played by the openly bisexual actor Alan Cumming. In addition, *X2* screenwriters Michael Dougherty and Dan Harris both openly identify as gay. Indeed, McKellen proclaimed that "*X-Men* was a gay man's delight, because it was full of the most amazing divas," citing especially his admiration of Halle Berry (playing Storm).[8] In effect, McKellen suggests that the *X-Men* set is a queer space, so much so that even an actress such as Berry, who does not identify as gay or bisexual, becomes readable as queer.

Discussion of real-world sexuality in the X-Men films would be remiss if its darkest side went unmentioned. Several men have accused Singer and his colleagues of sexual abuse in a manner that implicates *X-Men* and *X2*. In the late 1990s, Singer was a frequent guest at now-infamous parties hosted by tech entrepreneur turned film producer Marc Collins-Rector; he was also a minor investor in Collins-Rector's Digital Entertainment Network (DEN). In 2000, Alex Burton, who met Singer at one of these parties in 1998 and played Pyro in *X-Men* but was replaced for *X2*, sued the DEN founders, including Collins-Rector, for systematically raping and drugging him; though Burton eventually dropped the charges, in 2002, Collins-Rector was convicted of transporting minors across state lines for purposes of sex, making him a registered sex offender. In addition, in 2004, Brian Peck, a friend of Singer's who had cameo appearances in the first two X-Men films and was featured on the audio commentary for the *X-Men* DVD, was convicted of sexually abusing a minor. Finally, in 2017, Cesar Sanchez-Guzman sued Singer himself, alleging the director had raped him in 2003, when he was seventeen. Several more men have made on-the-record and anonymous allegations in a similar vein; one accuser, Victor Valdovinos, claims Singer molested him on the set of the film *Apt Pupil* (1998) when he was thirteen years old.[9] These events and allegations do not invalidate the cultural importance of Singer's X-Men films as historical documents, but they can influence their legacy—a matter addressed in the conclusion of this chapter.

The X-Men's long-standing discourse of otherness was well positioned to touch on the hot-button LGBTQ issues prevalent during the time of *X-Men*'s and *X2*'s production and release. The first film was produced under the presidency of Bill Clinton, a politician with a complex relationship with queer liberation. On the one hand, President Clinton enacted a series of legislative measures that were unambiguously detrimental to queer rights. The Defense of Marriage Act prevented full legal recognition of same-sex marriages, and "Don't Ask, Don't Tell" codified the military's ban on queers. On the other hand, Clinton vocally opposed sodomy laws, declared June "Pride Month," and was the first presidential candidate endorsed by the Human Rights Campaign. Another flashpoint of Clinton-era debates surrounding LGBTQ rights was the public outrage that followed the 1998 murder of Matthew Shepard, a case wherein evidence pointed to Shepard being attacked because he was gay. Shepard's murder compelled a considerable push to add queer victim identities to hate crimes legislation both at the Wyoming state level and the national level. Though both pushes were unsuccessful, the margins were close: the Wyoming bill failed with a 30–30 vote (a tie was insufficient to pass the bill), and although hate crime legislation passed in both the US House and Senate (due to the fact that the legislative and executive branches were all Democratic for the first time in over a decade), the provision regarding sexual identity was stripped by the House conference committee. Within this context, the unwillingness of the government in the first two X-Men films to protect mutants as a minority—and, indeed, its tacit support for anti-mutant discrimination—allegorizes a real-world desire for protection from anti-queer discrimination.

Navigating this ambivalence toward the state may be the single most significant theme in these X-Men films. In the first film, the impetus for the conflict between Professor X and Magneto is their differing posture toward the prospect of the "Mutant Registration Act" that would require all mutants to register with the US government. For Magneto, this registration evokes his experiences as a child at the Auschwitz concentration camp. "I've heard these arguments before," Magneto comments to Xavier, after showing the prisoner number tattoo he received at the camp. To prevent another genocide, Magneto believes it necessary to liberate mutants from humanity's oppression with a readiness to practice violence. Xavier, by contrast, has a more optimistic posture through the films, established in his retort to Magneto: "That was a long time ago. Mankind has evolved since then." Whatever oppression Magneto experienced during the Holocaust, Xavier is optimistic not only that similar actions will not happen again, but that state violence against mutants can be prevented by maintaining good relationships with the public and official channels.

In both films, the Brotherhood remains outside the legislative-political system that threatens it. As anti-mutant legislation gains traction, the Brotherhood threatens politicians and attempts to turn them into mutants in order to align their interests with the Brotherhood's, surely an act of violence by any definition. In contrast, while the X-Men largely remain unknown to the public in the first film, they nonetheless counteract anti-mutant legislation by working *inside* the legislative political system, efforts that ultimately help to protect that system: a "closeted" Jean Grey gives a speech to the US Senate, *X2* concludes with the X-Men reassuring the president of the United States that they will not harm humanity, and the X-Men as a team prevent nearly all facets of the Brotherhood's plot against humankind. The X-Men try to ensure that politics-as-usual remain uninterrupted, all while passing as regular humans to the powers that be. Indeed, Xavier and his students note that many parents are unaware that they sent their children to a school for mutants, as the school presents itself to the general public under the generic name Xavier's School for the Gifted. While using the guise of a private school to provide adolescent mutants a place to escape their family's judgmental gaze, Xavier also provides a closet for the adult X-Men, whom outsiders understand as mere "instructors."

Even as the films draw upon barely concealed queer discourse, they also encourage viewers to draw connections with Black liberation discourse. Magneto, for instance, forms a militant liberation group that is tellingly called the *Brotherhood* of Mutants, and he commonly refers to other mutants as "brothers." This evokes the use of *brother* as a term of

Black racial filiation and, in the Black liberation organization, the African Blood Brotherhood. There are also references to secret scientific experimentation on Wolverine and other mutants, recalling both experiments within concentration camps during the Holocaust and the Tuskegee syphilis experiments performed surreptitiously on Black men from 1932 to 1972 by the US government. Perhaps the single most explicit linkage between the Brotherhood of Mutants and Black liberation politics comes at the end of the first film, when Magento declares he will fight his oppressors "by any means necessary." This direct quotation of Malcolm X has lent credibility to commentators who understand the Magneto–Professor X conflict as analogous to the relationship between Malcolm and Martin; clearly identifying Magneto as a Malcolm-style figure encourages the viewer to see Xavier as a Martin Luther King Jr. analogue.

The films elaborate upon the Black liberation analogy in an exchange from *X2* between Nightcrawler and Mystique, both of whom have rich blue skin. Mystique, however, can shapeshift, which compels X-Men member Nightcrawler to ask, "Then why not stay in disguise all of the time? You know, look like everyone else." Mystique, a member of the Brotherhood, responds tersely: "Because we shouldn't have to." This exchange points to basic questions about privilege, skin color, and racial passing. One might recall Malcolm X's discussion of Black men straightening their hair (i.e., conking) to adhere more closely to white beauty standards. He describes the aftermath of his first conk in his autobiography:

> This was my first really big step toward self-degradation: when I endured all of that pain, literally burning my flesh to have it look like a white man's hair. I had joined that multitude of Negro men and women in America who are brainwashed into believing that the black people are "inferior"—and white people "superior"—that they will even violate and mutilate their God-created bodies to try to look "pretty" by white standards.[10]

Mystique has little interest in conforming to human norms of appearance, instead accepting her mutant body as beautiful by different standards. In addition, when Magneto meets Pyro, the Brotherhood leader asks the teenager what his name is, to which the latter replies "John." Magneto, unsatisfied with this answer, asks, "What's your *real* name, John?" To which the teenager responds, "Pyro." Here we are reminded of discourse on "slave names" and how many participants in Black liberation movements changed their names to ones that were not assigned to their ancestors by former owners; for instance, Malcolm Little took the names Malcolm X and Malik el-Shabazz, with the "X" symbolizing the lost name of his African ancestors.[11] Moreover, this exchange between Pyro and Magneto is nearly identical to a fictionalized scene in the 1992 film *Malcolm X*:

> Brother Baines: "What's your name?"
> Malcolm X: "Malcolm Little."
> Brother Baines: "No, that's the name of the slave masters who owned your family. . . . Who are you?"

The examples of both Malcolm X and Magneto assert that minorities cannot cultivate a sense of self-worth rooted in heritage without rejecting social norms that erase or diminish that heritage.

The use of (at least) two distinct political analogues has led many commentators to conclude that the X-Men films evoke a conflict that extends beyond racial and sexual boundaries, in the form of a universalized experience of oppression common to humanity in general. Singer himself states that within the first X-Men film "there's an underlying philosophy about prejudice, about feeling outcast, fear of the unknown, trying to find your place in the world," which Singer deems "very universal concepts."[12] Indeed, the films often blur lines between multiple discourses. Mystique tells the anti-mutant politician Senator Kelly that "people like you were the reason I was afraid to go to school as a child." Mystique's language is vague enough to evoke many different contexts. One can interpret her words as an evocation of the Little Rock Nine, who suffered physical and verbal abuse due to their role in desegregating Arkansas schools. Alternatively, this dialogue could recall the experience of virtually any "outsider" who was bullied by schoolmates, whether due to sexual orientation, economic status, disability, or other factors.

While a universalizing message of anti-oppression might be appealing, it is built upon an inadequate reading of these films. Black liberation metaphors are more often evoked by the Brotherhood of Mutants, whereas emancipatory queer politics are more often found among the X-Men. Given how these groups and their activities are heavily moralized, this characterization seems to serve a normative project advancing social interests within the so-called real world. I would like to adopt the language of Sara Ahmed to suggest that the proximity of discourses on queerness and the X-Men, and the proximity of Black liberation and the Brotherhood of Mutants, generates a shared "stickiness" between proximate categories that entails an exchange of attributes within these pairs.[13] These categories are deployed as part of a normative critique wherein the X-Men are positioned to discredit radical liberationist movements. To put it another way: these films show characters drawing upon the discourses of wildly different social formations (ones that are not even participating in the same cultural debates), but also stack the deck against movements critical of state and racial violence. Professor X and Magneto are not simple analogues to Martin and Malcolm, but rather are more akin to the Human Rights Campaign (with its emphasis on lobbying the government, quest for queer "equality," and noted diversity problems) and a racist caricature of the Nation of Islam (which is villainized and bears little resemblance to any groups of significance).[14] In these films, there is a salient distinction between assimilationist/integrationist politics and revolutionary politics; in addition, these politics are differently encoded with discourses on sexuality and race, and are imbued with moral authority constitutive of these discourses. In short, the first two X-Men films advance a deeply racialized politics of queer liberation that can be read as anti-Black. We might thus consider the first two X-Men movies as a homonormative project.

BIFURCATED POLITICS OF LIBERATION

Up to this point, this chapter has avoided giving much specificity to the X-Men films' depiction of queer emancipation. I will begin to address this by observing that a specifically *queer* form of political discourse functions as a source of the X-Men's moral authority. Xavier's politics are triangulated against anti-mutant fanatics (e.g., Senator Kelly, General Stryker) and Magneto's radical liberationism. It may be helpful to understand Xavier—and, because Xavier and his X-Men are the unambiguous heroes of the series, the X-Men films more generally—as promoting a politics that Lisa Duggan terms homonormativity, that is, "a politics that does not contest dominant heteronormative assumptions and institutions—such as marriage, and its call for monogamy and reproduction—but upholds and sustains them while promising the possibility of a demobilized gay constituency and a privatized, depoliticized gay culture anchored in domesticity and consumption."[15] Duggan notes that homonormative discourse in its current formation was born in the 1990s with the rise of "third way" politics in the geopolitical West. Since this time, various gay (and, less often, lesbian or transgender) groups have been founded on principles that reject both the anti-gay discourse perceived to be on the right and the radicalism perceived to be on the left. Duggan cites the founding principles of the Independent Gay Forum as an example, some of which are quoted here:

- We share a belief in the fundamental virtues of the American system and its tradition of individual liberty, personal moral autonomy and responsibility, and equality before the law. We believe those traditions depend on the institutions of a market economy, free discussion, and limited government.
- We deny "conservative" claims that gays and lesbians pose any threat to social morality or the political order.
- We equally oppose "progressive" claims that gays should support radical social change or restructuring of society.[16]

Homonormative discourse presents itself as a "third way" against its foes on the left and right, emerging as a viable alternative against excessively politicized foils. This rhetorical framework is commonly termed the "horseshoe" model of politics: the far right and far left are closer to each other than they are to centrists; all critique of the liberal-democratic status quo can be reduced to a broad category of "extremism," regardless of the reasons for opposing such a status quo and any differential in social power. By presenting itself as post-ideological, this rhetorical framework's deployment of whiteness is partially concealed through its disavowals of identity politics; gays indeed deserve rights, but "queerness" should not threaten prevailing systems of exploitation within global capitalism (here, "market economy" and "limited government").

Homonormativity is deeply imbued with respectability politics. Respectability politics locates the resolution of injustices against a dispossessed group in their adherence to dominant social norms; those who fail to adhere to respectable norms are thus responsible for any injustices they experience. Modern examples are numerous, but memorable instances in the recent past include media outlets' contrast of the ostensibly more "respectable" protests of Martin Luther King Jr. with the protests of Black Lives Matter (henceforth BLM). Within such contrasts: King's choice to wear suits is often compared unfavorably with more recent urban wear ("pull up your pants," as the saying goes), King's diction is praised in comparison with modern African American vernacular English, King's strict adherence to nonviolence is emphasized in comparison with recent confrontations with state authorities, and so on. The differences between respectable and unrespectable behavioral practices are used not only to explain the unrespectable member of society's experience of injustice, but also to discredit their protests and efforts at rectification; the implication is that protesters who do not dress and speak properly are not worth taking seriously. Respectability politics are particularly frustrating in activist circles because they tend to uphold classist assumptions dictating that the achievement of certain standards of normative decency should govern activist concerns more than rectification of injustice. Any metaphorical dirt can be sufficient reason for respectability advocates to veer away from sociostructural causes of injustice toward blaming individuals for their own circumstances.

Though the concept of respectability politics was developed in reference to Black liberation, it is also widely present in queer politics. In homonormative discourse, respectability politics distances "queer liberation" from any perceived threats to the hegemonic social order; good queers are framed as monogamous, educated, and consumer subjects that would contribute more to global capital if given the chance. Consequently, queer discourse grounded in respectability politics enhances the capacity of queers to act within the prevailing social order, especially via legislation; this would include gay marriage, repealing sodomy laws, inclusion in the military, political relations with "anti-gay" and "sex tourist" nation-states, and so on. In this formulation, queerness becomes, essentially, middle-class respectability preoccupied with *inclusion* within hegemonic social structures. While it is easy to understand why this formulation would be appealing to some, one consequence is that queers who are incapable of middle-class ascendency, or simply do not desire it, become further marginalized; within a homonormative framework, sex work, housing insecurity, HIV/AIDS and other precarious health care situations, gentrification, minimum wage, and mental illness are tangential or irrelevant either in toto or as specifically queer concerns, despite their disproportionate prevalence among queers (especially queers of color). The homonormative framework does not view these things as concerns because those suffering on account of them inhabit "unrespectable" bodies that cannot be incorporated into middle-class subjectivity. This respectability politics also disavows radical politics of liberation; queer critiques of state violence (especially marriage, the military, or the prison state) are increasingly rare, largely due to the mainstreaming of queer political discourse concomitant with the rise of queer respectability politics. Rather, the state discursively acts as a potential agent of liberation after shedding its counterproductive homophobia; queers are "good citizen subjects" that would contribute to the state if possible. Here, one might think of LGBTQ opposition to "Don't Ask, Don't Tell" that positioned queers as loyal soldiers, and support for the legalization of same-sex marriage that positioned queers as productive citizens.

Many radical queer activists have argued that the prevailing quest for "equality" in queer discourse is myopic in its failure to consider the intersectional issues at play, especially the role of "equality" in perpetuating state violence. For instance, Yasmin Nair observes that same-sex marriage was long a tertiary concern to queer activists, until wealthy whites became involved:

> When the secret history of gay marriage is finally written, it will reveal that gay marriage was foisted upon a community with few resources, held hostage by a wealthy few. The mid-90s onwards saw the rise of out gay men and women, mostly men and mostly white, who were powerful and wealthy and wanted a way to ensure that their aspirations to be seen as just like everyone else would be fulfilled and that their wealth would stay in their families and continue to enrich the financial interests they had so carefully nurtured. The secret history of gay marriage is that it has never been about "equality" in any real sense, but about ensuring that a small section of gay men and women are able to hold on to their wealth.[17]

Nair further observes that the rise of queer nonprofits focused upon marriage has had a negative effect on funding for organizations working on HIV/AIDS issues and the concerns of queer youth; indeed, since same-sex marriage is often presumed to be the end goal of queer activism, the concerns of more marginal queer populations are, in the wake of the legalization of gay marriage, more commonly dismissed. In short, there is reason to be suspicious of detectably "white" queer political discourse and its attendant calls for state intervention, as this discourse has a propensity to negatively effect and even exclude queers of color.

Returning to the purported Martin-Malcolm distinction between Professor X and Magneto in the first two X-Men films, it is clear that these films operate on a "horseshoe" model of politics. Magneto regularly claims that his plans are an ironic reversal of anti-mutant humans, at one point explicitly suggesting that mutants "play by [their oppressors'] rules." Xavier likewise asserts that both anti-mutant humans and Magneto are guilty of attempting to provoke a cataclysmic war between humans and mutants. As far as Xavier is concerned, both extremes lack moral authority; the center is where the solution to mutant-human relations will be found.

Through the comparison between Xavier's "good" mutants and Magneto's "evil" Brotherhood, these X-Men films delineate acceptable and unacceptable dissent. Acceptable dissent has two major characteristics in these films. First, acceptable dissent occurs inside oppressive systems—especially the nation-state—to facilitate a more equitable world for the oppressed. Second, the end goal of acceptable dissent is a state of peace between oppressor and oppressed. Though they are capable of "passing" as human in most circumstances, the X-Men desire a world where humans and mutants live alongside each other in peace. In short, the X-Men advance a privatized politics of mutant liberation, wherein being a "mutant" is a matter of concern limited to the private sphere of liberal discourse on tolerance. Magneto and the Brotherhood, in contrast, reject each of these elements of acceptable dissent. In their view, oppressive systems are essentially beyond repair and require radical intervention to be rendered just, mutants supersede humans evolutionarily and socially, and mutant liberation is an adamantly "public" discourse that is inherently political. This delineation of acceptable versus unacceptable forms of protest fits firmly within respectability politics. In these films, the state is inherently legitimate and radical forms of protest degenerate into unproductive violence, culminating in a "third way" politics via horseshoe rhetoric.

Recalling how Magneto and his Brotherhood evoke Black liberation politics, the films' endorsement of homonormative quietism becomes even more troubling. As one might guess, homonormative discourse has been subjected to ample critique by activists and academics on the left, who cite its willful ignorance of intersectional politics. Homonormative politics' preoccupation with inclusion is often criticized as promoting the ascendancy not only of the middle class but of whiteness more broadly. Jasbir Puar, for instance, observes how, in making queerness a component of the liberal West, homonormativity has also come to legitimate state violence.[18] Consider, for instance, how many European nations require prospective immigrants from Muslim-majority countries to take a questionnaire about their opinions on homosexuality; one wonders how many Americans would perform on such a questionnaire.

The vilification of Black liberation discourse within the first two X-Men films speaks to contemporary real-world events. Though preceding the emergence of the BLM movement by more than a decade, the X-Men films anticipate respectability politicians' polemic against BLM: violent dissent is illegitimate, it is better to work within political systems, the state is ultimately a benevolent force (aside from occasional bad apples), and the like. In this vein, one might consider the aforementioned Independent Gay Forum's dismissal of BLM protests:

> The Gay & Lesbian Alliance Against Defamation, in particular, has sought to align itself with Black Lives Matter despite BLM's incendiary denunciations of police officers—last year, the *New York Post* reported on the deadly rhetoric of the anti-cop movement, with activists calling for the murder of police officers. . . . Embracing BLM was never a good idea. But as I've noted before, now that gay legal equality in the U.S. has been achieved, LGBT left-progressive activists are looking for new causes, and recruiting LGBT battalions in the fight for the progressive agenda is increasingly their mission.[19]

In situating "equality" as the end goal of queer political activism and characterizing it as nearly synonymous with "gay marriage," this argument almost completely erases queers of color.

In a similar vein, the X-Men films not only place Black liberation discourse exclusively in the mouth of villains, but also skew this Black liberation politics to the point of caricature. In the first two X-Men films, "by any means necessary" no longer expresses a last resort to violence, but rather Magneto's eagerness to harm *homo sapiens*; Malcolm's advocacy of Black self-determination by separatism becomes mutant supremacy; and the self-defense of Black liberation becomes the Brotherhood's desire for anti-human genocide. As a result, state violence against the analogically Black Magneto and Brotherhood is rendered as not only acceptable but necessary; Xavier accepts the legitimacy of his friend Magneto's prison sentence, and the X-Men, both individually and as a team, refuse to mete out extrajudicial punishment on those who wronged them. The films' linking of Malcolm-Martin to the politics of Magneto-Xavier is especially pernicious because it maps onto existing uses of these figures in public discourse. Consider, for instance, the frequency with which Martin Luther King Jr. has come to be posthumously associated with the campaign for legalized same-sex marriage by white queers. Examples include the New Civil Rights Movement, think pieces on whether King would have endorsed same-sex marriage, and the trailer of the widely derided film *Stonewall* (2015), which included footage of King's "I Have a Dream" speech.[20] The position of Malcolm is more complicated, in that he has not been afforded the same status as King in the American canon of great men whose support, whether implicit or explicit, can authorize any political project. Rather, the long-standing tendency among whites (both queer and cis-hetero) to deride Malcolm X as an advocate of racialized violence is achieved obliquely; rarely depicted directly, Malcolm tends to be abstracted as a myopic and wild-eyed "Black Power movement" that serves as a foil for the more considered and peaceful civil rights movement (see, e.g., *Forrest Gump*, *The Butler*).[21]

The first two X-Men films do not participate passively in this heavily moralized Malcolm-Martin binary. Instead, the films actively discredit Magneto by evoking a distortion of Malcolm X and the Black Power movement, while it is Xavier's ostensive resemblance to both Martin Luther King Jr. and white queerness that legitimates his politics. It is *precisely because* Magneto is willing to achieve mutant liberation "by any means necessary" that the viewer recognizes he is a villain. Likewise, the queerness of Xavier and the X-Men constitutes their heroism; the need to "pass" and "come out," as well as the fact that they were "born that way" and are judged by their families, marks them as tragic heroes, and their refusal to practice violence against their oppressors further substantiates their heroism. Even on a visual level, the X-Men are costumed in relatively uniform garb, whereas the Brotherhood's refusal to conform is indicated by their wildly different (and even nonexistent) clothing: Magneto's cape adds a regal flair, Sabretooth's fur highlights his savagery, and Mystique's nudity represents the threat of her sexuality.

Perhaps most essential to this metaphor is the fact that while Xavier heroically seeks reconciliation with his oppressors, Magneto is marked as a villain because of his antagonism toward humans, regardless of their personal stance on mutant liberation. This allows the viewer to summarily dismiss efforts of Black liberationists to implicate whiteness as a category apart from personal prejudice; the viewer is reassured that any discourse implicating whiteness should only implicate individual whites who gleefully oppress others (here, African Americans and queers). We are also assured that radical Black liberationists differ little from the people they view as their oppressors, since both groups are ultimately oppressive. It is furthermore telling that Bryan Singer moralizes Xavier's assimilationist message as having a specifically American character: "[Xavier and Magneto] both embrace mutantkind. Magneto has a very separatist view. Professor X believes that *all men and mutants are created equal.*"[22] Here, Singer links characters he identifies as queer with the broader project of the American nation-state: white queers become Americans *par excellence*.

This is not to say that blackness is entirely irrelevant to the X-Men, as the Black (especially Jim Crow–era) experience of prejudice and oppression looms over all mutants. Neil Shyminsky observes that the mutant metaphor is sufficiently mutable that all readers are capable of identifying with the marginalized "other." Shyminsky also argues, however, that this universalism encourages appropriation: "The X-Men *actually* solicit identification from a similarly young, white, and male readership, allowing these readers to misidentify themselves as the 'other.'"[23] In the first two X-Men films, this appropriation comes across particularly clearly with the character Storm—the only Black mutant in these two films—and her adamant rejection of the radicalized politics of the Brotherhood of Mutants. In these films, Storm is visibly Black but culturally white; this is consistent with the complex history of her sexualization, as argued by J. Andrew Deman in the present volume. In this, her steadfast (and highly visible) loyalty to Xavier helps confirm the goodness of the X-Men's respectability politics while casting into further relief the immorality of Magneto and his allies, despite their greater affinity for Black liberation discourse.

CONCLUSION

This chapter certainly does not contend that queer metaphors are bad, or even that they are inherently bad in X-Men stories. Rather, it is my contention that the metaphorical depiction of queerness, as deployed in the first two X-Men films, is problematic to the extent that it reinforces historical and prevailing real-world anti-Black respectability politics. The first two X-Men films are emphatically *anti*-intersectional, in that queer liberation and Black liberation are placed in an antagonistic and ultimately irreconcilable relationship, wherein the former is lent legitimacy by its refusal of violence and insistence upon gaining inclusion within hegemonic social structures that perpetuate the marginalization of people of color. Same-sex attraction is prioritized above all other identities, setting aside vital questions of power, especially those relating to race but also those related to ethnicity, disability, class, and age. This neglect of the complexities of power inescapably recalls Singer's association with men who have been convicted of exploiting their power to commit sexual abuse against minors, as well as Singer's own alleged commission of similar acts.

Lest one assume that the first two X-Men films are an exception to the rule, X-Men comic books have rarely handled racial metaphors with grace or insight. One particularly ham-fisted effort at insight can be found during a scene from *Uncanny X-Men* #196 (1985), wherein one of Kitty Pryde's acquaintances at Columbia University, a mutantphobic Black teenager, asks Kitty if she is a "mutie," a derogatory slur for mutants. Kitty replies with a rhetorical question: "Gee, I dunno, Phil—are you a *nigger*?"[24] From there, Kitty proceeds to make a point that *all* name-calling hurts, regardless of race; this reminder is unfortunately reminiscent of the anti-BLM insistence that "all lives matter." On the one hand, it is hardly surprising that a comic book series dominated by white creative teams tends to reiterate hegemonic white perspectives; authors write about familiar topics and things they care about. Yet this episode is nonetheless particularly troubling in its rhetorical framing. This scene between Kitty and the Black classmate is presented as a teaching moment for the reader about being "intentionally hurtful" to others, but in order to make this point, anti-Black racism—an all-too *real* issue—is casually dismissed in order to highlight an entirely fictitious account of marginalization (i.e., the persecution of mutants) by a character who, while narratively Jewish, is visually white. The employment of a Black classmate enables this dismissal; it is as though Kitty is saying that fictional prejudice against mutants exceeds or is more important than real-life prejudices against Black people.

This tone-deaf exchange was not an isolated occurrence; similar scenes occur throughout the history of X-Men stories[25] and continue to crop up even now. For instance, in *Uncanny Avengers* #5 (2013) team leader and longtime X-Men member Havok rejects the label "mutant" while advancing a strongly assimilationist politics of mutant identity:

> Having an X-Gene doesn't bond me to anyone. It doesn't *define* me. In fact, I see the very word "mutant" as *divisive*. Old thinking that serves to further separate us from our fellow man. We are all *humans*. [. . .] We are defined by our *choices*, not the makeup of our *genes*. So please, don't call us *mutants*. The "M" word represents everything I hate.[26]

While the creative team probably intended this to be racially progressive rhetoric evocative of MLK, *Comics Alliance* columnist Andrew Wheeler rightly observed that it is "not good policy for any minority group, even a fictional one that exists as metaphor. It's not a position that any credible spokesman for a minority group would advance."[27] The possibility that this scene was intended to encourage mature debate is further undercut by writer Rick Remender's response to those it offended: on Twitter, Remender encouraged critics to "drown yourself [in] hobo piss."

In the end, although the X-Men's mutants provide a potent vehicle for political metaphors, most attempts at a "profound" message on American racial politics have merely reinscribed the legitimacy of white hegemony, albeit in a somewhat friendlier version than its present form. Consistent within these depictions is the supposition that "Black Power" is semantically and ideologically equivalent to the slogan "White Power" and the belief that race relations will only be rectified when Black antagonism toward whites and whiteness ceases. Too often, X-Men stories reduce the concept of racism to "race-based prejudice," an individual-attitudinal set of beliefs and practices intended to harm racial others. Where white creative teams and fans are concerned, this conception of racism is self-serving; it effectively places racism "over there," in the bodies of individual, monadic bigots, which in turn implicitly frees the accuser from participation in racist norms.[28] The problems and appeal of this definition are evident in the example of the first two X-Men films, which enable (white) fans to tell themselves, *I am not racist/anti-mutant, ergo Magneto must be a villain if he, like Malcolm X, condemns all whites/humans.* For X-Men stories to capitalize on their potential for an insightful discussion of American racial politics, it is necessary to first engage the *actual* workings of racism in the United States, rather than reinscribing the hegemonic ideology of race.

NOTES

Thanks to Ren Ito for conversations that culminated in this article. Michiko Bown-Kai, Laura Zeichman, and Anna Peppard also offered feedback that led to a much stronger article. Because this chapter refers to numerous digital publications, all links are collected at www.christopherzeichmann.com/x-men/ for ease of reference.

1. See Martin Lund, "The Mutant Problem: X-Men, Confirmation Bias, and the Methodology of Comics and Identity," *European Journal of American Studies* 10, no. 2 (2015).

2. E.g., see Marc DiPaolo, *War, Politics and Superheroes: Ethics and Propaganda in Comics and Film* (Jefferson, NC: McFarland, 2011), 238; Hilary Goldstein, "Xavier vs. Magneto: A Philosophical Debate," IGN, May 4, 2006, http://www.ign.com/articles/2006/05/05/xavier-vs-magneto-a-philosophical-debate; Mikhail Lyubansky, "Prejudice Lessons from the Xavier Institute," in *The Psychology of Superheroes: An Unauthorized Exploration*, ed. Robin S. Rosenberg and Jennifer Canzoneri (Dallas, TX: BenBella, 2008), 75–90, all cited in Lund, "Mutant Problem." See also the somewhat more nuanced discussion in Darowski, *X-Men and the Mutant Metaphor*, 30–32.

3. John M. Trushell, "American Dreams of Mutants: The X-Men—'Pulp' Fiction, Science Fiction, and Superheroes," *Journal of Popular Culture* 38 (2004): 154.

4. Quoted in John Rhett Thomas, *Marvel Spotlight: Uncanny X-Men 500 Issues Celebration* (New York: Marvel Comics, 2008), 5, 7. It is worth noting that a civil rights subtext originated in the later *Uncanny X-Men* stories written by Chris Claremont (1975–1991), though Lee is eager to retroactively claim it for himself. As Lund has demonstrated, Lee-Kirby stories consistently depicted Magneto and the Brotherhood of Evil Mutants as "terrorists and fanatics, not activists."

5. Erik Dussere, "The Queer World of the X-Men," *Salon*, July 12, 2000, https://www.salon.com/2000/07/12/x_men/.

6. Quoted in Michael Brown, "'Mutant' as a Codeword for 'Gay' in the X-Men Movies," *Townhall*, November 3, 2011, https://townhall.com/columnists/michael-brown/2011/11/03/mutant-as-a-codeword-for-gay-in-the-x-men-movies-n1216545.

7. Chad Thompson, "More Than Mutants," *Relevant*, July 26, 2006, https://relevantmagazine.com/culture/film/features/3383-more-than-mutants.

8. Quoted in Nigel M. Smith, "Ian McKellen: 'X-Men Was a Gay Man's Delight, Because It Was Full of the Most Amazing Divas,'" *Guardian*, November 21, 2015, https://www.theguardian.com/film/2015/nov/21/ian-mckellen-x-men-was-a-gay-mans-delight-because-it-was-full-of-the-most-amazing-divas.

9. For a thorough discussion of the allegations against Singer as of March 2019, see Alex French and Maximillian Potter, "Nobody Is Going to Believe You," *Atlantic* 323, no. 2 (2019): 50–65.

10. Malcolm X, *The Autobiography of Malcolm X* (New York: One World, 1992), 64.

11. Malcolm X, *Autobiography*, 229.

12. "Bryan Singer," *Charlie Rose*, July 14, 2000, https://charlierose.com/videos/3806.

13. Sara Ahmed, *The Cultural Politics of Emotion* (Edinburgh, UK: Edinburgh University Press, 2004).

14. Note the forceful criticism of the purported Martin-Malcolm metaphor among Black comic book critics, e.g., David Brothers, "Professor X Isn't Martin Luther King, and Magneto Isn't Malcolm X, Either," 4th Letter, April 3, 2013, http://4thletter.net/2013/04/professor-x-isnt-martin-luther-king-and-magneto-isnt-malcolm-x-either/; P. Djèlí Clark, "On Malcolm, Martin, and that X-Men Analogy Thing," The Musings of a Disgruntled Haradrim, February 21, 2015, https://pdjeliclark.wordpress.com/2015/02/21/on-malcolm-martin-and-that-x-men-analogy-thing/; J. Lamb, "Magneto Was Right," Nerds of Color, September 18, 2013, https://thenerdsofcolor.org/2013/09/18/magneto-was-right/; Orion Martin, "What If the X-Men Were Black?," The Hooded Utilitarian, December 16, 2013, http://www.hoodedutilitarian.com/2013/12/what-if-the-x-men-were-black/; Charles Pulliam-Moore, "It's Time for the X-Men's Stories about Discrimination to Evolve," io9, Gizmodo, September 26, 2017, https://io9.gizmodo.com/its-time-for-the-x-mens-stories-about-discrimination-to-1818715399; Smiley Yearwood, "For the Billionth Time, Magneto Is Not Malcolm X: Thoughts on Appropriation and Mutants of Color," Smiley in the Mirror, September 11, 2015, https://smileyyearwood.com/2015/09/11/for-the-billionth-time-magneto-is-not-malcolm-x-thoughts-on-appropriation-and-mutants-of-color/. Cf. Heather J. Hicks, "Impalement: Race and Gender in Bryan

Singer's X-Men," *Cineaction* 85 (2011): 52–62; Jason Smith, "Mutating Minorities: White Racial Framing and Group Positioning," in *The X-Men Films: A Cultural Analysis*, ed. Claudia Bucciferro (Lanham, MD: Rowman & Littlefield, 2016), 179–192.

15. Lisa Duggan, "The New Homonormativity: The Sexual Politics of Neoliberalism," in *Materializing Democracy: Toward a Revitalized Cultural Politics*, ed. Russ Castronovo and Dana D. Nelson (Durham, NC: Duke University Press, 2002), 179.

16. Independent Gay Forum, "About IGF CultureWatch," IGF CultureWatch, https://igfculturewatch.com/about/.

17. Yasmin Nair, "The Secret History of Gay Marriage," June 25, 2015, http://yasminnair.net/content/secret-history-gay-marriage.

18. Jasbir K. Puar, *Terrorist Assemblages: Homonationalism in Queer Times* (Durham, NC: Duke University Press, 2007).

19. Stephen H. Miller, "Cop Lives Matter," IGF CultureWatch, July 8, 2016, https://igfculturewatch.com/2016/07/08/cop-lives-matter/. In this post, the writer refers to the discredited claim that either New York or Dallas BLM activists chanted, "What do we want? Dead cops."

20. As has been widely discussed, King is a particularly potent site of collective memory, retroactively becoming a figure in service of various political projects. MLK has been linked to white queerness (see Yasmin Nair, "The Gay Marriage Campaign Shamelessly Exploits Martin Luther King," January 19, 2015, http://yasminnair.net/content/gay-marriage-campaign-shamelessly-exploits-martin-luther-king); MLK has been seen as a color-blind Reaganomics advocate (see Denise M. Bostdorff and Steven R. Goldzwig, "History, Collective Memory, and the Appropriation of Martin Luther King, Jr.: Reagan's Rhetorical Legacy," *Presidential Studies Quarterly* 35 [2005]: 661–690); MLK has been described as a respectable liberal (Jermaine M. McDonald, "The Canonization of Martin Luther King Jr.: Collective Memory, Civil Religion, and the Reconstruction of an American Hero" [Ph.D. diss., Emory University, 2015]), etc. For academic analysis on the collective memory of Malcolm X, see Cedric Dewayne Burrows, "The Contemporary Rhetoric about Martin Luther King, Jr., and Malcolm X in the Post-Reagan Era" (master's thesis, Miami University, 2005); James H. Cone, "Demystifying Martin and Malcolm," *Theology Today* 51 (1994): 27–37.

21. See, e.g., Shani Ealey, "What *The Butler* Didn't Reveal about the Black Panther Party," Black Women Unchecked, August 20, 2013, https://blackwomenunchecked.wordpress.com/2013/08/20/what-the-butler-didnt-reveal-about-the-black-panther-party/; Angel Evans, "*The Butler* Movie Review: New Film, Old Stereotypes," Mic, August 23, 2013, https://mic.com/articles/60669/the-butler-movie-review-new-film-old-stereotypes; Jane Rhodes, *Framing the Black Panthers: The Spectacular Rise of a Black Power Icon*, 2nd ed. (Urbana: University of Illinois Press, 2017), 12–29.

22. James B. Meigs, "Pickup Shots," *Premiere: The Movie Magazine* 128 (1997): 55. Emphasis added.

23. Neil Shyminsky, "Mutant Readers, Reading Mutants: Appropriation, Assimilation, and the X-Men," *International Journal of Comic Art* 8 (2006): 388.

24. Chris Claremont (w) and John Romita, Jr. (a), *Uncanny X-Men*, no. 196 (New York: Marvel Comics, 1985). Emphasis in original.

25. Anna F. Peppard documents several similar scenes in her article "Canada's Mutant Body: Nationalism and (Super)Multiculturalism in Alpha Flight vs. the X-Men," *Journal of the Fantastic in the Arts* 26, no. 2 (2015): 311–332.

26. Rick Remender (w) and Olivier Copiel (a), *Uncanny Avengers*, no. 5 (New York: Marvel Comics, 2013). Emphasis in original.

27. Andrew Wheeler, "Avengers Assimilate: Identity Politics in 'Uncanny Avengers,'" *Comics Alliance*, March 29, 2013, http://comicsalliance.com/uncanny-avengers-5-rick-remender-identity-politics-mutants/.

28. Sara Ahmed, "Declarations of Whiteness: The Non-performativity of Anti-Racism," *borderlands* 3, no. 2 (2004).

8

OVER THE RAINBOW BRIDGE

Female/Queer Sexuality in Marvel's Thor Film Trilogy

SAMANTHA LANGSDALE

INTRODUCTION

Over the last ten years, the films in the Marvel Cinematic Universe (MCU) have not only reintroduced superheroes to a mass audience but also helped confirm the superhero genre's capacity to offer meaningful reflections on social issues.[1] However, as the guiding research questions of this volume suggest, the superhero genre has infrequently offered meaningful explorations of sex and sexuality.[2] When sexuality has been explicitly present in the MCU, it has usually taken the form of scenes showing blurry-eyed women with tousled hair waking up in the beds of womanizing characters like Tony Stark/Iron Man or Peter Quill/Star Lord. We do not witness the full events leading up to these men being joined in bed by these (often nameless) women, nor do we get much explanation of what these sexual encounters mean for the characters in question.

Even rarer in the MCU is any exploration of female sexualities and sexual experiences. Characters like Black Widow are generally framed as "bombshells" through aesthetic styling and the reactions of male characters. But over the course of Black Widow's appearance in six MCU films, we see and hear virtually nothing of the character's own sense of her sexuality. This lack of representation results, at least in part, from the various ways sexism has influenced the film industry in general, the action film genre in particular, and the superhero film genre most acutely. As Yvonne Tasker has argued, "the action movie often operates as an almost exclusively male space,"[3] and as Blair Davis notes, "the entire Marvel and DC cinematic universes can be understood as action films."[4] Thus, it is unsurprising that there has been a paucity of female characters in the MCU. Of the female characters that do make it onto the screen, relatively few are superheroes, and almost all of them are positioned as love interests for the various male heroes. In general, the MCU operates within the heteronormative logic of the "male gaze," wherein women are either passive recipients of male desire or, especially in the case of female villains, possess a threatening, even deadly, sexuality.

Of course, as the various phases of the MCU have unfolded[5] and Hollywood box office trends have changed, representations of women have somewhat increased and diversified. These shifts are perhaps most obvious in the film *Black Panther* (2018), which includes multiple central female characters, all of whom are played by Black women. Although the characterizations in the Thor film trilogy, consisting of *Thor* (2011), *Thor: The Dark World* (2013), and *Thor: Ragnarok* (2017) (hereafter, these films shall be abbreviated as T1, TDW, and TR, respectively), are considerably less remarkable than those in *Black Panther*, they offer a particularly fruitful source for tracing the evolution of the representation of female sexualities in the MCU. This is true for two primary reasons: first, each Thor film was released in each one of the three phases of the MCU, allowing for the discussion of progress—or a lack thereof—over time; second, despite the trilogy centering on the Norse god of thunder, Thor, and his scheming brother, Loki, all three films incorporate multiple women who perform roles ranging from love interest to fighting companion to enemy. In conversation with feminist theory, film theory, and queer theory, this chapter will survey how the sexualities of the Thor trilogy's female characters illustrate these films' competing departures from and adherence to generic and cultural stereotypes, as well as the special anxieties—and possibilities—produced by the combination of female sexuality and power, super or otherwise.

PLAYING IT STRAIGHT

The representation of female sexualities in the Thor films is not unlike a rainbow—a spectrum that progresses from muted to more vibrant tones. Analogously, the first two Thor films are the most normative in their representations of gender, sexuality, and race, while the third film shows more nonnormative representations. The main female protagonists in the first two films, T1 and TDW, are the Asgardian Queen Frigga, the Asgardian warrior Lady Sif, and the astrophysicist Jane Foster and her intern Darcy Lewis from Earth. Despite occupying what seem to be powerful roles as queens, warriors, and scientists, all of these women succumb to problematic stereotypes. As a group, they also prove to be the least consequential, since all four disappear by the end of TDW. While there is some narrative justification for Frigga's disappearance (she falls prey to the grand comic book tradition of being "fridged"[6]), and even of Jane's (she apparently dumps Thor), Sif and Darcy's absences are entirely unremarked upon. Yvonne Tasker explains these common trends within action films generally:

> Whilst the woman in the action narrative may operate as some kind of symbolic guarantee, a place for the fixing of difference and heterosexual desire, she is simultaneously rendered increasingly marginal. . . . Sometimes she is simply written out of the more intense action narrative altogether. More often female characters are either raped or killed, or both, in order to provide a motivation for the hero's revenge.[7]

Pointing toward these problematic trends in both comics and cinema is not to suggest that there are not intriguing aspects of Frigga, Sif, and Darcy as characters. My contention, however, is that the first two Thor films perpetuate trends and plot devices that make it exceedingly difficult to read their female characters as anything other than a catalyst for the development of the more central male characters.

Frigga is, in many ways, the ultimate product of androcentric storytelling. She is primarily made known to viewers as the wife of Odin and the mother of Thor and Loki; consequently, she is recognizable only in relation to the male protagonists. Sif, although far more visible and central to the Thor films, is hardly treated better and does little to contribute to a more nuanced representation of female sexualities. In T1, Lady Sif is part of Thor's band of warrior best friends and something of a leader within the group. Throughout the film, she is unafraid to take the lead in battle, does not require rescuing any more than Thor's other warrior friends (or even Thor himself), and in total, has more speaking lines than any of the other Warriors Three.

Yet Sif starts to become a far more conventional character in TDW, where it is heavily implied that her relationship with Thor is not purely platonic. In addition to the fact that both the Norse mythology and the

Thor comics from which the films draw inspiration feature a heteronormative romance between Thor and Sif, TDW makes use of certain cinematic conventions to suggest that this kind of pairing is to be expected. In a banquet scene after a battle, Sif and Thor walk together, recounting battles past and joking about celebrations that spun out of control. Sif's voice is uncharacteristically soft and lacks some of the self-assurance we saw in the first film. She watches Thor as his mind drifts from the conversation and tries to reengage him by asking him to join her for a drink. When he declines, Sif confesses that "it has not gone unnoticed" that Thor disappears every night, and that as future king of Asgard, he has a duty to focus on all Nine Realms rather than just one (i.e., Earth). Sif's admonishment of Thor can reasonably be read not as actual diplomatic advice but rather as her attempt to redirect Thor's romantic interest. This interpretation is strengthened by the many unpleasant glances Sif gives Jane once the scientist arrives in Asgard. Here, Sif becomes the jilted member of a love triangle revolving around the film's central male character. This confirms the following problematic stereotypes: that women must compete for male attention and thus cannot be friends, and that cross-gender friendships are impossible.

Sif's character is additionally devalued through her physical representation. Tasker argues that within contemporary Hollywood action films, which have largely centered on the power and activity of male heroes, "images of women seem to need to compensate for the figure of the active heroine by emphasizing her sexuality, [and] her availability within traditional feminine terms."[8] In scenes where she is not in battle, Sif is dressed in traditionally feminine garments with militaristic accents, like a dress with delicate chain mail cap sleeves or a metallic sleeveless top and ornamental hair accessories. Although this combination of feminine and masculine characteristics has some subversive potential, it is difficult to read Sif's fighting armor, which includes high-heeled boots and a curved, breast-shaped chest plate, as anything other than intensely problematic. Numerous fans and pop culture websites have argued how practically ludicrous a breast-shaped chest plate—colloquially known as "boob armor"—is for characters that are frequently meant to be in battle.[9] This armor also essentializes the female body; Sif's "boob armor" suggests that her body is so stereotypically feminine, it cannot be accommodated by anything resembling traditional armor.

Dr. Jane Foster, a brilliant if somewhat unconventional scientist, and her oddball intern, Darcy Lewis, are introduced early in T1. The film opens in the New Mexico desert, where Jane and Darcy are joined by Erik Selvig (a colleague and family friend of Jane's) in order to observe and document unusual activity in the nighttime sky. While chasing what appears to be a tornado, Jane runs her van into a shadowy human figure standing in the middle of the storm. Thus, Jane's first interaction with Thor renders him unconscious. Jane and Darcy are remarkable insofar as they are both relatively central female characters who also appear to be friends, enjoying regular, witty dialogue throughout both T1 and TDW. Furthermore, Jane is never hypersexualized by tight or revealing clothing or gratuitous bedroom/shower scenes. She is generally dressed appropriately for her environments but is never made to look entirely unfashionable. Jane enjoys enough screen time for us to learn that she is tenacious, independent-minded, and capable of complex scientific theory and engineering, and that she has a sense of adventure. That Jane holds a PhD is notable in and of itself. Research on several decades of the Draw-a-Scientist Test has shown that gendered and racial biases, conveyed through education, social discourses, and media, embed themselves early in children's perceptions of what kinds of people become scientists. Diversifying representations of scientists has a direct impact on broadening children's perceptions, making them less likely to assume that only white men can be scientists.[10] Jane may contribute to addressing this long-standing problem. Adding to the depth of both Jane's and Darcy's characters are numerous instances in which they appear as sexual agents. From their first encounter with Thor, Jane and Darcy both exhibit sexual desire, Jane through a longing look and Darcy by offering to perform CPR (read: mouth-to-mouth) on an unconscious Thor. In a number of subsequent scenes in T1, Thor is turned into an object of Jane's and Darcy's gazes, such as when he briefly appears shirtless in the process of putting on borrowed clothes, or while he eats voraciously (Darcy finds the sight of Thor eating so appealing, she decides to document it on social media). What is intriguing about these scenes is that Thor is positioned as a thing to be looked at by two women who have already been established as unique characters as well as friends. This is not a love triangle, and Thor is a sexual spectacle not just for the audience (a point to which I will return) but also for characters whose broader desires and ambitions are known to us, allowing for their expressions of sexual desire to be read with some nuance.

When we see Jane and Thor talking about the Nine Realms on the roof of Jane's lab, we are being given hints about what attracts her. This scene establishes that in addition to a hard body, Jane is sexually attracted by other, personality-based traits, such as knowledge of the heavens. This represents at least somewhat of a departure from many action films, in which, as Tasker argues, "issues to do with sexuality and gendered identity [are] worked out over the male body."[11] Though Thor's body is certainly put on display in this film, we also see that he is desired for other reasons, lending complexity to his erotic display. Finally, Jane stretches the stereotypical mold of female sexuality in the ways she actively pursues the object of her desire. In the final scenes of T1, Thor pulls Jane toward him to offer a modest kiss on her hand. Jane responds by passionately kissing Thor on the mouth. The post-credits scene of TDW shows a similarly passionate kiss and embrace between Jane and Thor, though one that is mutually initiated. Jane is not a passive recipient of male desire, but an active agent pursuing her own desires.

It is also, however, necessary to examine the ways Jane adheres to the status quo. First, because Jane exhibits only heterosexual desire, and is seen directing that desire toward the stereotypically attractive and unimpeachably masculine Thor, she performs in normative ways that help to mitigate the latent homoeroticism that comes from making a spectacle out of male bodies in films that are "almost exclusively male spaces."[12] According to Tasker, within action films, because the "bodily integrity and heterosexuality" of male heroes "need to be maintained within the action narrative," the "woman as romantic interest performs, in this respect, a key narrative function. She both offers a point of differentiation from the hero and deflects attention from the homoeroticism surrounding male buddy relationships."[13] In T1, Thor's most emotionally intense, albeit tumultuous, relationship is with Loki, and after Erik Selvig helps Thor escape from captivity, they conclude a drunken brawl with declarations of love and admiration for each other. In both cases there is strong potential to see a framework of homoeroticism. Thus, even as the Thor films allow us to read Jane's desires with more nuance than is typically possible in similar films, it is also the case that she acts as a kind of guarantee that viewing Thor's bare chest is a heterosexual act. The progressiveness of Jane's status as a scientist is also somewhat diminished by heteronormative action film clichés. As Holly Hassel has argued, a readily observable trope in action films is the "babe scientist" who serves as "a romantic interest or buddy, or a combination of the two."[14] Echoing Hassel, Jeffrey A. Brown notes that "the young and sexy female scientists in films . . . explain complex plot devices and help the hero achieve his goals," giving her the appearance of having equal significance to her male counterpart.[15] Brown further suggests, however, that "the authority granted female characters with PhDs is really a chimera as the films typically show her as 'too bookish' and ultimately she needs to be saved by the more impulsive hero who survives on gut instincts."[16] While I do not believe that Jane is ever characterized as "too bookish," she does fit the pattern of "babe scientist" in most other ways. Her language at the beginning of T1 is highly technical; whereas Thor describes the heavens in terms of realms and rainbow bridges, Jane is forever in search of an Einstein-Rosen Bridge. She helps Thor attempt to get his hammer back in T1, and in TDW, she leverages what she has discovered to try and help Thor defeat the invasion of the Dark Elves. Yet as soon as she embarks on the mission to retrieve Thor's hammer in T1, Jane's seriousness as a scientist is undermined by her increasing infatuation with Thor. For example, Jane almost drives off the road because she is so giggly and nervous around Thor. By the time SHIELD (a worldwide law-enforcement organization) shows up to confiscate Jane's equipment, we no longer hear her being called "Doctor" but instead "Ms. Foster," and it is not Jane's initiative that saves the day but rather Thor's; it is Thor who steals Jane's diary, containing her most important life's work, and convinces SHIELD to return Jane's things, making possible the continuation of her research. The conclusion of T1, showing Thor and Heimdall standing at the end of the broken Rainbow Bridge, discussing the worlds below, includes Jane as an idea more than a protagonist and foregrounds her love interest role. In the last line of the film, Heimdall says of Jane, "She searches for you." While this line may seem innocuous, it detracts from the fact that Jane is down on Earth continuing the research she began before Thor's arrival, instead suggesting that the real purpose of her life's work is to once again locate the object of her romantic interest. Jane is similarly shunted into a stereotypically passive female role in TDW. In this film, while Jane's tenacious tracking of an anomaly in time and space begins to reveal the troubles Thor will face in Asgard, it also results in Jane being infected by the Aether (a mysterious, seemingly magical force that can convert matter into dark matter), a condition that Thor must save her from.[17] The film posters also heralded Jane's passive positioning by showing her either with her body facing Thor and her hand on his chest, as if in an embrace, or with Thor behind her, literally guarding her with his arm and hammer extended in front of her. In either case, a visual narrative of Jane as in need of protection is hard to dispute.

Though it almost goes without saying, Jane as well as Darcy, Frigga, and Sif additionally fail to break from the status quo insofar as they are all played by normatively beautiful, white, able-bodied, thin women. These female characters are, in the words of Richard J. Gray II, "masterful adherents to traditional sexual, racial, ethnic, and class stereotypes. Like their male counterparts, superheroines"—or, as I am suggesting, central female characters in superhero films more broadly—"are typically white, middle or upper class, and have strong heterosexual appeal."[18] None of these critiques render these characters unimportant or negate their complexity. Yet the potential to interpret the representation of female characters and their sexuality in TD1 and TDW in more "colorful" ways is paired with, and arguably severely limited by, heteronormative tropes that have long served to make superhero films androcentric at best and blatantly sexist at worst.

NOT A QUEEN OR A MONSTER

The next female character along the sexuality representation spectrum is Hela. Introduced as the primary villain in the third film, *Thor: Ragnarok* (2017), Hela also adheres to certain normative parameters for representations of female sexuality. The ways she disrupts and departs from those norms, however, are arguably more vibrant, and thus observable, than the ways the previously discussed female characters do. This may be due, at least in part, to the fact that TR as a whole is a much more colorful film, both literally and figuratively. Whereas T1 was shot in warm tones— dominated by golds, reds, and blues—and TDW was overwhelmingly shot in darker blues and greys, TR evokes all the colors of the rainbow. TR is also more vibrant in terms of the characters' costumes, some of which make direct visual reference to Jack Kirby's bombastic Silver Age designs and art. This film is additionally lighter in tone than the previous Thor films, partly because it features more humor, but also because of its genre-bending use of 1980s-inspired music as well as the ways it more openly evokes the sexual tastes and demeanors of its characters.[19] Jeff Goldblum as the Grand Master, for instance, defies many traditional ideals of heteronormative masculinity by sporting sparkling garments, makeup, and fingernail polish; being known for orgies; and being generally camp. The combined effect of these elements has led a number of pop culture writers to conclude that TR is the "gayest" of all Marvel movies.[20] It is perhaps little wonder, then, that the main female characters in the film embody and perform their sexualities in more dynamic, non-heteronormative ways.

Hela makes her entrance relatively early in TR, revealing herself to be the older sister of Thor and Loki and the true heir of Odin. She is immensely powerful, confident in herself and her aims, and entirely unimpressed with the legacy left by the Allfather. Like Frigga and Sif, the character of Hela draws both from Norse mythology as well as from the rewriting of that mythology present in the Thor comics. Cate Blanchett's portrayal of Hela, however, brings this character to life in uniquely seductive ways. Hela, like many women in action and superhero films, is dressed in a form-fitting black catsuit. Yet this catsuit is enhanced by metallic green piping that both accentuates the curves of her body and gives the impression of electrical wiring, lending visual confirmation of Hela as an embodiment of power. Her appearance also has a sharpness to it, emphasized by her helmet, which is accented by numerous black antlers that bend into thorny points. Her "piercing" aesthetic is solidified by her ability to produce all manner of blades from her body, a talent she exercises almost immediately upon her arrival and frequently thereafter.

While this combination of traits and visual cues may sound terrifying, Blanchett's Hela luxuriates in her own deadliness, giving the whole performance an erotic feel. As Charles Pulliam-Moore writes for pop culture site iO9:

> Hela also is an exquisitely campy, outsized personality who revels in the gauche, obsidian garishness of her divinity. Hela doesn't just transform her cascading hair into her antler-adorned helmet—she stops, luxuriates in her own lethality, and quite literally takes a moment to feel herself before she gets down to business. Hela is . . . undeniably feminine while also disrupting whatever ideas we may have about her gender.[21]

This moment of "feeling herself" acts as a sort of metaphor for Hela's sexuality more generally. As Pulliam-Moore argues, Hela is certainly sexy but never sexualized; the only body she caresses (rather than stabs, punches, or crushes) is her own, and she does so in a moment wherein she is preparing for violent engagement (figure 8.1). At no point does Hela exhibit desire toward another human-like character, and certainly never toward a man. Her seductiveness is plain, but because it is paired with such intense lethalness, and because her desires are only for her own flourishing, Hela's sexuality breaks with normative action film representations.

In fact, Pulliam-Moore goes so far as to suggest that Hela is a queer character, both because she disrupts heteronormative expectations of gender and sexuality and because she is evocative of queer culture. Turning again to her appearance, Pulliam-Moore writes that Hela performs "a kind of high-concept drag that transforms the horrors of death and war (concepts we traditionally associate with masculinity) into a gorgeous ensemble."[22] While I disagree with the assertion that death is traditionally associated with masculinity,[23] I agree with Pulliam-Moore's overall assessment of Hela's presentation. Her heavy eye makeup, dramatic headpiece, and overt disruption of gender norms does act as a kind of drag. That

FIGURE 8.1. Hela's auto-erotic sexuality. *Thor: Ragnarok* (2017).

this performative aesthetic is disruptive of the male gaze only adds to Hela's queerness. For example, Gray argues that black leather jumpsuits traditionally worn by female superheroes (or, in this case, a supervillain) reflect an inherent duality: "On one hand, it reveals the most intimate details of her body's topography; on the other hand, her costume reflects the needs of the character to keep her sexuality 'under wraps.'"[24] In Hela's case, the latter assertion is contestable. If we read her sexuality as auto-erotic, then she departs from the norms described, insofar as her sexuality is ever-present and readily observable. Moreover, because Hela seems to exude so much (seductive) self-confidence and is ceaselessly deadly, she may actively repel the desires of the male audience. According to Gray, "too much sex, too much 'ass kicking' may chase away the male audience. If one of the central functions of the 'male gaze' is to deny women agency, then the gaze must continually perpetuate that characteristic. With agency, women are no longer under the 'puppeteering' control of men."[25] From the moment of her emergence from her patriarchal prison, Hela literally throws off male control and subsequently defies any attempts made by men to abate or contain her. Her weaponized body enables her insatiable appetite for power; combined with her unshakeable sense of herself, these characteristics make Hela's pursuit of self-satisfaction particularly fatal. If Hela is anything, she is "too much," adding more weight to Pulliam-Moore's claim that she can be read as a queer icon. Relatedly, Hela may also be described as evocative of what Mary Russo identifies as "the grotesque body," a subject that "is open, protruding, irregular, secreting, multiple, and changing; it is identified with non-official 'low' culture or the carnivalesque, and with social transformation."[26]

Interestingly, Hela also disrupts the conventions of supervillainy more generally. Scholars such as Peter Coogan have suggested that, in direct opposition to the selfless motivations of superheroes, villains act out agendas that are entirely selfish.[27] Similarly, David A. Pizarro and Roy Baumesiter argue, "In tales of superhero versus supervillain, moral good and moral bad are always the actions of easily identifiable moral agents with unambiguous intentions and actions."[28] In addition to being somewhat reductive, neither of these characterizations sufficiently describes Hela's actions or motivations, nor do they entirely account for the actions of some of TR's "heroes." While it is certainly the case that she has her own interests at heart, Hela also fundamentally believes that she will be delivering Asgard to a higher state of existence. Hela's villainy is further complicated by the truth her presence reveals, that is, Odin's own overzealous campaign for power and glory. From a feminist perspective, Hela is not simply an agent of "moral bad," since her rebellion serves to expose the abuse, exploitation, and imprisonment she suffered at the hands of a patriarch whose motivations conveniently changed once he was securely in power and who does not take accountability for his actions, leaving the next generation of male heirs to perpetuate his mission to stifle and eradicate female power. Hela's plain disregard for the lives of others may be unambiguously evil, but her very existence queers neat definitions of "good guys" and "bad guys" and powerfully complicates assumptions about patriarchal power and lineage as inherently legitimate and morally right.

Yet as promising as Hela may seem as a powerful, self-directed, and self-desiring queer woman, her close association with what Barbara Creed has called "the monstrous-feminine" suggests that her character construction is not entirely devoid of sexist modes of representation. By investigating "seven faces" of the monstrous-feminine, Creed demonstrates how women in horror films are symbolic of men's fears of castration. The shared root of these seven variations is, of course, the *vagina dentata*. Creed explains that "male fears and phantasies about the female genitals as a trap" are common throughout myths and legends across numerous cultures and are evident, in the modern world, "in popular derogatory terms for women such as 'man-eater' and 'castrating bitch.'"[29] As a female character that quite literally slices her way through TR, Hela mirrors many of these conventions. Creed writes, "Castration can refer to symbolic castration (loss of the mother's body, breast, loss of identity) which is experienced by both female and male, or it can refer to genital castration."[30] Hela is feared, at least in part, because her arrival spells the end of Odin's life as well as the end of Asgard, both of which are crucial to Thor in defining his identity; thus, their destruction constitutes a significant attack on Thor's sense of self. While Hela never actually castrates Thor—she does not perform genital castration—she does cut out his eye. As numerous feminist theorists have argued, the eye in Western thinking has often been metaphorically aligned with the phallus; Carellin Brooks, for instance, explains that "the eye is an instrument for getting inside and another form of possession; as a phallic instrument it seeks entry and interprets truth."[31] Hela's violent acts also align with Creed's descriptions of castrating women: "Victims die agonizing messy deaths—flesh is cut, bodies violated, limbs torn asunder. Where the monster is a psychopath, victims are cut, dismembered, decapitated. Instruments of death are usually knives or other sharp implements."[32] The fact that Hela's body generates knives and swords cannot be overstated here; her primary means of murdering her enemies is precisely to cut, dismember, and decapitate.

Hela's relationship with and reliance on the wolf Fenris also resonates strongly with Creed's analyses. Creed writes, "In classical art the figure of a beautiful woman was often accompanied by an animal companion with open jaws and snapping teeth; the creature represented her deadly genital trap and evil intent."[33] Further, while many of these depictions couple women with wild cats, "other beasts" are not uncommon and "are frequently positioned near a woman's genital area."[34] In the artistic depictions of her past in the palace of Asgard and in various battle scenes near the conclusion of TR, Hela is shown riding on the back of Fenris, placing him between her legs. Finally, Hela's headpiece, worn specifically in times of violent conflict, gives her an appearance not unlike that of Medusa.[35] Creed explains that the snakes attached to Medusa's head are phallic symbols that, because they themselves have teeth, and because they are wielded by a vengeful woman, quite directly evoke castration.[36] Like Medusa's snakes, the antlers on Hela's helmet have a sharp appearance, and because they appear when she is wielding swords and knives (which are also phallic symbols), they similarly evoke a phallic, castrating power. And just as Medusa's castrating, phallic power could only be stopped by a man wielding a phallus (Perseus decapitates her with his sword), so too is Hela eventually vanquished by a male demon who plunges a giant sword deep into the heart of Asgard, and thus penetrates the source of Hela's power. The implications of these archetypes are that phallic power in the hands of women is deadly and horrifying, that female bodies are a threat, and that only when (heteronormative) men wield phalluses can the castrating dangers of the monstrous-feminine be stopped. Equally troubling are the ways these characteristics evoke what Julia Kristeva has identified as the abject. Hela is a character who evokes horror through the fluidity of her embodiment as well as through her violent disruption of hierarchical and bodily boundaries and her association with death; as abject, she is and continuously becomes "radically separate, loathsome."[37]

Because Hela embodies so many of the traits associated with abject monstrous femininity, we are once again forced to recognize how a female character with the potential to broaden representations of women and female sexuality is coupled with a perpetuation of harmful stereotypes. In her final fight scene with Thor in TR, Hela forcefully insists that she is "not a queen or a monster," and I think she is absolutely right. While Hela can certainly be read through a queer lens, wherein disruptions of heteronormative constructions of gender and sexuality become apparent, her close association with phallic violence also perpetuates patriarchal stereotypes of female sexuality as being deadly and castrating. Therefore, we cannot conclude that Hela is *only* a (drag) queen, nor can we characterize her as *entirely* monstrous. Instead, like the characters discussed above, Hela performs in ways that both depart from as well as adhere to norms of sexuality and gender in superhero films. I would suggest, however, that precisely through the intensity of her contradictions, Hela ultimately pushes representation of female sexualities forward in thrilling ways.

"IT'S THE BIFROST, NOT THE STRAIGHTFROST"

The final significant female character to make her debut in the Thor films is Valkyrie. Played by Tessa Thompson, an actress of Afro-Panamanian, Mexican, and European descent, Valkyrie is one of relatively few women of color among the predominantly white female cast of the Thor film franchise. She is also the only character with a documented non-heteronormative sexual identity in the comics.[38] Thompson, who in real-life self-identifies as queer, used social media to confirm the bisexuality of her performance of Valkyrie, much to the delight of LGBTQ fans: "Val is Bi in the comics," Thompson tweeted, "& I was faithful to that in her depiction."[39] Casting a woman of color for the role of Valkyrie—a traditionally white, blonde-haired, blue-eyed character—combined with recognizing the character's bisexuality certainly seems to trouble norms of race and sexuality in superhero films.

Valkyrie is an exceptional female character for a number of reasons, not least in terms of her embodiment. Black female characters have been central in action films since at least the 1970s, when blaxploitation became influential on the genre writ large. However, within blaxploitation films and beyond them, Black women have often been characterized in ways that exoticize them and contribute to stereotypes that frame Black men and women as hypersexual and animalistic.[40] These problematic trends have similarly dominated representations of Black female superheroes in comics. As Brown explains, "Black superheroines are often presented as hypersexual and metaphorically bestial. Moreover, popular black superheroines—like Storm, Vixen, Pantha, and the Black Panther—are explicitly associated with exoticized notions of Africa, nature, noble savagery, and a variety of Dark Continent themes, including voodoo, mysticism, and animal totemism."[41] Unlike her comic book peers, TR's Valkyrie is associated neither with "Dark Continent themes" nor bestiality. Instead, like all her fellow Asgardians, she is part of the mythological tradition of the Norse gods; her connection to the mystical is, therefore, indistinguishable from that of Thor or Loki. She is also part of an all-female order of warriors, contradicting T1's suggestion that Sif was the first of her kind.

In addition, unlike many of her Black female predecessors in film and in comics, it is difficult to characterize Valkyrie as hypersexual.[42] Throughout much of the film, she is dressed in sturdy boots, trousers, and a tough leather tunic, making the most visible part of her body her well-toned arms. Valkyrie is not wholly defeminized or desexualized: she wears her hair long in traditionally feminine styles, her tunic has contours evocative of breasts (though in a less exaggerated form than what Sif wears in T1 and what Valkyrie wears in the comics), and her male cohorts react to her in ways that indicate we are meant to recognize her feminine beauty. Yet this beauty is matched by—and inseparable from—Valkyrie's athleticism and skill as a warrior. She is every bit an equal to Thor, and while it may be the case that we occasionally witness brief moments of flirtation between the two, there seems to be very little indication that this "comrades-in-arms" relationship is meant to evolve into romance. These departures from action and superhero film norms create space for a character that is clearly marked by race and gender, but not boxed in by these traits or devalued as a result.

Unfortunately, however, similar to the women discussed above, Valkyrie also perpetuates stereotypes that detract from her impact as a truly progressive female character. Casting Thompson for the role of Valkyrie signaled to many a step forward in the struggle to increase diversity in Hollywood films.[43] Thompson, like the majority of women of color in action and superhero films, is, however, lighter skinned and mixed race. Brown argues that "when non-white women appear as action heroines in modern Hollywood, they are almost always portrayed by mixed race actresses."[44] The value of casting mixed race women "is not perceived as their ability to pass, but in being able to signify a tempered exotic Otherness."[45] This allows Hollywood "to include ethnic diversity on a superficial visual level"[46] while conveniently sidestepping the continued marginalization, stereotyping, and exclusion of darker-skinned actors. Valkyrie may also perpetuate a problematic trend associated with Black women in action films by virtue of her excessive drinking. Tasker explains how "Blackness is understood within Hollywood's symbolic in terms of marginality and criminality. This criminality has been most often expressed in action narratives of recent years not through sexualised images, but through the ideological figure of drugs."[47] For example, whereas white female heroes in action films are often motivated by a need to get revenge against their rapists, Black female heroes are less frequently exposed to this kind of sexual violence. This is a curse in disguise. Black female heroes are often considered incapable of falling victim to "unwanted" sex in part because they are assumed to be hypersexual; this causes them to instead seek revenge against themselves. Tasker argues that this "tortuous logic" seems to stem from the need to find an Other against which Black female heroes can fight: "This is . . . precisely where the ideological figure of drugs is introduced."[48] Valkyrie was a victim of trauma, and she does seek revenge against Hela, but it is largely herself that she subjects to abuse and harm. By intoxicating herself and waiting to die on Sakaar, she acts out a kind of self-punishment for surviving Hela's slaughter of the Valkyries.[49] In order to fully join Thor in his fight for peace and justice, Valkyrie must confront her own demons long before she actually confronts Hela. This story line does evoke sympathy and arguably provides a way for audiences to identify with the character. But critical questions must be asked of our viewing habits if the torture and self-abuse of a Black female character is the only way to engender such a reaction.

Finally, and perhaps most disappointingly, Valkyrie suffers the same fate as so many other bisexual characters in film in having the true nature of her sexual orientation all but erased. Despite Thompson's use of Twitter to confirm Valkyrie's bisexuality, and her reported imagining of another slain Valkyrie as her lover, there is no actual confirmation of Valkyrie's sexual orientation in TR. James Whitbrook, writing for iO9, reported, "Thompson lobbied director Taika Waititi to shoot a small moment including a woman walking out of Valkyrie's bedroom. Despite Thompson and Waititi fighting for the brief moment to stay in the film, it was eventually cut, because it was considered a 'distraction.'"[50] This cut perpetuates what numerous scholars, including Maria San Filippo, have identified as "bisexuality's cultural and representational '(in)visibility.'"[51] Bisexuality, San Filippo suggests, "unlike heterosexuality and homosexuality, seems to rely on a temporal component for its actualisation; at any given moment a bisexual person or character might appear monosexual depending on his/her present gender-of-object choice."[52] While we get glimpses of Valkyrie flirtatiously exchanging glances with Thor, the scene confirming her attraction to other women is erased, demonstrating the difficulty San Filippo describes. Whitbrook further argues that this kind of erasure is indicative of Hollywood's "play-it-safe politics of making mainstream, wide-appeal blockbusters."[53] The lack of explicit recognition is discouraging and, as Whitbrook asserts, "a grim reminder of where LGBTQ representation is at for these movies."[54] Despite this erasure, meaningful interpretations of Valkyrie as a bisexual woman can and have been made. In his analysis of fandom, sexuality, and superhero comics, Gareth Schott suggests that queer theory is a particularly useful framework for understanding how fans make meaning from the implied content of comic books. Queer theory, he writes, "is typically understood as a means of navigating the evolving terrain of both gender and sexual identity, but more broadly it functions as a process for articulating latent, potential, or hidden (closeted) identities and how they are brought to fruition."[55] Queer theory can aid scholars in recognizing and appreciating how fans locate latent meaning and employ it to interpret different meanings of superheroes' identities. Thus, it is possible to argue that the ways fans have embraced Valkyrie's bisexuality and chosen to interpret Thompson's performance as queer in spite of the edits described above must be important parts of any analysis of the character. Valkyrie may not be given the "necessary temporal components" in TR to make her bisexuality explicit, but for fans like independent artist Alena Lane, the character's sexual identity is clear. Tweeting out an illustration of Thompson's Valkyrie wearing a T-shirt that reads "Die Mad About It" and sunglasses painted in the characteristic colors of bisexual pride—pink, lavender, and blue—Lane included the message, "It's the Bifrost, not the Straightfrost, y'all!" (figure 8.2). Her tweet received more than three thousand likes and was retweeted

FIGURE 8.2. "It's the Bifrost, not the Straightfrost, y'all!" Fan art by Alena Lane, Portraitoftheoddity on Tumblr.

more than a thousand times. The request to buy the print was also made by so many people that Lane made it available for sale on her online art store. While this is just one example of the fan response to Thompson's Valkyrie, it is representative of how fans are able to interpret content in ways that make a character meaningful to them as members of an underrepresented community.

CONCLUSION

Ultimately, what is at stake in how superhero films portray sex and sexuality is not just our entertainment, but also "the larger forces at work that shape our societies, cultures, and identities."[56] As Tasker argues, "popular cinema forms one space in which identities can be affirmed, dissolved and redefined within a fantasy space. This space affirms a range of identities at the same time as it mobilises identifications and desires which undermine the stability of such categories."[57] Better representations of female superheroes and female sexuality cannot save us from the real-world abuses and setbacks faced by women and girls around the world. But they can remind us of our gains and triumphs and, perhaps most importantly, help us to imagine creative new strategies to fight for intersectional justice. As Carolyn Cocca explains, the overrepresentation of white men within the superhero genre and popular culture more generally "is not only unfair, but can curtail imagination. If you see heroes who look nothing like you, it may be easier to imagine someone in that group being a hero too. If you don't, it may be more difficult. Diverse representation benefits everyone, because it shows all of us that anyone can be a hero."[58] In seeing better representations of female superheroes with diverse sexualities, viewers are not actually being given the power to "stop locomotives, move faster than speeding bullets, or leap tall buildings in a single bound."[59] Nor are they going to entirely stop experiencing the oppression embedded in patriarchal gender norms. But complex, dynamic, and frankly *feminist* representations of female superheroes are crucial because, as Will Brooker asserts, they give us "something to embrace and aspire to. . . . We could be heroes."[60]

NOTES

1. One could potentially include the myriad Marvel TV shows that now exist in the MCU. However, owing to the differences between film and television as

mediums—including impact, audience demographics, and history of gendered representation—discussing both is beyond the purview of this chapter. For the purposes of this chapter, *MCU* will only refer to the film universe.

2. *Sexuality* is notoriously difficult to define. For the purposes of this chapter, the term is intended to indicate the combination of an individual's sexual desires, behaviors, and preferred identification.

3. Yvonne Tasker, *Spectacular Bodies: Gender, Genre, and the Action Cinema* (London: Taylor & Francis, 2002), 17.

4. Davis, *Comic Book Movies*, 23.

5. The MCU is defined by the Marvel Wiki in the following way: phase 1 includes the films from 2008 to 2012, phase 2 includes films from 2013 to 2015, and phase 3 includes films from 2016 to 2019.

6. The term "fridging" refers to an initiative started by comics creator Gail Simone to draw attention to the overwhelming tendency for mainstream superhero comics to treat female characters solely as plot devices. The term was inspired by a particular issue of the Green Lantern comics in which the main character finds his girlfriend dismembered in a refrigerator; using this incident as an example, Simone argued that female characters were frequently violently killed or mutilated in comics in order to provide a catalyst for male superheroes to spring into action. For more, see Simone's Women in Refrigerators blog.

7. Tasker, *Spectacular Bodies*, 16.

8. Tasker, *Spectacular Bodies*, 19.

9. Angie Dahl, "Hollywood Has a Boob Armor Problem, and It Needs to Stop," CBR.com, January 23, 2018, https://www.cbr.com/ant-man-wasp-costume-boob-armor/.

10. Jocelyn Steinke, Maria Knight Lapinski, Nikki Crocker, et al., "Assessing Media Influences on Middle School-Aged Children's Perceptions of Women in Science Using the Draw-A-Scientist Test (DAST)," *Science Communication* 29, no. 1 (2007): 35–64.

11. Tasker, *Spectacular Bodies*, 17.

12. Tasker, *Spectacular Bodies*, 17.

13. Tasker, *Spectacular Bodies*, 17.

14. Holly Hassel, "The 'Babe Scientist' Phenomenon: The Illusion of Inclusion in 1990s American Action Films," in *Chick Flicks: Contemporary Women at the Movies*, ed. Suzanne Ferriss and Mallory Young (New York: Routledge, 2008), 191.

15. Jeffrey A. Brown, *Beyond Bombshells: The New Action Heroine in Popular Culture* (Jackson: University Press of Mississippi, 2015), 68.

16. Brown, *Beyond Bombshells*, 68.

17. A similar analysis of Jane is developed by Terrence McSweeney. However, while I have tried to suggest that it is possible to read agency into the female characters in the Thor films, McSweeney argues that their roles merely provide "a superficial patina of progressivism." See Terrence McSweeney, *Avengers Assemble: Critical Perspectives on the Marvel Cinematic Universe* (New York: Wallflower Press, 2018), 384–445.

18. Richard J. Gray II, "Vivacious Vixens and Scintillating Super Hotties:

Deconstructing the Superheroine," in *21st Century Superhero: Essays on Gender, Genre and Globalization in Film*, ed. Richard J. Gray II and Betty Kaklamanidou (Jefferson, NC: McFarland, 2011), 77.

19. The director of TR, Taika Waititi, is also important to mention here. As a half-Polynesian New Zealander with a background in comedy, Waititi "brightened" TR not only through humor but also by including numerous visual references to indigenous Australian and New Zealand traditions, and by welcoming the local indigenous community to the set on the first day of production. See Shannon Connellan, "Taika Waititi Peppered 'Thor: Ragnarok' with Indigenous Australian and New Zealand References," Mashable, October 18, 2017, https://mashable.com/2017/10/18/thor-ragnarok-taika-waititi-references/#8RzOlv_ESmq7.

20. See, for example, Angela Watercutter, "*Thor: Ragnarok* Is Quietly the Queerest Superhero Movie Yet," *Wired*, November 3, 2017, https://www.wired.com/story/thor-ragnarok-lgbtq-visibility/. See also Kyle Buchanan, "What Is the Gayest Marvel Movie?" Vulture, July 9, 2018, http://www.vulture.com/2018/07/what-is-the-gayest-marvel-movie.html.

21. Charles Pulliam-Moore, "*Thor: Ragnarok*'s Hela Is Inadvertently Marvel's First Queer Icon," Gizmodo iO9, November 9, 2017, https://io9.gizmodo.com/thor-ragnaroks-hela-is-inadvertently-marvels-first-que-1820151270.

22. Pulliam-Moore, "*Thor: Ragnarok*'s Hela."

23. For an in-depth analysis of the ways femininity has historically been linked to death in Western visual culture, see Elisabeth Bronfen, *Over Her Dead Body: Death, Femininity and the Aesthetic* (Manchester, UK: Manchester University Press, 1992).

24. Gray II, "Vivacious Vixens," 89.

25. Gray II, "Vivacious Vixens," 91.

26. Mary Russo, *The Female Grotesque: Risk, Excess and Modernity* (New York: Routledge, 1994), 8.

27. Coogan, "Definition of a Superhero," 77–93.

28. David A. Pizarro and Roy Baumesiter, "Superhero Comics as Moral Pornography," in *Our Superheroes, Ourselves*, ed. Robin S. Rosenberg (New York: Oxford University Press, 2013), 20.

29. Barbara Creed, *The Monstrous-Feminine: Film, Feminism, Psychoanalysis* (London: Routledge, 1993), 390–391.

30. Creed, *The Monstrous-Feminine*, 392.

31. Carellin Brooks, *Every Inch a Woman: Phallic Possession, Femininity, and the Text* (Vancouver: UBC Press, 2006), 81.

32. Creed, *Monstrous-Feminine*, 392.

33. Creed, *Monstrous-Feminine*, 396.

34. Creed, *Monstrous-Feminine*, 397.

35. Loki also wears a helmet that is arguably phallic in nature, featuring two horns near the front of his head. However, scholar Alice Nuttall has suggested that Loki can also be read as queer owing to his association with (Frigga's) magic and because of the various ways he is emasculated by his father's and brother's

evocation of more traditional masculinity. Thus, he does not evoke the same type of threat that Hela does. For a more thorough discussion of Loki's gender presentation, see Alice Nuttall, "'I Am the Monster Parents Tell Their Children About at Night': The Marvel Films' Loki as Gothic Antagonist," *Gothic Studies* 8, no. 2 (2016): 62–73.

36. Creed, *Monstrous-Feminine*, 408.

37. Julia Kristeva, *Powers of Horror: An Essay on Abjection*, translated by Leon S. Roudiez (New York: Columbia University Press, 1982), 2.

38. Valkyrie's identity as bisexual became canon in Marvel's comic *The Fearless Defenders* (2013).

39. James Whitbrook, "*Thor: Ragnarok*'s Valkyrie Shows How Far We've Got to Go for LGBTQ Representation on the Big Screen," Gizmodo iO9, November 8, 2018, https://io9.gizmodo.com/thor-ragnaroks-valkyrie-shows-how-far-weve-got-to-go-f-1820188880.

40. Tasker, *Spectacular Bodies*, 20–23.

41. Brown, *Beyond Bombshells*, 120.

42. It is important to note, however, that scholars such as Tasker argue that long-standing racist and sexist stereotypes always already code Black female heroes as sexualized in action films, regardless of whether that sexuality is made explicit.

43. Recent iterations of Valkyrie in comics have been drawn in the likeness of Thompson's portrayal. See Christian Holub, "Tessa Thompson's Valkyrie Is Coming to Marvel Comics," *Entertainment Weekly*, January 8, 2018, http://ew.com/books/2018/01/08/tessa-thompson-valkyrie-marvel-comics/.

44. Brown, *Beyond Bombshells*, 80. On the use of multiracial actresses, see also Mary C. Beltrán, "The New Hollywood Racelessness: Only the Fast, Furious, (and Multiracial) Will Survive," *Cinema Journal* 44, no. 2 (2005): 50–67.

45. Brown, *Beyond Bombshells*, 80.

46. Brown, *Beyond Bombshells*, 82.

47. Tasker, *Spectacular Bodies*, 32.

48. Tasker, *Spectacular Bodies*, 32.

49. This reading is not inevitable. As Joan Ormrod has suggested, Valkyrie's drinking could be interpreted as making her "one of the boys." In more than one MCU film, Thor, too, is characterized as a heavy drinker, making it possible to argue that Valkyrie is demonstrating acceptable (masculine) Asgardian behavior rather than engaging in self-abuse.

50. Whitbrook, "*Thor: Ragnarok*'s Valkyrie."

51. Maria San Filippo, "The Politics of Fluidity: Representing Bisexualities in Twenty-First Century Screen Media," in *The Routledge Companion to Media, Sex and Sexuality*, ed. Clarissa Smith, Feona Attwood, and Brian McNair Smith (New York: Routledge, 2018), 71.

52. San Filippo, "Politics of Fluidity," 71.

53. Whitbrook, "*Thor: Ragnarok*'s Valkyrie."

54. Whitbrook, "*Thor: Ragnarok*'s Valkyrie."

55. Schott, "From Fan Appropriation," 21.

56. Davis, *Comic Book Movies*, 67.
57. Tasker, *Spectacular Bodies*, 165.
58. Cocca, *Superwomen*, 3.
59. Will Brooker, "We Could Be Heroes," in *What Is a Superhero?*, ed. Robin Rosenberg and Peter Coogan (Oxford: Oxford University Press, 2013), 17.
60. Brooker, "We Could Be Heroes," 17.

9

"NO ONE'S GOING TO BE LOOKING AT YOUR FACE"

The Female Gaze and the New (Super)Man in *Lois & Clark: The New Adventures of Superman*

ANNA F. PEPPARD

Among popular male characters with a longtime female love interest, Superman has been, for most of his history, exceptionally sexless. Sometimes, this is blamed on the obligations of his dual identity. Michael Kimmel offers a conventional reading of the Clark Kent/Lois Lane/Superman love triangle: "As Clark constantly pursued Lois Lane, seeking the comforts of marital stability, Lois had eyes only for the more manly alter ego, who could not, and would never be, tied down into a life of domestic drudgery."[1] Friedrich Weltzien puts the matter even more bluntly: "Manliness in the superhero genre seems to explicitly exclude love, family life, and tenderness. It is due to their double identity that they cannot carry on a 'normal' relationship with another person."[2] Larry Niven's infamous essay "Man of Steel, Woman of Kleenex," originally published in the men's magazine *Knight* in 1969 and reprinted with illustrations by Silver Age Superman artist Curt Swan in *Penthouse Comix* in 1995, offers a more graphic explanation:[3] if Superman had sex with Lois,

221

his super-penis would literally tear her to shreds, "ripping her open from crotch to sternum, gutting her like a trout."[4]

While Niven's interpretation has never been canonically confirmed, most Superman stories have similarly viewed supersex as a threat, whether to Lois, Superman, or the world itself. In the long-running comic book series *Superman's Girl-Friend, Lois Lane* (1958–1974), Lois's quest to convince (or, more often, trick) a reluctant Superman into marrying her routinely ends in catastrophe. And in Richard Lester's film *Superman II* (1980), "a relationship with Lois demands Superman essentially emasculate himself, by stripping himself of his superhuman strength."[5] Though *Superman II* confirms Superman's sexual desire for Lois as well as Lois's power over Superman, this desire and power ultimately threaten Superman's bodily integrity and the entire human race; the deflowered and depowered Clark Kent cannot stand up for himself in a bar fight, let alone save the world. Even in twenty-first-century stories that foreground the Lois/Superman romance, such as Grant Morrison and Frank Quitely's critically acclaimed twelve-issue comic book series *All-Star Superman* (2005–2008), sex is linked with death.[6] In this series, it is Superman's imminent demise that compels him to admit his love for Lois, and he expresses this love by working alone and in strict secrecy to devise a serum that will grant her superpowers for twenty-four hours, a premise that—intentionally or not—confirms the mere human Lois's incompatibility and inferiority, as inscribed in her relative lack of both power and knowledge.[7]

The television show *Lois & Clark: The New Adventures of Superman*, which aired on ABC from 1993 to 1997 and starred Teri Hatcher and Dean Cain in the title roles, presents a very different version of Superman's relationship with Lois Lane.[8] The show's title, which, as Kathleen Rittenhouse observes, puts Lois's name first in addition to referencing the Lewis and Clark expedition, is "a clue that this interpretation of the Superman material has as its principal theme the exploration of the uncharted territory of the relationship between Lois and Clark/Superman."[9] Developed by Deborah Joy LeVine from an idea by DC president Jenette Khan, *Lois & Clark* is, according to both LeVine and Hatcher, first and foremost a "romantic comedy,"[10] featuring more witty banter and conversations about feelings than superheroic action sequences. This genre hybridity proved very popular. At a time when it took Superman's death to convince more than one million people to buy a Superman comic book,[11] *Lois & Clark* attracted as many as twenty-two million viewers a week; no subsequent superhero television show has approached this level of popularity. *Lois & Clark*'s mix of action and romance undoubtedly appealed to a variety of demographics. Yet the key to its success is just as undoubtedly its direct appeal to girls and women. As Jackie Byars and Eileen R. Meehan observe, although many films and television shows of the 1980s and '90s exploit genre hybridity, the specific combination of traditionally masculine genres with more traditionally feminine ones evinces the growing importance of female viewers as a demographic.[12] This, combined with the fact that *Lois & Clark*'s hybridity privileges the more traditionally feminine genre, means this show can be described as a rare example of an iconic male superhero being (re)shaped by women with a female audience in mind.

This chapter interrogates this reshaping. In general, I am in agreement with existing scholarship on *Lois & Clark*, most of which has focused on the show's depiction of Lois as emblematic of the postfeminist ideal of "having it all" and the political shortcomings thereof.[13] Rather than reiterate these analyses, I am going to focus on what is, arguably, *Lois & Clark*'s more unique feature—namely, its unusually sexy depiction of Superman. I am deliberately using the term "sexy" rather than "erotic" to describe the general context of this depiction. Because *Lois & Clark* was a network show that aired, for most of its run, in a family-friendly Sunday evening time slot, its sexual content tends to be suggestive rather than overt. Yet despite and often *because of* its privileging of suggestiveness above explicitness, *Lois & Clark* makes Superman especially accessible to a desiring female audience; though the show certainly eroticizes Clark/Superman's muscular, waxed flesh, the character's broader sexiness also depends upon metaphors embedded in his transformations and gendered multiplicity. As a counterpoint, I consider how supersex is at the heart of the overarching conservatism *Lois & Clark* shares with so many other superhero stories. Even as *Lois & Clark* makes Superman unprecedentedly available to a female gaze and imagination, the supposed climax of this availability works to frustrate both; while *Lois & Clark*'s first three seasons foreground the sexiness of multiplicity, the title characters' commencement of a physical relationship following their marriage at the beginning of season four brings a descent into heteronormativity that undercuts the more deviant possibilities of the foreplay that proceeded it. Ultimately, my analysis suggests that the steep decline of *Lois & Clark*'s popularity in its fourth and final season may not be wholly blamed on the dissolution of its "will they or won't they" tension. Another factor may have been the show's failure to imagine supersex as anything other—or more—than perfect.

SEX AND THE NEW (SUPER)MAN

Lois & Clark's pilot episode—one of six first-season episodes written by LeVine—features several scenes that typify the show's sexy depiction of Clark/Superman. The "Clark/Superman" here is important, as *Lois & Clark* highlights the desirability of both Clark and Superman. As Michael G. Robinson observes, writer/artist John Byrne's 1986 comic book miniseries *The Man of Steel* laid the groundwork for *Lois & Clark* by emphasizing "the 'man' in Superman" and showing how Superman "became the disguise for Clark Kent."[14] Yet *Lois & Clark* differentiates itself by significantly amplifying both Clark's and Superman's sexiness while specifically highlighting both identities' appeal to women. Clark's interactions with his female officemates on his first day as a reporter for the *Daily Planet* function as a case in point. Upon her first glimpse of Clark, gossip columnist Cat Grant cranes her neck after his departing form, whistles, and asks Lois, "Who's the new tight end?" Cat's interest—or, perhaps, Clark's gentlemanly reaction to it—inspires Lois to begin seeing Clark in a new light. In the next scene, Lois is shown eyeing Clark from across the office. Shortly thereafter, she strides toward his desk and asks him—albeit reluctantly—if he wants to accompany her to Lex Luthor's charity ball. The pilot similarly emphasizes Superman's desirability. When the Man of Steel flies Lois into the newsroom in one of the final scenes, it is not only his costume and superpowers that inspire open-mouthed awe; his physical chemistry with Lois is equally spectacular. Cat, watching Superman and a breathless Lois gaze into each other's eyes, confirms as much. "I don't believe it," remarks Cat. Another female employee asks, "What—a man who flies?" to which Cat replies, "Lois Lane—finally, literally, swept off her feet."

Importantly, though, Clark and Superman are not desirable to everyone in precisely the same way, and their respective desirability shifts throughout the series. Lois initially finds the flashily heroic Superman more desirable than Clark, while other characters, such as Cat and a recurring season 2 love interest, district attorney Mayson Drake, find the sensitive and stylish Clark more desirable. In this way, the show exploits Clark's dual identity to present different types of attractive men that might appeal to different types of desiring women. Later, Lois finds Clark more desirable but is absolved from choosing between her loves when she discovers his dual identity at the conclusion of season 2. Once Lois possesses this knowledge, she in effect has simultaneous access to (at least) two types of men (a sensitive writer and a muscle-bound hero), with no moral qualms.

Clark's ability to embody different types of masculinity also, however, illustrates problematic aspects of the "new man" ideal that was born in the 1980s and persisted into the '90s. John Benyon describes one version of the new man: "Changing patterns in family life, with men marrying later or not at all, along with a willingness to take on a supportive role in a woman's career, resulted in the emergence of the new man as an ideal. He was the riposte to vilified 'old man', his father, and a refugee from the hardline masculinity epitomized by the paranoid, macho men with stifled emotions."[15] As Tim Edwards discusses throughout his book *Men in the Mirror: Men's Fashion, Masculinity and Consumer Society*, many popular representations of the new man were highly contradictory. The new man was frequently depicted as both newly sensitive and newly narcissistic, his desire to appeal to women manifesting in both a newly enhanced capacity for empathy as well as a newly vigorous embrace of masculine aesthetics, expressed through fashion, consumerism, and body maintenance, including both dieting and bodybuilding.

Like the new man, Clark is simultaneously contemporary and traditional: he is an artistically attuned and socially conscious journalist[16] whose stylish business clothes barely disguise a superpowerful male physique that is further glorified by the Superman costume, itself an iconic symbol of masculine strength, individuality, and heroism. Rowena Chapman argues that the new man's hybridity helped preserve men's cultural preeminence in the face of gender upheaval: although "the combination of feminism and social change may have produced a fragmentation in male identity[,] . . . the effect of the emergence of the new man has been to reinforce the existing power structure, by producing a hybrid masculinity which is better able and more suited to retain control."[17] *Lois & Clark*'s premise supports Chapman's argument. While the show's version of Lois has some access to hybridity—she often assumes disguises in her role as an investigative reporter, including on two occasions (the pilot and the season 2 episode "Chi of Steel") disguises involving male drag—Clark has more access to more types of hybridity, taking on investigative disguises in addition to living a double life every single day.

While Clark's hybridity obviously predates the rise of the new man ideal, it becomes additionally resonant within that context and in relation to *Lois & Clark*'s supposed embrace of female empowerment; Clark's hybridity enables his superheroism and vice versa, the new man ideal working in concert with the preexisting Superman mythos to make Clark's greater access to hybridity seem that much more natural and appropriate.[18] Throughout the show, empowering forms of hybridity are also demonstrated to be a privilege of whiteness. Despite taking place in a major metropolitan center analogous to New York, *Lois & Clark* relegates people of color to supporting roles that are almost exclusively nonrecurring and often tied to racial stereotypes that specifically foreclose the possibility of complexity.[19] For instance, the only prominent appearance of Asian Americans occurs in an episode about karate-wielding gangs in Chinatown;[20] in another episode, a Black illusionist (Cress Williams) tries to kill Clark with "voodoo";[21] and four episodes feature Lois's African American neighbor, Star (Olivia Brown), an eccentric, scatterbrained, but possibly magical psychic undoubtedly inspired, in broad strokes, by Whoopi Goldberg's character in *Ghost* (1990). Similar to Herman Gray's description of Goldberg's character, Star is "both a spiritual conduit from the world of the living to that of the dead and an affirmation that the triple sites of other—blackness, spirituality, woman—are, as [Toni] Morrison says, known and thus serviceable to that ultimate American fantasy—romantic love and the white heterosexual family."[22] The only nonwhite character to be featured in multiple seasons, Lex Luthor's personal assistant, Asabi (Shaun Toub), epitomizes the "inscrutable Oriental" trope.

Clark's privileged access to hybridity helps him ground (or disguise) his newly available sexiness in traditional trappings of heroic masculinity. Though Clark does not wear the "dark, broadly cut, double-breasted suits, striped shirts, [and] Oxford brogues" that Edwards describes as most typical of the new man's *"corporate power look,"*[23] he does stand apart from other reporters at the *Daily Planet* in always wearing a suit and tie. In addition, though Clark often favors softer colors such as brown, maroon, and beige, his suits are, in conversation with both '90s fashion and the 1930s and '40s style references that pervade the show, definitely oversized and, in their oversizedness, defiantly masculine; the broad shoulders and long lines of Clark's suits always make him appear wider and taller, fulfilling the conventional function of the suit as a form of clothing that is "used to cover yet accentuate the . . . masculine, mesomorphic physical shape."[24] Even as they reveal the body's potentially sensual curves, the full body covering, skintight costumes worn by most male superheroes, tend to function similarly. These costumes smooth and streamline the body, shrink-wrapping it in a seemingly impenetrable, condom-like sheath that symbolizes and preserves the superhero's phallic power. As Jeffrey A. Brown argues elsewhere in this volume, "the disparity between the phallus and the penis" is "magically resolved" in part through "the colorful costume that serves as a literal veil for the secret identity and the penis." "The costume as veil," continues Brown, "disguises the inherent weaknesses in the equation [of penis versus phallus] and presents the superhero/phallus as spectacular."[25] A male superhero's muscles can also protect him from being objectified or feminized. Chapman observes, "Even in passivity [the muscled body] . . . articulates action and potential, identifying the participants as active subjects, not passive objects, controllers rather than the dupes of destiny."[26] Dawn Heinecken similarly argues that a male action hero's muscles evoke "a 'hardness' that exists beyond the physical," representing, in the literalness of flesh, that the man is a "master over his environment," possessing "a control over his own body that has historically been denied to women, the weaker, 'softer' sex."[27]

TRANSFORMATIONS, MULTIPLICITY, AND THE GAZE

Yet even if *Lois & Clark* does not fully overcome the political shortcomings typical of both the new man movement and the famously sexist superhero genre, its depiction of Clark/Superman does severely test the protective function of suits, costumes, and muscles. The show does this, in part, by routinely stripping Clark of his suit and costume and revealing his muscled body in ways that make it particularly accessible to desirous female gazes. Another scene from the series pilot, which is highlighted by Matthew Freeman in his analysis of the show, is representative of *Lois & Clark*'s frequent depictions of Clark's partially naked body and the implications therein. The scene in question features, in Freeman's words, a "long shot to capture a scene of Clark in his apartment, on the phone to his parents, wearing nothing but a towel. Once Lois arrives at Clark's apartment, somewhat startled by the muscular physique of her new colleague, the camera's prolonged tracking of Clark's movement mirrors both the gaze of Lois and indeed the eye of most female audience spectators. . . . In this way, the 'to-be-looked-at-ness' typically associated with the male gaze theory is reversed."[28] I am hesitant to fully endorse Freeman's assertion that this scene might offer a wholesale reversal of male gaze theory. Here and elsewhere, male muscles function as Chapman and Heinecken argue they do—as signs of traditionally masculine power that resist the passivity usually associated with objectification. As I will discuss in due course, it is also fundamentally unclear whether male gaze theory *can* be so simply reversed. This scene does, however, make the male superhero unusually accessible, as a character and as an object of desire. Clark is caught in a decidedly private moment: alone in his apartment with his secret identity exposed, both in a physical sense, via his surprising muscles, and a narrative one, via the conversation he is having with his adoptive parents, who know his secret. His privacy is further penetrated by Lois, whose gaze we are encouraged to identify with, and who is introduced standing on the other side of the door, suggesting the classic voyeuristic scenario of looking through a keyhole.

It is also relevant that this scene depicts Clark within something of a transitional state, between his identities. He is, in effect, revealed—and eroticized—mid-transformation. Another scene from the pilot, wherein Clark tries on multiple potential versions of his Superman costume for the first time, further highlights the show's eroticization of his transformations (figure 9.1). Within a montage set to Bonnie Tyler's 1984 hit song "Holding Out for a Hero," Clark tests out costumes that include a head-to-toe hot pink leotard and a jungle hero–inspired leopard print spandex bodysuit paired with green tights and a studded belt. He also tries on several different masks and styles of tall lace-up and pull-on boots. Much of the montage is filmed from behind Clark while he poses alongside his adoptive mother, Martha (K Callan), facing a full-length mirror; throughout the sequence, the mirror reveals multiple angles of Clark's body as well as Martha's face working through a series of contemplative, frustrated, and admiring expressions. Other shots within the montage, which are spliced between views of Martha laboring over her sewing machine, dissect Clark's body; we are treated to close-ups of his feet, his face, and his bare shoulders, the last of which, because of the mirror, also provides a view of Clark's bare chest as Martha measures its impressive breadth. At one point, Clark examines his rear end in the mirror while Martha pokes and smooths his red underwear.

The montage concludes with Clark, finally dressed in a mostly complete version of his Superman costume, once again standing next to Martha in front of the mirror. This time, though, the camera is positioned alongside the mirror, so that we are looking at Martha's and Clark's faces as they look into it. After a moment of quiet contemplation, Martha offers the sarcastic quip, "Well one thing's for sure—nobody's going to be looking at your face!" She greets Clark's gentle admonishment with another quip: "Well they don't call them tights for nothing!" The first full view of the complete Superman costume begins with a slow pan across Clark's body, from his red-booted feet up his blue spandex-clad thighs to his chest and his face, his thoughtfully heroic countenance positioned next to and above the shorter Martha's almost tearful expression of pride. Amid a swell of dramatic music, Clark finally removes his glasses.

In showing Clark's process of becoming Superman in this way—that is, in another private moment, in which the male body is variously and

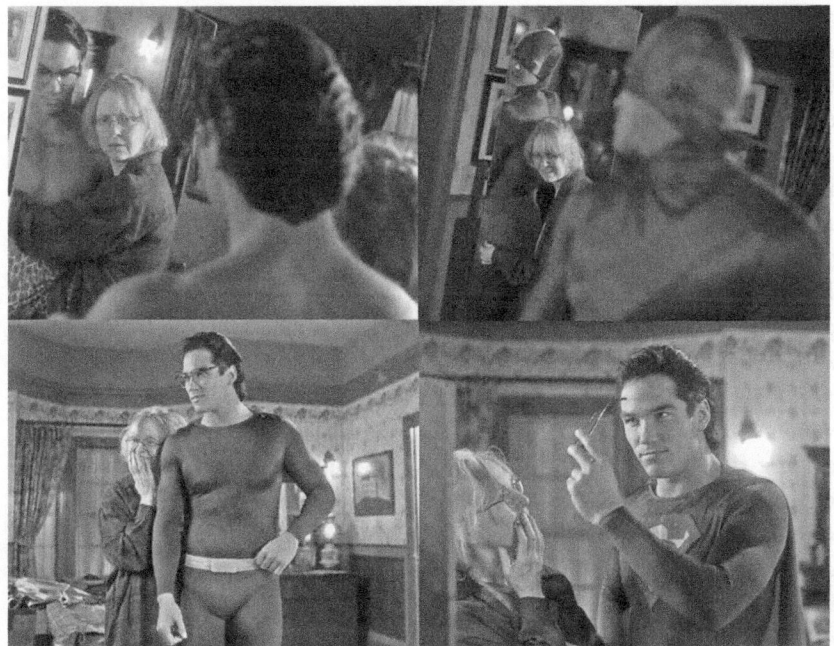

FIGURE 9.1. Martha helps (and watches) Clark try on costumes. Pilot episode of *Lois & Clark* (1993).

even simultaneously beautiful, powerful, and ridiculous—*Lois & Clark* subverts at least some of the male superhero's conventional phallic power. Weltzien argues that the male superhero's transformation between his two identities functions similarly to how Chapman posits the new man's hybridity functions—namely, as an advertisement for, and enactment of, (white) men's privileged ability to overcome, through incorporation, social and cultural changes that might otherwise threaten their preeminence. For Weltzien, superheroes are marked as both superheroic and supermasculine through "a superior ability in masking" that is less about women than about "the competitive relationship between men."[29] This superior ability in masking is foregrounded by the effortlessness of the male superhero's transformation, which occurs magically and/or in "absolute privacy."[30] Richard Reynolds similarly observes that for male superheroes, "the transformation into costume can best be achieved with something as instantaneous as Billy Batson's 'Shazam.'"[31] The gendered significance of this instantaneousness is highlighted by the generally quite different transformations of female superheroes. Because they typically involve more overtly erotic costumes and/or are drawn out in ways that male superheroes' transformations are not, the transformations of female superheroes "can (at least potentially) be viewed as the performance of an uncompleted striptease."[32]

By eroticizing the transformation of the male superhero and multiplying it—making one transformation a series of transformations evoking multiple degrees and/or types of masculinity—*Lois & Clark* both complicates the process of transformation and reveals its inner workings. Furthermore, by including women—both young, single working women and older, married mothers—as observers and even active participants in Clark's transformations, *Lois & Clark* makes the male superhero's performance of multiple masculinities something that can be both about women and for women. Though Martha's presence can be read as desexualizing the sequence, we do not have to believe that Martha sexually desires Clark in order for her to function, like Lois in the scene where she discovers Clark shirtless in his apartment, as a stand-in for the sexually desirous female audience. The savvy postmodern television audience can be expected to understand that Martha and the actor playing Martha are not one and the same; K Callan can acknowledge Clark/Superman's (or Dean Cain's) sexiness even as Martha's "official" reaction is nonsexual. In this, Martha's quips can function as winks from one wise woman to another (or many others). This is not, of course, the only audience these transformations might appeal to. Clark/Superman's heroic body can function as an ego ideal as well as an object of desire. In addition, the popularity of Tyler's song in gay and drag culture, along with the overtly "campy" nature of several of Clark's potential costumes, can, for properly attuned viewers, evoke a "gay vague" atmosphere of desire.[33] I am not denying these additional or alternative readings. I am, however, arguing that this show's depiction of Clark/Superman's transformations—in this scene and throughout the series—consciously includes and even prioritizes a desiring female audience.

There is a long but underexplored history of popular media using the performance of masculine multiplicity to appeal to female audiences. Among those who have explored this theme is Miriam Hansen, who discusses it within the context of theorizing the presence of a female gaze in films from the 1920s starring Rudolph Valentino. Because looking with the male gaze involves a patriarchal division of the filmic world into subject/object and passive/active binaries, many feminist film scholars have argued that the male gaze, and the patriarchy it reflects and reinforces, cannot be truly challenged except through a complication of these binaries. Scholars have typically looked for such complications in films and television shows starring female protagonists, including the "woman's film" of the 1940s, soap operas, or works produced within the feminist avant-garde.[34] Hansen takes a different approach that is particularly relevant to *Lois & Clark*. Rather than looking to female characters for a form of "instability, mobility, [and] multiplicity" capable of disrupting the "so-called normal vision" of "the male subject [that] controls the external world as well as the sexual field," Hansen looks to Valentino, a male performer whose films thematize multiplicity and attracted a famously devoted female fanbase.[35] Valentino's appeal, Hansen argues, is bound up in "the manner in which he combines masculine control of the look with the feminine quality of 'to-be-looked-at-ness.'"[36] Valentino's films do this by having the actor embody "two sides of a melodramatic dualism,"[37] wherein he both asserts the connotatively phallic, controlling power of the male gaze and is willingly eroticized in a connotatively feminine manner by the gazes of desirous female subjects within the film as well as desirous real women outside it. Valentino's hybridity is expanded into multiplicity via "a series of disguises and anonymous identities" as well as various "rituals of dressing and undressing"[38] that once again showcase the coexistence of connotatively masculine agency and connotatively feminine eroticism. According to Hansen, Valentino is ultimately "a figure of overdetermination, an unstable composite figure that connotes 'the simultaneous presence of two positionalities of desire' . . . and thus calls into question the very idea of polarity rather than simply reversing its terms."[39] In this, Valentino's example challenges theories of spectatorship that too easily associate maleness and masculinity with activity and subjectivity, and femaleness and femininity with passivity and objectification.

While American television of the 1990s obviously exists in a very different context from American films of the 1920s, *Lois & Clark*'s version of Clark/Superman is similar to Valentino in possessing both an unusually erotic body and an exaggeratedly powerful gaze; as Clark, he is an investigative reporter, and as Superman, he has X-ray and microscopic vision. Clark also, as discussed above, possesses a multiplicity that is foregrounded by the putting on and taking off of various disguises. Though Clark's disguises are more obvious than anonymous, inasmuch as he is always, to some extent, in disguise, his masculinity is, like Valentino's, self-consciously performative. Hansen's characterization of Valentino's appeal is furthermore strikingly similar to Clarissa Smith's reading of the Chippendales male stripper shows that, like *Lois & Clark*, were influenced by the rise of the new man ideal and surged in popularity alongside it. The Chippendales live shows Smith analyzes feature men clad in cuffs, bowties, and, at points, not much else, dancing their way through eroticized versions of "a number of Hollywood films, musical texts and performances alongside youth culture 'tableaux.'"[40] Although the Chippendales are all "clean cut, polished, manicured—'fantasy' men whose *individuality* seems to be limited to height and colour and length of hair, . . . 'the transformation of the body in its presentation and performance produces different ways of being male.'"[41] These different ways of being male, Smith argues, suggest different ways of looking at maleness and masculinity. The Chippendales shows are not "simply a role reversal of subject/object, male/female, looker/looked-at,"[42] nor do they offer a full-scale deconstruction of such binaries. These choreographed presentations of eroticized masculine transformations do, however, "perform male sexuality as fun, expressive and, crucially, desirous of women's pleasure and approval," which in turn "presents the spectacle of erotic male bodies in ways palatable and, essentially, accessible to women."[43] The Chippendales' accessibility is rooted in the multiplicity they embody as men who are at once demonstrably masculine and unconventionally erotic, and who act out, through their transformations, the play between such categories. It is this play between categories that makes even traditional masculinity— signaled by muscles and powerful gazes—erotically accessible; the fact that masculinity *can* be played with demystifies it, making it something that can be enjoyed without shame or masochism.

Appropriately, *Lois & Clark*'s honeymoon episode, season 4's "Soul Mates," most directly and extensively exploits the sexy potential of masculine multiplicity. Though LeVine ceased to have any direct input on *Lois & Clark*'s content after she left her executive producer role at the end the show's first season, "Soul Mates" demonstrates that the themes she helped establish pervade the show even in her absence. "Soul Mates" opens in Clark's apartment just as he and Lois are preparing to leave for their honeymoon in Hawaii, where they plan to escalate their physical relationship for the first time; up to this point, Clark is a virgin in the conventional sense (I will address the significance of this fact in the next section). The couple does not, however, make it to Hawaii. Clark, dressed as Superman, begins passionately kissing a supine Lois on his bed only to be interrupted by recurring associate H. G. Wells. In the universe of the show, the celebrated British writer possesses a real time machine that he repeatedly uses to thwart the evil schemes of an escaped future-dweller named Tempus. On this occasion, a past version of Tempus has placed a curse on Lois and Clark set to be triggered as soon as they, as Wells puts it, "consummate" their marriage. "Unless you go back to the time of the curse and stop it from being cast," says Wells, "tragedy will strike you down in every lifetime, every time you consummate. Usually it's . . . very painful."[44] Breaking the curse involves Lois and Clark traveling through time to inhabit versions of themselves from various historical periods; these are not actual relatives but bearers of what Wells characterizes as the couple's "soul energy." This premise can be viewed as a send-up of either/both *Superman II* or Niven's "Woman of Kleenex" essay, as well as a deliberate attempt to repair those and other stories' depictions of supersex as impossible or dangerous. Though Lois and Clark's relationship has historically been cursed, this version of the characters, this episode suggests, has the will and the power to intervene in the trope and change it.

Over the course of the episode, Lois, Clark, and Wells travel to a medieval Robin Hood–inspired scenario and a Western Lone Ranger–inspired scenario. In each scenario, Clark does not have his superpowers, but does have a dual identity that includes at least two different, sometimes flamboyant costumes featuring capes, masks, and lots of leather (his first questions after the initial time jump are: "Where are we? What am I *wearing*?"). Lois does not have a dual identity in either scenario, and most of her costumes are noticeably demure. As Maid Marion analogue Lady Loisette, she wears a crown and sheer headdress paired with a monochrome dress that features neither a corset nor décolletage. And as Lulu in the Wild West scenario, she wears an attractive but somewhat androgynous ensemble of wide-legged wool pants, a button-down white shirt, and a fitted, black leather vest. Most of Clark's costumes, meanwhile, are overtly sexy, whether in their substance, their articulation, the reactions they provoke, or all the above. At times, Lois is less than enthusiastic about prolonging the time-jumping experience. At one point, she laments, "I've heard of foreplay, but this is ridiculous"; at another, "Can't we just have a honeymoon like a normal couple?" Clark's costumes, however, repeatedly reignite her enthusiasm. When Clark makes his first change from Robin Hood analogue the Fox into his dual identity as a knight named Sir Charles, he steps into Lois's and the audience's view mid-transformation, wearing only a pair of tight-fitting, high-waisted black pants; Lois is so mesmerized by the sight that her words dry up mid-sentence, replaced with a glazed, jaw-dropped expression as her eyes journey across Clark's half-naked body (figure 9.2). The intensity of Lois's reaction prompts Clark to examine himself. "It's the pants, isn't it?" he asks, bending toward his glutes. "They're too tight." "No," Lois protests, glazed expression dissolving into a dreamy smile. "They're, uh, perfect. I just never get over how . . . *well-defined* you are." They kiss, with Lois's hand resting on Clark's bare abdominals, confirming their hardness with

FIGURE 9.2. Lois is struck speechless by Clark's transformation into Sir Charles. "Soul Mates" episode of *Lois & Clark* (1996).

her visible touch. Then, Lois helps Clark into a studded leather vest, carefully lacing it up his ribs as he settles it onto his ample, waxed chest. In the Western scenario, Clark, dressed as the Lone Ranger analogue the Lone Rider, hoists Lois onto the back of his horse for a dramatic escape, then lowers her, with a dancerly spin, into his arms. "Mmmm . . . ," Lois moans, "my hero." Clark smiles as he quips, "Pretty romantic, huh?" "Very," Lois agrees, returning his smile before dropping into his chest for yet another kissing session (no less than the sixth of eight such sessions within this forty-four-minute episode). When Wells interrupts the couple to warn of the villain's approach, it is Lois who steps out of Clark's arms to riffle through the saddlebags for a solution. "What are you looking for?" asks Clark. "Your secret identity," Lois replies. "I assume you have one." A moment later, Lois successfully retrieves the clothes of a man she humorously describes as a "mild-mannered telegraph operator."

Though "Soul Mates" features Lois performing more transformations than usual, it is still Clark who performs the most transformations the most spectacularly. This episode is, as such, less concerned with the traditional filmic spectacle of the female body as it is invested in watching Clark play dress up, watching Lois watch Clark play dress up, and encouraging viewers to watch Lois watching and dressing—and undressing—Clark. The available meanings here are complex and contradictory. In this episode, Clark is a man of action as well as a living doll, whose time-spanning sexiness advertises both multiplicity and immutability, either of which can be subversive or conservative; Clark is both an everyman and any man, both universally sexy and generically so, inasmuch as all of his masculinities are stereotypical and most of them are similar both to one another and to his usual performance of masculine multiplicity.

On the one hand, the genericness of Clark's masculinities presents the concept of masculinity—and specifically, masculine heroism—as a kind of unshakeable, universal truth. On the other hand, this genericness reveals this truth as a lie. Masculinity might be no more than a fetish, a disguise or costume that a man (or, perhaps, the right woman) can put on or take off as they need to or want to—less a biological fact than an erotic affectation. Even in this reading, though, traditional masculinity is upheld through the veneration implicit in its desirability; as in Hansen's reading of Valentino's films and Smith's reading of the Chippendales live show, Clark's multiplicity does not solve the problem of the female gaze so much as it illustrates underexplored aspects of that gaze's complexity. Clark's transformations in "Soul Mates" evoke additional complexity by extending the female gaze across eras and into other traditionally masculine genres, such as action-fantasy and the Western, that have traditionally—or at the very least officially—shunned it.

"Soul Mates" climaxes in a final series of quick transformations that are, this time, freely chosen and reciprocal. Back at the *Daily Planet* office in the twentieth century, Clark, dressed in what Edwards would describe as an *"outdoor casual"* look[45] consisting of a button-down plaid shirt tucked into faded blue jeans, once again scoops Lois into his arms. A dissolve and swooshing sound of flight returns the couple to Clark's apartment. As he did in the episode's opening scenes, Clark, now dressed as Superman, lays Lois down on the bed and climbs on top. They kiss until Lois extricates herself to perform her own transformation, running to the bathroom and emerging a few moments later in a black teddy with a small cape she quickly tosses off. Mirroring Lois in the scene where she first encounters Clark half-transformed into Sir Charles, Clark is momentarily stunned into speechlessness. Then he smiles and, before our eyes and hers, performs a fast-motion spin to change into a masculine version of Lois's outfit: black boxer shorts paired with a semi-sheer, unbuttoned black shirt (figure 9.3). The couple spends another long moment gazing at each other, then meet at the bed, where Lois peels Clark's shirt off his shoulders before Clark, for the third time in the episode, lowers Lois onto the bed and himself onto Lois. The newlyweds exchange long, passionate open-mouthed kisses as their blanket-draped bodies rise into the air above the bed. A dissolve pulls the camera back, outside the floor-to-ceiling window, and finally up into the starry sky to watch a flaming comet streak across it.

Despite the conventional phallic imagery that closes this episode, the preceding scene's emphasis on gazes founded in, to quote Hansen, "reciprocity and ambivalence, rather than mastery and objectification,"

FIGURE 9.3. Lois and Clark transform into versions of each other. "Soul Mates" episode of *Lois & Clark* (1996).

suggests what is most potentially subversive about such gazes:[46] unlike mainstream, heterosexual pornography, in which "male-female differences are reducible to bodily parts which are exclusively sexual in function,"[47] these gazes might offer "a different *kind* of sexuality, different from the norm of heterosexual, genital sexuality."[48]

DOMESTICATING DIFFERENCE

The season 3 episode "Virtually Destroyed"—which was, interestingly, cowritten by Cain—establishes that Clark is a sexual virgin prior to his marriage, whereas Lois is not. This choice is significant inasmuch as it subverts gender norms and unlinks masculine identity and heroism from the actualized performance of heterosexuality. In a different but related vein, *Lois & Clark*'s depiction of Clark as a man who actively desires marriage and family represents a dramatic departure from previous representations of the character, and of mainstream representations of masculine heroism more generally. Other prominent superheroes had been married before, and the Superman comic books had Lois and Clark become engaged prior to the launch of *Lois & Clark* and wed concurrently with it. Yet *Lois & Clark* is arguably unprecedented in setting up the male superhero's desire for marriage and family as a primary focus of his character journey. In *Lois & Clark*, Clark does not move to Metropolis and pursue a job at the *Daily Planet* because he wants to be a hero. Instead, in the show's pilot, Clark associates moving to Metropolis with his desire to "lead a normal life," which, to his mind, includes "living, working, meeting someone, having a family." *Lois & Clark*'s fourth season lets Clark fulfill this dream, but at the expense of the sexual deviance suggested by the nervous response of his adoptive father Jonathan (Eddie Jones). "Clark . . ." Jonathan begins, struggling to meet his son's eyes, "We don't know if that's possible."

This deviance is domesticated, first and foremost, through the conservative morality underpinning the couple's desire to be married in a Christian church before beginning a physical relationship. In addition, several post-marriage episodes deliberately eliminate aspects of Lois and Clark's relationship that might make it anything less than perfectly heteronormative: in "The People vs. Lois Lane," Lois and Clark abandon their city apartments for a house in the suburbs (complete with white picket fence); in "Ghosts," Lois agonizes about not fulfilling her wifely role due to her inability to cook, but learns the basics after being possessed by a domestically gifted ghost; and in "Stop the Presses," Lois rescinds a promotion to editor of the *Daily Planet* due to the negative effect it has on her relationship with Clark. Season 4 also features several episodes that resolve Clark's biological differences in a heteronormative direction. In "Brutal Youth," Lois is distressed to realize Clark will age much slower than she will. Upon discovering this, Lois has a vision of herself and Clark in a mirror wherein she is a much older woman, while Clark is still his thirty-something self. Whereas the costume montage in the show's pilot sanctioned and even encouraged postmenopausal women to gaze at Clark/Superman, in "Brutal Youth," the audience is meant to react to Clark placing his affectionate hands on the shoulders of a visibly older woman in much the same way Lois does—with terror and revulsion. By the conclusion of the episode, Clark has surrendered a portion of his "life force" to save Jimmy Olsen (Justin Whalin), resulting in his aging process assuming a normal (i.e., human) speed. Lois and Clark's biological incapacity to have children, meanwhile, is resolved, like their wedding, through unexplained magical intervention. The series' final episode, "The Family Hour," concludes with a baby in a Superman blanket being dropped off on the doorstep of Lois and Clark's suburban home.

The single season 4 episode that foregrounds a sexual theme strongly suggests that while sex—even supersex—within marriage is right and good, sex—*especially* supersex—that happens outside of it is either/both morally wrong or dangerous, capable of destroying not only individual lives but the world itself. In the episode "Sex, Lies, and Videotape," a tabloid reporter captures a photograph of Clark kissing Lois in a hotel room while he is dressed as Superman. A scandal erupts, which threatens Lois's and Clark's credibility as reporters and Superman's status as a hero; in the wake of the scandal, Lois and Clark are besieged by television crews and tabloid reporters, and the leaders of two fictional Middle Eastern countries reject the peace treaty Superman had been helping to negotiate, instead accelerating their war. When Clark suggests ending the scandal by revealing his dual identity, Lois's opposition to the idea is revealing. In a lengthy, passionate speech, she says: "There's a greater truth to protect here, and that's the *idea* of what Superman is. If you tell them you're *married*, that you have desires and feelings just like everybody else, then that image of a hero is shattered. It's *gone*. People need to believe in that mythic truth. *That* is what Superman is all about, and *that* is what you should protect above all else."[49] Though Lois protecting the idea of Superman is not out of character—she is, after all, the person who names him and routinely uses her writing to bolster his myth—her insistence that the scandal goes beyond Superman's supposed infidelity to the fact that he has a sexuality at all stands out as unusual. The season 3 episode "Chip off the Old Clark," in which Superman becomes embroiled in another sex scandal involving a woman who claims to have had his baby, features a great deal of public outcry concerning Superman's lack of financial support for the woman and her child, but never suggests the public is upset about the mere *idea* of Superman having sex. And yet "Sex, Lies, and Videotape" ultimately supports Lois's argument. After Lois and Jimmy discover the tabloid photographs are faked (the photographer's original film was destroyed in an accident), Clark agrees to tell a white lie, the wording of which eerily presages President Bill Clinton's famous denial of his affair with Monica Lewinsky, which would occur the following year. At a press conference, Clark, as Superman, declares, "I am not having, nor have I ever had, an illicit affair with Lois Lane." War is averted, and life returns to normal.

This episode's final scene confirms that supersex is only acceptable within clearly defined limits. Wearing nothing but a pair of boxer shorts, Clark joins a suggestively naked Lois under a blanket in front of a raging fireplace. Clark admits he is not completely comfortable with the lie he told the media but agrees that "there was a larger truth to protect here."

He and Lois promise to "be more careful" in the future and begin to move toward each other. Clark pulls back quickly, complaining that Lois's feet are freezing. Lois smirks and quips, "Warm 'em up." Clark ducks his head under the blanket. There is a buzz and glow of heat vision, a gasp, and then an exchange of playful smiles above the blanket. "You missed," Lois charges. "No," Clark replies, "I didn't." Lois giggles as she melts into Clark's embrace, the screen fades to black, and the episode ends. Given Superman's predominantly sexless history, showing him use his heat vision to, presumably, warm Lois's nether regions represents a significant departure from tradition. Yet this act is preceded by Lois and Clark agreeing that Superman's sexuality is inherently scandalous, requiring careful management; this scene, this episode, and this season as a whole sanction this management by replicating it.

CONCLUSION

Like several other contributors to this collection, I am compelled, in closing, to make a brief turn toward the personal. *Lois & Clark* was the first superhero story I ever loved, and I did so obsessively, with all the passion of a first romance. As a girl on the cusp of puberty, I taped all the episodes to rewatch dozens of times; I called a best girlfriend after each episode aired for a gush session full of squeals and giggles; I read the tie-in novels and when I finished those, turned to fan fiction; when I ran out of fan fiction, I wrote my own—a hundred-page magnum opus featuring time travel, alternate dimensions, and, of course, plenty of transformations and lots of smoldering gazes. Yet within this obsessive love, I was tortured by an angry indecision that possessed my body like a physical pain. I loved Lois, I loved Clark, and I loved Superman. But as much as I wanted to *have* Clark, I also wanted, more than I felt I had ever wanted anything in my life up to that point, to *be* him.

Partly, I wanted to be Clark because he was freer than Lois. Where Lois ended the series in a largely conventional female role—in suburbia, raising a baby with a presumably much-distracted husband—Clark never lost the ability to soar above it all. This was not, however, the only reason I identified with him. The same sexy transformations that made me want to have Clark enabled him to embody, more persuasively than Lois is permitted to do, struggles at the heart of both her female experience and mine. Clark's performance of gendered multiplicity metaphorizes the struggle to be sexy while remaining in control of that sexiness, as well as related struggles to live up to hopelessly contradictory expectations, and to be simultaneously normal and special. These struggles are also, of course, commonplace; most of us will experience them at some point, in some way. But for all its catering to a female audience, *Lois & Clark* does not treat them that way. Nor does most of the scholarship I have read in my more than ten years of researching and writing about superheroes, which too often treats female fans of the superhero genre as insignificant, invisible, and even impossible.[50] And every time I encounter this neglect, I remember my twelve-year-old self, watching *Lois & Clark*, and watching Lois watch Clark, wondering why falling in love had to feel so lonely, or make me so angry.

NOTES

1. Michael Kimmel, *Manhood in America: A Cultural History* (New York: Oxford University Press, 2006), 140.

2. Friedrich Weltzien, "Masque-*ulinities*: Changing Dress as a Display of Masculinity in the Superhero Genre," *Fashion Theory* 9, no. 2 (June 2005): 232.

3. The popularity of Niven's essay is evinced by the fact that it has been reprinted and shared widely since it was originally published. In addition to being reprinted in *Penthouse Comix*, it appeared in Niven's 1971 short story collection *All the Myriad Ways* as well as his 1990 collection *N-Space*. It was also reprinted in the 1978 anthology *SuperHeroes*, edited by Michel Parry, and was shared, in 1986, on Usenet (an early form of the World Wide Web). The essay is currently available on multiple websites.

4. Though most of Niven's essay dwells with fetishistic fascination on the details of how Superman's penis and sperm would destroy Lois, his conclusion does offer a boldly deviant solution to the problem of Superman's inability to reproduce. Writes Niven, "A better solution may be to implant the growing fetus in Superman himself. There are places in a man's abdomen where a fetus could draw adequate nourishment, growing as a parasite, and where it would not cause undue harm to surrounding organs. Presumably Clark Kent can take a leave of absence." The boldness of this suggestion is limited, however, by the transphobic tone of Niven's final sentences: "The mind boggles at the image of a pregnant Superman cruising the skies of Metropolis. Batman would refuse to be seen with him; strange new jokes would circulate the prisons." Larry Niven, "Man of Steel, Woman of Kleenex," accessed January 20, 2019, http://www.rawbw.com/~svw/superman.html.

5. Jessica Weiss, "Sex, the Single Girl, Superman, and the City: Lois Lane and Romance in *Superman: The Movie* through *Superman IV*," in *Examining Lois Lane: The Scoop on Superman's Sweetheart*, ed. Nadine Farghaly (Lanham, MD: Scarecrow Press, 2013), 141.

6. For examples of "best of" lists that rank this series highly, see Edward Wallace, "10 Essential Superman Comics You Need to Read," Fortress of Solitude,

May 9, 2017, https://www.fortressofsolitude.co.za/superman-comics-you-need-to-read/; Evan Narcisse, "The Best Superman Stories of the Modern Era," io9, Gizmodo, April 23, 2018, https://io9.gizmodo.com/the-best-superman-stories-of-the-modern-era-1825416272; and "The Best Superman Stories, Ranked," Ranker, https://www.ranker.com/list/best-superman-comics/ranker-comics.

7. This is, admittedly, a significant simplification of the long and tangled history of Superman and Lois's relationship as it has existed across many different comics, television shows, cartoons, and films over the past seventy years. Yet while Lois and Clark/Superman do enjoy a reasonably healthy romance and/or have children or get married in multiple DC-sanctioned properties, there remain far more stories where the characters' romance is endlessly deferred or ends in tragedy and death. For a more thorough account of this history, see Kathleen Rittenhouse, "Lois and Superman: Will Love Triumph?" in *Examining Lois Lane: The Scoop on Superman's Sweetheart*, ed. Nadine Farghaly (Lanham, MD: Scarecrow Press, 2013), 61–88. See also Matt Yockey's contribution to this volume, which discusses both additional stories linking sex with death and several notable exceptions to this convention.

8. *Lois & Clark: The New Adventures of Superman*, developed by Deborah Joy LeVine, aired September 12, 1993–June 14, 1997, on ABC. Hereafter, all episodes are cited by episode number and name.

9. Rittenhouse, "Lois and Superman," 78.

10. See Freeman, "Woman on Top," 190. See also Bruce Fretts, "TV Winners & Losers," *Entertainment Weekly*, no. 277, June 2, 1995.

11. *Superman* #75 (1992), in which supervillain Doomsday kills Superman, is the only Superman comic book from the 1990s to sell more than a million copies, selling approximately three million copies. "Top 10 Best Selling Comic Books of the Modern Era," Zap-Kapow Comics, May 10, 2019, https://www.zapkapowcomics.com/top-10-best-selling-comic-books.

12. Jackie Byars and Eileen R. Meehan, "Once in a Lifetime: Constructing 'the Working Woman' through Cable Narrowcasting," *Camera Obscura* 11–12, no. 3–1 (May 1994): 20–21.

13. In general, the show erases potential conflicts between career and romance by having Lois's professional and personal lives both revolve around Superman, often at the expense of independent action and character development. For a fuller discussion of this theme, see Rhonda V. Wilcox, "Lois's Locks: Trust and Representation in *Lois and Clark: The New Adventures of Superman*," in *Fantasy Girls: Gender in the New Universe of Science Fiction and Fantasy Television*, ed. Elyce Rae Helford (Lanham, MD: Rowman & Littlefield, 2000), 91–114; Mary D. Durden, "It's a Bird! It's a Plane! It's Lois Lane!: The Construction of a Super(ior) Woman in *Lois & Clark*," in *Examining Lois Lane: The Scoop on Superman's Sweetheart*, ed. Nadine Farghaly (Lanham, MD: Scarecrow Press, 2013), 171–188; Freeman, "Woman on Top," 189–210.

14. Michael G. Robinson, "*Lois & Clark*: What's New About *The New Adventures of Superman?*" *Studies in Popular Culture* 21, no. 1 (October 1998): 83–98.

15. John Benyon, *Masculinities and Culture* (Philadelphia, PA: Open University, 2002), 100.

16. In the pilot, Clark earns his job at the *Daily Planet* by writing what Lois denigrates as a "mood piece" about the proposed destruction of a historical theater. To write the piece, Clark spends time sympathizing with an older actress, watching her perform scenes from Anton Chekhov's *The Cherry Orchard*.

17. Rowena Chapman, "The Great Pretender: Variations on the New Man Theme" in *Male Order: Unwrapping Masculinity*, ed. Rowena Chapman and Jonathan Rutherford (London: Lawrence & Wishart, 1988), 235.

18. Tellingly, at no point is there ever any real suggestion that Lois might take over the superhero role. On the one occasion Lois does become a superhero—in the season 3 episode "Ultra Woman," wherein one of the show's many nefarious female scientists builds a red kryptonite laser capable of stripping and transferring Superman's powers—she not only gladly surrenders this role but follows this surrender with an acceptance of a more definite heteronormativity. In the concluding scene of "Ultra Woman," after she has returned Clark's powers, Lois tells Clark that experiencing how hard it is to be a superhero made her love him more. This revelation prompts Lois to accept Clark's wedding proposal from seven episodes before, albeit with the gender reversal of her proposing, on bended knee, to him.

19. Though Dean Cain, born Dean George Tanaka, has Japanese ancestry (his Wikipedia page indicates he is three-eighths Japanese), this ancestry is not obvious or directly referenced in *Lois & Clark*.

20. Season 3, episode 11, "Chi of Steel."

21. Season 4, episode 12, "Never on Sunday." Voodoo is invoked in the official episode summary. "Who do that voodoo? Wedding plans take a back seat when a master of magic haunts Clark with bizarre visions." See "Never on Sunday," *Lois & Clark: The New Adventures of Superman* Wiki, Fandom, https://lois-and-clark-the-new-adventures-of-superman.fandom.com/wiki/Never_on_Sunday.

22. Herman Gray, *Watching Race: Television and the Struggle for "Blackness"* (Minneapolis: University of Minnesota Press, 1995), 159.

23. Tim Edwards, *Men in the Mirror: Men's Fashion, Masculinity and Consumer Society* (Herndon: Cassell, 1997), 41. Emphasis in original.

24. Edwards, *Men in the Mirror*, 41.

25. See Jeffrey A. Brown's chapter in this volume.

26. Chapman, "Great Pretender," 237.

27. Heinecken, *Warrior Women*, 1.

28. Freeman, "Woman on Top," 195.

29. Weltzien, "Masque-*ulinities*," 242.

30. Weltzien, "Masque-*ulinities*," 233.

31. Reynolds, *Super Heroes*, 37.

32. Reynolds, *Super Heroes*, 37.

33. For the place of "Holding Out for a Hero" in drag culture, see Joe Morgan, "Know Your Herstory: Relive the Most Epic Lip Sync to Holding Out for a Hero Ever," Gay Star News, April 20, 2017, https://www.gaystarnews.com/article/

know-herstory-relive-epic-lip-sync-holding-hero-ever/#gs.5XG29pgB. For the song's relevance to gay culture, see Nick Bond, "Holding Out for Bonnie," *Star Observer*, Oct. 22, 2008, http://www.starobserver.com.au/artsentertainment/holding-out-for-bonnie/2304. "'Gay vague' refers to images that create an ironic understanding for those 'in the know' who are internal to a marginalized community (or are aware of its existence)." See Shari L. Dworkin and Faye Linda Wachs, *Body Panic: Gender, Health, and the Selling of Fitness* (New York: New York University Press, 2009), 57.

34. See Mary Ann Doane, *The Desire to Desire: The Woman's Film of the 1940s* (Bloomington: Indiana University Press, 1987); Ien Ang, *Watching Dallas: Soap Opera and the Melodramatic Imagination*, trans. Della Couling (New York: Methuen, 1985); Catherine Summerhayes, "Who in 'Heaven'? Tracey Moffatt: Men in Wet-Suits and the Female Gaze," *Journal of Narrative Theory* 33, no. 1 (Winter 2003): 63–80.

35. Miriam Hansen, "Pleasure, Ambivalence, Identification: Valentino and Female Spectatorship," *Cinema Journal* 25, no. 4 (Summer 1986): 14, 16.

36. Hansen, "Pleasure, Ambivalence, Identification," 12.

37. Hansen, "Pleasure, Ambivalence, Identification," 17.

38. Hansen, "Pleasure, Ambivalence, Identification," 17.

39. Hansen, "Pleasure, Ambivalence, Identification," 10.

40. Clarissa Smith, "Shiny Chests and Heaving G-Strings: A Night Out with the Chippendales," *Sexualities* 5, no. 1 (2002): 80.

41. Smith, "Shiny Chests," 71, 80.

42. Smith, "Shiny Chests," 78.

43. Smith, "Shiny Chests," 83–84.

44. Punctuation and use of emphasis within direct quotations of dialogue from *Lois & Clark* is meant to approximate the delivery of the lines within the show.

45. Edwards, *Men in the Mirror*, 41. Emphasis in original.

46. Hansen, "Pleasure, Ambivalence, Identification," 15.

47. Annette Kuhn, "Lawless Seeing," in *The Power of the Image: Essays on Representation and Sexuality*, ed. Annette Kuhn (London: Routledge & Kegan Paul, 1985), 35.

48. Hansen, "Pleasure, Ambivalence, Identification," 22.

49. The emphases I have included here are meant to mimic the emphases within Lois's speech.

50. For a fuller discussion of this tendency in superhero scholarship, see Peppard, "'This Female Fights Back!,'" 105–137.

10

THE VISIBLE AND THE INVISIBLE
Superheroes, Pornography, and Phallic Masculinity

JEFFREY A. BROWN

There is a curious, and much talked about, scene in the middle of *Thor: Ragnarok* (2017). Thor (Chris Hemsworth) and the Hulk (a computer-generated image) are stranded on the alien planet Sakaar and forced to do gladiator-style battle for the amusement of the masses. After their epic bout, the two most powerful Avengers share lavish living quarters, complete with an oversized hot tub. At one point, Thor is explaining his escape plans to the Hulk, who is taking a bath. As Thor continues to talk, the green behemoth casually emerges from the tub completely naked and makes no effort to conceal his loins. Thor is shocked and embarrassed; he stammers and tries to look away as the Hulk confidently strides past. "That's in my brain now," Thor humorously laments. James Dyer's review in *Empire* describes the moment as "a priceless reaction to the sight of Hulk's giant green penis."[1] Likewise, Carl Greenwood's review in the *Sun* claims: "The look on the poor God of Thunder's face will tell audiences everything they need to know about the Hulk and will have them roaring with laughter."[2] Though the Hulk's presumably giant green penis is never actually shown, this scene is nonetheless very revealing for precisely the reasons Greenwood identifies. By playing superhero sexuality for laughs and simultaneously showing and not showing the Hulk's penis, this brief scene exposes the complicated web of relations between superheroes, masculinity, and sexuality, as well as a widespread and assumed discomfort with examining those relations without the protective shield of sophomoric humor.

The issue I specifically want to investigate in this chapter is the way that hegemonic masculinity is produced and reinforced at multiple levels through the symbolism of the superhero. Even more specifically, I want to investigate how the masculine symbolism of the superhero is reinforced by the myth of the phallus. My case study for this investigation will be the increasingly popular subgenre of superhero porn parodies. Most mainstream depictions of superheroes, whether in comics, film, television, or video games, present almost ridiculously extreme symbols of phallic power while always keeping the penis safely out of view. But the pornographic versions of popular superheroes expose, literalize, and fetishize the superhero penis as the ultimate "proof" of masculine privilege. While inviting the audience to look at and admire the superhero penis would seem to invite subversion of the norms of superhero representation, my analysis of popular heterosexual superhero porn parodies will argue that these films do not meaningfully undermine or recontextualize the superhero genre, but instead reinforce the superhero's presumption of hegemonic masculinity.

DEFINING THE PENIS AND THE PHALLUS

As the naked Hulk scene suggests, the allegory of the phallus is an important reference point for fantasies about masculine ideals. Moreover, the fact that the naked Hulk scene both shows and *does not show* the mythical phallus parallels many of the ways that phallic masculinity both declares itself exceptional and averts scrutiny. The dynamic between what *is* and *is not* seen in relation to the phallus, and *how* it is presented, is integral to how hegemonic masculinity is valued as naturally superior. In reference to the presence and absence of the penis in popular media, Anja Hirdman argues, "Questions of visibility, of what can be seen and not seen, are crucial for the symbolic authority of masculinity, or the myth of masculinity."[3] Furthermore, Hirdman continues: "Invisibility has always constituted a significant component of a privileged position allowing for certain aspects of the subject to remain hidden from common visibility—and yet to appear as if there is nothing hidden, nothing that has to be concealed from the public gaze."[4] Superheroes are one of the most visible contemporary models of hegemonic masculinity, and they help perpetuate an abstract notion of the phallus that is supreme but always hidden from view. But with the seemingly ever-growing popularity of superhero movies spawning a tidal wave of pornographic parodies seeking to capitalize on our society's current fascination with all things superhero, the mythical phallus of these caped crusaders is at risk of being exposed.

Parodies generally ridicule or critique the premise of the texts they parody. Superhero parodies in comic book form, like Garth Ennis's series *The Boys* (2009–2012) or Mark Millar's mini-series *Nemesis* (2010) question the hypermasculinity of generic superheroes, as do live-action parodies such as *Dr. Horrible's Sing-Along Blog* (2008) and *Super* (2010). Yet many of these mainstream superhero parodies ultimately still allow the protagonist to save the day, even if he is a less than ideal model of masculinity.[5] Most contemporary heterosexual superhero porn parodies do not, however, intentionally ridicule the characters they focus on. Instead, they glorify them through a commitment to fidelity that includes the supposed fidelity of the superhero penis.

The process of fostering identification with masculine ideals such as superheroes has been a central tenet of film studies. In her seminal work "Visual Pleasure and the Narrative Cinema," Laura Mulvey notes that male leads exemplify the "more perfect, more complete, more powerful ideal ego" and that Classical Hollywood cinema employs an array of narrative and stylistic techniques to align viewers with that perspective.[6] Likewise, Steve Neale outlines how the visual conventions used to present heroic men offer viewers a form of "narcissistic identification" with masculine fantasies of "power, omnipotence, mastery, and control."[7] Jon Stratton, in his analysis of cultural fetishism and gender in relation to consumerism, explicitly links Neale's theory of narcissistic male identification to the metaphor of phallic authority: "The reason why male narcissism involves those fantasies Neale lists is because the man with whom the male viewer is narcissistically identifying exhibits, either in his body or in his actions, phallic power."[8]

To be clear, the phallus is a symbol or an idea of masculine power and privilege; it is not a body part. As Susan Bordo notes, "it is a majestic imaginary member, against which no man's penis can ever measure up."[9] The phallus and the penis are not synonymous, but they are representationally intertwined. The phallus is suggestive of the penis in a way that elevates the physical marker of masculinity to justify inequities as natural gender differences. As Richard Dyer describes, "the penis is also the symbol of male potency, the magic and the mystery of the phallus, the endowment that appears to legitimate male power."[10] Moreover, Dyer's general claims about the penis's inability to live up to the majesty of the phallus as depicted in popular culture is a near perfect description of the majority of male superhero characters: "The penis can never live up to the mystique implied by the phallus. Hence the excessive, even hysterical quality of so much male imagery. The clenched fists, the bulging muscles, the hardened jaws, the proliferation of phallic symbols—they are all straining after what can hardly ever be achieved, the embodiment of the phallic physique."[11] Where much male imagery may strive to embody an impossible phallic physique, the illustrated superhero figure in comic books and the digitally enhanced live-action performers in modern superhero movies, combined with the incredible powers afforded these fictional champions of justice, are able to embody phallic masculinity in an exaggerated manner that is relatively unfeasible for real men to achieve.

Though the phallus as the preeminent symbol of hegemonic masculinity is forever linked to the penis as the definitive marker of sexual difference—what Dyer refers to above as "the endowment that appears to legitimate male power"—the efficacy of the phallus is predicated on the absence of the actual penis. In order for the phallus to signify strength and power, the penis needs to remain invisible. As Jacques Lacan famously declared, "the phallus can only play its role when veiled."[12] This veiling that Lacan describes involves both obfuscating any association between the phallus and the penis that is too literal and the near constant censorship of the penis from public view. Penises must remain hidden to support the logic of the phallus for fear of revealing the truth of Dyer's assertion that "penises are only little things (even big ones) without much staying power[,] . . . not magical or mysterious or powerful in themselves, that is, not objectively full of real power."[13] Indeed, most considerations of the phallus stress the importance of the invisibility of the penis in relation to the spectacle of the phallic symbol. Peter Lehman argues that "silence about and invisibility of the penis contributes to phallic mystique."[14] The literal and symbolic erasure of actual penises from public view facilitates the mythical position of the phallus as pure symbol. "Phallocentrism is an imaginary idea," Hirdman notes, "relying on the invisibility of the penis in order to maintain its authoritative position in culture."[15] Likewise, Stephens maintains, "The penis is paradoxically both everywhere—disseminated through the proliferation of phallomorphic imagery and privilege—and nowhere, its specificity hidden from view."[16] The phallus needs to be ever visible to effectively signify masculinity as powerful, and the penis needs to remain ever invisible to avoid undermining the myth of the phallus.

Phallic symbols abound in the superhero genre—Thor's hammer, Wolverine's claws, the Punisher's guns, Cyclops's eye lasers, and so on. But nothing symbolizes and naturalizes superheroes' phallic masculinity as much as their heavily muscled bodies. Dyer bluntly observes that "muscularity is the sign of power—natural, achieved, phallic."[17] Impossibly massive shoulders, huge biceps, ripped quads, and sculpted abs are the standard bodily uniform for male superheroes. The comic book superhero body has only become more muscular over the years, to the point where many modern superheroes have bodies that professional athletes, underwear models, and bodybuilders might either envy or laugh at; the male superheroes drawn by the once record-breakingly popular artist Rob Liefeld, for instance, have been roundly criticized for being so excessively muscular that real-life versions would be unable to stand. Despite this comical excess, and while certain monstrously large and hard characters such as the Hulk and the Thing can occasionally be read as critiquing as well as celebrating phallic masculinity,[18] in general, the excessively muscular bodies of male superheroes imply that these characters' privilege, power, and superiority over others is natural and an innate part of masculinity. The visible muscularity of superheroes is so crucial that the actors who portray the caped crusaders in the current wave of live-action movies are frequently required to undergo extreme body makeovers to approximate the brawny form of the hero. Hugh Jackman, Chris Evans, and Chris Hemsworth had to pack on a formidable amount of muscle mass to play Wolverine, Captain America, and Thor, respectively, while Chris Pratt had to exchange forty pounds of fat for lean muscle to portray Peter Quill, a.k.a. Starlord, in *Guardians of the Galaxy* (2014). Even the more traditionally lithe Spider-Man required Tobey Maguire to bulk up. In general, the actors who portray superheroes are expected to achieve a body that implies the character is naturally powerful and will triumph over any challengers. As Stratton describes, these types of hypermasculine film heroes represent "the active ideal of the male, the strong and powerful man who has the phallus and, metonymically, can represent the phallus."[19] The super-muscular body of the superhero veils any weaknesses that might disprove the intrinsic supremacy of the phallus.

PHALLIC SYMBOLS IN THE SUPERHERO GENRE

Returning to the naked Hulk scene, we can see how it reinforces the association between muscularity and phallic symbolism by appearing to mock it through the excessively pumped-up body of Chris Hemsworth's Thor and the massive CGI characterization of the Hulk. In his review of *Thor: Ragnarok* for the entertainment news website Vulture, Kyle Buchanan explicitly addresses the hot tub scene and how it raises many of the issues about masculinity, power, muscles, and phallic symbolism that lurk just below the surface of superhero stories:

The gratuitous shirtless scene is a Marvel-movie staple, and few of its heroes have been paraded around half-nude more than Chris Hemsworth. As Thor, possibly the most swole superhero in the Marvel Cinematic universe, Hemsworth can be counted on to reliably remove his shirt for no reason whatsoever beyond marketing purposes. The latest Marvel movie, *Thor: Ragnarok*, readily continues that tradition—and yup, Hemsworth still has physical dimensions that would make any mortal man envious—but at the same time, Marvel realizes that the ante must be upped. . . . It falls to *Thor: Ragnarok*, then, to break that barrier in the most unexpected way, stripping the familiar purple skivvies off the Hulk in a nude scene. . . . So while Thor can manage an impressive shirtless scene, Hulk one-ups him by casually strolling past Thor in the nude, letting it all hang out. Thor reacts to the full-frontal glimpse reserved only for him but the rest of the audience has a moment to ponder Hulk's rear, and there's a whole lot there to ponder.[20]

This short passage from Buchanan's review contains several points worth noting in the context of superhero phallic symbolism. First, the recognition that every Marvel movie contains a "gratuitous shirtless scene" is an indication of how important it is, and how conventional it has become within the genre, to always display the muscularity of the actors. Second, the description of Chris Hemsworth's shirtless moment as evidence that he "still has physical dimensions that would make any mortal man envious" exposes the fact that the display of the hero's muscles is important both for male viewer identification and aspiration and as a sexual offering for heterosexual women and gay men in the audience; it is also recognition that Thor's exceptional muscularity is crucial to his status as a *super* man, that is, as an embodiment of phallic masculinity. Third, the physical excess of the Hulk's body, which is only possible as a CGI rendering, extends the logic that the bigger the muscles the more ideal the masculinity, and proves it through recourse to nudity, by showing the Hulk "letting it all hang out." Fourth and finally, it is important to note that the Hulk's presumed giant green penis is never actually seen by anyone other than Thor; we have to assume the Hulk's penis is exceptional based solely on Thor's reaction. In other words, the Hulk's penis is framed as a phallus precisely because audiences never actually see it, but only a reaction to it. Compounding things is the fact that *it* does not—and cannot—exist in reality anyway, as the Hulk's entire body is a computer-generated image.

The abundance of phallic symbols in the world of superheroes suggests the depth of insecurity about masculinity in our society. The mythic image of ideal masculinity inherently creates fears about not living up to impossible cultural standards, self-doubts linked to stereotypical notions about racial inequalities, feminizing influences, bodily characteristics, and even financial success. All of the formidable powers, muscles, and armor of male superheroes serve to dispel any possibility of weakness. In Neale's terminology, the superhero is a complicated ego ideal that may inspire anxiety as much as it does confidence. "The construction of the ideal ego . . . is a process involving profound contradictions," Neale argues. "While the ideal ego may be a 'model' with which the subject identifies and to which it aspires, it may also be a source of further images and feelings of castration, inasmuch as that ideal is something to which the subject is never adequate."[21] It is impossible for real men to live up to these fantastic fictional models of hegemonic masculinity. The fact that Neale describes the possibility that real men may feel anxiety about their inability to meet the unreasonable demands of ideal masculinity as "feelings of castration" again highlights the interrelated symbolism of the mythical phallus and the flesh-and-blood penis. The unremarkable normality of the penis haunts the mystique of the phallus. Similarly, the shadow of male insecurity that haunts the superhero genre—which is guarded against so vehemently (or exposed so obviously) by a surplus of phallic symbols—can be read as analogous to the themes of duality at the foundation of the superhero story. The superhero genre revolves around dual identities: the mild-mannered reporter who can become Superman, the timid teenager who turns into the amazing Spider-Man, the 4F civilian who becomes a super-soldier, the irresponsible playboy who is really a Dark Knight, and so on. The symbolic disjuncture between the phallus and the penis parallels the inherent duality of a genre that hinges on the differences between the superhero and the secret identity, wherein the secret identity is usually either average or ineffectual (and thus implicitly feminized).

The male superhero can be understood as the embodiment of phallic masculinity, and conversely, the symbolic logic of the phallus can be interpreted as similar to, or even constitutive of, major conventions of the superhero genre. To put it simply: the conventional traits that distinguish the male superhero from his civilian identity are comparable to the relationship between the phallus and the penis. In a binary frame, the phallus is to the penis as the superhero is to the secret identity (and vice versa). The phallus and the superhero are both strong and gifted with magical powers; they are both visible and public icons whose true secrets need to be disguised, masked, and veiled. On the other side of the divide, the penis and the secret identity are weak and lack any real power; thus, they have to avoid being exposed or unmasked for fear of revealing the mundane humanity behind

SUPERHERO		SECRET IDENTITY
Phallus	C	Penis
Superhuman	O	Human
Powers	S	Lack
Strong		Weak
Veiled	T	Exposed
Visible	U	Invisible
Masked	M	Unmasked
Public	E	Private

TABLE 10.1. Dual Identities and Dual Symbolism.

the fantasy. As disparate as the two sides are—as different as the superhero is from the secret identity and the phallus is from the penis—there is not a great distance between them. Yet the border between these two sides is clearly delineated and marked by the colorful costume that serves as a literal veil for the secret identity and the penis (see table 10.1). The contrast between the superhero and his secret identity encompasses a range of opposing characteristics that are magically combined within the superhero genre. These same qualities align in the disparity between the phallus and the penis, and the distinction between the phallus and the actual male organ is also magically resolved in the superhero narrative. The costume as veil disguises the inherent weaknesses in the equation and presents the superhero/phallus as spectacular.

The carefully maintained image of the superhero as an embodiment of the phallus is potentially endangered when the hero's sexuality becomes the object of the story. The rise of superhero porn parodies risk exposing (both literally and figuratively) the costumed hero's penis. X-rated depictions of superheroes are nothing new. In the first half of the twentieth century, the infamous Tijuana Bibles illustrated the explicit sex lives of popular characters,[22] including the likes of Superman, Batman, and Captain Marvel (the original, male version, now known as Shazam). Likewise, fan-produced slash fiction and fan art continues to depict the sexuality of superheroes, often in hard-core or "deviant" ways.[23] The emphasis in superhero comics on ideal bodies and skintight costumes easily suggests a fetishistic side to the adventures and marks the characters as ripe for (s)exploration. Even though there is a long tradition of underground or fan-based creations that venture into the realms of hard-core depictions of superhero sex, mainstream comic books, films, and television programs avoid any X-rated portrayal of sexual activities. In the market-dominating comic books from Marvel and DC, superheroes do have sex and glimpses of flesh are seen, but genitals are never illustrated, except in the form of ultra-smooth "packages" based more on underwear mannequins than on actual bodies. Instead, the stories tend to cut to postcoital scenes of Batman and Catwoman, or Daredevil and Elektra, that imply (or state) the sex was amazing.

THE RISE OF PORN PARODIES

With superhero movies currently raking in record-setting box office profits for Hollywood, the porn industry has sought to cash in on the superhero's popularity and erotic potential. Dozens of superhero porn parody movies are now released annually, and they are consistently among the most profitable X-rated videos produced. As Dru Jeffries notes in his analysis of these pornographic parodies, "the porn industry is following Hollywood's lead by taking superheroes more seriously than either had in decades past, and both are being rewarded with financial success and devoted followings."[24] The demand for superhero porn parodies is significant enough that the two largest adult film production companies have each developed their own line devoted to comic adaptations—Vivid Superheroes and Wicked Comix. "Parodies, once a cheaply filmed niche segment of the adult movie market, are big business these days," declared an Associated Press article that was picked up by hundreds of mainstream media outlets, including USA Today. These parodies, according to the AP story, are "filled with expensive special effects, real story lines, actors who can (sometimes) actually act and costumes that even comic-book geeks find authentic."[25] The porn parodies are an excuse to explore the sexual exploits of all these attractive characters running around in skintight fetish costumes. Now, fans can see Batman, Robin, and Catwoman having a threesome, or watch Spider-Man get a rooftop blowjob from Black Cat, or see Wonder Woman have sex with all of the men in the Justice League at the same time.

Axel Braun is the adult film director most associated with the superhero porn parodies. Braun has been credited with nearly single-handedly raising the quality of pornographic movies and reinvigorating the industry. Even mainstream news outlets have reported on Braun's achievements. For example, Fox News reported:

> Director Axel Braun has become the most in-demand X-rated director in the world by taking popular super heroes and creating super successful porn parodies. The adult film director has directed more than four hundred movies since 1990, but it was his work on Vivid's *Batman XXX: A Porn Parody* in 2010 that cemented his name when it became the best-selling and most-rented title of 2010.[26]

Since the success of *Batman XXX*, the prolific Braun has directed over seventy films, including a remarkable number of superhero characters in films such as *Avengers XXX*, *Wolverine XXX*, *Man of Steel XXX*, *Thor XXX*, *She-Hulk XXX*, *X-Men XXX*, *Captain America XXX*, *Wonder Woman XXX*, *Batman vs. Superman XXX*, *Supergirl XXX*, *Suicide Squad XXX*, *Avengers vs. X-Men XXX*, and *Justice League XXX*. In addition to the requisite XXX included in each of the titles, all of the films are subtitled either *A Porn Parody* or, more recently, *An Axel Braun Parody*. The designation of "parody" implies that the films mock, ridicule, or critique their subject matter, but Braun's style of superhero porn parody is only parody in a legal sense. The claim to parody allows the porn industry to use characters that are the corporate properties of Time-Warner (DC) and Disney (Marvel) without fear of lawsuits. As Axel Braun freely admits in interviews, his films are not making fun of comic book characters or story lines. In fact, Braun claims he is striving for a greater degree of fidelity to the original comics than many of the Hollywood film productions pursue.

As the leading creator of superhero porn parodies, Axel Braun's attention to detail, his fidelity to the look and characterizations of the original comic book source material, and his professed geekdom can situate his parodies as particularly well-funded fan films (with hard-core sex included). Both Jeffries and Iain Robert Smith insightfully discuss Braun's superhero porn parodies as akin to fan videos. Smith reasons that "the current cycle of porn parodies resembles less the exploitation features . . . than a commercialized form of fan film."[27] And Jeffries argues, "Braun's superhero parodies present a unique point of intersection between Hollywood, fandom, and the porn industry, appropriating transformative textual practices usually associated with fan productivity in order to attract hard-core fans to their hard-core product."[28] But, unlike other creative works produced by fans within gift economies, which often explore sexual relationships outside of official canon and subvert cultural norms through gender-bending or changing the sexual orientation of characters,[29] heterosexual superhero porn parodies adhere to very conventional and conservative interpretations of their sources. Whereas other types of fan-created works, as well as the distinct subgenre of gay superhero porn parodies, can often be read as critiquing the source texts through their recontextualizations of canon,[30] the Axel Braun–style superhero porn parodies—which are not really "parodies" and are trying to make money by capturing as many viewers as possible—stabilize conventional conceptions of male superheroes as exceptional models of masculinity, and thus reinforce and naturalize traditional conceptions of gender and power.

In his discussion of the potentially carnivalesque qualities of fan-produced slash and current porn parodies, including those directed by Axel Braun, Paul Booth maintains that while slash is inherently subversive, heterosexual porn parodies exaggerate gender norms. "Slash," writes Booth, "allows the reader (and the writer) to re-examine traditional notions of patriarchy within traditional society through *subversion* of the sexuality of the main characters." In contrast, "[heterosexual] porn parody does the opposite, [forcing] the audience to confront the patriarchal modes of contemporary media through overt *hyper-articulation*."[31] Superhero porn parodies may be an extreme fringe form of the dominant superhero narrative, but these pornographic versions nonetheless function to solidify ideas of phallic masculinity in a manner that is even more conservative than what is found in the original comic books. In heterosexual superhero porn parodies, not only does the hero always defeat the villains, he also sexually satisfies every woman he meets. Male anxieties about sexual performance and penis size have no place in pornographic fantasies, even if these issues have recently begun to creep into the mainstream comic books. For example, in *Guardians of the Galaxy* #4 (2013), notorious lothario Tony Stark (a.k.a. Iron Man) beds the green-skinned alien warrior Gamora but fails to impress her. Tony is left in bed ashamed and embarrassed as the disappointed Gamora shrugs and heads back to the bar. This type of upset to Tony's ego and reputation has no place in *Iron-Man XXX* (2013), where Stark easily satisfies numerous women, both heroic and villainous, individually and in groups.

In the X-rated depictions, the hero's penis is necessarily revealed, but through the narrative and visual conventions of pornography, the penis becomes the phallus and reinforces the association between the phallic symbol and the male organ it is based upon. Hirdman notes the importance of the penis's transition from invisible to eminently visible: "In hardcore pornography the penis is everything but invisible, and the connection to the phallus is not just on an imaginary level. Hence, this spotlight position brings with it a need for securing the penis as spectacular, as ever erected (and usually large)."[32] Because the overwhelming majority of superhero porn parodies are targeted at heterosexual viewers (male, female, and couples) the male porn star's penis is presented as remarkable, powerful, ever-hard, and always satisfying to women. The superhero penis that is shown in these films may not be as ridiculously oversize as the ones depicted in online erotic fan art and X-rated comics, but the superhero penis is equated with the professional porn star penis. The explicit representation of the porn star penis—a version of the male organ that Linda Williams refers to as "not just ordinary but quite spectacular"[33]—means that when the penis is visible in this media form it is presented as embodying phallic properties. Thanks to casting choices based on male physical endowments, careful editing of sexual scenes, and the scripting of female responses during intercourse, this "super-penis" of the superhero/porn star is routinely larger than average, never limp, never impotent, and never disappointing. Like the conventional male superhero, the super-penis is portrayed as powerful, hard, big, and conquering.

Like the mainstream movies they reference, the superhero porn parodies substantiate the hero's masculinity through fight sequences and special effects, albeit on a much smaller scale. But in the porn parodies, the hero's true superiority is confirmed by his sexual conquests. As is the norm in pornography, the hero has mind-boggling sex with almost every woman he encounters. Whether she is a civilian, a fellow superhero, or a supervillain, no woman can resist the hero's super-penis. For example, when Wonder Woman (Romi Rain) first meets Green Lantern (Xander Corvus) in *Justice League XXX* (2017), she initiates sex with him, claiming she needs to see if he is powerful enough to help fight alien invaders. After Green Lantern satisfies her with oral, vaginal, and anal sex, Wonder Woman declares him strong enough. Likewise, Black Widow (Peta Jensen) has sex with Captain America (Charles Dera) in *Captain America XXX* (2014) to determine if he is a traitor or the real hero. After Captain America brings Black Widow to a screaming climax, she declares him to be the legendary super-soldier. In *Superman vs. Spider-Man XXX* (2012), Superman (Ryan Driller) proves he really is a "man of steel" in a threesome with Mary Jane Watson (Capri Anderson) and Liz Osborn (Lily LaBeau). And in *X-Men XXX* (2014), Wolverine (Tommy Gunn) has sex with the villainess Polaris (Chanel Preston) that is so fulfilling she converts to the X-Men's side in their battle against her evil boss, Magneto.

The male superhero in these parodies manages to have triumphant sex with all manner of women. Female superheroes and villains alike are kept in line by, and in thrall of, the super-penis. In every case, the superhero's super-penis extends the phallic status of the character's hypermasculinity. The women in the movies "oooh" and "aahhh" over the costumed hero's penis, gasp at how big it is, and moan about how good it feels inside them. And, despite the porn starlets' own hypersexuality, the women are always left satiated by the superhero's performance. These pornographic conventions link the penis to the phallus. As Bordo argues, "the penis becomes a phallus when . . . it is viewed as an object of reverence or awe."[34] Chris Hemsworth's muscles combined with expensive special effects signify phallic masculinity in the Hollywood *Thor* films, but in *Thor XXX* (2013), the muscles and the special effects are not needed—the porn star penis alone conveys phallic power. Of course, even here the penis is not really the phallus, but it is narratively and visually presented as phallic. In other words, the super-penis is to the real penis as the superhero is to the secret identity, and as the phallus is to the penis.

The phallic masculinity bolstered in porn parodies is predominantly portrayed as white. Thus, the parodies reinforce and mirror the mainstream superhero films and comic books they reference. Despite the incredible number of superhero porn parodies that have been produced in the last decade, very few Black superheroes have been included. African American porn stars Lexington Steele and Nat Turner played Nick Fury and Luke Cage in *Avengers vs X-Men XXX: An Axel Braun Parody* (2015), and Lexington Steele also played Deadshot in *Suicide Squad XXX: An Axel Braun Parody* (2016), but all three of these roles were minor supporting characters. Racial stereotypes about nonwhite bodies and sexual appetites are common in mainstream pornography[35] and can present a qualifying problem for parodies that function to uphold a belief in white phallic masculinity. Age-old racial stereotypes about Black men as more bodily (read: larger, stronger, and better endowed) than white men are often embraced in pornography, especially in the common subcategorization of BBC (Big Black Cocks). In the simplest racial terms, if the parodies focused on Black superheroes in conjunction with the pornographic logic of BBCs, then white masculinity and the white super-penis might be undermined or presented as lesser than the almighty phallus it claims to be. Moreover, as Hirdman insightfully notes, part of the phallic mastery displayed by white male performers in porn involves the performer's almost mechanical control over passion and his own body. While porn is about giving in to corporeal pleasures, cultural scripts encourage white men to maintain control of their bodies at all times. Hirdman observes, "White men are so much more than their bodies. The white male is not confined to his corporeality. The white man's sexual drama, as evident in hard-core porn, concerns questions of how to have a sexual urge while controlling it, how to simultaneously be a body while denying this cultural position."[36] Just as the comic book superhero often struggles to maintain complete control over his powerful body, the porn superhero must demonstrate control over his corporeal pleasures. Black masculinity in pornographic terms adheres to an entirely different script of being excessively, even painfully large, and of embracing carnal pleasures. Both of these racially informed differences threaten to undermine the idea of white-heroic-phallic-masculinity that is mutually reinforced between the mainstream and the pornographic depictions of superheroes.

The conventions used in pornographic texts like superhero porn parodies uphold the myth that the white male organ legitimates male power—that the penis can be a phallus. Yet, even though these porn star penises are presented as phallus-like in their size, strength, power, and infallibility, the superhero costume remains an important part of the equation for bolstering the relationship between superheroes and phallic masculinity. The fidelity to various comic book and film versions of the superhero costumes in Axel Braun's movies is routinely singled out by critics, and by Braun himself, as a key part of the parodies' appeal. Hollie McKay's report for Fox News observes, "Braun is known for casting actors who can actually act, and for paying meticulous attention to every wardrobe detail."[37] Similarly, a profile of Braun in the *Chicago Tribune* declared, "Known for his 'geek porn' parodies like *Spider-Man XXX, Batman XXX, Iron Man XXX*, etc., his films are noted for having costumes that are often startling faithful to the comic book visuals."[38] Braun's desire to accurately reproduce superhero costumes was evident from his first huge success, *Batman XXX*, for which he went as far as tracking down the original fabric and colored dyes that were used to make the iconic costumes for Adam West and Burt Ward in the 1960s television series *Batman*. Ironically, superhero costumes are even more important when the characters are transferred to a genre whose central purpose is to reveal the body—to strip it naked and expose its secrets. As Williams has shown, modern video pornography is about far more than just nudity and a showing of genitals; it is about trying to capture and reveal the truth of bodies (particularly the mysterious female body) and sexual pleasures. Images of penetration in hard-core pornography provide evidence of actual intercourse, and the visual demonstration of penile ejaculation (or the "money shot") confirms male pleasure. But for women, who are assumed to lack any objective physical proof of orgasmic pleasure, pornography relies on what Williams refers to as a "frenzy of the visible." All the woman's moaning, screaming, convulsing, and verbal declarations of pleasure in pornography are meant to signify the truth of her excitement. These same conventions that testify to the phallic power of the superheroic penis offer, at a broader but interrelated level, "the visual evidence of the mechanical 'truth' of bodily pleasure caught in involuntary spasm; the ultimate and uncontrollable—ultimate *because* uncontrollable—confession of pleasure in the climax of orgasm."[39] The visible frenzy of the woman's body is meant to signify a truth of female sexual pleasure, and when this overwhelming pleasure is derived from the male organ, the penis becomes the phallus. The fact that in heterosexual porn parodies (most of) the male superhero costume tends to stay on during intercourse suggests that the superhero costume is more important than the exposed body as a means to transfer the phallic abilities of the pornographic super-penis to the super man and, circularly, to offer evidence of phallic power as rooted in the male organ. Here the costume is not a veil for the penis (which is portrayed as a phallus in itself), but is still needed to mark the wearer as powerful, special, bordering on omnipotent, and—in a word—phallic.

The costumes must remain on during the sex scenes not because it reveals the "truth" of sexual pleasure but because it visually confirms the "truth" of phallic masculinity personified by the superhero. The colorful costume in these porn parodies is the link between the phallus and the penis, and the penis *as* the phallus. Jeffries argues, "The graphic display of the naked body requires, first and foremost, a naked body, which would strip the superheroes of both their unique identities and their fetishistic charge." After all, "without the costumes they are not superheroes, they are just porn stars."[40] The more fantastical aspects of the superhero body, those which are routinely illustrated in comic books or produced through advanced digital technologies in mega-budget Hollywood films, are impossible to re-create in lower budget films. In the porn parodies, bodies cannot fly, burst into flames, turn to steel, or stretch like rubber. In fact, given the potential for innovative carnal possibilities, the sexual acts depicted are very standard; there is no floating sex in the clouds, no super-speed vibrating fingers during foreplay, no power-ring-generated green sex toys. Given these restrictions, the pornographic imperative to reveal the body is necessarily balanced with the need to maintain the pretense that these are superheroes engaging in various carnal acts, which means that the costume needs to remain on at all times, especially during intercourse. The costumes of the porn parody superheroes come complete with holes in the crotch so that the porn star penis can be revealed, and put into action, without taking off the iconic costumes. As in most heterosexual pornography, the female superhero and/or villain body is the primary object of sexualization, meaning that the women's costumes often open more to reveal breasts, buttocks, and vagina. But in virtually every case, the tights, boots, masks, and capes stay on for the duration of the sex scene. Vicki Karaminas argues that the superhero's costume is important because it "succeeds in signifying industrial strength associated with the ideal hyper-muscular superhero body: *the look* of power, virility and prowess."[41] The combination of the costume's "look of power" and the display of the porn star super-penis mutually reinforce the association between superheroes, hegemonic masculinity, and the mythical phallus.

Such is the power of the porn star super-penis that in the case of the porn parody version of the Hulk, it can step in to compensate for the burden of phallic symbolism usually borne by the character's impossibly large muscles. Given the budgetary differences between a Disney blockbuster movie and a quickly produced porn video, *The Incredible Hulk XXX: A Porn Parody* (2011) required a less expensive way to portray the Hulk in all his glory. Thus, it eschewed CGI technology and instead opted to mimic the nostalgic look of the television series *The Incredible Hulk* (1977–1982). In the pornographic version, Dr. David Banner's (Dale DaBone) experimentation with sexual frustration turns him into the Hulk (Lee Stone), a raging sexual beast. The alternation between the mild-mannered scientist played by DaBone and the more heavily muscled and green-skinned Hulk embodied by Stone mirrors the division between Bill Bixby as Banner and the green spray-painted bodybuilder Lou Ferrigno as the Hulk in the original television show. By choosing to present the Hulk through a relatively normal (but muscular) actor in green paint, the

X-rated film saves money and also adheres to pornography's imperative to demonstrate the "truth" of real bodies. In the parody, both Banner and the Hulk satisfy numerous sexually insatiable female swingers and prostitutes. And in the finale, Banner's research partner, Dr. Elaina Marks (Lily LaBeau), helps tame the Hulk's sexual rage through fornication that is extremely gratifying for both of them. Because the porn version can show the Hulk's penis, and because the Hulk's penis is performed by a professional porn star penis, the phallic symbolism of the exaggerated CGI muscles is not needed—it would, in fact, be redundant. A thin layer of green paint is costume enough to solidify the relationship between superheroism and phallic masculinity.

CONCLUSION

Williams clarifies the relationship between "phallus" and "penis" in hardcore porn as a presumption of sexual knowledge and mastery. Writes Williams, "Hardcore pornography is not phallic because it shows penises; it is phallic because in its exhibition of penises it presumes to know, to possess an adequate expression of the truth of 'sex'—as if sex were as unitary as the phallus presumes itself to be."[42] Extending Williams's observation to the specific subject of this chapter, the superhero porn parody is not phallic because it shows penises; instead, it is phallic because it presumes a unifying mastery of sexual knowledge and prowess as a form of masculine power. Furthermore, the comic book and Hollywood versions of superheroes are not phallic because of their muscles and powers—those are just phallic signifiers. Instead, they are phallic because they present masculinity as naturally dominant, authoritative, and infallible.

NOTES

1. James Dyer, "*Thor: Ragnarok* Review," Empire, October 23, 2017, https://www.empireonline.com/movies/thor-ragnarok/review/.

2. Carl Greenwood, "Green with Envy? *Thor: Ragnarok* Features Marvel's First Nude Scene," *Sun*, October 19, 2017, https://www.thesun.co.uk/tvandshowbiz/4724141/thor-ragnarok-features-marvels-first-nude-scene-as-a-beloved-character-strips-naked-in-front-of-a-window/.

3. Anja Hirdman, "(In)Visibility and the Display of Gendered Desire: Masculinity in Mainstream Soft- and Hardcore Pornography," *NORA–Nordic Journal of Women's Studies* 15, no. 2–3 (2007): 158–171.

4. Hirdman, "(In)Visibility," 159.

5. See Jeffrey A. Brown, "Superhero Film Parody and Hegemonic Masculinity," *Quarterly Review of Film and Video* 33, no. 2 (2016): 131–150.

6. Laura Mulvey, "Visual Pleasure and the Narrative Cinema," *Screen* 16, no. 3 (1975): 12.

7. Steve Neale, "Masculinity as Spectacle: Reflections on Men and Mainstream Cinema," *Screen* 24, no. 6 (1983): 11.

8. Jon Stratton, *The Desirable Body: Cultural Fetishism and the Erotics of Consumption* (Urbana: University of Illinois Press, 2001), 181.

9. Susan Bordo, *The Male Body: A New Look at Men in Public and Private* (New York: Farrar, Straus and Giroux, 2000), 94–95.

10. Richard Dyer, *Only Entertainment* (New York: Routledge, 1993), 113.

11. Dyer, *Only Entertainment*, 116.

12. Jacques Lacan, "The Meaning of the Phallus," in *Feminine Sexuality*, ed. J. Rose and J. Mitchell (New York: Norton Press, 1982), 82.

13. Dyer, *Only Entertainment*, 113.

14. Peter Lehman, "Will the Real Dirk Diggler Please Stand Up? *Boogie Nights*," *Jump Cut*, no. 42 (December 1998): 124.

15. Hirdman, "(In)Visibility," 165.

16. Elizabeth Stephens, "The Spectacularized Penis: Contemporary Representations of the Phallic Male Body," *Men and Masculinities* 10, no. 1 (2007): 85–98.

17. Dyer, *Only Entertainment*, 114.

18. See Robert Genter, "With Great Power Comes Great Responsibility: Cold War Culture and the Birth of Marvel Comics," *Journal of Popular Culture* 40, no. 6 (2007): 953–978.

19. Stratton, *Desirable Body*, 119.

20. Kyle Buchanan, "We Have Now Seen the Hulk's Butt, If You're into That," *Vulture*, November 3, 2017, http://www.vulture.com/2017/11/thor-ragnarok-has-a-hulk-nude-scene-a-first-for-marvel.html.

21. Neale, "Masculinity as Spectacle," 13.

22. Barry, "Eight-Page Eroticism," 227–237.

23. See Henry Jenkins, *Fans, Bloggers, and Gamers: Exploring Participatory Culture* (New York: New York University Press, 2006). See also Olivia Hicks's and Anne Kustritz's chapters in this volume.

24. Dru Jeffries, "This Looks Like a Blowjob for Superman: Servicing Fanboys with Superhero Porn Parodies," *Porn Studies* 3, no. 3 (2016): 276–277.

25. Associated Press, "Can Superhero Parodies Rescue the Porn Business?" *USA Today*, July 27, 2013, https://www.usatoday.com/story/news/nation/2013/07/27/can-superhero-parodies-rescue-the-porn-business/2592913/.

26. Hollie McKay, "Super-Hero Parodies Do for the Porn Industry What Super-Hero Blockbusters Do for Hollywood," Fox News, July 30, 2013, http://www.foxnews.com/entertainment/2013/07/30/super-hero-parodies-do-for-porn-industry-what-super-hero-blockbusters-do-for.html.

27. Iain Robert Smith, "Batsploitation: Parodies, Fan Films and Remakes," in

Many More Lives of the Batman, ed. Roberta Pearson, William Uricchio, and Will Brooker (London: MacMillan International, 2015), 115.

28. Jeffries, "This Looks Like a Blowjob," 279.

29. See Olivia Hicks's and Anne Kustritz's chapters in this volume.

30. For a discussion of how the gay variant of superhero porn parodies differs from the hetero version, see Joseph Brennan's chapter in this volume.

31. Paul Booth, "Slash and Porn: Media Subversion, Hyper-Articulation, and Parody," *Continuum: Journal of Media & Cultural Studies* 28, no. 3 (2014): 401. Emphasis in original.

32. Hirdman, "(In)Visibility," 165.

33. Linda Williams, *Hard Core: Power, Pleasure, and the Frenzy of the Visible* (Berkeley: University of California Press, 1989), 266.

34. Bordo, *Male Body*, 95.

35. For example, see Celine Parreñas Shimizu, *The Hypersexuality of Race: Performing Asian/American Women on Screen and Scene* (Durham, NC: Duke University Press, 2007); Jennifer C. Nash, *The Black Body in Ecstasy: Reading Race, Reading Pornography* (Durham, NC: Duke University Press, 2014); and Mireille Miller-Young, *A Taste for Brown Sugar: Black Women in Pornography* (Durham, NC: Duke University Press, 2014).

36. Hirdman, "(In)Visibility," 167.

37. McKay, "Super-Hero Parodies."

38. Elliot Serrano, "'Geek Porn' Director Axel Braun on Avengers' Quicksilver, Comic Book Costuming," *Chicago Tribune*, April 8, 2014, http://www.chicagotribune.com/redeye/redeye-axel-braun-quicksilver-interview-20140408-story.html.

39. Williams, *Hard Core*, 101.

40. Jeffries, "This Looks Like a Blowjob," 281.

41. Vicki Karaminas, "'No Capes!' Uber Fashion and How 'Luck Favors the Prepared': Constructing Contemporary Superhero Identities in American Popular Culture," *International Journal of Comic Art* 8, no. 1 (Spring/Summer 2006): 498. Emphasis in original.

42. Williams, *Hard Core*, 267.

"I THINK THAT'S MY FAVORITE WEAPON IN THE WHOLE BATCAVE"

Interrogating the Subversions of Men.com's Gay Superhero Porn Parodies

JOSEPH BRENNAN

INTRODUCTION

There is a long history of fans coding male superheroes as queer. This has been the case at least since Fredric Wertham's alarmist 1950s characterization of comics featuring Batman and Robin as a "wish dream of two homosexuals living together," and probably before then.[1] Beyond the potential—and occasionally intentional—eroticism of the superhero genre's exaggerated, spandex-clad bodies, such readings often draw comparisons between the anxieties that superheroes and queer youth may encounter in negotiating and managing the visibility of an identity that is both special (i.e., non-mainstream) and not always accepted,[2] negotiations that necessitate the superhero's "queer secrecy."[3] When gay culture adopts superheroes, this queer secrecy is often emphasized.[4] Because of superheroes' aforementioned potential for eroticism, and because pornography also plays a vital role in gay culture—with some critics describing gay

SUPERGAYHERO

	SCENES	VIEWS	DATES	SCENE #'s	TOPS	BOTTOMS	BOTH
ARROW	1	39K	3.13	1	Arrow	Villian	
BATMAN V SUPERMAN	3	158K	3–4.16	1 2 3	Superman Victim Superman	Victim Batman Victim	 Batman
X-MEN	4	115K	5–6.16	1 2 3 4	Wolverine Pyro Wolverine Wolverine	Cyclops Iceman Mystique Magneto	
CAPTAIN AMERICA	4	137K	6–7.16	1 2 3 4	C. America C. America B. Barnes C. America	Civilian B. Panther C. America Nick Fury	Cap, Civilian Cap, Panther
SPIDER-MAN	3	651K	7.17	1 2 3	Spider-Man Spider-Man Villain, Buddy	Buddy Victim Spider-Man	
JUSTICE LEAGUE	4	834K	11–12.17	1 2 3 4	Batman G. Lantern Bats, Buddy G. Lantern, Superman, Bats	Flash Aquaman Robin Flash, Robin	
	22	2.3M					

FIGURE 11.1. A snapshot of the content on offer via the Super Gay Hero website.

culture as especially "pornified"—the adoption and integration of superheroes into gay culture is often similarly pornographic.[5] This chapter employs textual analysis in the cultural studies tradition to read twenty-two scenes of gay superhero porn parody hosted on Super Gay Hero, a premium gay porn parody website.[6] This analysis focuses on the narrative structure of these texts, seeking to understand how the embodied, pornified performances of gay and superheroic identities coalesce and clash, most often through the (re)deployment of clichés inherent to gay porn and/or the superhero genre. An example would be a scene in *Justice League: A Gay XXX Parody*[7] in which "power bottom twink" Johnny Rapid, performing as the Flash, reveals his anus as a main source of inspiration for Batman,[8] reciting lines while being anally penetrated that include: "I'm in your batcave, while you're in my man cave"; "Use that bat[. . . .] I think that's my favorite weapon in the whole batcave."

This chapter acknowledges gay porn parody's potential to be a "productive mix of parodic comedy and dead-serious eroticism."[9] To this end, an emphasis on parody within the gay variant of superhero porn parody serves to highlight the form's political meanings, whether progressive, conservative, or both. This chapter's analysis finds some examples of parodies that are self-consciously political, capturing the potential of parody to supersede stereotypes, and of gay porn parody specifically to function at the level of visibility activism. Yet even as this chapter argues there is an inherent subversiveness to all superhero gay porn parody, it will also address the fact that most of the examples at hand feature problematic elements. Foremost among these problematic elements is the fact that within scenes where binary sexual performance constitutes the primary narrative, sidekicks, victims, and villains are almost always associated with receptive sexual roles (i.e., bottoming); this supports stereotypical gender hierarchies and reifies a form of masculinity defined by dominance over others. The chapter also includes a chart (figure 11.1) that provides a helpful overview of the superhero matchups at Super Gay Hero. Visualizing this data provides an important reference point for this chapter's qualitative readings while also demonstrating Super Gay Hero's tendency to align heroes and certain victorious villains with sexual activeness while associating sidekicks, victims, and more slender, youth-oriented heroes (i.e., the Flash and Spider-Man) with passive sexual roles.

WHAT IS SUPER GAY HERO?

Men.com is the second most visited gay porn site in the world.[10] Yet it actually consists of nine individual sites, each catering to a different niche. Among these is Super Gay Hero, which forms the case study here. Though inclusive of a range of parody texts—including parodies of *Star Wars*, *Game of Thrones*, *Pirates of the Caribbean*, and even the popular mobile game Pokémon Go—Super Gay Hero is, as its name suggests, especially keen on producing content parodying superhero franchises. To quote from the site's own marketing: "Who's your favorite superhero? Now imagine him with his big cock out going head to head with other superheroes in a hardcore scene."[11] Since the site's launch in March 2013, seven superhero series have received gay porn reimaginings. Often coinciding with the release of a blockbuster film or big-budget television series, the following titles have been the subject of parody on the site: the television show *Arrow*, film *Batman v Superman*, *X-Men* film franchise, recent *Captain America* films, *The Flash* television series, *Spider-Man* film franchise, and 2017 *Justice League* film. While the marketing materials for these parodies often mimic particular films or television series, generally, Super Gay Hero's parodies are archetypal, attending in general terms to the canons of the texts being parodied. With the exception of *The Arrow*, all of Super Gay Hero's superhero parodies are directed by Alter Sin.[12] From the seven superhero parody series hosted on Super Gay Hero, there have been a total of twenty-two scenes released, all of which are included in this chapter's analysis. Of course, these samples from Super Gay Hero do not compose the full range of superhero gay porn parody that is currently available; other recent notable examples of the genre include Colby Knox's Superman, Batman, and Daredevil parodies.[13] These samples do, however, provide insight into one popular location of the genre and enable reflection on the potential and problematics of the genre as a whole.

Figure 11.1 offers a snapshot of the content on offer via Super Gay Hero and illustrates the presence of certain trends and techniques. For example, we can see that, except early entrant *The Arrow*, parody series tend to be split into three or four scenes, which have been concentrated in the 2016–2017 period. We can also see a general increase in viewership across the series (with the exception of increased interest in *Batman v Superman: A Gay XXX Parody*, which can be read as evidence of the special appeal this particular pairing holds for gay men). Additionally, we see the distribution of these scenes across series, and that the sample at hand has attracted 2.3 million views (to the nearest one decimal place, as of January 1, 2018). Yet figure 11.1 is more valuable still for the way it invites reflection on the site's sex role lineup. By connecting each character with the anal sex role that is performed in each scene—insertive (top), receptive (bottom), or both (versatile)—figure 11.1 invites a game-match conception of the characters that is in keeping with the competitive, dichotomous logic of the superhero genre more generally, in which heroes fight—and measure themselves against—both villains and other heroes. As the data shows, typically, victims, civilians, and sidekicks feature in passive sex roles—83 percent, 67 percent, and 100 percent, respectively—and are thus associated with "defeat," a connotation that will be elaborated on in the forthcoming qualitative readings of these scenes. The data also reveals a general lack of sex role versatility, showing the importance of binary symbolism within these texts—only four characters adopt a "both" or negotiated position. This situation suggests a preference for separating characters into sex role categories that connote a clear "winner"—an active Superman triumphing over a more passive Batman, for instance. Interestingly, this clear separation of roles contrasts starkly with the reality of gay life; survey research suggests that approximately half of gay men self-identify as versatile in their anal sex.[14] The qualitative readings that follow will explore the meaning of this discrepancy, along with the possible significance of Captain America's negotiated sex role position and his submission to his best friend, Bucky Barnes; Superman's top-only status; and Spider-Man and the Flash's anal penetration by older "daddy"-type villains in the final scenes of their respective parodies.

READING THE SUPERHERO PORN PARODY

Scholarship on the superhero porn parody has so far been confined to the heteroporn context.[15] Some of this existing scholarship is, however, applicable to gay porn parodies. Dru Jeffries, for instance, explores the films of Axel Braun, using the analogy of the superhero doppelgänger to describe their function.[16] Jeffries observes that superhero porn parody "sometimes approaches Hollywood levels of quality and detail, and [can] routinely resemble the original comic book designs more closely than the mainstream adaptations."[17] A comparison between the posters of Super Gay Hero's titles and their mainstream cinematic and televisual counterparts reveals a similar trend.

Figure 11.2 presents the film posters of most of the parodies being analyzed in this chapter, alongside examples of posters from the texts up for parody. As I have argued in previous work, juxtaposing these posters demonstrates that in order to facilitate intertextual recognition, gay porn parodies often "model marketing campaigns on the style of the original."[18] Notice in the figure how typeface and staging of performers and props/effects is mimicked across the Super Gay Hero titles. In fact, one could easily mistake the parody versions for official posters from a specific entrant in each series, save perhaps for the "A Gay XXX Parody" disclaimer and casting recognition. This comparison reveals that the Super Gay Hero parodies, like the heteroporn parodies analyzed by Jeffries, aspire to a specific high-end look, mimicking, at least in their advertising, big-budget aesthetics.

Such high-end ambitions are not necessarily applicable to all gay porn superhero parody, but instead reflect Men.com's status as a popular (read: "mainstream") provider of gay porn. The Colby Knox site, conversely, is campier, featuring performers with painted-on suits that also accentuate the muscular/heroically formed sculpting of the men performing in the role. Connection can be made here between Men.com's superhero parodies and heteroporn examples, inasmuch as actors wear their costumes during sex scenes in most, but not all, cases. Yet Jeffries's claim that "many of the

FIGURE 11.2. Parody posters versus originals. Parody posters reproduced from the Super Gay Hero website; original posters are widely circulated publicity images.

pleasures that [porn parodies] offer fans ultimately have little to do with sex, and often undermine the expectations and norms of pornography as a genre," does not stand in the case of gay porn parodies (figure 11.3).[19]

This leads us to a consideration of the ways in which parodies transcend the texts they reference. According to Jeffries, Braun's heteroporn films are the equivalent of "an evil double" of the mainstream/original

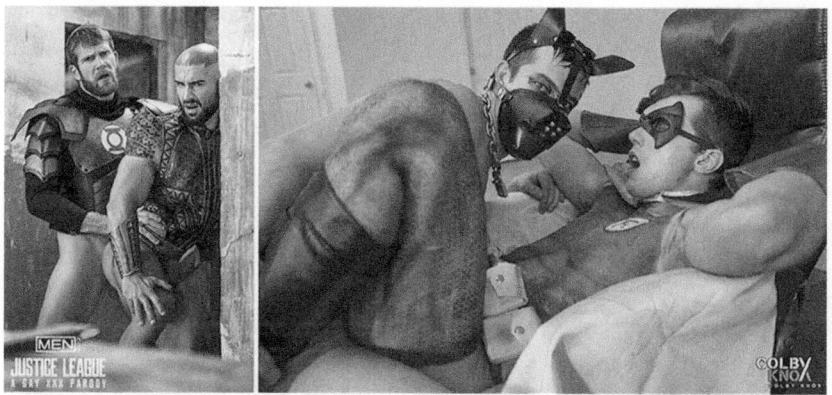

FIGURE 11.3. Men.com's high-end costuming versus Colby Knox's camp body paint and kink accessories.

superhero characters they parody, which "resembles [them] physically but whose morality is the inverse of [their] own."[20] In this view, heterosexual superhero porn parodies are antithetical to the dominant (i.e., non-pornographic, non-parodic) interpretation, being curiously described as "evil" and manifesting an inverted morality. This reading does not address parody's ability to change or reframe the meaning of the original text in potentially subversive ways, which can be true of both gay porn parodies and heteroporn ones. Paul Booth's reading of porn parodies, for instance, acknowledges the increased presence of women in heteroporn parody, at times through a gender-swapping process that is inherently—if not always actively—subversive.[21] Jeffries further defines superhero porn parodies as "basically [. . .] fan films" that are geared toward "servicing fanboys" who are "perennially dissatisfied with the ways in which Hollywood adaptations deviate from their comic book source material."[22] This characterization of superhero porn parodies as fan films that appeal, in part, through their loyalty to the comic book canon does not quite fit the context of gay porn parodies, wherein characters who are not canonically gay are reenvisioned as such. Nor does Jeffries's assumption of an exclusively male audience—gay male porn tends to attract a diverse audience, with male homoerotic reinventions of heteronormative texts being demonstrably popular among female fans.[23] Thus, despite some valuable observations that will inform later parts of this chapter, Jeffries's analysis ultimately presents a somewhat limited (and limiting) view of the subversive/political potential of superhero porn parodies.

The heteroporn texts discussed by Jeffries are marked by aspirations of

FIGURE 11.4. Aquaman holds a newspaper announcing that Green Lantern is gay. Super Gay Hero's *Justice League* parody.

fidelity that quash the possibility of nonnormative sexualities. For instance, Jeffries describes the heteroporn parody *Batman XXX* as "replicat[ing] the style of the original 1960s television series while thoroughly neutralizing the original's subversive homosexual subtext."[24] In contrast, the gay superhero porn parodies of Super Gay Hero are, by their very nature, dedicated to transformation and transgression, primarily through the actualization of latent homoerotic/homosexual desire. Inasmuch as gay superhero porn parody contributes much-needed diversity to universes that routinely ignore and even edit it out, it could actually be argued that it resides on the side of the moral and the inclusive.[25] The second scene of Super Gay Hero's *Justice League* parody is a case in point. In it, Aquaman (portrayed by François Sagat) is enticed from the sea by a newspaper masthead announcing that Green Lantern (portrayed by Colby Keller) is gay (figure 11.4). Sagat's character seeks out Green Lantern in order to ask what it means to be gay, a question that Keller answers by fucking him. This scene serves as an explicit realization of the Green Lantern character as carrying homosexual cues. The existence—and canonical rejection—of these cues is present in Stan Lee's rumored refusal to hire Gil Kane, who drew the original adventures of the Hal Jordan version of Green Lantern, because he drew men "too gay."[26] This scene also aligns itself with a specific aspect of the comic book canon—namely, DC Comics' "outing" of original Green Lantern Alan Scott in their alternate "Earth Two" universe, a narrative that garnered widespread media coverage.

The *Justice League* gay porn parody could, however, be read as braver or more progressive than the official DC version of Green Lantern's outing, since it does not rely on alternate universes but rather portrays the Green Lantern of the "main" universe as openly gay.

It is worth noting, too, that DC's Earth Two version of Green Lantern is highly atypical; mainstream superhero comics rarely feature any gay male characters at all, even in alternate universes.[27] Green Lantern acknowledges this context in a remark to Aquaman in the *Justice League* parody: "I guess people think it's a big deal that I'm the first gay superhero." The rarity of gay male superheroes in mainstream comics makes Super Gay Hero parodies, in which homosexuality is posited as the norm, inherently political, offering subversive reimaginings of a straight-washed world. Thus, although gay superhero porn parodies exploit and in some ways (such as aesthetics, costuming, and marketing) aspire toward what is present in blockbuster adaptions of familiar (almost folk) narratives, they always exceed what is typically considered exhibitable within such blockbusters; this is true not only because these parodies feature explicit sex, but also because they explicitly feature same-sex desire. All of this makes gay superhero porn parody inherently subversive not only of the superhero genre but of the hegemonic society and culture that informs it; this subgenre is always pushing the envelope in terms of what types of physical acts and desires are acceptable to show and experience within our heteronormative society. Central to this subversiveness is the fact that the gay variant of superhero porn parody places a greater emphasis on parody, which is a distinction worth reflecting on.

THE FUNCTION OF PARODY

The *parody* in gay superhero porn parody distinguishes the texts being discussed in this chapter from other pornographic contexts in which gay superheroes frequently appear. Relevant non-parodic contexts include instances in which well-known gay porn stars are described in metaphorical terms as "superheroes," whether of sexual endurance, prowess, or erotic abandon.[28] Other gay porn texts feature more symbolic appropriations of superhero imagery. Gustavo Subero, for instance, reads the iconography of the "masked wrestler" as a "superhero against evil forces" in two Mexican gay porn films, *La Putiza* and *La Verganza*,[29] while Shaka McGlotten discusses masked sexual performance and superhero motifs in The Black Spark, an amateur gay porn project.[30]

Parody requires a degree of subversion of an original narrative or dominant, external text. Yet gay porn parodies also allow for the seriousness of sexual arousal and climax. This is in keeping with the importance of parody to gay porn and gay culture more broadly, which Richard Dyer describes as underscored by "an awareness of something's style with a readiness to be moved by it."[31] Such texts are also specifically devoted to refusing the heteronormativity of an original/dominant text. This process is akin in certain respects to queer reading, which has long been enacted with characters such as Batman and Robin. Will Brooker illustrates the subversion at play in such reading strategies when he draws a comparison between gay readings of the relationship between Batman and Robin in 1950s comics and similar readings of physique magazines of the same era, the latter of which have often been coded as gay porn by virtue of the masturbatory function these texts served for many gay men at a time when more explicit homoeroticism was not available.[32] Both Batman comics and physique magazines were texts with an "official," or sanctioned, non-gay narrative—a professional homosocial bond between superhero and sidekick and the aesthetic promotion of muscle development, respectively—alongside an "unofficial, 'deviant' meaning."[33] Brooker's analysis demonstrates the tradition of fashioning homosexual meaning from mid-twentieth-century texts, the homoerotic potential of which was "an open secret" for many.[34] We should always remember, though, that these were subtextual readings and were enacted in a climate wherein public, official meanings were often strictly policed by producers and other institutions of power; homoerotic interpretations of both superheroes and beefcake models have frequently been vociferously rejected by the producers of these texts,[35] and the development of the Comics Code is one of many institutional responses inspired, in part, by a fear of gay reading.[36] Gay superhero porn parodies embody an especially "active" form of queer reading,[37] inasmuch as they involve not just imagining but actually creating alternative gay realities. Such parodies open up possibilities that, though suggested by latent cues in the main text, are not explicit, or "validated." It is here that gay parody's important political function is performed.

Having established the general political context of gay superhero porn parodies, it is now possible to turn to specific examples of the potential and problematics of Super Gay Hero's parodies. In the interest of facilitating in-depth readings, the following analysis will focus on a single common potential and a single common problematic element of these texts, beginning with the potential for these texts to function on a political level as a form of queer visibility activism.

ON THE POTENTIAL OF SUPERHERO GAY PORN PARODY

In pointing out the applicability of queer theory to the construction of the superhero, Gareth Schott reminds us that these characters constitute a resistance to what Michael Warner describes as "regimes of the normal."[38] Superheroes are, according to Schott, "already at odds with heterosexual society due to their super human qualities."[39] Superhero origin narratives, for instance, often mimic gay coming-of-age tales, as both cases involve a protagonist (or "hero") coming to terms with a nonnormative identity. Of course, there are a number of metaphors that can be ascribed to superheroes; caped crusaders have also been read as symbols of arrested maturity, for instance.[40] Yet the plight, especially, of mutation-based superheroes in series starring the X-Men and Spider-Man, wherein the heroic protagonists must come to terms with being treated as "freaks of nature" by a generally hostile society, makes for much metaphorical "gay sense."[41] Elsewhere in this volume, J. Andrew Deman, Brian Johnson, and Christopher B. Zeichmann discuss various ways in which both comic books and films have intentionally emphasized the thematic links between the X-Men's mutant metaphor and experiences of queerness.

William Earnest also notes, however, that despite the "intentional framing" of films from the X-Men franchise as metaphors for homosexuality and gay rights, directors and screenwriters simultaneously equip these texts "with the rhetorical stealth needed to fly below the gaydar of many critics and audience members."[42] This is where much of the liberating potential of gay superhero parody lies—namely, in the actualization of queer readings. While queer readings of superheroes are reasonably plentiful in both scholarly and audience contexts,[43] queer acts (let alone actual gay sex acts) are seldom shown in mainstream texts. This absence has prompted a vocal movement for manifest queerness in representations, and a call for more than "rhetorical stealth" tactics. Fans have even created a term, "queerbaiting," to label and criticize instances of homoerotic suggestiveness in mainstream texts that fall short of fully validating queerness.[44] In its own way, gay superhero porn parody answers this call for manifest queerness. Of the texts analyzed here, *Captain America: A Gay XXX Parody* is the most self-conscious in its interaction with this call. *Captain America: A Gay XXX Parody* contains four scenes, the first three of which are of particular interest. Scene 1 pairs the newly-in-the-present-day Captain America (portrayed by Alex Mecum) with a stranger (portrayed by Jay Roberts) from his apartment block. While initially taken aback when the male stranger kisses him, our hero ultimately displays an open mind to the pleasures of male-male sex; he does not resist the kiss, which progresses to Cap first fucking and then being fucked by the male stranger. Scene 2 pairs Cap with Black Panther (portrayed by "Anonymous") in a rare interracial scene[45] that once again presents Cap as open to a diversity of sexual roles (i.e., both insertive and receptive anal sex). Scene 3 offers the opportunity for our hero to "show his best friend how close they really are" when Cap's WWII-era partner, Bucky (portrayed by Paddy O'Brian), turns up in the present day; in this scene, Cap adopts the receptive sexual role, allowing Bucky to penetrate him.[46] This is a pairing of particular significance for queer and slash fans, many of whom have employed queer reading and remix strategies to make sense of the Cap/Bucky Barnes relationship within the Marvel Cinematic Universe.[47] Seeing Cap being receptive to penetration is a refreshing subversion of the cultural expectation placed on male heroes (and Western men in general) to remain "stiff" and impenetrable.[48] And yet, unlike the many transformations of Cap's body that occur in the genderbending fan works discussed by Anne Kustritz elsewhere in this volume, within the confines of Super Gay Hero, Cap's flexibility is atypical, and narratively explained by Cap's out-of-time ignorance of contemporary gender norms. On balance, there is much more that is problematic about Super Gay Hero's typical coupling of sexual roles with character archetypes. The site's problematic couplings will be discussed throughout the remainder of this chapter. But first, to put these problematic couplings in context, we need to situate Super Gay Hero within the broader gay porn landscape.

SPIDER-MAN: WEBBING A SEGUE TO THE PROBLEMATIC

It is worthwhile at this point to make the delineation between gay and queer porn. Whereas queer porn describes a form of alternative pornography inclusive of a "multiplicity and variety of bodies and genders" together with more "alternative pleasures,"[49] gay porn is hyperbolically and often archetypally gendered male, and it prioritizes white bodies and fantasies. Generally speaking, gay porn features "mansex": male-male sexual adventures populated by characters that often mimic and exaggerate a masculine ideal—think the "clone" iconography made popular by Finnish homoerotic fetish artist Tom of Finland. This is not, of course, applicable to all gay porn, which has its own variants championing more diverse body types and forms of sex.[50] The sample at hand, however, which comes from what can be described as the commercial gay porn mainstream (Men.com being, at the time of this writing, the second most popular gay porn studio), definitely features hyperbolic masculine performance and stereotypical bodily ideals. Additionally, diversity of color among performers is also lacking, with the *Captain America* parody, which features two interracial scenes (scenes 2 and 4), once again standing out as an exception.[51] The limited racial diversity of the performers is in keeping with Men.com's status as a mainstream (and American) producer of gay porn, and what John Mercer describes as the genre's "fact of whiteness."[52]

As I have observed elsewhere, Men.com's porn performers and stars are presented in a "rather monolithic" manner, conforming to "narrowly defined sex roles" and "privileged alignment of opposing positions (top/bottom) and prototypes" that "connect action, power, and penetration with extraordinarily sized, masculine men."[53] It is hardly surprising, therefore, that similar top/bottom dichotomies would be carried over into Men.com's parody texts, with the archetypal dominant-top construction generally reserved for the superheroes with the greatest perceivable masculine prowess. The carryover of such dichotomies suggests that Super Gay Hero replicates tried-and-tested gay porn conventions, rather than using parody to subvert them. Such carryover is best demonstrated through *The Flash: A Gay XXX Parody* and *Spider-Man: A Gay XXX Parody*, both of which overlay the heroes' sexual journeys with bottom-defeat/top-triumph conventions.

Both of these parodies exploit the mutation-as-gay-metaphor reading previously discussed. Containing three scenes, *The Flash* details how Barry Allen (portrayed by Johnny Rapid) is convinced to submit himself to testing and take up the burden of becoming the Flash after he is observed moving through city streets at superhuman speeds by a bystander (Dr. Wells, portrayed by Jessy Ares). Barry is hesitant, expressing the familiar reluctant-hero position. "I just want to be normal," he tells Dr. Wells in scene 1. In the third scene, it is revealed that Dr. Wells, the man who had observed Barry in the streets and convinced him to submit to tests, is in fact a villain who possesses the same abilities. The narrative paints the disclosure of mutation as a process of trust as well as betrayal, as Dr. Wells's identity as the murderer of Barry's mother is revealed. Wells-as-villain, who had feigned being confined to a wheelchair, fucks the Flash in the final scene. The Flash becomes a fallen hero here as he succumbs to the villain's advances, allowing himself to be taken over with desire: "I hate you, but I forgive you."[54] Our hero, who had performed the active sexual position in the first two scenes (penetrating

Gabriel Cross as Dr. Snow and Pierre Fitch as "Raymond," respectively),[55] is finally made sexually subservient to the older man who had deceived him. The finale presents queer seduction as villainous, with the Flash, previously a sexual instigator, made to submit to a larger, more mature male who is able to dominate him, both in terms of size and in terms of cunning and access to information. *Spider-Man* utilizes a near-identical narrative: the hero penetrates a friend and victim he saves in scenes 1 and 2, respectively, only to be penetrated by the arch-villain, the Green Goblin (portrayed by Myles Landon) and the Goblin's son (portrayed by Tobias) in the final scene. These texts' use of active/passive sexual positions as symbolic of victory/defeat brings us into the realm of the problematic. This is represented visually by figure 11.1, with the Flash and Spider-Man both finding themselves in the "bottom"/losing column by the end of their parody series.

In part, the narrative arcs of Super Gay Hero's *The Flash* and *Spider-Man* align with established readings of the superhero/supervillain relationship as being haunted by an obsession with possessing and penetrating bodies. Jes Battis, for instance, argues that the villain is obsessed with the hero's body, "with finding his weakness, with penetrating or shattering or inflicting violence upon him."[56] In this regard, the villain is a "failed version" of the hero, not content with ruling the world but obsessed with "ruling the hero's body" as well.[57] This interpretation makes particular sense within the context of the Super Gay Hero parodies. In the cases of the site's versions of *The Flash* and *Spider-Man* especially, the villain's intense, and indeed overriding, desire to possess and penetrate the hero's body is overt rather than implied.

But even as Super Gay Hero produces parodies that rub against the superhero genre, it exists in a different context. The texts of Super Gay Hero are primarily gay porn, produced for an audience interested in watching gay sex. As such, compared to mainstream superhero texts, Super Gay Hero's texts also have different narrative goals. In superhero gay porn parody, heroes and villains are not primarily motivated by desires to preserve or destroy the social order or each other; instead, penetration and sex are their primary motivators and markers of triumph, possession, and control. Even with such replacement, traces of destructive impulses remain, both as an anchor point to the original text and as part of the adaptive process of parody. Yet the fact that Super Gay Hero's texts are located within gay porn traditions also presents possibilities for more nuanced performances and readings, an example of which is developed below.

VARIATIONS/COMPLICATIONS OF THE PROBLEMATIC

To return to Dr. Wells and his success in penetrating and possessing the hero in *The Flash*: when situated within the gay superhero porn subgenre, this narrative event has significance beyond the hero/villain comic book archetype. Johnny Rapid, who portrays the Flash, is currently among the best-known porn stars; he was recently voted Best Gay-4-Pay Performer at the 2017 Str8UpGayPorn Awards, among many other industry awards and nominations. Such fame creates a context of its own. Rapid, after all, connotes a particular porn "prototype": the power bottom.[58] The construction and maintenance of such a persona is vitally important within gay porn.[59] For knowledgeable viewers, this persona transcends the character the performer is parodying. For example, in the parody of *The Flash*, within the first scene of the nonsexual narrative "webbing" that precedes the hard-core sex, Rapid pulls away when his soon-to-be sexual partner, Dr. Snow, comes in for an initiating kiss.[60] "Don't get me wrong, I like you," Rapid explains. "I just have this thing with kissing." In this case, the thwarted kiss serves as a wink and nod to a knowing audience. Rapid is notorious as a gay-for-pay performer; in real life, he is married to a woman with whom he has a child, and in porn films, he often refuses to kiss men during his scenes. In this moment, Rapid ceases to be an adult entertainment actor turning his hand at a well-trodden character and allows his porn persona to shine through. The sex then proceeds as expected, minus any kissing.

In this same vein of persona recognition, there is an element of naturalness—of coming home—to *The Flash*'s final scene. This scene features Rapid completely abandoning his superhero masquerade in favor of his well-known porn persona. Therefore, this final scene represents an ultimate return to form and porn convention. As I explain elsewhere, "Johnny Rapid is the current best-known representation of the power bottom twink"; as a result, no porn feature starring him would be truly satisfying without his powerful performance of sexual passivity.[61] If the power bottom is, as Mercer describes, "an autonomous sexual adventurer" who "orchestrates sexual situations,"[62] then Dr. Wells revealing that he is not in fact confined to a wheelchair and is at least as strong (if not stronger) than the Flash leads to the promise of a "hate-fuck" from an opposing force (in this case, the hero's parental killer) that is perhaps too alluring for Rapid-as-sexual-adventurer to resist. This makes for an especially spectacular display of Rapid's bottoming talents, fulfilling his porn

FIGURE 11.5. Power bottom twink Johnny Rapid performs his iconic O-face. Super Gay Hero's *Justice League* parody.

persona's longing for "a well-endowed, prototypical top who will satisfy his need for anal sex."[63] This scene importantly recognizes the textual literacy and intertextual competence that gay porn audiences can bring to a parody such as *The Flash*.

That Rapid's power bottom persona takes precedence over his portrayal of the Flash is additionally confirmed by Rapid's reprise of his role in scenes 1 and 4 from *Justice League*. In his first appearance, Rapid consoles Batman about his feelings of inadequacy following the death of Superman. He does this first with his words ("I saw you fight. [. . .] You can do anything[; . . .] you just need some encouragement"), then with his anus ("I think that's my favorite weapon in the whole batcave"). Ever orchestrating the sexual adventures, in the finale Rapid first deflects the advances of Wonder Woman (portrayed by drag queen Manila Luzon) toward him ("Not a chance, hon") then procures penetration from two prototypical tops, Batman and the resurrected Superman. And he does so with tremendous vigor, his bottoming athletic (at one point, he is suspended from a rope) and accompanied by his now-iconic "O-face," a defining characteristic of the power bottom (figure 11.5).[64]

This reading of Rapid as an active and self-reflexive force despite his stereotypically passive sexual role(s) does not contradict this chapter's earlier (and forthcoming) reading of Super Gay Hero as a space wherein the sexual positions on offer generally reaffirm problematic power hierarchies. What this illustration of Rapid's active role(s) *does* do is highlight the different viewing positions on offer in gay superhero porn parody. It also further emphasizes that, unlike heteroporn parodies, which Jeffries argues prioritize their relationship to their superhero genre source texts, gay superhero porn parodies are as indebted to the gay porn genre as to the superhero genre, enough so that they often prioritize the conventions of the former while keeping certain signifiers of the latter (via fucking in costumes, for instance).

It should also be emphasized, however, that Rapid is a unique case—the exception, not the rule. Viewers' likely recognition of his persona comes from his status as a "porn star" rather than a mere "porn performer"; the latter label describes the vast majority of actors in Super Gay Hero's features.[65] In the other scenes analyzed in this chapter, the conventions of mainstream superhero narratives more closely align with the conventions of gay porn; the most politically troubling aspects of these scenes reside within the merging of these generic contexts.

HEROES ON TOP; VICTIMS, VILLAINS, AND SIDEKICKS ON THE BOTTOM

As the example of Johnny Rapid illustrates, taking on a receptive sexual role (i.e., bottoming) should not automatically be equated with defeat. Gay sex—and, indeed, all sex—is more complex than that; the pleasure any of us derive from sex or porn is located on a spectrum that does not obey reductive top/bottom logic.[66] This chapter's author certainly does not subscribe to Dworkinesque assessments of gay porn,[67] such as those advanced by Christopher N. Kendall, who interprets gay porn in this way: "Gay men are not only penetrated like women but are expected to lust after pain and degradation like women are thought to under male dominance."[68] It is also, however, important to acknowledge that superhero narratives are, by and large, driven by binary symbolism such as good/evil, light/dark, strong/weak, speed/lethargy, active/passive, victory/defeat, top/bottom, and the like. It is also important to note that there is some evidence of such binaries resonating with lived gay experiences, wherein a normally anally receptive partner "getting on top" (i.e., switching to the penetrative sexual role) is perceived by some individuals as a conscious resistance to the perception of the bottom being dominated by the anally insertive partner.[69] This binary symbolism is most clearly on display in *Batman v Superman: A Gay XXX Parody*, which was the Best Porn Parody winner at the 2017 Cybersocket Awards.

This parody consists of three scenes featuring the following pairings: Superman/victim, Batman/victim, Superman/Batman/three victims. In scene 1, Superman (portrayed by Topher Di Maggio) rescues a young man (portrayed by Damien Crosse), "fending off his attackers and then drill[ing] his hole with his fat Superman cock."[70] In both this description and the scene itself, Crosse is clearly coded as a helpless victim. The narrative webbing for the scene, for instance, includes a close-up shot of Crosse's crotch, which dampens with urine during the altercation with two masked assailants. Crosse offers up his anus to be used by Superman's erect phallus following the rescue; this reads as the least he can do to show his gratitude, and all such an obviously vulnerable man has to offer the Man of Steel. Batman is a voyeur during the scene, watching from the shadows. Scene 2 presents Batman (portrayed by Trenton Ducati) with the opportunity to save the day, yet in this case, the victim (portrayed by Paddy O'Brian) fucks the hero. While it may seem progressive for a hero character to be depicted as preferring the receptive sexual position, when scene 2 is compared with the third and final scene, Batman's submission instead becomes conventional, and problematic in that conventionality. O'Brian foreshadows in scene 2 while fucking Batman: "Well, you're no Superman," setting up Batman to bottom in his eventual showdown with his hero rival.

The series' "orgy finale [. . .] has Superman and Batman joining forces to rescue three cock hungry studs."[71] This time, however, there is no narrative connecting the action sequence to the sex orgy, no rationale or even a "Thanks for saving me; now let's fuck" statement from the victims. The action simply ends, the threat is removed, the suspense music ceases, and the fucking begins, with the sound of men groaning (a veritable chorus of "oh yeah"s) taking over. With the exception of the crash of one of the cages in which the victims had been held falling to the ground halfway through the action, this scene features few other non-fucking, action-oriented elements. The "cock hungry" victims (Allen King, Dario Beck, and Massimo Piano) do not get to penetrate the heroes, nor even each other; they are passive receivers for the entirety of the scene. Batman and Superman both take part in fucking the "cock hungry" victims, but the narrative focus of the scene is on the Batman vs Superman element. "You're not as strong as I thought you were," Superman tells Batman, who then promptly falls to his knees, removes Superman's penis from beneath the suit, and puts it in his mouth. Toward the scene's conclusion, Superman says, "Now it's my turn." He then comes up behind Batman, disrupting Batman's penetration of one of the victims, and slides his cock inside him. The statement cuts through the moans and non-narrative-driven sexual action, ending the series by returning to the competition of the title. Batman ejaculates with Superman inside him, and Superman is the last of all to climax, which he does across Batman's face and mask—a powerful symbol of domination of one hero over another. Batman then diligently sucks Superman's spent penis clean. This final act delivers a definitive victory for Superman.

To unpack the significance of a top/bottom, victory/defeat narrative, we can look to scholarship on the masculine performance of male superheroes in more general, nonpornographic (i.e., mainstream/traditional) contexts. The superhero genre has always prioritized hegemonic masculine ideals, associating muscles with power and the capacity of men to wield power over others with individuality, freedom, and even goodness.[72] Edward Avery-Natale's analysis of seventy-seven DC comic books from the 1940s to the 2000s furthermore argues that "the bodies of superheroes have become far more sexualized, exaggerated, and unrealistic in recent years."[73] This has resulted, Avery-Natale argues, in "an intersection of spectacle and narrative that cannot be disconnected from both the physical body and the costume of the hero."[74] Avery-Natale also notes that despite the recent integration of gay superheroes into the DC and Marvel universes, these heroes "fit every element of embodied hegemonic masculinity."[75] Throughout the superhero genre, then, the measure (and success) of male superheroes is inextricably linked to their performance of hegemonic masculinity. This becomes especially clear in contrast with the representation of "others"—namely victims, villains, and characters with some queer trace—in the comics tradition. All such characters are, to some degree, examples of failed masculinity, for they, to paraphrase Friedrich Weltzien, lose control over their own process of identity transformation.[76]

Though Avery-Natale provides some valuable insights about what is "typical" within the superhero genre, it is important to differentiate between what is typical and what is true of all characters. In addition, the look and logic of hegemonic masculinity has changed in significant ways from the 1940s to the present.[77] Yet Avery-Natale's analysis is particularly apt within the context of this chapter's sampling of gay superhero porn parodies, all of which can be described as exaggerated portrayals of masculinity, in both a gay porn and superheroic sense. The gendered conventions Avery-Natale identifies play out again and again in Super Gay Hero's parodies. To illustrate via example, in chronological order of production: in the one-scene parody *The Arrow*, the hero (portrayed by Liam Magnuson), who is hard and scarred with a painted green eye mask, fucks into submission and silence the villain, a man (portrayed by Spencer Fox) who is trying to expose his real identity. Another example, *X-Men: A Gay XXX Parody*, contains four scenes. In scene 1, Wolverine (portrayed by Colby Keller), a character who, similar to Green Arrow, is a gruff, "brooding and ruthless vigilante,"[78] fucks Cyclops (portrayed by Brenner Bolton). Scene 2 pairs Pyro (Paul Canon) with Iceman (Mike De

Marko). Iceman was revealed to be gay in a 2015 comic;[79] that he bottoms here couples manifest homosexuality with bottoming, especially given the binary symbolism of Pyro (as associated with fire) penetrating Iceman (as associated with ice, which melts in contact with heat). When read along the binary chain, we arrive at: fire/ice, hot/cold, hothead/frigid, male/female, active/passive, top/bottom. Wolverine returns in scene 3 and fucks Mystique, a canonically female, shape-shifting villain who has deceived Wolverine into thinking she is Colossus (portrayed by Landon Mycles). Here the bottoming is connected with the "trickster" archetype; imagining gay men as effeminate tricksters was especially popular during McCarthy-era America[80] and persists into the present. The stealth metaphor also evokes Earnest's "rhetorical stealth" description of queer representation in mainstream superhero texts, which references a history in which gay men have been required to experience and perform their sexuality by means of stealth. The series concludes with Wolverine fucking Magneto (portrayed by Paddy O'Brian), an anti-hero known for his perverse morality. When the hero (victorious) partner is the penetrator, and the villain (defeated) partner is being penetrated, bottoming comes to double as punishment. Additional support for this argument can be found in scholarship on other types of hero narratives, wherein evil is often equated with being queer (Disney villains come to mind[81]), as well as scholarship within gay studies that considers associations between the receptive sexual role (bottoming) and failed masculinity/effeminacy.[82]

One final problematic element of this topping/bottoming dynamic that once again harkens back to the conventions of the superhero genre lies in the depiction of the sexually actualized relationship between the hero and his sidekick. Batman and Robin are the most well-known example of a hero and sidekick duo, and queer interpretations of their dynamic have attracted much attention spanning some six decades.[83] In Super Gay Hero's texts, sidekicks join victims and villains as passive receivers of the hero's phallus. In scene 3 of *Justice League*, for instance, Robin (portrayed by Paul Canon) is seen seducing Batman's housekeeper, Alfred (portrayed by Manuel Skye). When the pair are caught by Batman *in flagrante delicto*, Batman delights in instructing Alfred on exactly how he should fuck Robin, and has a go himself, too. "Now I want you to fuck him; I want to see you fuck him," Batman says. In this scene, Robin is not Batman's equal nor his sexual match; he is an object, rather than a subject, whose youth and comparable innocence are fetishized by the older male characters who can be read as stand-ins for the intended audience.

CONCLUSION

Deep Throat was the first porn film to be both financially successful and receive a wide release.[84] And with its surprising success came the predictions of social commentators that hard-core sex was poised to spill over into mainstream cinema. It did not happen, at least, not in the way these 1970s cultural commentators thought it would. While porn has become ubiquitous on the internet, the only cinema screens where it regularly appears belong to porn theaters that are rapidly becoming a thing of the past; it seems that despite the supposed "pornification" of our culture, porn itself continues to be viewed as unfit for public consumption. Gay porn parody is even less likely to become publicly acceptable in this author's lifetime. And yet, it continues to have value. Like disaster films of the 1970s, gay superhero porn parodies have the potential to serve a powerful metaphoric function,[85] providing space for heroes who have been remade as openly gay to step beyond the "public, political realm" within which mainstream characters, who are "stuck in their colourful uniform tights," are often confined.[86] Superhero sexuality is worthy of study in part because the narrative of the superhero often serves as "the rhetorical equivalent of a gay, lesbian, or bisexual teenager's 'coming out' ritual."[87] And porn parodies of such narratives carry the potential to turn rhetoric into real, tangible representation rather than the "below the gaydar" tenor of typical superhero genre fair[88] that, when it does include LGBTQ characters or storylines, too often does so for purposes of titillation or in a facile manner that neglects LGBTQ culture[89] and the realities of LGBTQ sex.

As this chapter has demonstrated, gay superhero porn parodies also, however, have the potential to confirm, precisely through their presentation of explicit gay sex between superheroes, villains, and their victims, problematic gendered roles and hierarchies that have long informed both the superhero genre and the gay porn genre. Interestingly, Jeffrey A. Brown's essay in this collection on the "myth of the phallus" and the reinforcement of "the superhero's presumption of hegemonic masculinity" in heteroporn parodies draws similar conclusions.[90] Despite the fact that superhero gay porn parody's political possibilities and problems exist simultaneously, the (literally) explicit nature of the latter routinely threatens to consume the former. This chapter's analysis is, admittedly, limited by its focus on the texts of a single pornographic site and the vision of all but a single director. It will be up to future scholars to determine whether the trends examined in this chapter hold true for all gay superhero porn parodies. Certainly, this author would like nothing more than for future scholars to find other examples that challenge the overarching conservatism of Super Gay Hero's fantasies.

NOTES

1. Wertham, *Seduction of the Innocent*, 190.
2. See Will Brooker, *Batman Unmasked: Analyzing a Cultural Icon* (London: Bloomsbury, 2000); Jes Battis, "The Kryptonite Closet: Silence and Queer Secrecy in *Smallville*," *Jump Cut*, no. 48 (2006), http://www.ejumpcut.org/archive/jc48.2006/gaySmallville/index.html; Schott, "From Fan Appropriation," 17–29.
3. Battis, "Kryptonite Closet."
4. See Sarah Panuska's chapter in this volume.
5. Stephen Maddison, "Comradeship of Cock? Gay Porn and the Entrepreneurial Voyeur," *Porn Studies* 4, no. 2 (2017): 139.
6. www.supergayhero.com.
7. Alter Sin, dir., *Justice League: A Gay XXX Parody* (Men.com, 2017).
8. Joseph Brennan, "'Bare-Backing Spoils Everything. He's Spoiled Goods': Disposal and Disgust, a Study of Retired Power Bottom Twink Jake Lyons," *Porn Studies* 3, no. 1 (2016): 29.
9. Scott Herring, "The Sexual Objects of 'Parodistic' Camp," *Modernism/Modernity* 23, no. 1 (2016): 5–8.
10. Joseph Brennan, "Size Matters: Penis Size and Sexual Position in Gay Porn Profiles," *Journal of Homosexuality* 65, no. 7 (2018): 915.
11. www.men.com/sites/.
12. Alter Sin, dir., *Batman v Superman: A Gay XXX Parody* (Men.com, 2016); Alter Sin, dir., *X-Men: A Gay XXX Parody* (Men.com, 2016); Alter Sin, dir., *Captain America: A Gay XXX Parody* (Men.com, 2016); Alter Sin, dir., *The Flash: A Gay XXX Parody* (Men.com, 2016); Sin, *Justice League*; Alter Sin, dir., *Spider-Man: A Gay XXX Parody* (Men.com, 2017).
13. www.colbyknox.com.
14. See Domonick J. Wegesin and Heino F. L. Meyer-Bahlburg, "Top/Bottom Self-Label, Anal Sex Practices, HIV Risk and Gender Role Identity in Gay Men in New York City," *Journal of Psychology and Human Sexuality* 12, no. 3 (2000): 43–62.
15. For an introduction to parody in cinema, see Dan Harries, *Film Parody* (London: British Film Institute, 2000).
16. Dru Jeffries, "This Looks Like a Blowjob," 276–294.
17. Dru Jeffries, "This Looks Like a Blowjob," 277.
18. Joseph Brennan, "Not 'from My Hot Little Ovaries': How Slash Manips Pierce Reductive Assumptions," *Continuum* 28, no. 2 (2014): 256.
19. Brennan, "Not 'from My Hot Little Ovaries,'" 279.
20. Brennan, "Not 'from My Hot Little Ovaries,'" 276.
21. Booth, "Slash and Porn," 405.

22. Jeffries, "This Looks Like a Blowjob," 276–277.

23. Lucy Neville, *Girls Who Like Boys Who Like Boys: Women and Gay Male Pornography and Erotica* (Cham, Switzerland: Palgrave Macmillan, 2018).

24. Axel Braun, dir., *Batman XXX: A Porn Parody* (Vivid Entertainment, 2010). Jeffries, "This Looks Like a Blowjob," 290.

25. The recent editorial decision to deny the bisexuality of Marvel's Hercules could be an example of "editing out" historically established/preexisting queerness; see Jack Shepherd, "Marvel's Diversity Problem Continues as Once Bisexual Character Hercules Confirmed Straight," *Independent*, August 3, 2015, https://www.independent.co.uk/arts-entertainment/books/news/marvels-diversity-problem-continues-as-once-bisexual-character-hercules-confirmed-straight-10435249.html.

26. Josh Flanagan, "Green Lantern: Where Do I Start—Updated!," iFanboy, June 15, 2011, https://ifanboy.com/articles/green-lantern-where-do-i-start-updated/.

27. Edward Avery-Natale, "An Analysis of Embodiment among Six Superheroes in DC Comics," *Social Thought and Research*, no. 32 (2013): 71–106.

28. For example, see Benjamin Scuglia, "The Last Days of Gay Porn," *Psychology & Sexuality* 6, no. 1 (2015): 115.

29. Gustavo Subero, "Gay Pornography as Latin American Queer Historiography," in *LGBT Transnational Identity and the Media*, ed. Christopher Pullen (Basingstoke, UK: Palgrave Macmillan, 2012), 216; Jorge Diestra, dir., *La Putiza* (Mexico: Mecos Films, 2004); Jorge Diestra, dir., *La Verganza* (Mexico: Mecos Films, 2005).

30. Shaka McGlotten, "The Élan Vital of DIY Porn," *Liminalities* 11, no. 1 (2015): 13.

31. Richard Dyer, "Idol Thoughts: Orgasm and Self-Reflexivity in Gay Pornography," *Critical Quarterly* 36, no. 1 (1994): 60–61.

32. Will Brooker, "Hero of the Beach: Flex Mentallo at the End of the Worlds," *Journal of Graphic Novels and Comics* 2, no. 1 (2011): 28.

33. Will Brooker, "Hero of the Beach," 28.

34. Thomas Waugh, *Hard to Imagine: Gay Male Eroticism in Photography and Film from Their Beginnings to Stonewall* (New York: Columbia University Press, 1996), 222.

35. Brooker, *Batman Unmasked*, 105–106.

36. See Anna F. Peppard's introduction to this volume for a more thorough discussion of the relationship between homoerotic fears and fantasies and the development of the Comics Code.

37. For discussion of the active nature of queer reading, see Alexander Doty, *Making Things Perfectly Queer* (Minneapolis: University of Minnesota Press, 1993).

38. Michael Warner, "Introduction," in *Fear of a Queer Planet: Queer Politics and Social Theory*, ed. Michael Warner (Minneapolis: University of Minnesota Press, 1993), xxvi.

39. Schott, "From Fan Appropriation," 21.

40. See Isaac Cates, "On the Literary Use of Superheroes; Or, Batman and Superman Fistfight in Heaven," *American Literature* 83, no. 4 (2011): 831–857.

41. William Earnest, "Making Gay Sense of the *X-Men*," in *Uncovering Hidden Rhetorics: Social Issues in Disguise*, ed. Barry Brummett (Los Angeles: Sage, 2008), 215–232.

42. Earnest, "Making Gay Sense," 216; also see Zeichmann in this volume.

43. For example, see Brooker, *Batman Unmasked*; Battis, "Kryptonite Closet"; Schott, "From Fan Appropriation."

44. See Joseph Brennan, ed., *Queerbaiting and Fandom: Teasing Fans through Homoerotic Possibilities* (Iowa City: University of Iowa Press, 2019).

45. The anonymity of the Black Panther performer, which is further ensured by the fact that he remains masked throughout the scene, makes it more implicitly than explicitly interracial.

46. Scene description.

47. See Francesca Coppa, "Slash/Drag: Appropriation and Visibility in the Age of *Hamilton*," in *A Companion to Media Fandom and Fan Studies*, ed. Paul Booth (Hoboken, NJ: Wiley-Blackwell, 2018), 189–206; also see Catherine Coker, "Earth 616, Earth 1610, Earth 3490—Wait, What Universe Is This Again? The Creation and Evolution of the Avengers and Captain America/Iron Man Fandom," *Transformative Works and Cultures*, no. 13 (2013), http://journal.transformativeworks.org/index.php/twc/article/view/439/363; Proud Arunrangsiwed, "Heroic Role and Attractiveness as the Cause of Creating Slash or Yaoi Fan Art," *BU Academic Review* 16, no. 1 (2017): 18–30.

48. Susan Faludi, *Stiffed: The Betrayal of the American Man* (New York: HarperCollins, 1999).

49. Shawna Lipton, "Trouble Ahead: Pleasure, Possibility and the Future of Queer Porn," *New Cinemas* 10, no. 2–3 (2012): 197.

50. For more on alternative gay pornographies, see Joseph Brennan, "Gay Porn Networks," *International Journal of Cultural Studies* 22, no. 1 (2019): 140–156; for another exceptional case, namely examples of positive representations of fat men in gay porn, see Nels P. Highberg, "More Than a Comic Sidekick: Fat Men in Gay Porn," *Performing Ethos* 2, no. 2 (2011): 109–120.

51. Another potential exception is the casting choice of François Sagat to play Aquaman. Yet despite being famed for his striking Arab aesthetic, Sagat is in fact "a Caucasian actor . . . inspired by Arab culture . . . [and] discovered peripherally by consumers searching for Arab men"; Mehammed Amadeus Mack, *Sexagon: Muslims, France, and the Sexualization of National Culture* (Oxford: Oxford University Press, 2017), 235.

52. John Mercer, *Gay Pornography: Representations of Sexuality and Masculinity* (London: I. B. Tauris, 2017), 147.

53. Brennan, "Size Matters," 927–928.

54. Scene 3.

55. In a gender-bent casting, the all-male porn is loosely based on *The Flash* (United States: CW Network, 2014–) TV show.

56. Battis, "Kryptonite Closet."

57. Battis, "Kryptonite Closet."

58. See John Mercer, "Homosexual Prototypes: Repetition and the Construction of the Generic in the Iconography of Gay Pornography," *Paragraph* 26, no. 1–2 (2003): 280–290.

59. Jeffrey Escoffier, *Bigger Than Life: The History of Gay Porn Cinema from Beefcake to Hardcore* (Philadelphia, PA: Running Press Book Publishers, 2009).

60. Mercer, *Gay Pornography*, 53.

61. Brennan, "Bare-Backing Spoils," 29.

62. John Mercer, "Power Bottom: Performativity in Commercial Gay Pornographic Video," in *Hard to Swallow: Hard-Core Pornography on Screen*, ed. Claire Hines and Darren Kerr (New York: Columbia University Press, 2012), 220.

63. Mercer, "Power Bottom," 220.

64. Brennan, "Bare-Backing Spoils," 23–25.

65. See Jeffrey Escoffier, "Porn Star/Stripper/Escort: Economic and Sexual Dynamics in a Sex Work Career," *Journal of Homosexuality* 53, no. 1–2 (2007): 182; exceptions include other "big names," such as Colby Keller and François Sagat.

66. For examples of this range of desires in viewing porn, see Todd G. Morrison, "'He Was Treating Me Like Trash, and I Was Loving it . . .' Perspectives on Gay Male Pornography," *Journal of Homosexuality* 47, no. 3–4 (2004): 167–183.

67. For example, see Andrea Dworkin, *Pornography: Men Possessing Women* (New York: Plume Press, 1989).

68. Christopher N. Kendall, *Gay Male Pornography: An Issue of Sex Discrimination* (Vancouver: University of British Columbia Press, 2004), 67.

69. See Susan Kippax and Gary Smith, "Anal Intercourse and Power in Sex between Men," *Sexualities* 4, no. 4 (2001): 413–434.

70. Scene description.

71. Scene 3 description.

72. See Jeffrey A. Brown's chapter in this volume.

73. Avery-Natale, "Analysis of Embodiment," 71.

74. Avery-Natale, "Analysis of Embodiment," 71.

75. Avery-Natale, "Analysis of Embodiment," 100.

76. Weltzien, "Masque-*ulinities*," 244.

77. For an example of such change, see Keith Friedlander's analysis of the Young Avengers franchise in this volume.

78. Wright, *Comic Book Nation*, 277.

79. Brian Michael Bendis, *All-New X-Men* no. 40 (New York: Marvel, 2015).

80. Craig M. Loftin, ed., *Masked Voices: Gay Men and Lesbians in Cold War America* (Albany: State University of New York Press, 2012).

81. See Craig M. McGill, "'This Burning Desire Is Turning Me to Sin': The Intrapersonal Sexual Struggles of Two Disney Singing Villains," *Queer Studies in Media & Popular Culture* 3, no. 1 (2018): 27–49.

82. For example, see Andrew Reilly, "Top or Bottom: A Position Paper," *Psychology & Sexuality* 7, no. 3 (2016): 167–176.

83. For a review of this literature, see Edward Schneider and Roxanna Palmer, "Archiving, Accessibility, and Citation: The Relationship between Original

Materials and Scholarly Discussion in Homosexual Interpretations of the Batman Franchise," *Journal of Graphic Novels and Comics* 7, no. 1 (2016): 20–34.

84. Gerard Damiano, *Deep Throat* (United States: Bryanston Pictures, 1972).

85. See Fred Kaplan, "Critical Dialogue on Disaster Films: Drugged Popcorn," *Jump Cut*, no. 8 (1975): 19–20.

86. Robert Voelker-Morris and Julie Voelker-Morris, "Stuck in Tights: Mainstream Superhero Comics' Habitual Limitations on Social Constructions of Male Superheroes," *Journal of Graphic Novels and Comics* 5, no. 1 (2014): 101.

87. Earnest, "Making Gay Sense," 215.

88. Earnest, "Making Gay Sense," 216.

89. See Sarah Panuska's chapter in this volume.

90. See Jeffrey A. Brown's chapter in this volume.

12

"THAT'S PUSSY BABE!"
Queering Supergirl's Confessions of Power

OLIVIA HICKS

In his introduction to volume 1 of *The Tijuana Bibles*, comics historian R. C. Harvey argues that superheroes and pornography are generic bedfellows: "Turgid superheroic musculature evokes at a subconscious level images of the similarly engorged sex organs that are flaunted in the eight-pagers."[1] Harvey draws on the work of cultural critic Gershon Legman, who argues that many comic book depictions of violence are thinly veiled metaphors for sex, substituting blood for semen and crime for coitus.[2] Thus, there is a scholarly history of equating the superhero with pornography and an impetus for using porn studies to examine the superhero. Where female superheroes are concerned, however, existing analyses tend to focus on the sexist objectification of these characters at the expense of other possibilities, including that of female superheroes becoming vehicles of female power fantasies and queer desire. This chapter will address this neglect by exploring mainstream and alternative texts starring Supergirl. Gendered power and difference are central to the character of Supergirl, who has historically struggled to be recognized as a woman without being dismissed as one within a world dominated by the patriarchal power of Superman.[3] Related to this, a gendered response to Supergirl's powers can be found in both the character's officially sanctioned stories and unsanctioned pornographic fan works.

Supergirl's struggle with her powers can be read as a struggle with her powerful sexuality. In a variety of texts, her sexuality threatens to either dominate or destroy her male love interests. There have been attempts in both official comic book narratives and unofficial fan texts such as *The Tijuana Bibles* to provide a solution to this superpowered—and potentially super-subversive—sexuality, but these solutions have often been constructed from a male heterosexual standpoint. As a result, they have generally taken the form of conservative attempts to contain Supergirl's sexuality. By contrasting these male-directed depictions with pornographic constructions of Supergirl's sexuality and powers developed and consumed within communities of self-identified queer women, this chapter will consider an alternative set of responses to this iconic character's sexuality.

This chapter begins with a discussion of Supergirl's sexuality in her original comics incarnation juxtaposed with male heterosexual fan responses to the problem of a superpowered female sexuality. It then proceeds to a discussion of the fandom surrounding the *Supergirl* television series (CBS and the CW Television Network, 2015–present), incorporating examples of fan fiction, fan art, and comments/conversations from online fan forums. The main focus of this discussion is the Supercorp fandom, wherein fans wish to see a romance develop between Supergirl, played by Melissa Benoist, and Lena Luthor, played by Katie McGrath. Supercorp was the most popular "femslash ship" (a romantic pairing involving two women) on the social media website Tumblr in 2017 and 2018, and McGrath was the most popular actress across the entire website in 2017.[4] This analysis will argue that differences in the heterosexual/male and queer/female visions of Supergirl echo similar debates about the construction of female sexuality in heterosexual versus queer pornography, and demonstrate how the same media can be interpreted very differently by heterosexual male fandoms versus female and queer fandoms. This chapter will use queer theory, porn studies, genre theory, and fan studies to unpack these dynamics.

"ARE YOU A GIRL OR A GRIZZLY BEAR?" SUPERSEXUALITY AND THE MALE FAN IMAGINARY

Supergirl, the younger cousin of Superman, debuted in *Action Comics* #252 (1959) (figure 12.1). She initially arrives on Earth as a teenager, decades after her cousin Superman, who is already established as a hero. Armed with the superpowers she has gained from the Earth's yellow sun, Supergirl has to learn not only how to control her powers but also how to

FIGURE 12.1. *Action Comics* #252 (1959).

assimilate with the people of Earth. This involves following her cousin's example in taking up a secret identity. In Supergirl's eponymous television series, this identity is Kara Danvers. In the comics, she has had several alter egos, but the most common is Linda Danvers.[5] Most importantly, within the comics and, to a lesser extent, within the television series, Supergirl struggles to escape from Superman's shadow and become a hero on her own terms. Comics scholar Alex Link argues that the "early Supergirl is most readily recalled as Superman's obedient cousin . . . while the later Supergirl is a transparent appeal to adolescent boys' fantasy."[6] In Link's characterization, Supergirl is caught between two patriarchal positions: an obedient prop and a sexualized object.

In his foreword to the Supergirl collected comics volume *Many Happy Returns* (2003), writer Peter David argues, "What [fans of Supergirl] remember, and pine for, when you strip it all down, is the sweet, innocent Kara back when she was first introduced. . . . I wanted to use *that* Supergirl. The girl who was either every fanboy's kid sister or first crush."[7] In this quote, David assumes a male identity for Supergirl fans that is also a misremembering of the original Supergirl stories, which were "intended deliberately to appeal to young girls."[8] Thus, David is replicating a wider erasure of female superhero fans in both academic scholarship and the comics industry.[9] By removing female fans from the history of Supergirl, David places the character in a nostalgic patriarchal framework where (male) fans yearn to either protect or woo her. The original version of Supergirl, who appeared in *Action Comics* and *Adventure Comics* throughout the 1960s, continues to hold power over the (male) fan imaginary. It is tensions from these adventures that David is still attempting to resolve in 2003, and that, according to David, twenty-first-century (male) fans still want to see addressed.

Supergirl's adventures in *Action Comics* and *Adventure Comics* are inordinately concerned with female power and female sexuality, which are presented as being in conflict with male power and sexuality. Linda Williams argues that the primary ideological conflict within hard-core pornography is between male and female power.[10] This primary conflict is evident in Supergirl's debut in *Action Comics* #252. The cover of this issue depicts Supergirl exploding out of her crashed rocket ship with a triumphant grin on her face while Superman looks on, aghast. Superman is about to land next to her, but from his body language, he could be recoiling in horror. "Great guns!" Superman exclaims. "A Girl, *flying*! It—uh—must be an illusion!" "Look again, *Superman!*" Supergirl crows back. "It's me *Supergirl*! And I have *all* your powers!"[11] This image and exchange not only presents Supergirl as a threat to Superman, but also frames the relationship between Supergirl and Superman as a gendered power struggle. Superman's astonishment is directed not merely at Supergirl's powers, but also at the fact that it is a *girl* who wields them. Supergirl's riposte, meanwhile, is an obvious threat to Superman's position as the dominant authorial figure in the comic book universe. Supergirl dares to be his equal, and as she is not only female but a teenager, Superman finds this to be not only unbearable but also unimaginable, declaring her presence "an illusion" and "impossible."[12] Superman attempts to contain Supergirl by ordering her to keep the existence of a superpowered girl a secret from the rest of the planet. Instead, she must masquerade as the mousey Linda.[13] However disguised, the threat of Supergirl remains; her fearsome powers quickly become a metaphor for a terrifying and emergent female sexuality.

Supergirl's powers are presented as a threat to others as well as herself; within *Action Comics* and *Adventure Comics*, her powers routinely threaten to "out" her as distressingly different from her peers, friends, and potential lovers. This theme has significant sexual connotations. In his seminal book *The History of Sexuality*, Michel Foucault argues that knowledge and sexuality exist as part of a larger framework of "power-knowledge-pleasure" that "sustains the discourse on human sexuality in our [i.e., the Western] part of the world."[14] For Foucault, confession functions as a central aspect of Western society's exercise of control over knowledge, sexuality, and pleasure.[15] Williams draws on Foucault in her discussion of hard-core pornography, arguing that the genre acts as a "confession" of female pleasure even though, paradoxically, female sexual pleasure is what the genre can never truly guarantee: "While it is possible in a certain limited and reductive way, to 'represent' the physical pleasure of the male by showing erection and ejaculation, this maximum visibility proves elusive in the parallel confession of female sexual pleasure."[16] The supposed elusiveness of female sexuality necessitates the performance of many graphic confessions that fundamentally structure the genre's objectifications of the female body. In hard-core pornography, female bodies must be ultra-visible (and usually, ultra-vocal) to provide "documentary evidence" of their pleasure and confirm male power over that pleasure.[17]

The original *Supergirl* stories similarly emphasize the elusiveness of female sexuality—or, more broadly, female subjectivity—and include the reader in multiple confessions. In the concluding scene of "The Day Supergirl Revealed Herself!" a miserable Supergirl thinks, "I wonder how people on Earth would react if they learned there is a *Supergirl* on Earth? <Sigh> Because of my promise to *Superman*, I guess I'll never know!" An

FIGURE 12.2. Dick Malverne asserts his knowledge of, and control over, Lena. *Action Comics* #296 (1963).

unseen, extratextual narrator responds, "But *we* know, *Supergirl!*"[18] This scene situates the readers of the comic in a voyeuristic position, recipients of Supergirl's hidden "confessions" of her true identity. This voyeurism is further realized through the character of Dick Malverne (first appearance: *Action Comics* #256 [1959]), a boy who dates Supergirl's alterego, Linda (figure 12.2). Dick suspects Linda is Supergirl, and he constantly watches for "evidence" of her true identity, attempting, on numerous occasions, to force a "confession." His investigative attentions are paired with romantic ones. In a brief interlude where he suspects Lena Luthor of being Supergirl, he spurns Linda for Lena. As Supergirl/Linda watches, Dick sweeps the startled Lena into a kiss, declaring, "Lena, you were *marvelous*! You saved that pilot's life with your *super-breath*! I could *kiss* you!"[19] Dick's attraction to Supergirl's powers, and his association of her super-abilities with her desirability, highlights the metaphorical link between her sexuality and her powers. It also emphasizes the sexualization of Supergirl's secrets. Dick's desire is inseparable from his need to elicit Supergirl's confession, and his (imagined) knowledge of her secret identity entitles him to take control of her body.

Williams argues that hard-core pornography attempts to "resolve" the question of male/female difference in a sexual union that confirms traditional gender identities and hierarchies.[20] Similarly, Supergirl's early stories attempt to resolve her difference by continually seeking a male partner for her. Time and again, however, Supergirl's power makes the task impossible. Due to the comics' patriarchal bias, any male partner of Supergirl must be able to dominate her physically and sexually. This rules out a number of "normal" young men that Supergirl attempts to date. In "The Jilting of Supergirl" from *Adventure Comics* #385 (1969), Supergirl makes it clear that ordinary men woefully fail to stimulate her. In the opening of the story, Supergirl, in the guise of Linda Danvers, is out dancing with Phil, who, we are told, is the "grooviest guy in school."[21] However, despite his popularity and handsomeness, he is unable to excite Supergirl:

> PHIL: The group is rocking, dream doll! Ready to fly?
> SUPERGIRL: Blast off, Phil! All systems are go—go—go!
> CAPTION: But to Linda's mounting dismay, even amidst the feverish festivity surrounding her . . .
> SUPERGIRL [thinks]: It's no use! He's not only *not* sending me into orbit. . . . I haven't even left the *pad*![22]

From Supergirl's chanting of "go—go—go!" to the "feverish" actions of her date, which are likened to the phallic imagery of a rocket, to Supergirl's final announcement that she has not "even left the *pad*!" this scene has clear sexual overtones. It is additionally clear that Supergirl's silent "confession" is not one of pleasure but rather of intense disappointment with her male companion. On other occasions, Supergirl's superstrength terrifies "normal" men. In "Supergirl's Shattered Marriage!" from *Action Comics* #370 (1968), Supergirl becomes engaged to the campus Casanova, Gary Sparks. However, using a computer-predictor she has invented, Supergirl learns that Gary will be a terrible husband, and that the inevitable outcome of their marriage is that an infuriated Supergirl will murder him; as such, Supergirl resolves to break her engagement. Although she has performed many superheroic feats for Gary, she has not subjected him to her full strength, and it is this that she uses to break the engagement. Pretending that she is overjoyed at seeing him, Supergirl lifts Gary off his feet, spins him so fast that he becomes dizzy, and hugs him so hard that he exclaims, "Are you a *girl* or a *grizzly bear*?"[23] Supergirl then treats Gary to a "super-kiss." As Gary struggles to break Supergirl's embrace, he desperately thinks, "Her super-kiss is drawing out my breath like a *vacuum cleaner*! *I can't break the suction!*"[24] (figure 12.3). Gary promptly decides to end the engagement, as Supergirl's "true" sexual

FIGURE 12.3. Supergirl's deadly sexuality. *Action Comics* #370 (1968).

self—which has obvious vagina dentata connotations—will prove fatal to him.

Even as mortal men are incapable of satisfying Supergirl, her series of super-boyfriends, including Jerro the Merman, Brainiac V, and Comet the Super-Horse, seemed to have failed to satisfy her readers. In his aforementioned introduction, David does not even consider these super-boyfriends to be suitors, referring to them only as "pals."[25] David seeks to resolve the question of Supergirl's sexuality by pairing her with Superman, having the two marry in the story arc *Many Happy Returns*, which ran in *Supergirl* #75–80, published between 2002 and 2003.[26] Due to some complicated alternate universe maneuvering, Supergirl is not related to the version of Superman she ends up marrying. Yet because Supergirl has such a long, canonical history as Superman's cousin, and because the possibility of a romance between the versions of the characters who *are* cousins is alluded to several times in the original comics, this relationship maintains a hint of taboo.[27] In addition, because *Many Happy Returns* was the final story line before the *Supergirl* title was temporarily canceled, the marriage of Supergirl and Superman can be seen as a final resolution rather than a temporary containment. David solves the "problem" of Supergirl by enforcing a patriarchal framework. Supergirl is effectively paired with an older family member who also happens to be one of the few beings in the universe more powerful than she is. Thus, David contains Supergirl's potentially disruptive power/sexuality and makes her accessible to (male) fans as both a younger relative in need of protection and a dream girl who may be safely romanced.

David's patriarchal solution is characteristic of heterosexual pornography. In *Hard Core*, Williams writes, "That the 'solutions' to the problems of sex [in pornography] are most often constructed from the dominant power knowledge of male subjectivity should come as no surprise."[28] This reaffirmation of male power is echoed in pornographic superhero fan works aimed at heterosexual men. In his examination of the superhero porn parodies of director Axel Braun, for instance, Dru Jeffries argues, "In practice . . . Braun is a producer, selling a product to a particular kind of fan that does not want to creatively transform the text but rather wants to 'celebrate the story the way it is.'"[29] In other words, Braun and the fans of his parodies want to see sexual encounters that reify traditional (read: patriarchal) gender roles and hierarchies. Elsewhere in this volume, Jeffrey A. Brown similarly argues that superhero porn parodies aimed at heterosexual men uphold the superhero genre's historical and conventional veneration of phallic masculinity. Supergirl's appearances in the pornographic Tijuana Bibles also address a presumed male heterosexual audience and posit solutions to the "problem" of Supergirl that are strikingly similar to what David devises in the non-pornographic *Many Happy Returns*. "Linda Lee's Delimma [sic]" (early 1960s, reprinted in *The Tijuana Bibles Volume 3*) plays on the ineffectualness of Dick Malverne. In this story, Supergirl propositions Superman, informing him that they are going to have sexual intercourse as their alter egos, Clark Kent and Linda Lee. Supergirl explains, "Linda never experienced any satisfaction on dates—so, you are going to give her that satisfaction!"[30] Of course, Superman performs admirably, and Supergirl is, at last, satisfied. Another Tijuana Bible story, "Last Day on Krypton" (early 1960s, reprinted in *The Tijuana Bibles Volume 4*), sees Zor-El, Supergirl's father, teach Supergirl "the facts of life" before she departs for Earth. Pairing Supergirl with her father is, from a patriarchal perspective, a logical solution to the problem of her sexuality/power; the taboo of incest is used to titillate even as it is implicitly sanctioned by canonical suggestions of a similarly taboo relationship with Superman. The story concludes with Supergirl exclaiming, "Oh oooh—Dad-dy——I'm coming—and it's all yours—ooh—o-o-oh!"[31] This dialogue—and, of course, the graphic images that accompany it—leaves no doubt that Supergirl is a "daddy's girl," in every sense of the term.

But is this the only way the gendered tensions bound up in Supergirl's sexuality/power can be resolved? The desire of (heterosexual male) fans to reaffirm the original texts' patriarchal gender roles and hierarchies is not universal. It can be contrasted with aspects of gay porn parodies (see Sarah Panuska and Joseph Brennan in this volume) as well as the desire of many female fans to "critically address what they perceive to be the shortcomings of the franchises they are so invested in, creatively reshaping them to fit their own interests and desires."[32] An example of this desire can be seen in an edit of comic book art posted by Tumblr user Nerdmikhail (figure 12.4). In this post, Nerdmikhail rewords two panels from Supergirl's debut in *Action Comics* #252. In the original comic, the first panel shows Superman's continued questioning of Supergirl's presence, and in the second panel, Supergirl begins to tell him her origin story. In the reworked version, Superman is not doubting Supergirl's existence but her sexuality: "Wait, so let me. Get this straight. So what you're saying is that you are in fact in *love* with a *Luthor*. More specifically *Lena Luthor*?" Supergirl replies, "That's Pussy Babe!"[33] Whereas the original comic focused on the tension between male and (unacknowledged) female power, the reworked version focuses on the tension between the House of El and the Luthor family, and how this tension is successfully resolved through a queer union. The Supercorp fandom further explores this possibility.

FIGURE 12.4. "That's Pussy Babe!" Fan art by Nerdmikhail on Tumblr.

SUPERGIRL (2015) AND SUPERCORP

The *Supergirl* television series premiered on the CBS network in October 2015; subsequent seasons appear on the CW network.[34] The CW network has a history of targeting younger female audiences but in recent years has sought out older male audiences by developing several superhero television series.[35] *Supergirl* represents a bridge between the network's already strong female viewership and its newer male-targeted superhero fare. This is, however, an unstable bridge. This is emphasized by the fact that *Supergirl* does not take place in the same dimension as the other series; various universe-hopping devices are employed to have Supergirl appear in the channel's superhero crossover events.

The move to the CW network in season 2 saw *Supergirl* undergo several dramatic changes, including the introduction of Lena Luthor, the adopted sister of classic Superman villain Lex Luthor. In her original *Action Comics* appearances, Lena is Supergirl's best friend, and unaware that she is related to Lex Luthor. Because of Lena's ESP powers, however, Supergirl is constantly worried she will unwittingly "confess" her true identity to Lena. In addition, because she knows who Lena's brother is, Supergirl continually doubts the veracity of Lena's friendship. The television series imports these tensions while slightly rearranging their specifics. Because Lena is a Luthor, she is mistrusted by most people in National City. The key exception is Supergirl, who, for the most part, trusts Lena has good intentions, even as she continues to keep the identity of her alter ego a secret from her. Lena herself notes that her friendship with Supergirl exists "against all odds": "Who would've believed it? A Luthor and a Super, working together."[36] The emotional drama of the friendship that develops between both Lena and Kara as well as Lena and Supergirl is bolstered by these tensions and by the onscreen chemistry between Benoist/Supergirl and McGrath/Lena. This in turn fuels fans' championing of a romantic interpretation of the two's relationship.

The television series frequently and self-consciously highlights identity politics. In season 1, episode 1, when Supergirl questions whether the label "Super*girl*" is anti-feminist, her boss, Cat Grant—portrayed by 1990s postfeminist icon Calista Flockhart—gives the impassioned (and fittingly postfeminist-informed) reply: "And what do you think is so bad about 'girl'? I'm a girl, and your boss, and powerful, and rich, and hot, and smart. So if you perceive 'Supergirl' as anything less than excellent, isn't the real problem you?"[37] The series also generates a sense of female community and intersectional feminism by creating the character of Alex Danvers, Supergirl's powerful, supportive, and protective adoptive sister, who is a lesbian. The series has also reinterpreted and updated the source material by casting an African American actor, Mehcad Brooks, as Jimmy/James Olsen, Superman's best friend, who, since his first named comics appearance in *Superman* #13 (cover dated 1941), had appeared as white.

Despite these progressive moves, however, the series has continued to be conservative in the ways it has romantically positioned Supergirl. Although Supergirl is romantically paired, in the first season, with the non-powered, nonwhite James, the first episode of season 2 sees her and James suddenly end any attempts to start a relationship. Supergirl's main love interest then promptly becomes Mon-El, a white, heterosexual superpowered man. The relationship between Mon-El and Supergirl is conservative inasmuch as it focuses on Supergirl's redemption of Mon-El, who prior to meeting Supergirl was a self-centered, unheroic, slave-owning prince. This links female power to a maternal and nurturing role, undermining the show's feminist branding. Popular culture news website io9, for instance, describes Mon-El as "the complete antithesis of what the show should be—a brash dude who always knows best and whose story always comes at the expense of the show's robust group of women."[38] The unpopularity of the pairing of Supergirl and Mon-El (referred to by fans as "Karamel") relative to the popularity of Supercorp suggests it is out of step with the desires of a significant portion of the show's audience. A search for "Kara Danvers/Mon-El" on the popular fan fiction site Archive of Our Own (AO3) shows that there are, as of this writing, just over two thousand entries focusing on a romance between Supergirl and Mon-El. In contrast, a search for "Kara Danvers/Lena Luthor" reveals over eight thousand entries. The popularity of the Supercorp fandom is significant in and of itself, but also because it is generally understood to be predominantly made up of fans who have, historically, been tremendously underserved by mainstream superhero texts—namely, queer women. In the notes to her fan fiction "I Have to Confess (You Look So Good in That Dress)," author Jazzfordshire argues that Lena/McGrath is dressed in form-fitting, sultry career clothes by the costume department specifically because "they need us thirsty wlw [women who love women] to keep watching."[39] In its creation of popular pornographic content targeting queer women rather than the straight men who are the usual presumed audience for superhero texts, Supercorp showcases several important revisions to the questions that have traditionally surrounded Supergirl's power/sexuality.

Although Supercorp-affiliated fan art and fan fiction feature a samesex pairing and frequently seek to transform the patriarchal framework within which Supergirl's powers/sexuality have historically been placed, it is important to note that this is also, in many ways, a conservative pairing. Some Supercorp fans have reacted antagonistically to the nonwhite actors who have been paired romantically with McGrath in the television show.[40] Within this context, it is worth noting that McGrath is not only white but has her whiteness regularly fetishized within fan art created by Supercorp shippers, who often present her as either significantly paler than Kara or, on occasion, without any skin color at all.[41] While it would be very difficult to prove these artistic choices are deliberately racist, the widespread fetishization of McGrath's whiteness can be linked to long-standing cultural prejudices surrounding race. Sean Redmond argues that stardom and fetishized whiteness are linked through mythic tropes, which are embodied by the white female star.[42] Although stars are objects of desire for their fans, projecting a promise or possibility of "great sex with the fantasy figure," Western culture codes white women in mixed relationships as impure or deviant.[43] To maintain her purity and status as an available object of desire, Lena must be paired with—and, as will be discussed below, aggressively "claimed" by—the white Supergirl. Despite its queerness, then, the Supercorp fandom risks a tired retelling of the same racist politics that have long been attached to nonwhite men and white women in Western narratives, with white female sexuality needing to be policed and protected from nonwhite men.[44]

This chapter will conclude with an exploration of some of the general themes and trends that inform Supercorp fan fiction, and a close reading of the pornographic fan fiction of Jazzfordshire, who has written a number of particularly popular works around the *Supergirl* television show.[45] As of this writing, Jazzfordshire has contributed twenty-three separate fan fictions to AO3, with the most popular story garnering over fifty-three thousand "hits," placing it within the most popular 1 percent of Supercorp fan fictions. That Jazzfordshire is well known within the fandom is demonstrated by fan discourse surrounding her work. For example, a Twitter account dedicated to posting Supercorp fan fictions publicized a recent work by claiming "Jazzfordshire strikes 😳 [the emoji for embarrassment]," to which another Twitter user replied, "I'm a simple Supercorp shipper and quality smut fan—I see Jazz, I click!"[46]

Jazzfordshire, who identifies as a "Big Lesbian," is also representative of the common interaction between fan writing and the wider fan community, and the importance of this interaction for marginalized voices. Jazzfordshire's very active Tumblr account shows that Supercorp discourse on that site has influenced her writing; similarly, Jazzfordshire's writing has influenced the creation of other fans' Supercorp content on Tumblr (figure 12.5).[47] Tamara Packard and Melissa Schraibam argue that lesbian pornography "offers a location for lesbians to gather and form

FIGURE 12.5. Accompanying fan art for the Jazzfordshire story "Gonna Make You Sweat." Sangoundercover on Tumblr.

a necessary political, social, and sexual community.... Because sexuality is so central to lesbian identification, visible and honest discussion among lesbians of sexuality is critical in creating and maintaining a strong, political, and diverse lesbian community."[48] Clearly, the Supercorp fandom grew out of the *Supergirl* television series rather than Jazzfordshire's work. Yet Jazzfordshire's work has provided a space where queer women can discuss sexuality. In the comments section of the fan fiction "Touch Me (Tell Me What You Want Me to Do)," which features a lengthy depiction of anal intercourse, several commenters have discussed how the fan fiction changed their perceptions of this sex act.[49] In addition, Jazzfordshire has received so many requests for advice that she has started a separate Tumblr, ask-jazzfordshire.tumblr.com. Thus, her work has made a significant contribution to the Supercorp fandom and the discussions and explorations of queer female sexuality that occur with it.

"ASK . . . AND YE SHALL RECEIVE": NEGOTIATING SUPERGIRL'S POWER IN QUEER FEMALE FAN CONTEXTS

As Packard and Schraibam observe, pornography made by women for women is an important space in which "women can formulate and show sexualities that are not male-defined."[50] Even though "slash" fiction (fan fiction that romantically pairs two characters of the same sex) traditionally focuses on male same-sex couples, fan studies scholar Henry Jenkins argues that "slash stories . . . offer insights into female sexual fantasy; slash contains much Russ (1985) finds lacking in pornography aimed at a predominantly male audience."[51] Jenkins argues that slash fiction has a relatively simple generic pattern, and, like hard-core pornography, resolves cultural conflicts in sexual act: "The narrative formula of slash involves a series of movements from an initial partnership, through a crisis in communication that threatens to disrupt that union, towards its reconfirmation through sexual intimacy."[52] While Supercorp stories do not always precisely obey this trajectory, the theme of finding solutions for interpersonal as well as cultural conflicts through sexual acts is a staple feature of most stories, including those by Jazzfordshire. Importantly, though, whereas the fan narratives of the Tijuana Bibles attempt to unite Supergirl with a patriarchal figure and refrain from the use of superpowers within sexual scenes, even the name "Supercorp"—an amalgamation of "Supergirl" and "L-Corp," Lena's company, which is in turn easily reinterpreted as a reference to lesbianism (*The L Word*)—alludes to the erotic appeal of superpowered and/or superpowerful female bodies. The work of Jazzfordshire is particularly keen to explore Supergirl's supersexual prowess.

In some ways, the Supercorp fandom is organized around the figure of Lena Luthor rather than Supergirl; Lena typically works as a self-insert character, and stories are frequently told from her perspective and/or constructed to prioritize her point of view. Tumblr user katiemccgrath argues that "the Supercorp fandom is just a bunch of bottoms self-projecting onto lena luthor and that's Valid."[53] One effect of this conventional pattern is that, instead of reifying a patriarchal framework that would seek to contain Supergirl's supersexuality, the Supercorp fandom celebrates Supergirl's abilities and her sexual dominance of Lena. Although some fans do openly identify with Supergirl and make Lena/McGrath the object of their sexual desires, they appear to be in the minority. In some fan conversations, lusting after Lena is even (jokingly) disapproved of; some Supercorp shippers react as if it places the fan in competition with the all-powerful Supergirl, who has already "claimed" Lena.[54]

In Supercorp stories, there is a strong focus on using Supergirl's powers (such as superstrength, flight, cold breath, etc.) in a sexual setting. However, there is also an emphasis on Supergirl as a caregiver who nurtures Lena. This dichotomy is represented in the fan fiction "Touch Me (Tell Me What You Want Me to Do)," in which Jazzfordshire writes, "Kara is pure Supergirl in her aftercare—gentle but unyielding, pure focus on Lena's every twitch and noise."[55] This mix of "unyielding" and "gentle," which is mirrored in the contrast between the strong public façade of Supergirl and the shy alter ego of Kara, echoes what Jenkins calls slash fiction's "play with androgyny," wherein characters are presented with a "mix and match [of] traditionally masculine and feminine traits, sliding between genders."[56] This also relates to Janice Radway's work on romance fiction, which argues that the male hero of romance stories often fulfils a maternal nurturing role, offering emotional support to the heroine.[57] This mixing of traditionally gendered traits helps Jazzfordshire evoke a fantasy of Supergirl putting her powers at the service of the readers, tending to their every physical and emotional need. This fantasy is especially evident in the following section from "Touch Me (Tell Me What You Want Me to Do)": "Kara's iron grip on [Lena's] hip is a stark reminder of who exactly is doing this to her—the power of the being splitting her open, a god turned gentle in her eagerness to please. It gives [Lena] the thrill of power, knowing that Kara will do anything it takes to make her feel good."[58]

Although there are similarities between heterosexual male fans' and queer female fans' desire to be able to command Supergirl's attentions, there are some key differences. First, there is the aforementioned emphasis on Supergirl's powers in queer female fan fiction, which is not present in texts produced by and aimed at heterosexual males. Second, Jeffries argues that in the porn parodies of Axel Braun, anal sex "is rare . . . and only desired by villainous ("deviant") characters like Livewire and Joker."[59] However, three separate works by Jazzfordshire discuss anal sex extensively: the aforementioned "Touch Me (Tell Me What You Want Me to Do)," "Two Heroes Are Better Than One," and "The Best Kind of Apology." Jazzfordshire depicts anal sex within an explicitly consensual, intensely erotic environment: "The fact that Kara is going to be fucking her *that way* makes it even dirtier, makes her feel positively *molten*."[60] Not only is this contrary to those fantasies catering to heterosexual men, but it is also an unusual sexual act to include in lesbian media, and studies of same-sex female couples have found that anal sex is a relatively unpopular practice.[61] This heightens the subversiveness of Jazzfordshire's work, even within queer female circles.

The deliberate subversiveness of Jazzfordshire's work is furthermore evident in the fact that she often draws on Western Christianity in an ironic way. The fan fiction "I Have to Confess (You Look So Good in That Dress)" begins with the authorial note: "Ask . . . and ye shall receive."[62] The aforementioned "Two Heroes Are Better Than One," which features a three-way between Supergirl, who has been split into two, equally superpowered identities, and Lena, ends with the authorial note: "I THINK I NEED JESUS."[63] Finally, "Touch Me (Tell Me What You Want Me to Do)" opens with images of salvation/purity and damnation/smut, with the authorial notes informing us, "I'm giving you 4000 words of the purest smut I could think of, so I hope you're grateful. May god have mercy on my soul."[64] This request for mercy places the writing within a confessional context; we are reading the confessions not only of the fictional Supergirl and Lena, but of a real-life queer woman, whose stories appeal to a wider queer female fan imaginary.

This religious imagery extends into the stories. In "Of Piercings and X-ray Vision," Supergirl discovers that Lena has multiple tattoos and piercings. Her ensuing sexual obsession with them leads to the two becoming involved romantically. We are told that "Kara opens and closes her mouth, trying to conjure words to describe the feeling of wanting to worship every inch of Lena's perfect body, finding every secret it holds until she knows absolutely *everything*."[65] This sentence not only continues the religious overtones of the authorial notes but once again incorporates the Foucauldian power dynamics of the "confessional" that Williams argues is a structuring tension of pornography. The body of Lena is imbued with divinity, yet it is a body with "secrets." In this case, the secrets are her multiple hidden tattoos and piercings, rather than a potentially evil hidden identity. But in almost every case, these secrets are revealed—or confessed—to Supergirl over the course of the story. This story also echoes the Foucauldian dynamic of power-knowledge-pleasure; by giving Lena pleasure ("[worshipping] every inch of Lena's perfect body"), Supergirl gains a knowledge of Lena that will redistribute the power balance of their relationship, which has been disrupted by her realization that she does not know *everything* about Lena. After discovering that Lena has a nipple piercing, "[Supergirl] spends the whole day with Lena's parting words rattling around in her head like a hamster ball, throwing her off. They make her unbalanced, distracted, and she has more trouble than usual moderating her powers."[66] Supergirl's lack of knowledge about Lena results in a lack of control that undermines her powers, mirroring her loss of power in the relationship.

Power, knowledge, and pleasure are held in balance throughout Jazzfordshire's work, which focuses on "truths" that have to be uncovered in order for power balances to be restored and pleasure to be granted. These are, at their heart, utopian fictions, whose central fantasy is the establishment of a romantic and sexual equality that directly contradicts mainstream (read: patriarchal) depictions of heterosexuality. The most important truth that has to be unveiled is the truth that Supergirl and Kara Danvers are the same person; in every one of Jazzfordshire's stories, Lena either already knows this secret or learns it throughout the story. In this way, the author is rectifying one of the biggest power imbalances in Kara/Supergirl and Lena's friendship, one that is present in both the comics and the television series. The secondary truth that must be discovered for Supergirl and Lena to begin a relationship is Supergirl's homosexuality. An example of this can be found in "When I Think about You (Well, You Know the Rest)." After a moment of clarity in which Lena realizes that Supergirl and Kara are the same person—a moment that comes, fittingly, as she masturbates—Lena embarks on two investigations. First, she has to secure a confession that Kara truly is Supergirl; second, she seeks a confession of Kara's queerness.[67]

On the surface, this need to elicit Supergirl's confession(s) suggests a similarity between Supercorp stories and the heterosexual and patriarchally informed texts previously discussed. There are, however, important differences, which become clear when the specifics of these stories are further unpacked. The *Supergirl* comics and heterosexual male–produced fan works routinely imagine Supergirl as possessing an intimidating power that threatens to emasculate Superman and/or the "normal" men who attempt to date her. In these texts, Supergirl is a terrifying sexual powerhouse whose illogical and unnatural existence can only be resolved by her being dominated sexually by Superman or her father. The *Supergirl* television series seemingly resolves the "problem" of Supergirl's power by having her pursue a romance with Mon-El, a heterosexual, white, super-powered man who, in the second season, is established as more important to Supergirl than her vocational calling to be a reporter, and who, by the third season, is proving his dominance on-screen by training her with skills he has honed as a member of the Legion of Super-Heroes. In contrast, rather than seeking a partner to dominate Supergirl, the Supercorp fandom eroticizes Supergirl's physical dominance.

In "Your Sunday Best (Looks Best on My Floor)," Jazzfordshire draws attention to the erotic potential of Supergirl's powers:

> It's almost like, now that her body knows what it's like to be fucked by Supergirl, nothing else will do. Not her fingers, not toys, *nothing*. Nothing can hit the right spots, can go *hard* enough. She can't imitate the coolness of Kara's freeze-breath tongue or the way she can make her fingers practically vibrate with super-speed, and she can't stop thinking about the raw strength Kara was holding back. Lena is ruined for anyone else, even herself, and it's killing her slowly.[68]

In this and other stories, the potential threat of Supergirl's strength is nullified by Lena's intelligence and wealth. In the story series *You Look Way Too Good (To Leave This Up to Luck)*, Lena builds a red sun lamp that dampens Supergirl's powers, and in the stand-alone fiction "Of Piercings and X-ray Vision," Lena creates a green kryptonite tongue piercing. Once Lena's physical safety is assured, any damage to Lena's possessions (beds are inevitably broken, and in "Of Piercings and X-ray Vision," Supergirl punches and burns a hole in Lena's ceiling) is treated lightly due to Lena's billionaire status. Within these stories' sex scenes, Supergirl's losses of control and displays of power in moments of pleasure work as visual markers of the female "confession" of sexual pleasure. Similarly, Jazzfordshire details the visual "evidence" of Lena's arousal, which Supergirl "claims":

> Lena groans, legs shaking slightly, and Kara reaches down to gather some of the embarrassing slick from Lena's inner thighs. She traces her wet fingers over Lena's lower back—*is she spelling something?*
> Kara. She's spelling Kara.[69]

Just as Jazzfordshire's work subverts the heterosexual male need to "resolve" Supergirl's superpowers (read: supersexuality) by instead celebrating its erotic potential, so too does it subvert the problem of making the supposedly invisible confession of female pleasure visible, by presenting an undeniable deluge of evidence of Lena's arousal. Jazzfordshire draws deliberate attention to Lena's vaginal wetness, which is an important signifier of female pleasure in pornography made by women. In her discussion of pornographic manga aimed at female readers, Deborah Shamoon writes, "Ladies' comics emphasize vaginal wetness as a sign of female arousal, and frequently female characters use it as a demand for satisfaction. . . . Fluids gush forth in a tide of unbridled sexual excitement."[70] Whereas the hard-core pornography discussed by Williams is informed by a misogynist, patriarchal perspective that wants to make female sexuality visible in order to investigate and control it, Jazzfordshire's fan fiction both frames confessions within a quest for equality and makes visible sexual desires and physical responses that our heteronormative society views as deviant. In Jazzfordshire's fan fiction—and within the Supercorp fandom more generally—making female pleasure visible is an act of rebellion; it is about liberation rather than control. The confessions in these stories are similarly rebellious, in that what is confessed—namely, queer love and a general embrace of female (super)sexuality—is something that patriarchal audiences of mainstream pornography, and mainstream superhero texts, have shown little interest in hearing. To put it another way: these confessions are important statements of existence. By foregrounding and "showing" queer female desire and pleasure as well as the eroticism of female power, Jazzfordshire's fan fiction defiantly asserts the presence of a queer female gaze and fan community that has, to date, been all but erased in both officially sanctioned Supergirl stories and academic accounts of Supergirl's career.

CONCLUSION

The Supercorp fandom has found ways to view Supergirl's power not as a problem but rather as a possibility, one which is both erotic and liberating. Admittedly, this vision of erotic liberation is not always as inclusive as it could be. As discussed above, the pairing of Supergirl and Lena Luthor generally privileges—and fetishizes—white, upper-class identity; this is, to paraphrase Williams, the "dominant power knowledge" of this fandom. Nevertheless, Jazzfordshire's embrace and eroticization of Supergirl's power points toward ways that female superheroes might be conceptualized outside of the patriarchal, heteronormative frameworks that have historically dominated understandings of their power, as well as their gender and sexuality. Within the Supercorp fandom, Supergirl's power is less a problem than it is a solution, and superpowered female sexuality is not a source of anxiety but rather a cause for very enthusiastic celebration.

NOTES

1. The Tijuana Bibles are underground eight-page pornographic comic books that reappropriate popular figures; they were circulated from the 1920s to the 1950s.

2. Quoted in Robert C. Harvey, "Getting Our Pornograph Fixed," in *The Tijuana Bibles: America's Forgotten Comic Strips Volume 1*, ed. Michael Dower (Seattle, WA: Eros Comix, 1996), 6.

3. In the comics, Supergirl is traditionally a teenager, but in the television series she is a woman in her twenties, which enables her to be a more independent figure.

4. Fandom on Tumblr, "2017's Top Actresses," Tumblr, November 29, 2017, https://fandom.tumblr.com/post/168017030884/tumblr2017-actresses; Fandom on Tumblr, "2017's Top Ships," Tumblr, December 4, 2017, https://fandom.tumblr.com/post/168182191859/tumblr2017-ships; Fandom on Tumblr, "2018's Top Ships," Tumblr, November 28, 2018, https://fandom.tumblr.com/post/180587157019/2018-ships.

5. In the comics, Supergirl is known by several civilian names: her Kryptonian name is Kara Zor-El, but upon arriving on Earth she chooses the name Linda Lee for herself. After she is adopted by the Danvers family, she becomes known as Linda Danvers.

6. Alex Link, "The Secret of Supergirl's Success," *Journal of Popular Culture* 46, no. 6 (2013): 1177.

7. Peter David (w) and Ed Benes (a), *Supergirl: Many Happy Returns* (New York: DC Comics, 2003), 4.

8. Link, "Secret of Supergirl's Success," 1177.

9. Peppard, "'This Female Fights Back!,'" 108.

10. Peppard, "'This Female Fights Back!,'" 135.

11. Otto Binder (w), Al Plastino (a), and Curt Swan (a), *Action Comics*, no. 252: "The Supergirl from Krypton!," in *DC Showcase Presents: Supergirl Volume 1*, ed. Bob Harras and Bob Jay (New York: DC Comics, 2007), 33.

12. Binder, Plastino, and Swan, "Supergirl from Krypton!," 33, 35.

13. Binder, Plastino, and Swan, "Supergirl from Krypton!," 39.

14. Michel Foucault, *The History of Sexuality, Volume 1: An Introduction* (New York: Pantheon Books, 1978), 11.

15. Foucault, *History of Sexuality, Volume 1*, 19–20.

16. Williams, *Hard Core*, 49.

17. Williams, *Hard Core*, 50.

18. Jerry Siegel (w) and Jim Mooney (a), "The Day Supergirl Revealed Herself!," in *DC Showcase Presents: Supergirl Volume One*, ed. Bob Harras and Bob Jay (New York: DC Comics, 2007), 203.

19. Jerry Siegel (w) and Jim Mooney (a), "The Girl Who Was Supergirl's Double!," in *DC Showcase Presents: Supergirl Volume One*, ed. Bob Harras and Bob Jay (New York: DC Comics, 2007), 188.

20. Williams, *Hard Core*, 133.

21. Robert Kanigher (w) and Win Mortimer (a), *Adventure Comics*, no. 385 (New York: DC Comics, October 1969), 16.

22. Kanigher and Mortimer, *Adventure Comics*, no. 385, 17.

23. Leo Dorfman (w) and Kurt Schaffenberger (a), *Action Comics*, no. 370 (New York: DC Comics, December 1968), 24.

24. Dorfman and Schaffenberger, *Action Comics*, no. 370, 25.

25. David and Benes, *Supergirl*, 4.

26. In *Many Happy Returns*, the Supergirl from the 1990s timeline (who is not related to Superman) swaps places with the classic 1950s Supergirl in order to prevent her from dying in the events of *Infinite Crisis*. It is while she is living in the 1950s Supergirl universe that she falls in love with Superman and marries him.

27. Jerry Siegel (w) and Jim Mooney (a), "Superman's Super-Courtship!," in *DC Showcase Presents: Supergirl Volume One*, ed. Bob Harras and Bob Jay (New York: DC Comics, 2007), 105.

28. Williams, *Hard Core*, 152.

29. Jeffries, "This Looks Like a Blowjob," 278.

30. "Linda Lee's Big Dilemma," in *The Tijuana Bibles: America's Forgotten Comic Strips Volume 3*, ed. Michael Dowers (Seattle: Eros Comix, 1998), 70.

31. "Last Day on Krypton," in *The Tijuana Bibles: America's Forgotten Comic Strips Volume 4*, ed. Michael Dowers (Seattle: Eros Comix, 1999), 103.

32. Jefferies, "This Looks Like a Blowjob," 277.

33. Nerdmikhail (@Nermikhail.tumblr.com), "I sure golly do! . . .," Tumblr, https://nerdmikhail.tumblr.com/.

34. Although the show was not popular enough for network television, it has done very well on the CW network, where it has recently been renewed for its sixth season.

35. Jeanine Poggi, "Why the CW Is Happy to Grow Up," *AdAge*, April 2, 2015, https://adage.com/article/media/cw-happy-grow/297888/.

36. *Supergirl*, season 2, episode 5, "Crossfire," directed by Glen Winter, aired November 7, 2016, on the CW network.

37. *Supergirl*, season 1, episode 1, "Pilot," directed by Glen Winter, aired October 29, 2015, on the CW network.

38. Alex Cranz, "*Supergirl* May Have Finally Fixed Its Mon-El Problem for Good," io9, April 24, 2018, https://io9.gizmodo.com/supergirl-may-have-finally-fixed-its-mon-el-problem-for-1825486463.

39. Jazzfordshire (https://archiveofourown.org/users/Jazzfordshire/profile), "I Have to Confess (You Look So Good in That Dress)," Archive of Our Own, January 17, 2018, https://archiveofourown.org/works/13396245.

40. BicBiro, "[Video Interview] Rahul Kohli on His Experience with the SuperCorp Fandom," video, Reddit, 2017, https://www.reddit.com/r/supergirlTV/comments/6l8gca/video_interview_rahul_kohli_on_his_experience/. Princess Weekes, "Why I'm Upset About Mehcad Brooks' James Olsen Leaving *Supergirl*," The Mary Sue, July 29, 2019, https://www.themarysue.com/why-upset-over-mehcad-brooks-james-olsen-leaving-supergirl/.

41. Examples of fan art where Lena is portrayed as significantly white or absent of color:

Yuanslove (@yaunslove.tumblr.com), Tumblr, March 19, 2018, https://yuanslove.Tumblr.com/post/172393772120/2018-3-30-SuperCorp; Airstripyaks (@airstripyaks.tumblr.com), Tumblr, May 23, 2018, http://airstripyaks.tumblr.com/post/174192207436/someone-on-twitter-requested-a-SuperCorp-kiss; and DKships (@dkships.tumblr.com), Tumblr, accessed December 23, 2019, https://dkships.tumblr.com/post/170670805401.

42. Sean Redmond, "The Whiteness of Stars: Looking at Kate Winslet's Unruly White Body," in *Stardom and Celebrity: A Reader*, ed. Sean Redmond and Su Holmes (London: Sage Publications, 2017), 165.

43. Redmond, "Whiteness of Stars," 268; Ruth Frankenberg, *White Women, Race Matters: The Social Construction of Whiteness* (Minneapolis: University of Minnesota Press, 1993), 77.

44. Frankenberg, *White Women*, 76.

45. This analysis only considers work by Jazzfordshire that is within the Supergirl television show canon (as opposed to, for instance, stories that take place in "Alternative Universes," in which Supergirl is a normal woman rather than a superhero).

46. Supercorp Fanfictions (@SupercorpFics), "she loves control (sometimes)," Twitter, October 21, 2018, https://twitter.com/supercorpfics/status/1054093765223182336/.

47. Jazzfordshire (@Jazzfordshire.tumblr.com), bio, Tumblr, http://jazzfordshire.tumblr.com/; Jazzfordshire, "Casual Fridays Will Be the Death of Mc" (end notes), Archive of Our Own, December 21, 2017, https://archiveofourown.org/works/13092759#work_endnotes; Jazzfordshire, "I Made a Playlist...," Tumblr, May 27, 2018, http://jazzfordshire.tumblr.com/post/174318336412/mooosicaldreamz-i-made-a-playlist-for-lena-and. For accompanying fan art, see Sangoundercover (@sangoundercover.tumblr.com), Tumblr, January 27, 2019, http://sangoundercover.tumblr.com/post/182351430917/art-forjazzfordshires-awesome-fic-view-the.

48. Tamara Packard and Melissa Schraibam, "Lesbian Pornography: Escaping the Bonds of Sexual Stereotypes and Strengthening Our Ties to One Another," *UCLA Women's Law Journal* 4, no. 2 (1994): 313–314.

49. Jazzfordshire, "Touch Me (Tell Me What You Want Me to Do)," Archive of Our Own, February 15, 2018, https://archiveofourown.org/works/13697754.

50. Packard and Schraibam, "Lesbian Pornography," 310.

51. Henry Jenkins, *Textual Poachers: Television Fans & Participatory Culture* (London and New York: Routledge, 1992), 192.

52. Jenkins, *Textual Poachers*, 206.

53. Katiemccgrath (@katiemccgrath.tumblr.com), "The supercorp fandom is just a bunch of bottoms . . .," Tumblr, July 1, 2018, https://katiemccgrath.tumblr.com/post/175438285874/the-supercorp-fandom-is-just-a-bunch-of-bottoms (link disabled).

54. See the following Tumblr asks: Sangoundercover (@sangoundercover.tumblr.com), October 2, 2018, http://sangoundercover.tumblr.com/post/178675166527/dude-the-fight-that-will-start-over-lena-will-be; and Sangoundercover, October 2, 2018, http://sangoundercover.tumblr.com/post/178674999072/ok-you-guys-occupy-kara-ill-take-lena.

55. Jazzfordshire, "Touch Me."

56. Jenkins, *Textual Poachers*, 193.

57. Janice Radway, *Reading the Romance: Women, Patriarchy, and Popular Literature* (Chapel Hill: University of North Carolina Press, 2009), 140.

58. Jazzfordshire, "Touch Me."

59. Jeffries, "This Looks Like a Blowjob," 288. Emphasis in original.

60. Jazzfordshire, "Two Heroes Are Better Than One," Archive of Our Own, July 1, 2018, https://archiveofourown.org/works/15120893.

61. Jacqueline N. Cohen and Sandra E. Byers, "Beyond Lesbian Bed Death: Enhancing Our Understanding of the Sexuality of Sexual-Minority Women in Relationships," *Journal of Sex Research* 51, no. 8 (2013): 896.

62. Jazzfordshire, "I Have to Confess," notes.

63. Jazzfordshire, "Two Heroes Are Better Than One," notes.

64. Jazzfordshire, "Touch Me," notes.

65. Jazzfordshire, "Of Piercings and X-ray Vision," Archive of Our Own, April 28, 2018, https://archiveofourown.org/works/14457534.

66. Ibid.

67. Jazzfordshire, "When I Think about You (Well, You Know the Rest)," Archive of Our Own, January 22 2018, https://archiveofourown.org/works/13454346.

68. Jazzfordshire, "Your Sunday Best (Looks Best on My Floor)," Archive of Our Own, January 7, 2018, https://archiveofourown.org/works/13302201.

69. Jazzfordshire, "Touch Me." Emphasis in original.

70. Shamoon, "Office Sluts," 91.

MEET STEPHANIE ROGERS, CAPTAIN AMERICA
Genderbending the Body Politic in Fan Art, Fiction, and Cosplay

ANNE KUSTRITZ

From Mr. Fantastic's endless expansion to Spider-Man's animal-human hybridization, superheroes' bodies frequently house metaphors for frightening excesses of a malleable and permeable corporeal self. Yet superheroes also become icons whose physical solidity and impenetrability embody and ideologically stabilize institutions like gender, heterosexuality, and the nation. Fan fiction refers to amateur writing drawn upon a preexisting source, and genderswap is a subgenre that reverses or reconfigures characters' canon sex and/or gender. Genderswap fan fiction that dramatically alters the sexual biology of Captain America thus investigates the intersection of the superhero body's iconicity and instability as a signifier of national masculinity. Such fan fiction makes adhesions between gender, sex, sexuality, and national belonging visible by showing how the meaning of a story changes when, for example, the representation of America's strength becomes physically female, or when a male-embodied Captain America becomes sexually open. The problematic is encapsulated in the synopsis of fan author TamrynEradani's story "Stephanie Rogers Reporting for Duty," which illustrates the painful irony of why the physical transformation of superheroes remains so culturally significant: "When Stephanie comes out of the ice and finds out she's in the future, she expects there to be an adjustment period. What she doesn't expect is to be told that the world still isn't ready for Captain America to be a woman." This chapter argues that examples of fan works that envision Captain America as both muscular and female illustrate the pervasive gendered limits of hegemonic imaginings of national muscle and construct a collaborative alternate vision of female-centered national strength.

EMBODYING THE STATE: SYMBOLIZING NATIONAL STRENGTH

A codependent relationship exists between cultural assumptions about bodies and cultural modes of representing the nation. As in the classic gendered dichotomy between nature and culture documented by Sherry Ortner, scholars including Richard Slotkin and Michael Kimmel argue that female-gendered embodiments of the nation, such as Blind Justice, Lady Liberty, La Malinche, Mother Ireland, and Mother India, commonly represent the land itself, passive virtues, or familial bonds,[1] who then require the cultivation of masculine citizens to defend, tame, and secure.[2] Male embodiments of the nation thereby represent national strength and agency, often in the form of the citizen, cowboy, colonial agent, and soldier. Such gendered patterns make implicit arguments about both the intimate body and the body politic. Because they appear across various cultural registers, they form what Lauren Berlant calls part of the "national symbolic," that is, representations, icons, and symbols that can readily be called upon by anyone to signify and stand in for the nation.[3] Henry Jenkins likewise uses the terms "civic imagination" and "cultural vernacular" to argue that it is not just that popular culture contains politics, but that politics can be spoken using the iconography of popular culture.[4] Captain America, like Uncle Sam, Rosie the Riveter, and the Statue of Liberty, is a piece of the civic imagination, or national symbolic, with potent power to represent and (re)imagine the nation. Yet, as such, he is also part of a common language—the cultural vernacular—that remains vulnerable to appropriation and resignification for a variety of political (and libidinal) uses. Reconfigurations of Captain America's iconic body and narrative thereby not only bear significance for his specific story but also implicitly disrupt the gendered logic of American identity.

Despite considerable social transformations in sex/gender norms in the wake of first-, second-, and third-wave feminism, muscle continues to present a strangely intransient symbol of sexual difference. Studies of female athletes by Precilla Choi, Jan Brace-Govan, and Angela Ndalianis suggest that even when muscle is necessary to athletic performance or intrinsic to sporting achievements, female athletes are still discouraged from developing visible muscle to their full physical potential.[5] Choi explains that even in bodybuilding, which is, by its very nature, about building muscle, the competition rules of the International Federation of Bodybuilders (IFBB) penalize women whose muscles become "too large," stating that "the goal is to find an ideal female physique. . . . Muscle development must not be carried to such an excess that it resembles the massive musculature of the male physique."[6] Choi argues that as female bodybuilders advanced in their sport, developing larger and more visibly prominent muscles, the IFBB neutralized the implied threat of female strength by creating a new women's "fitness" category, whose rules require little to no visible muscle while emphasizing scopophilic qualities such as "facial beauty," "grace," and "charm." As Choi notes, these norms encourage women to lift lighter weights than they are actually capable of lifting, reinforcing the notion that the female body is "naturally" weaker. Susan Douglas, in her analysis of the rise of aerobics culture in the 1980s, similarly argues that the aerobics body idealizes a punishing notion that women should discard all the visible fat associated with femininity, especially on the butt and thighs, while somehow simultaneously avoiding the muscular bulk associated with masculinity.[7]

It is even more telling that within the superhero genre, wherein vita rays, magic, and alien biology offer ways for bodies to expand and wield strength far beyond the natural limits of a non-superhuman, large, well-defined muscles remain almost exclusively the domain of male characters. For example, while She-Hulk is one of the most muscled female characters in comics, she is much less so than the male Hulk. According to Marvel's online database, both characters have the same level of strength (class 7), but the angry male Hulk is 7'6" and 1,150 pounds, while She-Hulk is a comparatively modest 6'7" and 700 pounds.[8] This disparity goes beyond average physical sex differences to reinforce an ideal extreme physical dimorphism between men and women, central to the construction of heterosexuality. As argued by numerous theorists, heterosexual desire—literally conceptualized from Richard von Krafft-Ebing's *Psychopathia Sexualis* in 1892 as "different-sexual"—anchors itself in a highly polarized understanding of men and women.[9] Thus, in Judith Butler's work on performativity, spectacles like drag both question essential sex differences and undermine the foundation of heterosexuality.[10] Similarly, Adrienne Rich's classic work "Compulsory Heterosexuality and Lesbian Existence" argues that queer sexuality is almost inevitably interpreted as an attack on the normative gender system.¹¹ Thus, the codependence between heterosexuality and gender (as well as patriarchy) means that deviations from gender norms also destabilize heteronormativity. Consequently, physically muscled women both pose a threat to hegemonic femininity and are metaphorically queer, inasmuch as they raise the specter of a heterosexuality unmoored from difference and male dominance.

As hyper-gendered figures, superhero bodies often shore up the notion of physical sexual difference upon which normative heterosexuality depends. As Aaron Taylor notes, although Wonder Woman and Superman have gone through many incarnations, their consistent morphological divergence—that is, the fact that Superman always sports much larger muscles despite the fact that he and Wonder Woman are similarly strong—emphasizes the importance of extreme muscle as the preeminent symbol of superheroic hetero-masculinity. Writes Taylor, "Super-sexuality has been carefully constructed according to highly visible binaries[:] . . . chiseled brutes and buxom babes."¹² Taylor quotes comics artist Bart Sears, who explains the importance of maintaining visible markers of femininity in female superheroes: "You have to be careful not to draw them bloopy or dumpy, but at the same time, if you draw them too hard and chiseled, they start to look masculine, which is definitely not good."¹³ It is important to keep in mind that female superheroes are not average women but rather literally superhuman women, representing the height of physical achievement. As such, like bodybuilders, their strength should logically appear on their bodies as visible muscle. However, again and again, even those female superheroes who are supposedly as strong or stronger than their male compatriots are not allowed to make that strength visible as muscle. When it came time to cast Wonder Woman for the 2017 film, it was not a trained athlete with a body like CrossFit champion Stacie Tovar, Olympic weightlifting medalist Sarah Robles, wrestling medalist Helen Maroulis, or gymnastics phenom Simone Biles who took the iconic tiara, but svelte model Gal Gadot, who, despite real-life military training and well-publicized efforts to "bulk up" for the role, still embodies the fitness or aerobic ideal of "toned" but not "overly" muscular thinness.

Physical muscle thus resolutely acts as a chief signifier of masculinity. In his analysis of mixed messages within male pin-up photos, Richard Dyer argues that visible muscle "[draws] attention to the body's potential for action."¹⁴ In evoking the dominance, violence, and force associated with muscle, Dyer argues that male pin-ups undermine the viewer's ability to establish visual mastery over the male photographic subject(s). Choi similarly argues that due to its synecdoche fusion with strength and violence, muscle has become perhaps the preeminent visual signifier of masculinity and sexual difference.[15] Consequently, muscle also becomes part of the rhetoric of national power, on a purely metaphorical level but also as part of a disciplinary strategy that encourages individual men to cultivate themselves into ideal national subjects.Historically, panics about the strength of the nation and the physical strength of the individual men who make up the body politic go together. Thus, in an 1889 article titled "National Muscle," Charles Beresford, then a British admiral and member of Parliament, directly connects the average man's masculinity and physical fitness to the success of the nation, writing, "Amongst the many matters which occupy the public mind at the present time, there is surely none that should command more interest than the health and manliness of the people."[16] While Beresford was primarily concerned with the cultivation of muscle to increase the capacity of working-class men to perform labor and military service, Jeffrey Montez de Oca argues that during the Cold War era, American rhetoric stressed the need to inculcate physical "hardness" into young men to inoculate them against the dual seductions of communism and the welfare state.[17] Oca argues that fears about generational racial degeneration were projected upon young white men's bodies, with the college-educated elite of the Cold War viewed as lacking in comparison to the American elite of earlier times, exemplified by President Theodore Roosevelt's rhetoric of the "strenuous life," which urged men of all classes to test themselves both within combat and against nature on the frontier.[18] Quoting the President's Council on Physical Fitness, Oca argues that a transparent cultural association had been forged between masculinity and national security: "As our muscles get softer, our missile race becomes harder."[19]

This intertwining of muscle, masculinity, and the nation also affects the portrayal of politicians (literal representatives of the state) as studied by Michael Messner, Mary McDonald, and Samantha King. In his article "The Masculinity of the Governator," Messner argues that Arnold Schwarzenegger's history as a muscle-bound bodybuilder remained the dominant component of his public image, which contributed to his success as governor of California and helped rhetorically connect masculine toughness with Republican policies.[20] On the flip side, McDonald and King argue that President Barack Obama walked a thin line in representations of his bodily muscle and athleticism. As a Black man, McDonald and King argue, Obama risked being stereotyped as hypermasculine and threatening when framed as a physically dexterous basketball player, while simultaneously facing feminization as a Democrat and a member of "the elite."[21] For example, commentators described photos of Obama bowling as "dainty" and "prissy," which recalls a long history of framing upper-class men as effete. Yet, one may also recall similar incidents that positioned Obama as "typically" athletic and dexterous because of his masculinity and race, as when he snatched a fly out of the air during a television interview.[22] These examples all demonstrate a long history of entanglements between the strength of the nation, the masculinity of the body politic, and the muscularity of individual representatives of the nation.

The body may seem like an odd terrain of mythological struggle in an era of technological warfare.[23] Yet the image of national brawn remains compelling and ideologically indispensable. The particularly iconic nature of a character such as Captain America intensifies the ideological effect of sex/gender disruptions because the established story is so well known and directly imbricated in the iconography of state masculinity. As discussed by Jason Dittmer, similar to Superman, who explicitly fights for "the American way,"[24] Captain America has repeatedly been used to represent American moral authority, national identity, and the cultural zeitgeist, especially during World War II and following 9/11.[25] With his origin story as an impoverished and sickly boy who is transformed through scientific ingenuity into a super-soldier, Captain America's body unites the corporeal and scientific realms. Yet his childhood growing up in the slums of Brooklyn anchors the character in the mythos of wholesome working-class muscle. Captain America's famous dislike for bullies and willingness to protect the defenseless, even before his technological enhancement, further help to define the national strength he embodies as virtuous and purely defensive.[26] At the present moment, Captain America's popularity also taps into an embodied iconography of moral and masculine authenticity and wholesomeness that shores up ideological gaps in the picture of dehumanized and calculated drone warfare.[27] Therefore, transforming Captain America into a woman illuminates remaining structural limits of gendered embodiment and national imagination.

THE RHETORIC OF NATIONAL MUSCLE: RE-GENDERING THE BODY POLITIC

Literary and artistic play with sexual embodiment is a long-standing form of social critique and experimentation. Characters who undergo sexual transformations—whether these transformations are dramatized in specific stories or take place extratextually through the serial process of retelling and adaptation—allow authors and artists to reflect upon the relationship between biology, performance, and subjectivity. They also enable reflection on the cultural conditions that structure the lives of those socially recognized as women and men, and the manner in which collective understandings of concepts as wide-ranging as the nation-state, nature, and war rely upon hegemonic definitions of sex and gender opposition for their iconography and connotative resonance. Replacing a male-bodied character with a female-bodied character in the same story teaches us how sexed bodies construct different meanings. Thus, fan fiction about a physiologically altered Captain America takes part in a lengthy genealogy of thought experiments exploring the ways in which biological sex has historically been entangled with gender, the social order, legal standing, and the political imagination.

Contemporary fan productions interact with a legacy of transformation stories that expose sex and gender hierarchies by casting female-to-male transformations as an increase in status, and male-to-female transformations as a dangerous loss of status. Historically, female characters take on male roles and appearance primarily to gain greater social mobility and power, which they often must give up at the story's close, as in Shakespeare's iconic "breeches roles" or the legend of Mulan. According to Cristina Bacchilega, Susan Redington Bobby, and Jack Zipes, many contemporary feminist fairy tale retellings target this precise pattern for reversal when female characters who dress and act as men forge an alternative ending by refusing to give up their breeches and newfound freedom.[28] In contrast, the sexual transformation of male characters repeatedly presents a dangerous threat to their privilege and status as men. Often, feminization is form of punishment and humiliation, as in classical mythology when Hercules must dress as a woman for one year as a slave to the sister of a man he murdered, or when Hera transforms Tiresias into a woman for seven years for the crime of killing a snake. Other cases, such as the film *Some Like It Hot* (1959), use female guise for comic effect. However, Eve Kosofsky Sedgwick notes that some male characters such as Lord Byron's Don Juan and Horner in William Wycherley's Restoration comedy *The Country Wife* deliberately invite the social stigma of effeminacy in order to enter female-only spaces and increase their overall masculine mastery through sexual conquest.[29] The wolf in Little Red Riding Hood is often interpreted within this framework as a seducer who hides his animal appetites inside grandmothers' clothing to gain private access to Little Red.[30]

Of course, in both real life and stories, different social meanings and consequences also constrain these embodiments. Historians such as Valerie Traub speculate that the much larger number of men who suffered torture and death for homosexuality and transvestism in medieval Europe resulted from a need to protect the social preference for masculinity.[31]

While female-bodied people who refuse feminine dress and behavior have certainly suffered from pathologization, both Traub and Carroll Smith-Rosenberg argue that male drag creates a different sort of social threat.[32] As this strand of logic goes, female bodies who pass for men require social policing, but their desire for greater power and influence is understandable, and thus, sympathetic; in contrast, if being a man is preferable, why would anyone want to become a woman?[33] This logic illustrates some of the intersectional underpinnings of homophobia, transphobia, and misogyny, and the lingering taboos at stake in male characters' sexual transformations.

Like the classical and fairy tale structures described above, fan fiction, fan art, and cosplay that mobilize female versions and transformations of Captain America often draw on the notion that masculinization of female characters offers women empowerment, while feminization of male characters can make women's cultural disempowerment visible in new ways. Because making male characters female or putting them into poses, clothes, or roles associated with women can invoke ridiculous humor, castration, or a loss of power and pathos, these processes make gender hierarchies obvious; feminization can only be experienced as loss or violence if there is something to lose. Fan projects that genderswap or otherwise transform Captain America's canonical body thus perform public pedagogy and intervene in hegemonic systems of mass representation. By appropriating highly recognizable icons of masculinity, femininity, heterosexuality, and nationhood, fans may directly challenge the semiotic structures of ideological reproduction. Situated within Butler's theorization of performativity, such fan productions circulate aberrant reiterations of hegemonic forms, putting reimagined cultural ideals back into discourse in order to make the familiar strange and open space for doing culture differently.[34]

Similar fan projects exist for other culturally resonant characters—what Jenkins would describe as elements of the modern vernacular and Berlant would call the icons of the national symbolic. For example, sexual reversals of Disney versions of fairy tales in feminist literature and high art as well as fan art create interesting thought experiments because the characters are not only well known but deeply implicated in the cultural imagination of romance, heterosexuality, and gender identity. Many of these images are circulated within the framework of constructing more empowered princesses as role models for girls by providing them with male roles and dress, while others reverse the gender of all the characters in a Disney film, which challenges assumptions about gendered social roles. For instance, a series of popular YouTube videos by user

DisneyCartoonLover morphs the bodies and dress of Disney characters back and forth between female and male presenting,[35] while a series of drawings shared on Tumblr by user Sakimichan depicts a gold-bedecked male Esmeralda smiling enticingly and a bemused female Beast looking down adoringly at a petite male Beauty.[36] A set of drawings by Christopher Stoll shared on DeviantArt are particularly interesting within the context of this chapter, as they fuse Disney princesses with the male characters from the Avengers superhero franchise, including a representation of Pocahontas as Captain America.[37] While Chad Barbour discusses the politics of erasure at play when the Marvel limited series *1602* featured a seventeenth-century version of Captain America in Native American dress, the image by Stoll appropriates Captain America to tell a very different sort of story.[38] This image begins to suggest the ways in which altering Captain America's race and sex can challenge ideologies implicit within embodiments of American power: How could we imagine the nation differently with a Native American woman at its center? Which people and causes would Pocahontas use her superhuman strength to defend, and who would bear the brunt of her vigilante justice? (figure 13.1).

However, most of these images, with the exception of a hulked-out Snow White by Stoll and Belle as Beast by Sakimichan, do little to challenge gendered conceptions of the physical body. Other fan initiatives much more directly engage the embodiment of sex, gender, and national heroism. In recent years, fans have increasingly called attention to pervasive gender disparities in comics and industry assumptions about audience preferences. For instance, to draw attention to the overly sexualized, physically impractical clothing and stance of female comics superheroes, the Hawkeye Initiative project on Tumblr invited fans to replace unrealistic images of women with the male Avengers character Hawkeye.[39] Fans responded with drawings as well as photos of physical attempts to replicate female superhero poses while wearing a Hawkeye costume. Some Hawkeye Initiative images specifically engage the question of female empowerment, skewering the notion that anyone would feel powerful while mostly naked and twisted into the characteristic pretzel shape or "broke back" pose that provides viewers with visual access to the character's chest and ass at the same time.[40] Men dressed as Hawkeye who try to pose like female superheroes often add commentary about how difficult and painful the poses are and how useless they would be for combat. By implication, these images also engage with the converse discourse, which acknowledges that the bodily semantics of power are gendered male. As Butler argues, gender performances come to feel natural not because they are inevitable but because audiences become accustomed to them through

FIGURE 13.1. From left to right: Pocahontas by Christopher Stoll on DeviantArt, Snow White by Christopher Stoll on DeviantArt, Beauty and the Beast by Sakimichan on Tumblr.

repetition.[41] Thus, while the often bizarre body positions and proportions of female superheroes become unremarkable through repetition, placing a male superhero in the same costumes and contortions makes the gendering of their appearance obvious and denaturalizes the connection between body and gender performance.

The Hawkeye Initiative thus directly destabilizes the juncture between bodies, gender, and image. Linda Williams and Laura Mulvey document early structures of film and photography that position women as visual spectacles and men as viewers.[42] Thus, Suzanne Scott notes that the Hawkeye Initiative not only parodies specific comics but also radically disrupts a history of images that protect men from queer and female desiring gazes[43] using what Steve Neale calls "armoring" tactics like violence, narcissism, and copious stubble.[44] Because feminization of male characters via sexual objectification often functions as humor in mass culture—which is another "armoring" strategy to disavow the sexual potential of such images—the Hawkeye Initiative is often framed as comedic. Julie Levin Russo makes a similar argument regarding the "misreading" of slash, that is, same-sex fan videos. She explains that videos designed and circulated for female fans' erotic pleasure have often been interpreted in mass media as homophobic comedy.[45] Yet it is worth noting that like slash fan videos, the Hawkeye Initiative has also produced numerous images of the character as a sexual object that can be read as visually pleasing, especially because the fundamentally gendered visual semiotics of representing human bodies make images of objectified men so rare.

Fan costuming, art, and fiction that put Captain America in a showgirl costume or picture Stephanie instead of Steve Rogers behind Captain America's mask act as a provocation against existing industry standards, as well as the mythology of hetero-masculinity underlying national iconography. Perhaps unsurprisingly, when many male fans create Captain America costumes, they often add prosthetic muscle to live up to a superhuman standard of masculine display—a clear example of what Mark Simpson and Judith Butler call "men performing masculinity." Non-muscled women who cosplay as Captain America can immediately ironize the hypermasculinization of the character by contrasting the iconic clothing with their significantly less ripped bodies and sometimes overtly sexualized poses, a strategy reminiscent of Butler's argument that drag makes the construction of gender obvious through juxtaposition. Conversely, female cosplayers may also borrow the visual language of Captain America to construct a kind of female masculinity, one that presents a completely sincere but female reproduction of the character; precisely through their sincerity, these types of performances challenge the boundaries of who can embody

FIGURE 13.2. Captain America genderswap cosplay by Imatangelo on DeviantArt.

national muscle. The range of women who embody Captain America in fan spaces begins to open up possibilities for considering who can inhabit the sacred space of national heroism and what sort of strength female bodies can, if given the opportunity, make visible (figure 13.2).

REWRITING NATIONAL MUSCLE

Unlike cosplayers or fan artists, fan fiction writers are not bound by any constraints of the human body, nor can they rely on visual juxtapositions between signifiers of the physical body and gendered signifiers of nationalism. Instead, fan fiction takes at least four forms in exploring the embodied subjectivity of a female Captain America, thematizing closeting, invisibility, utopian norm reversal, and physical transformation. Many stories posit that the science fiction–based super-soldier enhancement serum would produce a female Captain America with a stature and musculature that is the same or very similar to that of the male Captain America. These stories thus offer opportunities for unthinking naturalized associations between gender, muscle, and national power. In her book *The Queen of America Goes to Washington City*, Berlant notes the passive nature of most female American symbols and speculates on the radical disruption a sword-wielding, African American Queen of America could deliver to the national psyche. Fan fiction stories that construct female versions of Captain America engage in a similar project of national imagining, charting how a female embodiment of national might disrupts hegemonic order within both public and interpersonal realms.

In the subset of stories that thematize closeting, many fan authors speculate that Captain America had always been a woman but had been forced to masquerade as a man because Americans buying bonds and enlisting during World War II would not have placed confidence in a female super-soldier. The story "Stephanie Rogers Reporting for Duty" revolves around when and under what circumstances the government, as represented by the army and SHIELD, would allow Stephanie Rogers to "come out" as a woman.[46] This context allows the story to reflect, at length, on the progress women have, and have not, made in society since World War II. Upon being revived after spending the years since the war frozen in the arctic, Stephanie considers how the world might have changed: "She has so many questions she wants to ask Darcy: are women more respected now, are there women generals, are there women presidents, can I reveal who I am and will people accept me?" Given the uneven treatment of women in mainstream American superhero comics and society, there is strong evidence to the contrary; this reality is reflected in the story, wherein Stephanie is not, at first, permitted by SHIELD to tell her new teammates her true identity and must remain constantly masked. She bitterly reflects, "Aliens are believable but a woman soldier isn't? That's not right. She's supposed to be in the future." These contradictions mirror other contemporary debates about women and LGBTQ people in the army and society more generally, especially arguments that women and gay men disrupt "unit cohesion."[47] At their core, these are anxieties about what Mary Douglas would call "matter out of place," and they attest to the resiliency of sex and gender hierarchies.[48]

A second thematic group of Captain America sex/gender reversal stories similarly proposes that Captain America has always been a woman but depicts her as never trying to mask or hide this fact. In these stories, the dominant cultural imagination has merely *perceived* Captain America as male due to an inability to see—or even imagine—national muscle as female. For example, in the story "Feminist Theories" by starrdust411, Captain America fanboy Phil Coulson is faced with the fact that his boyhood hero was a woman the whole time, and only a kind of deliberate blindness prevented him from seeing it.[49] As Nick Fury explains, "people see a six-foot-two figure in uniform commanding troops and automatically assume they're looking at a man." Here, being able to see Captain America as a woman becomes a sort of activist litmus test for the ability to see past cultural ideologies that constrain gender expression. Thinking about the "feminist theories" of women who had told him the truth all along, "Coulson thought about Suzy Liebowitz and the handful of other feminists he had met in his college days. They had all been admirers and had painted their own pictures of what the female Cap would have looked like before going off to rallies." This type of story emphasizes that a legacy of physically strong, variously gendered women has always existed. It thereby shows that they can serve as an empowering and challenging example of what women can be when they succeed in becoming visible and recognized.

A third group of stories offers a utopian picture of a parallel universe wherein the female embodiment of Captain America draws no particular attention. These stories often engage what Jenkins would call the civic imagination, in that they "imagine alternatives to current cultural, social, political, or economic conditions; one cannot change the world unless one can imagine what a better world might look like."[50] Many of them fall under the "Rule 63" genre of fan creativity, which uses the logic of quantum mechanics to posit that opposite sexed and/or gendered versions of all characters exist in parallel narrative universes. Such experimentation with parallel timelines containing differently gendered characters is common in superhero comics, which endlessly restart their characters' stories with a slightly different premise, time period, or set of genre rules. Fan stories based on Rule 63 are relatively unlikely to comment upon gender directly because they tend to imagine a world that is either completely equal in terms of sex/gender or significantly less sexist. These stories' social commentary is more implicit; the protest is embedded in the difference between readers' own experiences of society—including their experiences of typical mainstream superhero stories—and how things could be, or should be, were women able to seamlessly embody national muscle. In other words, in these stories, critique lies in the non-event of characters' lack of reaction to Captain America's female embodiment.

Finally, some stories deal with a Captain America who undergoes a sex or gender transformation within the story, or who has sexually variant biology from the outset, often either influenced by alien or animal DNA. These stories construct the sexual body as endlessly permeable and malleable. In doing so, they draw upon both the uncanny world of the superhero and the older, topsy-turvy body of fairy tales, mythology, and legend.[51] By making the body not a matter of fixed natural properties but instead a site of inherent unpredictability, these stories undermine the basis of Captain America's function as a symbol of physical strength and solidity who biologically anchors national mythology. While such stories rarely directly engage in critique of national or international politics, and most often use such tropes for erotic ends, their ability to instantly make Captain America pregnant, female, half-dog, or an infant still fundamentally disturbs Captain America's body as a settled achievement of American ingenuity and masculine iconicity. Perhaps the most subtly radical form of such stories begins with the premise that the same technological breakthrough that transformed sickly little Steve Rogers into a super-soldier also simultaneously gave him female physiology. In such cases, the connection between male physiology, masculinity, and national muscle become radically dislocated, with the superheroic musculature of Captain America becoming intrinsically tied to female biology. Some stories with this premise directly discuss gender norms in society, but many, like "Good Becomes Great" by hotchoco195, focus on romance. Yet despite and even *because* they focus on romance, these stories cannot help but compel readers to imagine a complete reordering of both the sexual body and the body politic.[52] In "Good Becomes Great," Captain America's muscular female body disrupts culturally sacred memories of American boys fighting in World War II, and at the same time upends fixed notions of femininity and sexual desire based on difference. In this story, a lighthearted conversation with a friend about Steve's attraction to another soldier reflects a deft reordering of the entwined personal and political stakes of female embodiment of national muscle:

> "Well, what can I do?" Steve looked down at her tea, "There's no guarantee he's noticed me. I don't wanna ruin things."
> "Why wouldn't he notice you?" Velma tutted, "You're gorgeous, smart, real sarcastic, and you can bench-press a refrigerator. You're a catch."[53]

The narrative persistently echoes Velma's insistence that a woman who can bench-press a refrigerator is both more sexually desirable and more useful to the nation than one who dies inside of them, as in the Green Lantern story that inspired the now-infamous term *fridging* to describe the misogynistic treatment of women as disposable commodities within male-driven stories.[54] As such, "Good Becomes Great" and other, similar fan works destabilize the fixity of the male body and undermine clear associations between men, muscle, and the strength of the nation, which in turn opens up the possibility of imagining an affirmative vision of female strength at the center of the national symbolic.

Speaking more directly of the erotic significance of such stories suggests at least two further vectors of radical significance for the physically transformed Captain America. As argued by Pauline Greenhill, folk stories that eroticize animal-human relationships and physical transformations embrace a radical vision of alterity.[55] Greenhill argues that any number of social others, including women, have been socially excluded and controlled by the charge that they are animalistic in comparison to straight white men—that they are irrational, emotional, feral. The animal transformation story and human-animal romance embrace these associations and deploy them against the hetero-patriarchal order by revaluing precisely the animal-like bodily excesses and pleasures that are used to justify oppression of such groups. These stories are thus a rejection of respectability politics and a glorification of grotesque, carnivalesque, erotic excess.[56] Captain America frequently stars in "A/B/O" or "Omegaverse" stories, a highly popular fan genre of animal-human hybridization most often featuring extremely graphic sexual scenes in which human and dog physiology merge.[57] In such tales, the usually stoic, highly strategic Captain America is overcome by the animal instincts of his body—he cries, becomes moody, and, most especially, develops a desperate desire to be sexually penetrated and impregnated as he goes into heat. There is clear pleasure to be found in taking a male character iconic of national masculinity, implicating him in every stereotype used to exclude women from national belonging and leadership, and then having him revel in his abjection. In these stories, Captain America becomes a bitch in every sense of the word: he is at once feminized, animalistically feral, and rebelliously strident.

Although typically less extreme in its eroticization of abjection, the female-transformation story pivots around a recognizably similar metaphorical axis, inasmuch as it negotiates the same network of bodily rhetoric regarding physical stability and openness. In "Good Becomes Great," Steve wakes up from the super-soldier serum process in a healthy, superstrong female body, able to breathe deeply and move without pain in a way he never could in his old, male body. Yet he is immediately offered profuse apologies that the experiment was a disaster and given monetary compensation. On the one hand, the incident evokes the sexist norm that male bodies are more valuable than female bodies. On the other hand, as a muscled woman, Steve finds himself thrown adrift from the normative hetero-patriarchal matrix, because not only has he lost his valued male body but he has not gained a recognizably female one. Struggling to learn how to use makeup, he explains, "I don't wanna get stuck as a frumpy old maid with lipstick on her teeth that other people feel sorry for. I don't want to be some pathetic lost person, not a man or a woman, just an odd mix of both." This statement can be read as a gender-dysphoric identity crisis and an indictment of transphobia, but it is also a gateway for exploring Simone de Beauvoir's famous dictum that "one is not born, but rather becomes, a woman"[58] and Butler's suggestion that every iteration of gender performance is also an opportunity to imagine gender differently. "Good Becomes Great" goes on to detail Steve's process of becoming his own kind of woman.

Steve finds that his new body allows him to imagine new possibilities for his life, including bisexual attractions he had repressed. In his (in)famous article "Is the Rectum a Grave?" Leo Bersani argues that the specter of anal sex creates fear and disgust partly because it opens the rhetorically closed and impenetrable male body.[59] Jessica Benjamin notes that *The Story of O* exemplifies the way that the female body, in contrast, semiotically unifies the shape of the female genitals with the idea of sexual openness, submissiveness, and vulnerability.[60] In his exploration of the AIDS crisis in 1980s Japan, John Treat notes that this sexual semiotics of the body bears national significance, as Japanese politicians repeatedly explained that AIDS could not penetrate Japan's borders because Japanese men (supposedly) do not have anal sex; this rhetoric synchronizes the meaning of closed borders with closed male bodies and omits the possibility of the body politic's penetration by foreign bodies of the immigrant, phallic, or microbial form.[61] The female-embodied nation thus semiotically becomes sexually open and available for penetration, insemination, invasion, and influence. In "Good Becomes Great," Steve's muscled but female body, and the bisexual desire that preceded his bodily transformation, creates a queer third term in this matrix of national signification, suggesting a non-abject form of hybrid identity and sexuality. The female body wherein Steve finds himself at peace, and wherein he discovers and is able to express great pleasure, conjures an image of a national body that is at once strong and yielding, open, yet not vulnerable.

CONCLUSION

Fan works enable the public to powerfully engage in representational struggles over how sex, gender, and citizenship can, should, and will be configured in the future. By borrowing from shared culture, fans are able to level critiques of existing norms and offer alternatives in what I have elsewhere called a "genre commensurate form"—that is, by countering the emotive and aesthetic strengths of mass media on their own terms.[62] Fan art can provide striking images that utilize the visual language of national colors and the bodily logic of anatomy to present thoughtful juxtapositions between femininity and American strength. Cosplayers cannot take on the superheroic proportions possible in art and film special effects, but they can draw attention to gaps between masculine ideals and the shapes and limits of real bodies; they can also provocatively attribute masculine mastery to female bodies. Fan fiction lacks the immediate visual register of art, performance, or photography, but with only the quick tap of a keyboard, it can fundamentally destabilize the national order by transposing fixed markers of national goodness and strength onto female-embodied characters, then invite readers to empathize with these muscular women by providing deep access to their interiority. Following the journeys of Stephanie Rogers navigating the 1940s or the present as a female embodiment of national power allows readers to experience the painful limitations still placed on women's development of physical strength and invites them to begin to imagine the profound rearrangement of social and political norms necessary to build a national identity with female muscle at its center.

NOTES

1. Sherry Ortner, "Is Female to Male as Nature Is to Culture?," *Feminist Studies* 1, no. 2 (1972): 5–31; Richard Slotkin, *Regeneration through Violence: The Mythology of the American Frontier, 1600–1860* (Middletown, CT: Wesleyan UP, 1973). Kimmel, *Manhood in America*.

2. Lauren Berlant, *The Queen of America Goes to Washington City* (Durham, NC: Duke UP, 1997); Suruchi Thapar-Bjӧrkert and Louise Ryan, "Mother India/Mother Ireland: Comparative Gendered Dialogues of Colonialism and Nationalism in the Early 20th Century," Women's Studies International Forum 25, no. 3 (2002): 301–313.

3. Lauren Berlant, *The Anatomy of National Fantasy: Hawthorne, Utopia, and Everyday Life* (Chicago: University of Chicago Press, 1991).

4. Henry Jenkins, Sangita Shresthova, and Gabriel Peters-Lazaro, eds., *Popular Culture and the Civic Imagination: A Casebook* (New York: New York University Press, forthcoming 2020).

5. Precilla Choi, "Muscle Matters: Maintaining Visible Differences between Women and Men," *Sexualities*, Evolution & Gender 5, no. 2 (2003): 71–81; Jan Brace-Govan, "Weighty Matters: Control of Women's Access to Physical Strength," *Sociological Review* 52, no. 4 (2004): 503–531; Angela Ndalianis, "Muscle, Excess & Rupture: Female Bodybuilding & Gender Construction," *Media Information Australia* 75, no. 1 (1995): 13–23.

6. Choi, "Muscle Matters," 73.

7. Susan Douglas, *Where the Girls Are: Growing Up Female with the Mass Media* (New York: Three Rivers Press, 1995).

8. Bruce Banner/Hulk biography, In Comics Full Report, Marvel, accessed October 20, 2018, https://www.marvel.com/characters/hulk-bruce-banner/in-comics; Jennifer Walters/She-Hulk biography, In Comics Full Report, Marvel, accessed October 20, 2018, https://www.marvel.com/characters/she-hulk-jennifer-walters/in-comics.

9. See Judith Butler, *Undoing Gender* (New York: Routledge, 2004); Jacques Derrida, "Geschlecht: Sexual Difference, Ontological Difference," *Research in Phenomenology* 13 (1983): 65–83; Diana Fuss, *Inside/Out: Lesbian Theories, Gay Theories* (New York: Routledge, 1991); Sara Heinämaa, "What Is a Woman? Butler and Beauvoir on the Foundations of the Sexual Difference," *Hypatia* 12, no. 1 (1997): 20–39; Luce Irigaray, *This Sex Which Is Not One* (Ithaca, NY: Cornell University Press, 1977); Jonathan Katz, *The Invention of Heterosexuality* (Chicago: University of Chicago Press, 2007); Richard Krafft-Ebing, *Psychopathia Sexualis: A Medico-forensic Study* (New York: GP Putnam's Sons, 1965).

10. Butler, *Gender Trouble*.

11. Adrienne Rich, "Compulsory Heterosexuality and Lesbian Existence," *Signs: Journal of Women in Culture and Society* 5, no. 4 (1980): 631–660.

12. Taylor, "'He's Gotta Be Strong,'" 345, 351.

13. Taylor, "'He's Gotta Be Strong,'" 353.

14. Richard Dyer, "Don't Look Now," *Screen* 23, no. 3–4 (1982): 61–73.

15. Choi, "Muscle Matters," 71–81.

16. Charles Beresford, "National Muscle," *The New Review* 1, no. 1 (1889): 62.

17. Jeffrey Montez De Oca, "'As Our Muscles Get Softer, Our Missile Race Becomes Harder': Cultural Citizenship and the 'Muscle Gap,'" *Journal of Historical Sociology* 18, no. 3 (2005): 145–172.

18. Michael Egan, "Wrestling Teddy Bears: Wilderness Masculinity as Invented Tradition in the Pacific Northwest," *Gender Forum* 15 (2006).

19. Egan, "Wrestling Teddy Bears," 147.

20. Michael Messner, "The Masculinity of the Governator: Muscle and Compassion in American Politics," *Gender & Society* 21, no. 4 (2007): 461–480.

21. Mary McDonald and Samantha King, "A Different Contender? Barack Obama, the 2008 Presidential Campaign and the Racial Politics of Sport," *Ethnic and Racial Studies* 35, no. 6 (2012): 1023–1039.

22. See Maureen Dowd, "Obama's Fly Move," op-ed, *New York Times*, June 20, 2009, https://www.nytimes.com/2009/06/21/opinion/21dowd.html; Angela Smith, "Mediated Political Masculinities: The Commander-in-Chief vs. the New Man," *Social Semiotics* 26, no. 1 (2016): 94–110.

23. This may equally be said of earlier eras of superhero, since the age of technological warfare arguably began with World War I if not before. See Thomas Andrae, "From Menace to Messiah: The Prehistory of the Superman in Science Fiction Literature," *Discourse* 2 (1980): 84–112; Scott Bukatman, "A Song for the Urban Superhero," in *The Superhero Reader*, ed. Charles Hatfield (Jackson: University Press of Mississippi, 2013), 170–198.

24. Only some versions of Superman used this catchphrase, which originated in the 1940s radio show "The Adventures of Superman" and became standard in the 1950s. See also Wendy Wall, *Inventing the "American Way": The Politics of Consensus from the New Deal to the Civil Rights Movement* (Oxford: Oxford University Press, 2009).

25. Jason Dittmer, "Captain America's Empire: Reflections on Identity, Popular Culture, and Post-9/11 Geopolitics," *Annals of the Association of American Geographers* 95, no. 3 (2005): 626–643; Robert Jewett and John Shelton Lawrence, *Captain America and the Crusade against Evil: The Dilemma of Zealous Nationalism* (Grand Rapids, MI: Eerdmans Publishing, 2004).

26. It is particularly clear that Captain America is good due to Steve Rogers's character because others who have inhabited similarly technologically augmented bodies have not been nearly so heroic, notably the villain the Red Skull.

27. Lisa Parks, "Drones, Vertical Mediation, and the Targeted Class," *Feminist Studies* 42, no. 1 (2016): 227–235; Lisa Parks and Caren Kaplan, eds., *Life in the Age of Drone Warfare* (Durham, NC: Duke University Press, 2017).

28. Cristina Bacchilega, *Postmodern Fairy Tales: Gender and Narrative Strategies* (Philadelphia: University of Pennsylvania Press, 2010); Susan Redington Bobby, *Fairy Tales Reimagined: Essays on New Retellings* (Jefferson, NC: McFarland, 2009); Jack Zipes, *Don't Bet on the Prince: Contemporary Feminist Fairy Tales in North America and England* (New York: Routledge, 2014).

29. Eve Kosofsky Sedgwick, *Between Men: English Literature and Male Homosocial Desire* (New York: Columbia University Press, 2015).

30. See Hélène Cixous and Annette Kuhn, "Castration or Decapitation?," *Signs: Journal of Women in Culture and Society* 7, no. 1 (1981): 41–55; Pauline Greenhill and Steven Kohm, "Little Red Riding Hood and the Pedophile in Film: *Freeway, Hard Candy*, and *The Woodsman*," *Jeunesse: Young People, Texts, Cultures* 1, no. 2 (2009): 35–65.

31. See Valerie Traub, "The (In)Significance of 'Lesbian' Desire in Early Modern England," in *Erotic Politics: The Dynamics of Desire in the Renaissance Theatre*, ed. Susan Zimmerman (New York: Routledge, 1992), 150–169; Valerie Traub, *The Renaissance of Lesbianism in Early Modern England* (Cambridge, UK: Cambridge University Press, 2002).

32. See Carroll Smith-Rosenberg, *Disorderly Conduct: Visions of Gender in Victorian America* (Oxford: Oxford University Press, 1986); Carroll Smith-Rosenberg, "The Female Animal: Medical and Biological Views on Woman and Her Role in Nineteenth-Century America," *Journal of American History* 60, no. 2 (1973): 332–356; Carroll Smith-Rosenberg, "The Hysterical Woman: Sex Roles and Role Conflict in 19th-century America," *Social Research* 39 (1972): 652–678.

33. Esther Newton, *Mother Camp: Female Impersonators in America* (Chicago: University of Chicago Press, 1979).

34. Butler, *Gender Trouble*.

35. DisneyCartoonLover, "Disney Characters Genders Reversed—Part 1," YouTube, Oct 5, 2015, https://www.youtube.com/watch?v=ZbbvLlQ6HtU.

36. Sakimichan (@sakimichan.tumblr.com), "Beauty and the Beast and Esmeralda," Tumblr, April 4, 2014, http://sakimichan.tumblr.com/post/81721945483/beauty-and-the-beast-and-esmeralda-i-hope-you.

37. Christopher Stoll, "Princess Avengers: CAPTAIN AMERICA," DeviantArt, November 9, 2012, https://www.deviantart.com/christopher-stoll/gallery/37232032/Princess-Avengers?rnrd=69913.

38. Chad Barbour, "When Captain America Was an Indian: Heroic Masculinity, National Identity, and Appropriation," *Journal of Popular Culture* 48, no. 2 (2015): 269–284.

39. The Hawkeye Initiative, http://thehawkeyeinitiative.com/.

40. Carolyn Cocca, "The 'Broke Back Test': A Quantitative and Qualitative Analysis of Portrayals of Women in Mainstream Superhero Comics, 1993–2013," *Journal of Graphic Novels and Comics* 5, no. 4 (2014): 411–428.

41. Butler, *Gender Trouble*.

42. Mulvey, "Visual Pleasure," 14–26.

43. Suzanne Scott, "The Hawkeye Initiative: Pinning Down Transformative Feminisms in Comic-book Culture through Superhero Crossplay Fan Art," *Cinema Journal* 55, no. 1 (2015): 150–160.

44. Steve Neale, "Reflections on Men and Mainstream Cinema," in *Screening the Male: Exploring Masculinities in Hollywood Cinema*, ed. Steven Cohan and Ina Rae Hark (New York: Routledge, 1993), 9–22.

45. Julie Levin Russo, "User-Penetrated Content: Fan Video in the Age of Convergence," *Cinema Journal* 48, no. 4 (2009): 125–130.

46. TamrynEradani, "Stephanie Rogers Reporting for Duty," Archive of Our Own. Link deactivated.

47. See Aaron Belkin, "Don't Ask, Don't Tell: Is the Gay Ban Based on Military Necessity?," *Parameters* (2003): 108–119; Elizabeth Kier, "Homosexuals in the US Military: Open Integration and Combat Effectiveness," *International Security* 23, no. 2 (1998): 5–39. Although women and LGBT people may now serve openly in the US armed forces, the Trump administration's reversal on inclusiveness policies of the Obama administration demonstrate that these gains remain tenuous. See John Peterson, "Present at the Destruction? The Liberal Order in the Trump Era," *The International Spectator* 53, no. 1 (2018): 28–44.

48. Mary Douglas, *Purity and Danger: An Analysis of Concepts of Pollution and Taboo* (New York: Routledge, 2003), 35.

49. Starrdust411, "Feminist Theories," Archive of Our Own, June 26, 2014.

50. USC Annenberg Civic Imagination Project, "Civic Imagination: Theoretical Foundation," 2017, https://www.civicimaginationproject.org/theory.

51. Stories involving Captain America's co-Avenger Thor transforming from man to woman and back again neatly connect superheroes to fairy tales and legends, with a story that originated in Norse mythology reappearing in modern comics and fan works.

52. Hotchoco195, "Good Becomes Great," Archive of Our Own, January 19, 2016.

53. Hotchoco195, "Good Becomes Great."

54. See Michael Dittman, "Women in Refrigerators: The Growing Dialogue between Comic Creators and Fan Communities," *Works and Days* 63/64, 32, no. 1–2 (2014–2015): 241–248; Kyra Nelson, "Women in Refrigerators: The Objectification of Women in Comics," *AWE (A Woman's Experience)* 2, no. 2 (2015): 9; Scott, "Fangirls in Refrigerators," 1–20.

55. See Pauline Greenhill, "'Fitcher's [Queer] Bird': A Fairy-Tale Heroine and Her Avatars," *Marvels & Tales* 22, no. 1 (2008): 143–167; Pauline Greenhill, "Wanting (to be) Animal: Fairy-Tale Transbiology in the Story-teller," *Feral Feminisms* 2 (2014): 29–45.

56. See Duggan, "New Homonormativity," 175–194; Steven Seidman, "From Identity to Queer Politics: Shifts in Normative Heterosexuality and the Meaning of Citizenship," *Citizenship Studies* 5, no. 3 (2001): 321–328.

57. See Kristina Busse, "Pon Farr, Mpreg, Bonds, and the Rise of the Omegaverse," in *Fic: Why Fanfiction Is Taking Over the World*, ed. Anne Jamison (Dallas, TX: SmartPop, 2013): 316–322; Milena Popova, "'Dogfuck Rapeworld': Omegaverse Fanfiction as a Critical Tool in Analyzing the Impact of Social Power Structures on Intimate Relationships and Sexual Consent," *Porn Studies* 5, no. 2 (2018): 1–17.

58. De Beauvoir, *Second Sex*, 283.

59. Leo Bersani, "Is the Rectum a Grave?," *October* 43 (1987): 197–222.

60. Jessica Benjamin, *The Bonds of Love: Psychoanalysis, Feminism, and the Problem of Domination* (New York: Pantheon, 2013).

61. John Whittier Treat, *Great Mirrors Shattered: Homosexuality, Orientalism, and Japan* (New York: Oxford University Press, 1999).

62. Anne Kustritz, "Re: Public Sphere Theory," discussion following "Gender and Fan Culture (Round Thirteen): Anne Kustritz and Derek Johnson," 2007, hosted by Fandebate on Livejournal, http://fandebate.livejournal.com/5330.html?thread=181458#t181458, accessed August 31, 2007; Russo, "User-penetrated Content."

EPILOGUE

THE MATTER WITH SIZE

RICHARD HARRISON

I first wrote of superheroes as images through which my condition as a man could be illustrated, and perhaps redeemed, in a poem I published in my second book, *Recovering the Naked Man* (1991):

BATMAN

This is the look of all my heroes:
a man, sheathed, pure,

poured from the idea of himself,
a ripple in the fall of cream.

Gone are all the awkward protuberances:
earless, he hears across the bald drum
of his cowl,
without a nose, he breathes, we do not know how hard,
through the triangle of his mask.

He has paved the nature of his hands and feet,
the uneven growth of his hair.

His cock, also, his testicles,
lie dormant in his hero suit, bound,
not painfully, but adequately for his true
action which is to save

and not to want. He is the man
women feel safe around, whose touch is powerful,
full of technique, but does not intrude, even to fulfill
what they might desire together. In short,

there is nothing to make fun of.

There is nothing weak,

and nothing for the weak to fear.

When villains shoot him, they aim for his die-cast chest.
He says only enough to fill a word balloon.[1]

That was written half my life ago, and since then, blessed with the opportunity of doing the difficult, traumatic, and hopeful work of reassessing everything we knew about sex and sexuality, we have understood more, accepted more, and inquired more. And for those of us for whom superheroes and their stories have provided a vocabulary for the interplay between our fantasies and the real world, the superheroes are here again, both part of the question and part of the measure of its answer. Feminism taught us that everything personal is political, too, so this paper, political as it is, has to begin with what I've learned about myself over the span of years that began with the writing of "Batman" and ended (however unfinished) in the stories my mother told me while we waited together for the medically assisted death she had chosen to arrive.

My sexuality was born in 1939, in an England at war, when the British government put the ironically named Operation Pied Piper in motion and sent thousands of children out of London to be spared the German air attack everyone knew was coming.[2] Some readers may remember this historic moment best as the reason the children in C. S. Lewis's *The Lion, the Witch, and the Wardrobe* are sheltered in that mysterious house in the countryside that becomes their doorway to Narnia, a land of magic and adventure as well as the backdrop for Lewis's argument for Christianity's faith, sacrifice, and salvation.[3] My mother, then twelve, was part of that exodus of the young.

But Hitler did not attack Britain that year, and the parents of many of those children, against official advice, decided to bring them home, so great was the pain of their separation. My mother wanted to return too. She was an only child, which would have been reason enough for her to be especially desirous of a reunion with her parents. But the far more significant influence was the fact that the father in the house where she had been sent for her safety was yet another of those men whose sexually predatory behavior is being dragged more and more often from the shadows where it has traditionally and prodigiously thrived. Behind the blackout curtains, this man fondled girls and had them stroke his erection. From him, my mother learned what a grown man's body was. She learned that men used their power to give or withhold based on the gratification they got, or didn't. She felt guilty and fearful about it all her life, and of all the stories she told my brother and me while she was waiting to be spared from the cancer closing in on her, the one about this man was among the last, as if the gargoyle that entered her world then, and bound itself to ours, was returning to take its final bow as her life's traumatically defining feature.

And I strongly suspect it was. My mother hated my father's penis. She hated his sex, his desire, his smell. I began to learn all this when I was around ten, and safe to confide in. I learned that a man's body was built around an ugly object whose power was, more than anything else, the power to frighten, and in whose power men became both helpless and monstrous at once. This background made me ripe, in the 1970s and '80s, for the branch of feminism found in writers like Andrea Dworkin, who argued on cultural grounds that all heterosexual sex was a kind of rape,[4] or Elaine Morgan, who argued the same on evolutionary ones.[5]

It's been over ten years since I wrote my part of *Secret Identity Reader: Essays on Sex, Death, and the Superhero*.[6] Since then, it's become increasingly clear how many have been, like my mother, harmed, how many have been made to bear the humiliation of being made to watch, or touch, or take it. The terrible aloneness of the victimhood my mother lived with is being relieved. The culture itself is changing accordingly, hopefully forever, and for everyone's good, even for those who fear losing what is lost when what is lost is power. In this accounting and reckoning, there is so much for everyone to gain. For if we define seeing the beauty of a person as perceiving in them the promise of pleasure, then I was raised to know, and we are acknowledging more profoundly than before, the ways in which male power is the antithesis of male beauty. In my father's life, and for much of mine, the use of male power eclipsed male beauty in the eyes of the very people whom we as men needed to see in us any beauty we had.

My father's real body was beautiful, his face handsome, his body athletic and muscles strong, trained through sports and the army. But it wasn't beautiful enough to stay ahead of my mother's pain, to stop the engines of memory that drove her away from him, or to leap over history and just be what it was. His body wasn't beautiful enough to persuade me that mine was or might be. But the male superhero body was all that my father's wasn't: it existed without a connection to real and disappointing life, and in its stories it was perfect to all who saw it. So I loved it instead.

We are living in a revolutionary time in both the history of sex and its representation in comics, an art form that, not so long ago, was considered a thoroughly inappropriate, and even dangerous, place to show or talk about it. When I think of graphic novels that I've read recently that most thoroughly address a heterosexual man's relationship with his identity and desires in the Anglo-American world, I land on Chester Brown's *Paying For It* and *Mary Wept Over the Feet of Jesus*.[7] These are not superhero stories, but I include them here because they are told in the same medium where superhero stories first appeared, and because these two books, similar to superhero fictions, are stories about the contradictions and secrets in their protagonists' identities. I've argued in the past that what makes superhero stories distinct isn't so much the parts of those stories about superpowers, but rather their function as secret identity fictions. These are stories built around the idea that what we are in our ordinary lives isn't all that we are. Simply by existing, the superhero says, *If only you knew who I really was, you would see me as greater than you ever thought.*

It's a fine fiction for anyone, male or female, though we know that the superhero shift in American comics from the early 1960s on was a shift orchestrated by predominantly male creators toward male readers and masculine fantasies. Many Golden Age comics and the vast majority of Silver Age ones are the perfect fiction for young men who either don't fit in or who, I would argue, are living on the edges of the adult world they are both eager and terrified to join. When superheroes and their adventures were largely confined to the pages of American comic books, it was common to think of their readers as the obvious male outsiders: nerds, geeks, outcasts, the effeminate boys who either really were, in the clinical language of the time, homosexual, or perceived to be within its spectrum by their closed-minded peers. But the migration of my childhood comic book heroes from the 1960s and '70s into the mainstream of the Marvel and DC cinematic and television universes suggests that whatever the appeal was to those on the fringes, that same appeal is working just as well if not better among a sizeable portion of the population at large. Much of that appeal exists, I would argue, in the superheroic specialness of the superhero body.

For most of its existence, the body of the male superhero was exaggerated in what Burne Hogarth, in his 1958 textbook *Dynamic Anatomy*, calls "an affirmative view of artistic proportion developed from the admiration, affection and enthusiasm of the population as whole" (figure 14.1).[8] Hogarth was, among other things, the artist for the daily newspaper strip *Adventures of Tarzan*. Twenty years later, in *How to Draw Comics the Marvel Way* (a book that remains in print to this day), Stan Lee calls this figure "heroically proportioned."[9] John Buscema, the book's primary illustrator and, for many years, the lead artist on some of Marvel's top-selling superhero series as well as the adventures of the brawny and often nearly naked Tarzan homage, *Conan the Barbarian*, echoes Hogarth's vision of such a man in virtually every drawing. This includes his sketch of Reed Richards (figure 14.2), who is, to most intents and purposes, the template for the comic book universe's "average" superhero. Batman, of course, is even better built than that.

Hogarth's ideal figure is not drawn according to the seven-heads-tall proportions of Greek statuary, which were, he argues, expressions of the ideal human body when that ideal was shaped and limited by nature alone. Hogarth's ideal figure is, instead, an eight-and-a-half-head-tall body that stands as "a figure of endurance, vitality and vigor."[10] And Hogarth, the Dr. Abraham Erskine of graphic artists, welcomingly foresees the body of this man of universal awe as "taking its physical attributes from the fields of hygiene, physiology, and medicine" to become "the prototype of the best standards of twentieth century civilization."[11] Nature, then, is no longer the standard for excellence in the human body. The new, modern standard is rooted in what we can make of it: our ideals as expressed in art are no longer descriptions; they are plans.

Such a figure appears lifelike enough to be believable even though it was, in Hogarth's time, almost impossible to achieve beyond the canvas or drafting table. It was not until the 1980s, with the advent of body-altering technologies, that real bodies could approximate this figure, and many men did so enthusiastically, sometimes painfully distorting themselves for a few years of showmanship only to later either quit the game or die playing it. Consider just some of the larger-than-life characters of professional wrestling who, through training or chemicals or both, maintained the spectacle of the superhero physique: Randy "Macho Man" Savage, Big John Studd, Davey Boy Smith, Chris Benoit, Paul "Mr. Wonderful" Orndorff, Curt "Mr. Perfect" Henning. These men could have been comic book characters, and they knew it. The most famous of them, Hulk Hogan, took a comic character's name as his own.

Hogan and his contemporaries altered the body type of the professional wrestler, deliberately shifting it from the thick-waisted bulky form of men like Haystack Calhoun, the Sheik, and Angelo Mosca. Whereas Calhoun and his brethren were strong because they did heavy work either

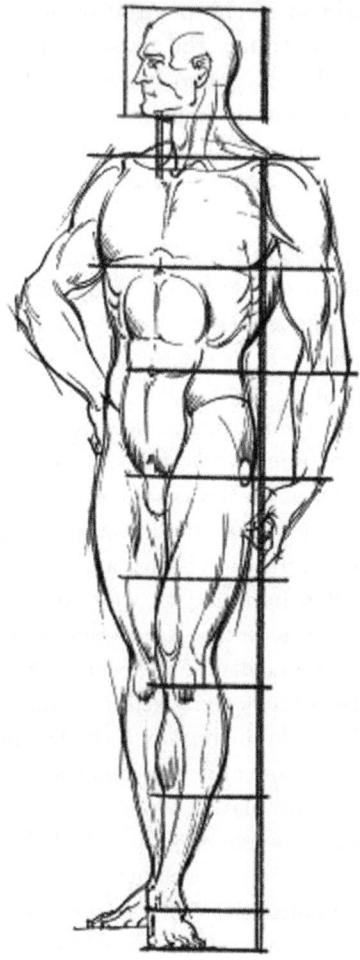

FIGURE 14.1. "The figure proportion *necessary to art*[,] . . . the figure of modern aspiration, inspiration, and human nature." Burne Hogarth, *Dynamic Anatomy* (1960).

in the world or in the sports they played before they wrestled, the New Men of the 1980s and '90s were strong because they built their bodies that way. These men attended to the aesthetics of their shoulders, arms, legs, and chests; they shaved their skin clean; they reduced their waistlines and body fat to evoke wedges of power; they cultivated regimens of antibiotics to bolster immune systems diminished by the redistribution of the body's resources; and they augmented their natural muscle-building systems with supplements that accelerated the accumulation of tissue with

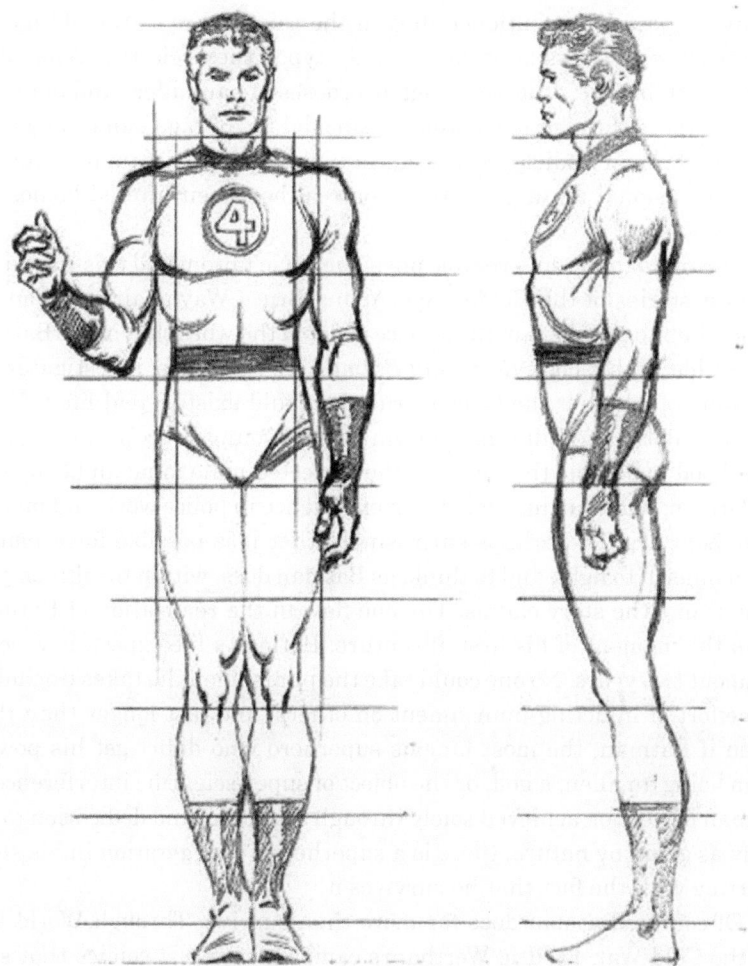

FIGURE 14.2. Burne's proportions applied the Marvel Way to Reed Richards as Stan Lee's "Heroic Proportions"—the male body not merely turned but transformed below the waist in the move from frontal to profile view. John Buscema, *How to Draw Comics the Marvel Way* (1978).

work. These weren't always beautiful bodies; sometimes, their largeness could be monstrous in its asymmetrical excess. But they were undeniably spectacular, exciting both in action and at rest.

Many of these men also, of course, played larger-than-life characters in fantasy and comic book movies; Hulk Hogan's "Thunderlips" in *Rocky III* and Macho Man's "Bonesaw McGraw" in *Spider-Man* come to mind.[12] Yet for all the cultivation of superhumanity in this new breed of wrestler, many of those I've mentioned died in the same years as the old men of the sport whose less superheroic body types they rejected. Some died from organ failure, others through overdoses of painkillers and addictive drugs, others through murderous or suicidal fits of rage induced by what they made their bodies become, all in pursuit of the dream of making a two-dimensional fantasy figure into a real boy, their altered bodies the key to riches.[13]

The route to the superheroic physique wasn't promoted this way in the earliest stories of the Golden Age. Young Bruce Wayne already had the riches, but he put them in the service of doing the work that made Batman believable. In his book *Becoming Batman*, E. Paul Zehr investigates the question of whether the Caped Crusader could exist in real life.[14] Using the 1939 Bob Kane/Bill Finger origin story of young Bruce's training from childhood to become the image of the perfected male mind and body that is Batman, and drawing on his own experience in police work and martial arts, Zehr argues, perhaps surprisingly, that it is possible for a man to train himself to fight, and to think, as Batman does, within the fifteen-year time frame the story claims. The one flaw in the realization of Batman: from the moment of his first adventure, Batman's life expectancy would be about two years. No one could take the punishment he takes (including the effort of inflicting punishment on others) and last longer than that. Even if Batman, the most famous superhero who didn't get his powers from being an alien, a god, or the object of super-scientific interference, is human perfection achieved solely through discipline and dedication to the body as given by nature, there is a superheroic exaggeration in his story, starting with the fact that he survives it.

Of course, Batman does far more than survive. Through World War II, the Cold War, Fredric Wertham's campaign against comics that shut so many comics down,[15] the revolutionary '60s, the materialist backlash in the decades that followed, and the trauma of 9/11 and beyond, Batman thrives and triumphs. He also protects, and though his relationship with the city that owes him its existence goes through its ups and downs according to the politics of the day, he is still always the object of boyish (and mannish) love and admiration, despite the enormous difference between what he is and who his readers are or will ever be. It's a love that starts in childhood and, for those smitten, lasts decades. For some reason, despite the unreality of Batman's existence, we believe him, and believe *in him*: we use the language of his life (and those with lives like his) to reach for words to describe our own.

Batman's body is at the center of this belief. The superhero body has been subject to a great deal of critical analysis already. Much of this analysis reads the exaggerated bodies of superheroes as one more sign of the Western world's impossible, millennia-long project of clearly defining and dividing male and female, a project with detrimental real-world consequences for everyone along the continuum of gender. Some commentators view these exaggerated bodies as unwitting parodies of that essentializing project. In this reading, superbeings may superficially resemble the standard definitions of "male" and "female," but their features as members of different (and opposite) genders are no more significant than the differences in their powers or planets of origin. If either of these readings were widely accepted among the contemporary audience for superhero stories (including their realizations in film), then those who read those stories, or watch them (or both), should be unhappy with the relationship between themselves and the superheroic bodies they are shown. Further, the more closely those bodies are compared with their own, the unhappier they should be.

And yet, every Comic-Con and Comic Expo I've attended has included fans in possession of the thousand natural shapes that flesh is heir to, dressed as every possible version of their heroes. Cosplay favorites include Captain America, Iron Man, Batman, Superman, and Wonder Woman. Of these, I've found Wonder Woman attracts fans with the greatest diversity of body types; she is also the character I've seen played most by fans regardless of gender. Certainly, every well-attended Comic-Con features intimidatingly powerful bodybuilding men painted up as Kratos from *God of War*, or dressed as the Punisher or Cap or Superman, and female cosplayers who are as voluptuous as some versions of Wonder Woman, Mystique, or Red Sonja. But those who could convincingly look the part in a movie about the superheroes whose costumes they joyously wear are, as expected, in the minority, and that's the point: there is something beyond physical resemblance in the moment of identification represented by the putting on of the other's clothes for the carnival. In some sense, I would venture, dressing as one's chosen hero is less an evocation of that hero's bodily presence, or even an attempt to emulate it, than it is an expression of that hero's meaning.

I acknowledge that my anecdotal observations of both costume-wearing and cosplay do not, on their own, substantiate an argument for the behavior of large numbers of people. So let me be more specific: in many ways, I agree with the analyses of the superhero body as problem, but if it is a problem, then it is a problem with an art object, and a work of art is many meanings at once. Regarding these meanings, what if it's the case that the male superhero body isn't an ideal that drives some young men to despise their own because they cannot live up to it, but is instead something both impossible and satisfying at the same time, which provides young men, within the context of the fictional world in which they're found, a body that is powerful, beautiful, and loved?

Let me turn to Aaron Taylor and his analysis of the self-negating sexuality of the male superhero in which he quotes Reitberger and Fuchs:[16] "Another anatomical inexactitude further undermines the virility of the male superheroes. 'Super-heroes . . . seem to have absolutely nothing under their tight fitting tights; they all appear to be androgynous beings—hermaphrodites who lack the primary sexual organs.'"[17] Although the rippling physiques represent an absurdly exaggerated ideal of Western anatomical perfection, they are underwritten, Taylor writes, in "a sterile, 'clean' world. . . . In a fictional universe in which any part of the anatomy has the potential to be super-powered, the superpenis is still strictly taboo."[18]

Fortunately, since Batman's romantic life has typically been full of all the excitement and reluctance of a typical twelve-year-old boy's, he hasn't had as much need for his penis as for every other part of himself. But that mix of character traits alone wouldn't change a man's anatomy. Indeed, when Batman, and all the other men whose bodies are versions of his own, are translated into television and film and have to be played by real men with proportional genitalia, those men often have to have their groins taped or otherwise contained so that the obvious effect of skintight clothes on the male body is mitigated. In "Batman: Behind the Tights," Jim Mitchell quotes Burt Ward from his autobiography:

> "Dancer's belts, jockstraps, double-thick jockey shorts, dong socks, testicle supports, padded underwear[,] . . . nothing reduced the swelling! Not even ice packs!" . . . As Ward tells it, it was Boy Wonder's green-clad bulge that was of particular concern to the Catholic Legion of Decency, who had raised the issue with broadcaster ABC, with the "crotch crisis" potentially jeopardizing the show.[19]

The contentious, perhaps show-stopping relationship between audience morality and acknowledgment of the reality of the penis in superhero films has continued into the twenty-first century. As part of a cast interview on Jimmy Kimmel's late night talk show, and at the prompting of his fellow *Avengers* actors, Mark Ruffalo offered this spin on his having to wear a specialized "CGI leotard" so that his on-screen Hulk identity has a genital-free body, the obvious unreality of which doesn't seem to affect the audience's acceptance or enjoyment of the character: "I call it 'man-cancelling' because it makes you look small everywhere you wished you looked big." He then, interestingly, refers to the impossibly exaggerated musculature of the rest of the Hulk's body, adding, "and big everywhere you wished you looked small."[20] But all of this analysis and talk treats comic book art as if it's representational, as if the purpose of the artwork in a comic book is to draw characters as though they were human beings dressed up to play their superheroic or supervillainous roles. Comic art is, instead, a species of graphic art precisely because the drawings aren't drawings of how characters look but of what the artists are telling the readers about them through the pictures. As Will Eisner argues in *Comics and Sequential Art*, comic art is about drawing on what he calls "the common storehouse" of images shared by the artist and the audience in order to create a visual language between them through which they can share their common understanding, not just of the physical world, but the moral world in which comic book stories, as twentieth and twenty-first-century fables and mystery plays, are told.[21]

In that language, to use Eisner's examples, bushy eyebrows, as opposed to smooth ones, signify a character's bestial nature; villains grimace through delineated teeth, whereas the hero's smile is a pure white space; body size, particularly height, is the rough measure of a character's power; blue eyes are ones readers can trust, while dark eyes ought to raise suspicion; and so on. Of course, much of this "common storehouse" draws upon and reinforces ugly stereotypes. The deep interconnections between comic art and stereotyping undoubtedly inform the inherently conservative, and sometimes retrograde, nature of most superhero comic books. In many ways, superhero comics creators who want to make the form and genre progressive have to work against the established language of the medium in which they operate. People like G. Willow Wilson, creator and primary writer of the adventures of the latest Ms. Marvel—Kamala Khan, a Pakistani American, Muslim teenager—have embraced this challenge, tackling stereotypes head-on and transforming them, much as Kamala herself transforms, in her introductory issues, from a nerdy, brown-skinned teenage girl into a version of the white, blonde, Amazon-proportioned former Ms. Marvel, Carol Danvers, only to realize that both the Caucasian body and Carol's costume make her feel self-betraying rather than powerful; in subsequent issues, Kamala's transformations reflect—and enrich—her own unique heroic identity.[22] Confronting and transforming stereotypes is work worth doing because, as everyone who analyzes comics agrees even as they disagree about the value of comic book messages, comics are influential; they have meaning; they teach.

Kamala Khan's body is obviously meaningful. But given that my search begins in my own childhood experience of superheroes, I am compelled to look at the male and mostly white bodies that have historically dominated the superhero genre and ask, "What are you telling me?" I played at being these characters. I dressed up as them. I drew pictures of them to have them closer to me than they were when I only owned pictures of them someone else drew. I told my own stories with them because an infinitely long series of stories about characters that capture the imagination always has room for one more.

My question about the exaggerated male body of Batman and all his kind should, perhaps, be further refined as, "If your body does not and never will show me how I should look, what is it telling me about how I should think of what I am and will become?"

A month ago, I visited the National Gallery of Canada. There I saw *The Shepherd Paris*, painted by Desmarais between 1787 and 1788 (figure 14.3). It's one of those standard post-Renaissance paintings that Europe produced by the hundreds after the rebirth of classic Greek art's adoration of the nude. It's a wonderful painting to contemplate: the nearly naked and beautiful young Paris is holding the golden apple over which, ultimately, the Trojan War will begin. He's weighing it as if he can feel both the glory and the danger it holds. In the upper left corner of the painting, you can see the faint image of Eris, the Goddess of Discord, whose "gift" to the most beautiful of the goddesses has set the tragedy in motion. She is departing, her work done, but she's only just now appearing to us. Originally, Desmarais had her in the painting; then, deciding that her presence should be felt in Paris's own posture rather than seen by us, he painted over her. But Discord is not that easy to remove. Over time, through the painted clouds that were meant to obscure her, she is returning to our sight.[23] The painting both tells a story and is one; it presents the beginning of the narrative of a man who will condemn his people to war and ultimately extinction because of his sexual desire, and suggests the story of the erasure of female presence and agency from that epic tale. It suggests other stories, too, precisely through its minimization of suggestiveness. Even though Paris has a body that would be right at home among comic book superheroes, and is a notorious lover and appreciator of feminine beauty, his sex organs are obviously and deliberately tiny: a mere wisp of cloth covers them.

For all that I see in *The Shepherd Paris*, it is a minor masterpiece, more receiver of artistic influences than their source. But the disproportionality I see there goes back to the work of one of the greatest representative artists of the Christian age: consider Michelangelo's rendition of Adam awakened by God (1508–1512). There, Adam's penis is a baby's

FIGURE 14.3. Paris contemplates the choices ahead of him. Jean-Baptiste Frédéric Desmarais, *Le Berger Pâris* (The Shepherd Paris), 1787.

penis on a man's body. And what a man's body it is: big, heavy, beautifully muscled, pleasingly posed. This Adam could be Batman, and maybe that's because Batman's body, to all intents and purposes, is this Adam's.

Maybe Batman is the way he is because of that Adam, because the meaning that Adam's and Batman's artists are both depicting is the same meaning encoded in the tiny penis, whether it appears in the sex-suppressing Christian era or the supposedly sex-loving world of the ancient Greeks that inspired the Renaissance artists that later inspired late nineteenth-century bodybuilders and, finally, Batman: the penis is a "problem" that interferes with our ability to view the male body as either/both powerful or beautiful. The pagan Greeks were slightly less repressive in this regard; their depictions of satyrs and centaurs frequently celebrate exaggerated male organs and the libidinal freedoms of the mythic world. Yet a hero like Hercules, who may have been half god but was definitely, unlike the satyrs or centaurs, all man, is usually depicted, as in the example of the *Farnese Hercules*, as considerably less well endowed.

To read Batman, Adam, and the *Farnese Hercules* as versions of one another means reading through distinctions between ancient statuary, the high art of the Renaissance, and comic book art of the twentieth and twenty-first centuries. It also means breaking down the distinction between "representational" and "graphic," because in this instance, the terms don't divide into two kinds of art; they apply to ancient statuary and Renaissance art as well as superhero comic books. In all of these contexts, artists are making choices within the visual language of their chosen forms to say something about what they are using those forms to make their audiences think.

As I was contemplating the difference (or lack thereof) between the representational and the graphic in both the past and the present, I found myself thinking, again, about my own past, and yet another image of the male body that had a hand in shaping it: a drawing I saw in a grade school science class of Cortex Man. This drawing depicted, as all such drawings do, a caricature of the body in which the space in the brain devoted to various body parts and functions is clearly laid out. In the grade school version I saw, the eyes, ears, nose, and feet were big; the legs, arms, and chest were thin. The mouth was huge, and just to show us how important language is, Cortex Man's tongue was hanging out. His penis was tiny; some pictures of him didn't show it at all. Clearly, for the brain, it was an unimportant bodily nub.

In high school, though, I saw another picture of Cortex Man (figure 14.4). In every respect, he was almost the same as he'd been when I met him years before. Only now he had quite a large penis; in subsequent

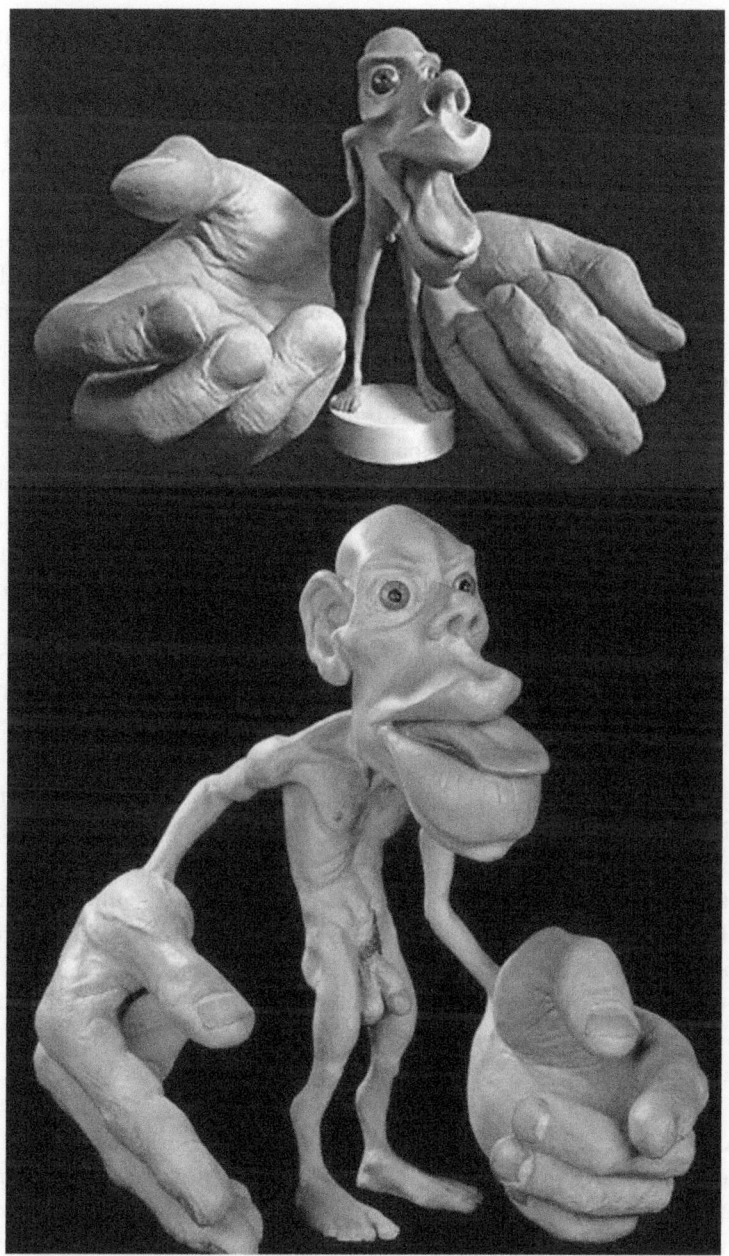

FIGURE 14.4. The Cortex Man of my first acquaintance (depicting what was presented as the relative importance of the body's parts to the brain) versus Sensory Cortex Man (the other picture of the brain's perception of the man). "Cortical homunculus," Wikipedia.

pictures I encountered of him, it was even larger, rivaling even his hands and feet. At the time, I thought I'd been deceived about what was being given to me as scientific knowledge. I thought the second Cortex Man was the truth and the first had been censored in order to keep the reality of his sexual nature away from us children, along with the rest of the content of any sex education that spoke of the value of pleasure.

But if my younger self had been the recipient of censored documents, it wasn't censorship through an alteration of the drawing *of* Cortex Man, but the choice of *which* Cortex Man to show and how he was identified. Cortex Man is twins. The figure with the large penis is a map of the body as seen by the sensuous brain, the part that feels the flesh and the world. The figure with the kind of penis Adam has is the willful brain—the part that exercises control over the body, the part that chooses. It was as if those two scientific drawings had reproduced the ancient sculptures of huge-penised satyrs—male sex at its most ridiculous and despised—and tiny-organed ancient and Renaissance heroes—male sex at its most properly undervalued—and said, *Here is the choice science tells us your own body presents: Which kind of man are you going to be?*

What if the meaning of Hercules or Adam is that everything in a man except his sex is what defines him, or should do so? What if it's that all the work a man can do, and everything in his body he can perfect except his cock, are both the important part of him and the route by which he can be beautiful, as in worthy of proportionate if not ennobling representation in art? If the distinctive power of the phallus is its arousal, the male superhero body is that phallic power distributed throughout its frame. What is the transformation from the soft, secret identity of a Clark Kent or a Bruce Wayne to the dramatically revealed hardbody of a Superman or Batman? A statement of enlargement as power? Emergence as identity? An emphasis on the importance of a body designed to act violently and to endure the acts of violence that may be visited upon it? We might also consider these bodies as idealized depictions of male sexual power in the form of physical power distinctly depicted as male.

All these meanings succeed (to the extent that they do succeed) because what the idealized male body, from Hercules through Adam to Batman, does is separate the male heroic body from the male sexual one. The male hero isn't androgynous; instead, he's male if heroic maleness had nothing to hide. To put the sex back on him is to do what drawing a dick on *anything* does: it satirizes it, diminishes any awe we may feel for it or any respect we might have for its beauty or power.[24] We might say that male superheroes are effectively sexless because they are still, at least in part, what they were in their beginning: artwork made for children. But not for children per se: rather, for children in their own particular place in a culture and its history, children for whom the adult world is, as the word *adult* implies, a corruption of the ideal. Male superheroes and both the ancient Greek and Renaissance depictions of the ideal man are the inheritors of an agreement that the penis is something to hide; its revelation, and the revelation of its power, is at best an embarrassment and at worst a shame.

The suppression of the knowledge of the incidence of sexual abuse is also the suppression of the knowledge of that abuse's effects. Here I'm reading, I know, from the point of view of someone raised by a sex abuse victim who never recovered. How many women like my mother are out there? And how many of us are raised with the sense, justified by patriarchal institutions and by so many men's behavior, that maleness itself is an evil? The male superhero, drawing on the imagery of the Greek hero, the Knight of the Round Table, Robin Hood, and Zorro, is the argument through fiction that evil isn't necessarily endemic to men themselves even as the antagonist is also almost always male as well.

The biggest lie within these fictions of male heroism might well be the suggestion that the evils of manhood can be defeated only by the actions of the men who are "good," with goodness being intertwined with, and symbolized by, sexlessness. In this, I find a disheartening and paradoxical convergence. The very comic book fictions that gave me male bodies to admire because they lacked that which brought so much harm to my mother, to my father, and to me gave me the same message that my mother's experience of abuse taught her to teach: male sexual organs, and hence male sexuality, were inherently the opposite of heroic. It would be easy to take the route of gendered self-pity and say that male sexual abusers are looking for the beauty they never see in themselves because of the underlying message of the almost-sexless Adam and all the depictions of men that follow from him. But things are more complicated than that. From where I sit now, having thought my way here in the months after my mother's death, I think that Batman took me as far as he could with his image of the good male body as a distorted one, enlarged one way, diminished another. But erasing the shame of male sexuality isn't a matter of drawing its most obvious organs out of the picture. To do so, for whatever "higher" purpose, is to reinforce such organs' ugliness and unacceptability. We need to go beyond that if we are to succeed in making tomorrow's world better for more people than today's world has proven to be.

What would it look like, though, to get "beyond" that? From the 1990s onward, mainstream superhero comics have included stories of a more adult nature, including stories about sex and violence, and sexualized

FIGURE 14.5. Adam West as Batman guides a group of schoolchildren across the road. Video recording from May 1967.

violence. But for the most part, these stories have done so without altering their conventional renditions of male or female bodies. Many of today's mainstream superhero comics, I'd argue, present even greater "heroic" exaggeration than before. Whatever I loved in the superhero body in the 1960s is still on offer, and still embraced, today.

So perhaps my ultimate question is this: What is the answer to loving what you used to love when you thought it was perfect, when now, instead, you see its limitations, its reversal of what you thought it told you? Superhero stories have grown up in some respects, but not everything in them has. Then again, maybe not everything in them can or should. In Aesop's greatest fables, animals talk, and what lets those fables speak to us metaphorically is that necessary disjunction between what we know is true about tortoises and hares and what is deliberately false about them. Maybe that Creation-of-Adam body that Batman has is all he can have in order to be Batman—not a character in life but a character in a fable that has something to teach me. Perhaps Batman's faith in his body as the means to do what good a man can do is the key to his meaning in so many lives, mine included.

Here's a photograph: it's Adam West's Batman, heroic enough in look, but in body only slightly more muscular than what was ordinary for the time, and still perhaps the most beloved version of the hero (figure 14.5). He's showing a group of schoolchildren how to properly cross the street in a 1967 British safety film.[25] Adam's been playing Batman for a year and a half by this time, so as far as the world is concerned, he is him. Batman will see the kids across the street; that's his job. But where they go once they arrive is a matter for the rest of their lives, and while the Caped Crusader's single act of kindness won't give them the model for everything they'll have to do, every decision they'll have to make in detail, it does give them a moment, and a feeling that may be the touchstone by which to act: it is the moment they were right there when their hero did the kind thing, and taught them to do the same.

NOTES

1. Richard Harrison, *Recovering the Naked Man* (Don Mills, ON: Wolsak & Wynn, 1991), 35.

2. "Operation Pied Piper" was actually three evacuations: the first, in 1939, was implemented when war was declared; the second, which reevacuated many of the children who returned from the first evacuation after there was no attack on Britain, began when the Blitz began; and the third commenced (again, after many children returned home post-Blitz) when V1 and V2 rocket attacks began in 1944. My mother was taken in the first. I would also note that the Pied Piper of Browning's poem, after which this operation was named, led the children out of Hamelin not to save them but to punish the city. And those children never returned. For a modern reflection on the sociological impact of Operation Pied Piper, see Amy Wang, "What World War II's Operation Pied Piper Taught Us about the Trauma of Family Separations," *Washington Post*, June 19, 2018, https://www.washingtonpost.com/news/retropolis/wp/2018/06/19/what-world-war-iis-operation-pied-piper-taught-us-about-the-trauma-of-family-separations/.

3. C. S. Lewis, *The Lion, the Witch, and the Wardrobe* (London: Geoffry Bles, 1950).

4. Andrea Dworkin, *Intercourse* (Glencoe: Free Press, 1987).

5. Elaine Morgan, *The Descent of Woman* (Toronto, ON: Bantam Books, 1973).

6. Lee Easton and Richard Harrison, *Secret Identity Reader: Essays on Sex, Death, and the Superhero* (Hamilton, ON: Wolsak & Wynn, 2010).

7. Chester Brown, *Paying for It: A Comic Strip Memoir about Being a John* (Montreal: Drawn & Quarterly, 2011); Chester Brown, *Mary Wept over the Feet of Jesus: Prostitution and Religious Obedience in the Bible* (Montreal: Drawn & Quarterly, 2016).

8. Burne Hogarth, *Dynamic Anatomy* (New York: Watson-Guptill, 1960), 70.

9. Stan Lee and John Buscema, *How to Draw Comics the Marvel Way* (New York: Simon & Schuster, 1978), 46.

10. Hogarth, *Dynamic Anatomy*, 70.

11. In the origin stories of Captain America, Dr. Abraham Erskine (a.k.a. Josef Reinstein, depending on which comics you read) is the one whose super-soldier serum transforms spindly Steve Rogers into the first of those intended to be the next step in human perfection. Hogarth, *Dynamic Anatomy*, 70.

12. Sylvester Stallone, dir., *Rocky III*, United Artists, 1982. Sam Raimi, dir., *Spider-Man*, Columbia Pictures, 2002.

13. See David Rhodes, "Why Do Professional Wrestlers Die So Young?" BBC News, August 8, 2015, https://www.bbc.com/news/magazine-33817959, which links to Herman, Anna S. C. Conlon, Melvyn Rubenfire, et al., "The Very High Premature Mortality Rate among Active Professional Wrestlers Is Primarily Due to Cardiovascular Disease," *PlosOne* 9, no. 11 (November 5, 2014), https://journals.plos.org/plosone/article?id=10.1371/journal.pone.0109945; and Benjamin Morris, "Comparing the WWF's Death Rate to the NFL's and Other Pro Leagues'," FiveThirtyEight, April 24, 2014, https://fivethirtyeight.com/features/comparing-the-wwfs-death-rate-to-the-nfls-and-other-pro-leagues/. Morris argues that professional wrestlers not only had a higher mortality rate than athletes in any other professional sport, but were also the only group of athletes studied who experienced a higher mortality rate than the general population.

14. Paul Zehr, *Becoming Batman: The Possibility of a Superhero* (Baltimore, MD: Johns Hopkins, 2008).

15. See Anna F. Peppard's introduction to this volume for a more thorough discussion of Wertham.

16. Reinhold Reitberger and Wolfgang Fuchs, *Comics: Anatomy of a Mass Medium* (Boston: Little, Brown, 1972), 120.

17. Taylor, "'He's Gotta Be Strong,'" 352–353.

18. Taylor, "'He's Gotta Be Strong,'" 353.

19. Jim Mitchell, "Batman: Behind the Tights," *SBS*, December 12, 2017, https://www.sbs.com.au/guide/article/2017/07/24/batman-behind-tights.

20. *Jimmy Kimmel Live*, "Mark Ruffalo on His 'Man-Cancelling' Avengers Outfit," YouTube, April 14, 2015, https://www.youtube.com/watch?v=TKawIuc7KGo.

21. Will Eisner, *Comics and Sequential Art: Principles and Practices from the Legendary Cartoonist* (New York: W. W. Norton, 2008 [1985]).

22. G. Willow Wilson and Adrian Alphona, *Ms. Marvel Volume 1: No Normal* (New York: Marvel Comics, 2015).

23. From the National Gallery information card accompanying the painting.

24. Anna F. Peppard's discussion of the Batman penis controversy of October 2018 in the introduction to this volume excellently demonstrates this point. As Peppard observes, the first-ever DC-sanctioned appearance of Batman's penis in a comic book was censored less because of moral outrage than because of the laughter it provoked, which the publisher felt diminished the intended seriousness of the comic.

25. "Adam West's Batman Helps Kids Cross the Street Safely," video recorded May 1967, Boingboing, April 16, 2008, https://boingboing.net/2018/04/16/adam-wests-batman-helps-kids.html; @kyle_vanover, "What other Batman would you see doing that? . . . ," Twitter, August 19, 2017, "https://twitter.com/kyle_vanover/status/898930326126436352.

CONTRIBUTORS

JOSEPH BRENNAN is an independent scholar residing in Far North Queensland, Australia. He has published extensively on gay pornography in leading scholarly journals, including *European Journal of Cultural Studies, Journal of Homosexuality, Porn Studies, Sexuality & Culture,* and *Psychology & Sexuality,* where he also serves as an editorial board member. His first book, *Queerbaiting and Fandom: Teasing Fans through Homoerotic Possibilities,* was published by University of Iowa Press in 2019.

JEFFREY A. BROWN is a professor in the Department of Popular Culture and the School of Critical and Cultural Studies at Bowling Green State University. He is the author of numerous academic articles about gender, ethnicity, and sexuality in contemporary media, as well as four books: *Black Superheroes: Milestone Comics and Their Fans* (University Press of Mississippi, 2000), *Dangerous Curves: Gender, Fetishism and the Modern Action Heroine* (University Press of Mississippi, 2011), *Beyond Bombshells: The New Action Heroine in Popular Culture* (University Press of Mississippi, 2015), and *The Modern Superhero in Film and Television* (Routledge, 2016). He is currently completing the book *Batman and Multiplicity: The Contemporary Comic Book Superhero as Cultural Nexus* for Routledge Press.

J. ANDREW DEMAN is a full-time lecturer at the University of Waterloo. His research on comics is published in *Critical Survey of*

Graphic Novels, American Visual Memoir after the 1970s, English Studies Forum, TRANSverse, Canadian Graphic Life Narratives (recipient of the 2017 Gabrielle Roy Prize), and his recent book *The Margins of Comics* (Nuada Press, 2015). He is currently the project lead for "The Claremont Run," a Social Sciences and Humanities Research Council of Canada–funded, data-driven study of Chris Claremont's run on *Uncanny X-Men* comics.

KEITH FRIEDLANDER is a communications instructor at Olds College in Alberta. He completed his doctoral thesis on British Romanticism in 2016 through the University of Ottawa. His research focuses on both nineteenth-century print culture and the modern comic industry, examining the relationship between the market conditions of publishing and conceptions of authorship and public identity.

RICHARD HARRISON is a professor in the Department of English at Calgary's Mount Royal University. A frequent public speaker on the comics and graphic novels, he introduced Neil Gaiman for the University of Calgary's Distinguished Writers Program, interviewed Adam West on stage for Calgary's Comic Expo, and presented on the historical development and connections between the origin stories of Superman and Batman for the Comic Arts Conference at the San Diego Comic-Con. With his colleague Lee Easton, he is the coauthor of *Secret Identity Reader: Essays on Sex, Death, and the Superhero*. His sixth book of poetry, *On Not Losing My Father's Ashes in the Flood*, won the 2017 Governor General's Literary Award.

OLIVIA HICKS is a PhD student at the University of Dundee. Her research interests are the superhero genre, British and American girls' comics, feminism, queer theory, and postcolonial and whiteness studies. Her PhD topic is twentieth-century British and American superheroines.

BRIAN JOHNSON is an associate professor in English at Carleton University, where he teaches courses on contemporary literature, theory, comics, and popular genres. Recent publications include a series of articles on H. P. Lovecraft's influence and sexuality; an article on *The New Teen Titans* and queer masculinities is forthcoming. Currently, his research focuses on queer and closeted practices of reading soap opera, superheroes, and romance.

ANNE KUSTRITZ is an assistant professor of media and culture studies at Utrecht University. Her work focuses on fan creativity, digital economies, and queer theory. Her publications appear in *Camera Obscura, Feminist Media Studies*, and the *Journal of American Culture*. She serves on the board of *Transformative Works and Cultures*.

SAMANTHA LANGSDALE is a senior lecturer in the Department of Philosophy and Religion at the University of North Texas, where she teaches courses on philosophy, feminism, and environmental ethics. Her academic research has been published in the journal *Animation Practice, Process & Production* and in the anthologies *Sacred Texts and Comics: Religion, Faith, and Graphic Narratives* (University Press of Mississippi, 2018) and *Fantasy/Animation: History, Theory, Culture* (Routledge, 2018).

SARAH M. PANUSKA earned her PhD from Michigan State University in 2019. She studies queer theory and its intersections with film. Her dissertation uses queer theory to reconsider conceptions of camp by looking at the ways that camp has been used with methodologies of curation in the work of queer and lesbian filmmakers working in the last decades of the twentieth century.

ANNA F. PEPPARD holds a PhD in literature from York University. Her writing on representations of race, gender, and sexuality in television, comics, and other popular media appears in *Canadian Review of American Studies, International Journal of Comic Art, Journal of the Fantastic in the Arts, Journal of Fashion Studies, Feminist Media Histories, Journal of Graphic Novels and Comics, Studies in Comics, The Walrus*, and the anthologies *Make Ours Marvel: Media Convergence and a Comics Universe* (University of Texas Press, 2017) and *#WWE: Professional Wrestling in the Digital Age* (Indiana University Press, 2019).

RICHARD REYNOLDS teaches at Central Saint Martins in London. He is also a former publisher and occasional broadcaster. He has written, lectured, and broadcast widely about aspects of the superhero, the comics medium, and their context since 1991. His best-known work on comics is *Super Heroes: A Modern Mythology* (University Press of Mississippi, 1992). Currently, his research interests focus on the relationship of the superhero to issues of gender and sexuality, and on the superhero's relationship to the philosophy of excess and the omnipresence of the superhero in contemporary culture.

relationship to the philosophy of excess and the omnipresence of the superhero in contemporary culture.

MATT YOCKEY is an associate professor of film and media studies at the University of Toledo. He is the author of *Batman* (TV Milestones Series) (Wayne State University Press, 2014) and the editor of *Make Ours Marvel: Media Convergence and a Comics Universe* (University of Texas Press, 2017).

CHRISTOPHER B. ZEICHMANN is an instructor at Emmanuel College in the University of Toronto and Ryerson University. He has previously published articles on the racial and ethnic politics of superhero stories, including "Black like Lois: Confronting Racism, Configuring African American Presence" and "Champion of the Oppressed: Redescribing the Jewishness of Superman as Populist Authenticity Politics."

INDEX

adaptation, 6, 20, 80, 98, 253, 269, 271, 273, 278, 322
adolescence, 83, 104, 155–156, 177, 182, 294. *See also* teenagers
AIDS/HIV, 19, 116, 133, 135, 137–138, 141, 187–188, 333–334
Altman, Teddy (character). *See* Hulkling (character)
androgyny, 83, 87, 96, 233, 307, 350, 356

Barnes, Bucky (character), 154–155, 266, 269, 276
Batman (character): "Batman's penis controversy," 9–11, 14; character tropes of, 32, 34, 41, 52; as epitome of masculinity, 341, 348, 252, 354, 357–359; and homoerotic subtext, 1–2, 4, 6, 15, 105, 265, 274; in pornographic contexts, 4, 253–254, 258–259, 266, 268, 272, 281–284; publishing history of, 59–60; romantic and sexual relationships of, 6, 253, 350
Batson, Billy (character). *See* Captain Marvel (character)

Batwoman (character), 4, 6
Berlant, Lauren, 22, 318, 324, 329; with Michael Warner, 166
Bersani, Leo, 333
bisexuality: "bi erasure," 213–214; and bisexual coding, 98; and creators/performers, 111, 180; legal contexts for, 159; representations of in fan culture, 214, 333–334; and subjectivity, 13. *See also* LGBTQ (identity cluster); queerness; representations of in mainstream media, 6, 162, 211–212, 285
Bishop, Kate (character). *See* Hawkeye (character)
Bizarro (character), 18, 57, 59, 67–72, 76
Black Fury (character). *See* Miss Fury (character)
Black identity: and Black liberation movements, 20, 176–177, 179, 182–194; fictional representations of, 14, 18–19, 79, 183, 191–193, 200, 212–213, 257–258, 276; historical contexts for, 183, 321; news media representations of, 111–112, 321;

and theories of representation, 15, 82, 91, 98, 143, 212, 226, 258, 321
Black Panther (character), 110, 200, 212, 276
Blaire, Alison (character). *See* Dazzler (character)
Braun, Axel, 254–255, 257–259, 269–270, 299, 308
breasts, 8, 202, 210, 212, 260
Bronze Age, 18, 81
Brown, Jeffrey A., 21, 204, 212–213, 226, 245–264, 285, 299
Bukatman, Scott, 12–13, 31, 65–66, 69, 108
Butler, Judith, 12–13, 36–37, 74, 319, 324–325, 327, 333

camp (cultural practice), 1, 14, 111, 206–207, 230, 269
Captain America (character): in fan culture, 22, 317–318, 323–333, 349; as nationalist symbol, 318, 322; in pornographic contexts, 22, 254, 257, 275–277; queer subtext for, 108, 269; representation of in comics, 154–159, 161, 163, 166; representation of in film, 249, 267
Captain Marvel (character/Billy Batson/Shazam), 4, 60, 229, 253
Captain Marvel (character/Carol Danvers). *See* Danvers, Carol (character)
castration, 209–211, 251, 324
Catwoman (character), 6, 53, 253–254
censorship, 2, 11–12, 107, 109, 129, 248, 356. *See also* Comics Code Authority
Chavez, America (character), 143–146, 161–162, 166, 169
cheesecake (art style), 111, 116–118
Claremont, Chris, 18–19, 79–81, 83, 90–91, 93–96, 98–99. *See also* mutants; X-Men
class (socioeconomic): and prejudice/stereotypes, 187, 321–322; and privilege, 34, 40, 163, 205, 311; relation of to power, 192; values of middle, 20, 72, 104, 152, 187, 189

closet, the (concept): closeted existence, 104–105, 142, 151; metaphorical representations of, 4, 40, 105, 110, 125, 154, 162, 182, 214, 329
Cocca, Carolyn, 15, 79, 81, 83, 216
comics (formal properties): queer metaphors in, 1, 104, 146–147, 153, 214; relation of to sexuality, 11–14, 253, 291, 311, 344; stereotyping in, 13–14, 319–320, 325, 345, 351, 358; subversive qualities of, 13, 89, 91, 94; symbolic qualities of, 64–65
Comics Code Authority, 2–6, 17–18, 64, 109, 274. *See also* censorship
cosplay, 16–17, 22, 317, 324, 327–329, 334, 349. *See also* costume
costume: erotic qualities in, 3–4, 53, 82, 84–85, 229–230, 254; for female superheroes, 4, 18, 32, 34–38, 40, 45, 51, 84, 87–90, 95–96, 351; for male superheroes, 61, 135, 224–230, 233, 235, 237, 259, 261, 269; symbolic implications of, 161, 191, 206, 208, 258–261, 303, 325, 327, 349; theories of, 16, 31, 34, 35, 87–88, 154–156, 226–227, 252–254, 283. *See also* cosplay
cross-dressing, act of, 40, 323. *See also* drag
Cyclops (character), 98, 248, 283. *See also* mutants; X-Men

Danvers, Carol (character), 145–146, 351
Danvers, Kara (character). *See* Supergirl (character)
Dazzler (character), 19, 103–105, 110–125. *See also* mutants; X-Men
DC Comics: approaches of to representation, 64, 109, 129, 253–254, 272–273, 283; brand identity of, 6, 9–10, 64
deviance, 1, 3–4, 13, 88, 90, 118, 163, 223, 237, 253, 274, 304, 308, 311
disability, 13–14, 16, 58–59, 68, 98, 176–177, 184, 192, 205

Disney, 254, 260, 284, 324–325
diversity: of audiences, 16, 17, 132, 203, 216, 271, 306, 349; racial, 115, 185, 200, 213, 277; sexual, 6, 16–17, 19, 130–131, 138, 146, 151, 153, 161, 166–168, 216, 272, 276
drag (cultural practice), 113, 161, 166, 207, 211, 225, 230, 280, 319, 324, 327. *See also* cross-dressing, act of
Drake, Bobby (character). *See* Iceman (character)
Drake, Marla (character). *See* Miss Fury (character)
Dworkin, Andrea, 281, 343

Eco, Umberto, 64
embodiment: embodied symbolism, 65–67, 73, 82, 108, 159, 163, 207, 251, 260, 266, 308–310, 318, 320–322, 325, 329–334; and fashion/costumes, 35, 42, 45, 47–48, 53, 87, 89, 231; and representations of female bodies, 96, 111, 118–119, 202, 207–212, 259, 260, 278, 295, 304, 319, 324, 327, 349; and representations of male bodies, 203–204, 225–230, 232, 234, 239, 247–251, 253, 256, 260, 277, 283, 317, 323, 343–352, 354, 356–359; and representations of racialized bodies, 183, 212, 258, 351; and social construction of bodies, 44, 66, 73–74; and unstable bodies, 12–13, 69, 73, 76, 187, 209–212, 276, 317
eroticism: and fashion/costume, 35, 87; and female bodies, 93, 118, 123, 207–208, 310–311; as genre trope, 3–4, 265; and male bodies, 21, 204, 223, 228, 230–232, 235; queer, 22, 106, 122, 131, 169, 246, 267, 273, 306–308, 327, 331–333; and racial identity, 89; relationship of to pornography, 6, 12, 253, 256. *See also* homoeroticism
ethnicity, 3, 33, 86, 89, 97, 192, 205, 213

family: and melodrama, 122–123, 155, 300; representations of nontraditional, 4, 18, 57–59, 61–62, 66, 72–73, 77, 82, 137, 144, 156–157, 180, 188; representations of normative/nuclear, 21, 52, 104, 108, 119, 166, 221, 223, 225–226, 236–237, 299, 318
fan art, 16–17, 22, 131, 169, 215, 253, 256, 292, 301, 303–305, 317, 324, 329, 334
fan culture: and fan works, 21–22, 131, 292, 303–304, 306–307, 324–325, 327–335; and interpretations of texts, 9–10, 83, 104–106, 109, 111, 123–124, 153, 167–169, 202, 211, 275–276, 302, 349; and theories of fandom, 135, 194, 214, 216, 240, 253–255, 265, 270, 294, 299–300, 311–312, 325–325. *See also* cosplay; fan art; fan fiction; Hawkeye Initiative, the; social media
fandom. *See* fan culture
fan fiction, 16–17, 22, 239, 292, 303–304, 306–308, 311, 317, 323–324, 329, 334
fatherhood: personal reflections on, 343–344, 357; representations of, 6, 68, 70, 103, 119, 122, 237, 300; symbolism of, 206, 225, 310
Fawaz, Ramzi, 15, 85–86, 89, 100, 108–110; with Darieck Scott, 1, 13, 146–148, 153
female gaze. *See* gaze, the: female
femininity: representations of, 32, 36, 47; stereotypes of, 74, 86, 110, 118–119, 155, 202, 223, 307, 319; subversions of, 1, 94, 96, 98, 111–113, 207, 209, 211–212, 231, 320, 324, 331, 334
feminism: and critiques, 8, 82, 107, 209–210, 225, 230–231, 318, 342–343; post-, 20, 223; representations of, 5, 9, 32, 89–90, 116, 118–119, 123, 125, 216, 302–303, 323–324, 330
fetishism: of bodies and costumes/fashion, 34–35, 47–48, 82, 85, 118,

235, 246–247, 253–254, 259, 284, 304, 311; and fetish art, 4, 276; of whiteness, 304, 311
Flash, the (character), 266–267, 269, 277–280
Forge (character), 91, 93, 95–97. *See also* mutants; X-Men
Foster, Jane (character), 201–205
Foucault, Michel, 66, 107, 295
Freudianism, 13, 63
fridging (trope), 13, 93, 201, 217, 332. *See also* sexual violence

Gay Comix, 19, 129, 132–143, 146–147
gay identity: and fans, 9, 104–105, 106, 109, 110–111, 168, 250, 274–275; legal contexts for, 159–160, 181, 187–188, 330; representations of in comics, 1, 4, 6, 19, 24, 40, 107, 109, 118, 125, 129–38, 139–43, 146–148, 151–154, 167–168, 177, 273; representations of in film, 206; representations of in pornography, 21, 255, 266–281, 283–286, 300; social contexts for, 87, 100–101, 103–104, 108–109, 129–138, 139–143, 146–148, 179–180, 185–186, 190, 230, 265, 268–269, 181
gaze, the: female, 203, 223, 227–228, 230–232, 235–237, 311, 327; male, 49–50, 82, 91, 118, 200, 208; multiple gazes, 41, 45; queer, 135, 327; theories of, 21, 52
Golden Age, 41, 344, 348
Grayson, Dick (character). *See* Robin (character)
Green Lantern (character), 6, 13, 217, 257, 272–273, 332
Grimm, Ben (character). *See* Thing, the (character)

Harper's Bazaar, 36, 46
Hawkeye (character), 130–131, 147, 162, 325, 327
Hawkeye Initiative, the, 325, 327. *See also* fan art; fan culture; social media
Hela (character), 206–211, 213, 219

heteronormativity: representations of, 16, 65–67, 106–108, 116–119, 130, 133, 149, 160, 166, 185, 191, 200, 202, 204–206, 211, 223, 226, 237, 292, 299–300, 319–320, 343; subversions of, 4, 57–59, 66, 73–74, 96, 153–154, 162, 168, 206–207, 236, 271, 273–275, 308–309, 311–312, 317, 324, 327, 332–333, 344
homoeroticism, 1, 4, 204, 271–272, 274–276. *See also* eroticism; gay identity; homosexuality; lesbian identity; queerness
homonormativity, 153, 185–187, 189
homophobia, 10, 107, 109, 187, 324. *See also* homosexuality
homosexuality: censure of, 1, 3, 105, 124, 135, 152, 160, 189, 265, 323, 344; representations of, 107, 109–110, 118, 153–154, 177, 214, 272–275, 284, 309. *See also* gay identity; homophobia; lesbian identity; LGBTQ (identity cluster); queerness
Hulk, the (character), 24, 109, 155, 158, 175, 245–246, 249–250, 260–261, 319, 345, 350–351
Hulkling (character), 130–131, 147–148, 151–155, 157–159, 161–164, 167–169. *See also* Young Avengers
Human Torch, the (character), 108, 110, 113

Iceman (character), 6, 132, 142–144, 146, 150, 179, 283–284. *See also* mutants; X-Men

Jeffries, Dru, 253, 255, 259, 269–272, 280, 299, 308
Justice League (superhero team), 108, 254, 257, 266, 268, 272–273, 280, 284

Kaplan, Billy (character). *See* Wiccan (character); Young Avengers
Kent, Clark (character). *See* Superman (character)

Khan, Kamala (character/Ms. Marvel), 351
King, Martin Luther, Jr., 175–176, 183, 186, 190–191, 196
Kirby, Jack, 175, 195, 206

Lacan, Jacques, 248
Lane, Lois (character), 5–6, 11, 20–21, 57–61, 63–64, 68, 70, 72–76, 221–242
Latinx identity, 14, 144–145, 161, 169, 214, 285
Lee, Stan, 175, 177, 272, 345, 347
lesbian identity: and fans, 304, 306; representations of, 6, 18, 110, 140, 144, 146, 161, 285, 303, 308; social contexts for, 87, 132, 180, 186–187, 190, 319; stereotypes of, 118–119. *See also* gay identity; homoeroticism; homosexuality; LGBTQ (identity cluster); queerness
LGBTQ (identity cluster): cultural contexts for, 111, 137–138, 140–141, 146, 153, 160–161, 165, 167, 180–181; legal contexts for, 17, 188, 330; as love interest, 4, 13, 57, 200, 205, 221, 224, 292, 303; representations of, 6, 19, 107, 129–133, 141–143, 145–148, 152, 166, 167–168, 170, 211–212
Luthor, Lena (character), 22, 292, 296, 300, 302–304, 306–311
Luthor, Lex (character), 22, 70, 76, 224, 226, 302

Magneto (character), 167, 176–177, 180, 182–185, 188–194, 257, 284. *See also* mutants; X-Men
Malcolm X, 175–177, 183–185, 188, 190–191, 194
male gaze. *See* gaze, the: male
marriage: legal contexts for, 181, 187–188, 190; representations of, 60–65, 70, 223, 323, 236–238, 297, 299; theories of, 185
Marvel Cinematic Universe (MCU), 20, 199–200, 206, 216–217, 219, 250, 276, 344

Marvel Comics: approaches of to representation, 6, 81–82, 118, 129–132, 145, 151, 153, 159, 162, 283, 325: brand identity of, 5–6, 109, 113, 115–116, 142, 159, 168–169, 176, 253, 319, 345, 347
masculinity: representations of, 5, 21–22, 116, 226–227, 230–232, 234–236, 247–251, 255–261, 299, 327, 344; stereotypes of, 1, 32, 42–43, 49, 58, 106, 118, 204, 222, 267, 276–277; subversions of, 85, 91, 206–207, 236, 307, 331, 333–334; theories of, 74, 156, 225, 229, 245–247, 250–51, 258, 283–285, 317–324
metamorphosis. *See* transformation
Mills, Tarpé, 18, 31–37, 39–42, 44–145, 48–55. *See also* Miss Fury (character)
misogyny, 5–6, 9, 16, 22, 31, 324, 332
Miss America (character). *See* Chavez, America
Miss Fury (character), 18, 31–34, 36–38, 40–44, 50–55
Mother (character), 163–164, 166–167
mothers/motherhood: personal reflections on, 342–343, 357; representations of, 97, 103, 122, 144, 159–160, 179, 201, 228, 230; symbolism of, 82, 163–164, 210, 318
Ms. Marvel (character/Carol Danvers). *See* Danvers, Carol (character)
Ms. Marvel (character/Kamala Khan). *See* Khan, Kamala (character/Ms. Marvel)
multiplicities: of bodies, 13, 209; of identity, 34, 37, 39, 143, 147, 160, 223, 230–231, 234–235, 239, 295; of interpretative possibilities, 4, 18, 59, 79, 184, 276
Mulvey, Laura. *See* gaze, the
mutants: as minority metaphor, 90, 159, 175–185, 188–194; as queer metaphor, 19–20, 105, 108, 110, 113, 123–125, 275. *See also* X-Men
Mystique (character), 183–184, 191, 284, 349. *See also* mutants; X-Men

Index 371

Neale, Steve, 247, 251, 327
Nightcrawler (character), v, 82, 125, 180, 183. *See also* mutants; X-Men
Niven, Larry, 221–222, 233, 240
Nyberg, Amy Kiste, 2

Olsen, Jimmy, 57, 59, 61, 237–238, 303
otherness, 13–14, 59, 67, 88–90, 101, 176, 181, 192, 194, 213, 226, 283

Parker, Peter (character). *See* Spider-Man (character)
parody: in comics, 5, 58, 133, 135, 137–138, 141, 247; in non-pornographic film, 247; in pornographic film, 253–255, 257, 260–261, 266–275, 277–285; and social media, 111
patriarchy: representations of, 5, 93, 116, 122, 211, 216, 291, 294, 297, 299–300, 306, 309; subversions of, 47, 49, 79, 208–209, 255, 303, 307, 311–312, 320, 332–333; theories of, 13, 20, 230, 357
penis: personal reflections on, 343; representations of, 5, 9–11, 14, 21, 222, 245, 251, 253, 259, 282–283, 352, 356–357; as symbol, 226, 245–248, 250–253, 256–261, 350, 354
phallic power: representations of, 5, 21, 231, 235, 246, 282, 284, 297, 299, 356, 361; subversions of, 229; theories of, 210–211, 226, 245–251, 255–260, 285, 334
pornography: in comics, 82, 291; in fan works, 6, 291–292, 299, 303–304, 308, 311; in film, 6, 21, 245–247, 253–261, 265–286, 299; theories of, 9, 11–12, 236, 294–296, 299, 306, 311. *See also* Tijuana Bibles
postfeminism. *See* feminism
pregnancy, 240, 331, 333. *See also* reproduction
Professor Xavier (character), 88, 125, 176, 182–183, 185, 188–192. *See also* mutants; X-Men
Pryde, Kitty (character), 85, 87, 89, 125, 192–193. *See also* mutants; X-Men

queerness: association of with villainy, 207–209, 283; cultural contexts for, 161, 166, 180, 207–209; metaphors of, 4, 13–15, 19, 52, 83–84, 105, 108–111, 113, 116, 118–119, 122, 176, 178–180, 182, 192, 211, 265, 284; political contexts for, 181, 185–191; and queerbaiting, 275; and queer fans, 91, 103–105, 109–111, 113, 223–225, 274, 276 291–292, 303, 311; and queer theory, 103, 106–108, 146–147, 153–154, 184, 214, 319–320; representations of, 8–9, 20–22, 87, 130, 135, 143–144, 166, 168–169, 300, 304, 306–309, 311, 327, 334. *See also* bisexuality; gay identity; homosexuality; lesbian identity; LGBTQ (identity cluster)

race: historical inattention to, 33, 109; and intersectionality, 143; and multiracial identity, 157–158; norms/stereotypes about, 22, 175, 205, 212–213, 322, 325; and racialized representations, 87, 185, 192–194; and racism in fan culture, 304. *See also* Black identity; ethnicity; Latinx identity; white identity
rape. *See* sexual violence
reproduction, 18, 58–61, 63–74, 76, 106, 185, 240. *See also* pregnancy
Robin (character), 1, 4, 6, 15, 52, 105, 254, 265, 274, 284
Rogers, Steve (character). *See* Captain America
romance: conventions of, 3, 20, 83–84, 96, 123, 204, 226, 307, 324; heterosexual, in comics, 57, 60–61, 74, 76, 91, 93, 95–97, 130, 222, 296, 299, 350; heterosexual, in film, 202, 205, 212, 222; heterosexual, in television, 223, 234, 303–304, 310; personal reflections on, 239; queer, in comics, 130–131, 151–153, 161, 164, 169; queer, in fan works, 292, 302, 305, 306, 308–309,

331–332; queer-coded, 116; and romantic fashion, 50

Schott, Gareth, 15, 147, 168, 214, 275
Sedgwick, Eve Kosofsky, 103, 106–107, 159, 323. *See also* closet, the
Seduction of the Innocent. *See* Wertham, Fredric
sexism, 16, 122, 148, 199, 206, 209, 219, 227, 291, 331, 333. *See also* misogyny; patriarchy
sexual violence: conventions of, 13, 201, 213; personal reflections on, 22, 343, 357; representations of, 5, 109, 116, 209; and Bryan Singer allegations, 20, 180–181, 192. *See also* fridging; violence
She-Hulk (character), 6, 34, 53, 116, 118, 254, 319
Sif (character), 201–202, 205–206, 212
Silver Age, 15, 18, 57–59, 63–67, 69, 72, 76, 206, 221, 344
Singer, Bryan, 20, 111, 175, 178, 180–181, 184, 191–192
social media: representations of, 145, 164–165, 203; Tumblr, 111, 300–301, 304–307, 325–326; Twitter, 9–10, 193, 211–212, 214–215. *See also* Hawkeye Initiative, the
Spider-Man (character), 103, 156, 158–159, 249, 251, 254, 257–258, 267, 269, 275–278, 317, 347
Spider-Woman (character), 116, 118
stereotypes: cultural, 90, 200, 251; gender, 22, 40, 87, 89, 201–202, 204–205, 234, 267, 277, 333; racial, 2, 81–82, 86, 97–98, 212–213, 226, 258, 321, 351; relation of to comics form, 13, 351; sexual, 107, 118, 130–131, 137, 211, 267, 280
Storm (character), 18–19, 79–91, 93–99, 125, 180, 192, 212. *See also* mutants; X-Men
Storm, Johnny (character). *See* Human Torch, the (character)
subversion: of gender and sexual norms, 9, 21, 79, 119, 125, 202, 229, 234, 236, 246, 255, 267, 271–274, 276, 292, 308; of other identity norms, 3, 67–68, 73; of story conventions, 63. *See also* deviance
Superboy (character), 68–70
Supergirl (character), 4–6, 21–22, 57, 60–61, 70, 254, 291–292, 294–300, 302–304, 306–312
Superman (character): in fan culture, 349; in pornographic contexts, 4–5, 253–254, 257, 267–269, 280–283, 300; relationship of with Supergirl, 291–292, 294–295, 309–310; in romantic and sexual relationships, 6, 18, 20–21, 57–77, 221–240, 299; secret identity convention of, 41, 251, 356; tropes, 11, 133, 135, 320, 322
supervillains. *See* villains

Tasker, Yvonne, 200–204, 213, 216
teenagers: as fans/readers, 2, 6, 8–9; representations of, 13, 20, 57, 130–131, 152, 156, 164, 179, 183, 193, 251, 285, 292, 295, 351. *See also* adolescence
Thing, the (character), 108, 110, 249
Thor (character), 20, 154, 175, 199–206, 210–214
Tijuana Bibles, 4–5, 21, 253, 291–292, 299–300, 306. *See also* pornography
transformation: of identity, 32, 36–37, 41–42, 73, 95–96, 104, 106, 123–124, 137, 283, 318; narrative, 18, 79, 83–84, 98–99, 255, 272, 299, 303; physical, 11–12, 18, 21, 40, 60, 72–73, 76, 87, 90, 207, 228, 232–236, 239, 276, 317, 322–324, 329, 331–334, 347, 351, 356; symbolism of, 34, 48–49, 68, 209, 229–230, 256
transgender, 6, 185, 240, 324, 333
transvestism. *See* cross-dressing, act of

Uncanny X-Men. *See* X-Men
underground comics, 4–5, 15, 19, 129, 132, 146–147, 253. *See also* Tijuana Bibles

Valkyrie (character), 6, 211–214, 216, 219
villains: and conventions of representation, 13–14, 209, 278; fashion/costume of, 31, 37–38, 40; and gender themes, 21, 42, 115, 118–119, 200, 208–209, 260, 267–269, 277–279, 283–285, 308; and racial themes, 20, 190–191, 194; reformed, 155, 257; and subversion of tropes, 158; sympathetic, 177. *See also* Hela (character); Luthor, Lex (character); Magneto (character); Mother (character)
violence: censorship of, 1–2, 64; critiques of, 135; political contexts of, 186–190; representations of, 9, 123, 176, 178–179, 182, 185, 190–192, 207, 356–358; symbolism of, 3, 13, 65, 93, 176, 210–211, 278, 291, 320, 327. *See also* sexual violence
virginity, 83, 232, 236
Vogue, 35, 49

Warner, Michael, 20, 153, 160; with Lauren Berlant, 166
weddings. *See* marriage
Weisinger, Mort, 59–60, 62–64, 72, 76–77
Wertham, Fredric, 1–2, 4, 12, 14, 105, 107, 265, 348. *See also* censorship; Comics Code Authority
Wheeler, Andrew, 84, 167–168, 193
white identity: and beauty norms, 183, 304; as cultural identity, 113; and feminism, 116, 123; as privileged norm, 20, 34, 58, 72, 79, 132, 143, 158, 179, 186, 188–195, 203, 205, 211–213, 216, 225–226, 257–258, 216, 216, 225–226, 257–258, 276–277, 311, 332, 351; and white supremacy, 8, 14, 16
Wiccan (character), 130–131, 147–148, 151–154, 159–164, 167–169, 171
Williams, Linda, 9, 256, 259, 261, 294–296, 299, 308, 311, 327
Wolverine (character), 81–83, 125, 179, 183, 248–249, 254, 257, 283–284. *See also* mutants; X-Men
Wonder Woman (character), 1–2, 6–8, 11, 14–15, 31, 41, 51, 81, 254, 257, 280, 320, 349
World War II, 41, 154, 276, 322, 329, 331, 348

X-Men: mainstream contexts for, 6, 18–20, 79–88, 90–92, 94–99, 103–104, 108, 110–111, 113–114, 123, 125, 127, 142, 147, 159, 175–185, 188–195; pornographic contexts for, 254, 257, 267, 275, 283. *See also* Claremont, Chris; mutants

Young Avengers (superhero team), 19–20, 130–131, 143, 147, 151–170. *See also* Hulkling (character); Wiccan (character)
Yukio (character), 83–85, 87, 90–91, 95–96